FROMMER'S

COMPREHENSIVE
TRAVEL GUIDE

Chicago '95

by Michael Uhl

MACMILLAN • USA

ABOUT THE AUTHOR

Michael Uhl, a freelance writer, has contributed articles to numerous national magazines and is the author of *G.I. Guinea Pigs* (with Tod Ensign) and *Exploring Maine on Country Roads and Byways*. Uhl is currently at work on a book about the German-American experience. A longtime resident of New York City, he now lives in Maine.

MACMILLAN TRAVEL

A Prentice Hall Macmillan Company
15 Columbus Circle
New York, NY 10023

ISBN 0-02-860054-1
ISSN 1040-936X

Design by Michele Laseau
Maps by Ortelius Design

Special Sales

Bulk purchases (10+ copies) of Frommer's Travel Guides are available to corporations at special discounts. The Special Sales Department can produce custom editions to be used as premiums and/or for sales promotion to suit individual needs. Existing editions can be produced with custom cover imprints such as corporate logos. For more information write to: Special Sales, Prentice Hall, 15 Columbus Circle, New York, NY 10023.

Manufactured in the United States of America

Contents

List of Maps

Invitation to the Readers

In researching this book I have come across many fine establishments, the best of which are included here. However, I'm sure that many of you will discover other wonderful hotels, restaurants, shops, and attractions. Please don't keep them to yourself. Share your experiences, especially if you want to comment on places that I have covered in this edition that may have changed for the worse. You may address your letters to:

Michael Uhl
Frommer's Chicago
Macmillan Travel
15 Columbus Circle
New York, NY 10023

A Disclaimer

Readers are advised that prices fluctuate in the course of time and travel information changes under the impact of the varied and volatile factors that affect the travel industry. Neither the author nor the publisher can be held responsible for the experiences of readers while traveling. Readers are invited to write to the publisher with ideas, comments, and suggestions for future editions.

Safety Advisory

Whenever you're traveling in an unfamiliar city or country, stay alert. Be aware of your immediate surroundings. Wear a moneybelt and keep a close eye on your possessions. Be particularly careful with cameras, purses, and wallets, all favorite targets of thieves and pickpockets.

For Wilbur and Margaret

Acknowledgments

The author would like to acknowledge Meg Gerken and Gordon Quinn for aid and comfort, and the substantial assistance in researching this guide I received from Dorothy Coyle of the Chicago Office of Tourism. I wish to acknowledge in particular the contributions and kindnesses of Susan Chernoff, who has been a mainstay of support for this guide over several editions, and of Mary Wagstaff, to whom the current edition owes a great deal. Many other individuals contributed valuable time, information, and suggestions during the updating of this guide. They include M.J. Gapp, Pat Kremer, JoAnn Bongiorno, Ann Ridge, Pat O'Brien, Joyce Saxon, Deborah Lucien, Gloria Garofalo, Daniel F. Roberts, Russell Salzman, Marc Schulman, Michael Lash, Mary Denis, and Kate Myers. Their assistance is greatly appreciated.

What the Symbols Mean

★ **FROMMER'S FAVORITES**—hotels, restaurants, attractions, and entertainments you should not miss

$ **SUPER-SPECIAL VALUES**—really exceptional values

In Hotel and Other Listings

The following symbols refer to the standard amenities available in all rooms:

A/C   air conditioning
MINIBAR   refrigerator stocked with beverages and snacks
TEL   telephone
TV   television

The following abbreviations are used for credit cards:

AE   American Express
CB   Carte Blanche
DC   Diners Club
DISC   Discover
ER   enRoute
JCB   (Japan)
MC   MasterCard
V   VISA

Trip Planning with This Guide

Use the following features:

What Things Cost   To help you plan your daily budget

Calendar of Events   To plan for or avoid

Suggested Itineraries   For seeing the city

What's Special About Checklist   A summary of the city's highlights

Easy-to-Read Maps   Walking tours, city sights, hotel and restaurant locations

Fast Facts   All the essentials at a glance: climate, currency, embassies, emergencies, information, safety, taxes, tipping, and more

Frommer's Smart Traveler Tips   Hints on how to secure the best value for your money

Other Special Frommer Features

Cool for Kids   Hotels, restaurants, and attractions

Did You Know?   Offbeat, fun facts

Famous People   The city's greats

Impressions   What others have said

1

Introducing Chicago

A CERTAIN AMOUNT OF SKEPTICISM ATTACHES ITSELF TO CHICAGO. LET'S face it, Chicago just isn't the first place you'd think of visiting as a tourist. Trade show? Convention? All right. But just for the fun of it? Not likely. Somehow the major metropolis of the heartland doesn't trigger the special curiosity or excitement associated with so many other cities. Maybe it's because Chicago has become so saturated in its own clichés—gangster land, hog butcher, second city, windy city—that the underlying reality of the diverse, sophisticated, and entirely livable city that exists on the flip side of the myths has not been allowed to shine through. Well, I'm here to tell you that Chicago is not only a bona fide leisure destination, but that as cities go, this is one of the great ones.

Let's take a closer look at those clichés one at a time.

GANGSTER LAND   When Al Capone and company operated with impunity outside the law here, Chicago had yet to celebrate 100 years of existence. The constant waves of immigrants that made the city's population swell from a few thousand to a few million over the course of several generations kept Chicago from being polished into a genteel, provincial burg like a thousand other towns and cities that were settled along the frontier during the westward expansion of the Republic. Today's Chicago (it need hardly be said) has long shed both its frontier rawness and the gangland warfare that lent so much drama to Prohibition. Sure, organized crime still operates in Chicago, but its visibility and style are no different from that of their cousins in a host of other American cities.

HOG BUTCHER   The poet Carl Sandburg gets the credit for Chicago's "hog butcher" image. Sandburg's Chicago poems—once anthologized in every high-school literature text in the country— idealized the impact of immigration and industrialization on his city, as if somehow these phenomena were intrinsic to Chicago's very topography, rather than resulting from phases of its economic and social development. Indeed, this is understandable given the power of those images in the Chicago of his day, where the rank, unsanitary stockyards and meat-packing plants employed at subsistence wages some 80,000 workers, many just off the boats from Europe or up from the sharecroppers' farms of the American South.

Today the stockyards are gone, meat packing has relocated elsewhere, and the successful union movement of the past five decades has improved the living conditions of the working family in general far beyond the vision of life in Chicago that Sandburg memorialized. Today Chicago has extremes of both polish and poverty, but it's the vast middle ground occupied by the city's numerous working- and middle-class neighborhoods that offers so many possibilities for the adventuresome visitor.

SECOND CITY   Chicagoans themselves are responsible for the idea of their city as second best. The term *second city* came into fashion as a bit of local puffery. Chicago's population grew large within a remarkably short time, outstripping several old culture capitals of

What's Special About Chicago

Beaches
- Oak Street Beach occupies a favored position on Lake Michigan along the Gold Coast, near some of the city's best hotels, shops, and restaurants.
- Lincoln Park offers different beach environments for a variety of lifestyles.

Architectural Highlights
- Suburban Oak Park is saturated with fine examples of Frank Lloyd Wright's homes and buildings.
- Some of Louis Sullivan's greatest works, including the Auditorium Building and Theater (1888) and the Carson Pirie Scott department store (1899) on State Street.
- Many examples of the work of Bauhaus wizard Ludwig Mies van der Rohe adorn the city, such as the IBM Building on the Chicago River.
- Chicago has two of the world's tallest buildings: the John Hancock Center and the Sears Tower.

Museums
- The Museum of Science and Industry is the most-frequented museum in the Midwest.
- The Field Museum of Natural History has many interactive displays.
- The Art Institute has one of the nation's great collections and is home to Grant Wood's famous *American Gothic.*
- The Chicago Historical Society has wonderful displays that make history accessible to all.

Events/Festivals
- The Chicago Blues Festival in June, the Taste of Chicago food fair in July, and the Jazz Festival in September are the most popular events.

For the Kids
- The Lincoln Park Zoo, the Museum of Science and Industry, the Children's Museum, the Shedd Aquarium, the Field Museum, the Adler Planetarium, and the suburban Brookfield Zoo are the top hits for the kids.

Shopping
- The Magnificent Mile, with Chicago's fanciest shops and department stores.

Evening Entertainment
- Dozens of blues clubs and 120-plus theaters.

the East Coast, such as Philadelphia and Boston; for a time, the only American city that surpassed Chicago in population was New York.

Thus, Chicago became—and was proud to see itself as—the "second city."

But who ever heard of anyone bragging about being Number Two? The point is that Chicago is a real city, with a rare vitality and diversity that some bigger and more famous cities (Los Angeles, Paris) don't have. While no longer strictly Number Two, the "second city" mania continues to reflect in Chicago the defensiveness of a populace in the provinces looking for the respect and appreciation their city deserves. Chicago today, after all, is no longer the ugly duckling, but the swan; and it shouldn't take real city lovers among the traveling public too much longer to discover this fact.

WINDY CITY   There is some dispute as to how Chicago earned its nickname as the "windy city." But the climate, apparently, had nothing to do with it. Over the years Chicago has been host to more presidential nominating conventions than any other American city. It is said that some "windy" politician at one of those conventions in the late 19th century is the true source of the nickname, not the howling air currents off Lake Michigan that sometimes chill the city and its denizens to the bone. In the popular mind, however, "windy city" is synonymous with cold, and for some, Chicago has the reputation of being uninhabitable in the wintertime. In reality, Chicago is neither better nor worse in this respect than the other Great Lakes and north country cities. People who hate the cold should not only avoid Chicago in the winter but all of New England and the Northwest as well.

1   HISTORY

Dateline

- 1673 French explorers Marquette and Jolliet discover the portage at Chicago that links the Great Lakes region with the Mississippi River Valley.
- 1781 The first European settlement at Chicago is founded by the Afro-French-Canadian trapper, Jean Baptiste DuSable.
- 1794 Gen. "Mad" Anthony Wayne defeats the British

➤

Chicago was created as the great engine of America's westward expansion. It was all a matter of location. The particular patch of land where Chicago would someday stand just happened to straddle a key point along an inland sea route that linked Canada, via Lake Erie, to New Orleans and the Gulf of Mexico by way of the Mississippi River.

The French, who were expanding their own territory in North America throughout the 17th and 18th centuries, were the first Europeans to survey the topography of the future Chicago. The French policy in North America was simple—to gradually settle the Mississippi Valley and the Northwest Territory (modern Michigan, Illinois, Wisconsin, and Minnesota). The policy rested on an alliance between religion and commerce: The French sought a monopoly over the fur trade among the Native Americans, whose pacification and loyalty they would attempt to ensure by converting them to Catholicism.

The team of Marquette, the Jesuit, and Jolliet, the explorer, personified this policy to perfection. In 1673 the pair found a very short portage between two critically placed rivers, the Illinois and the Des Plaines. A mere isthmus, "but half a league of prairie," reported Marquette and Jolliet, separated these two rivers, with one connected to the Mississippi, and the other to Lake Michigan via the Chicago River and then onward to Montréal and Québec.

Chicago owes its existence to this strategic $1^1/_2$-mile portage trail that the Native Americans had blazed in their own water travels over centuries of wandering throughout this territory. Marquette himself was on the most familiar terms with the Native Americans, who helped him make his way over the well-established paths and byways of their ancestral lands. The Native Americans, of course, could not foresee how intolerant the land-starved Europeans would be in the wake of the fur traders and the priests, especially if the "savages" happened to occupy real estate coveted by the settlers.

FIRST SETTLEMENT   Over the next 100 years, the French used this waterway to spread their American empire from Canada to Mobile, Alabama. Yet the first recorded settlement in Chicago, a trading post built by a Frenchman, Jean Baptiste Point DuSable, did not appear until 1781. By this time the territory had already been conquered by the British, the victors in the 70 years of intermittent warfare that cost the French most of their North American holdings. After the American War of Independence, the Illinois Territory was wrested from British/Native American control in a campaign led by the Revolutionary War hero Gen. "Mad" Anthony Wayne that ended with a treaty in 1795 ceding the land around the mouth of the Chicago River to the United States.

Dateline

in the battle of Fallen Timbers, and the disputed Illinois Territory is finally ceded to the young American Republic by treaty a year later.

■ **1803** The garrison of Fort Dearborn is created in Chicago and is commanded by the grandfather of artist James McNeill Whistler.

■ **1812** Threatened by an attack by Native Americans trying to reclaim their lost territory, the residents of Fort Dearborn are slain while attempting to flee the garrison.

■ **1816** Fort Dearborn is manned anew, and the military presence is reestablished in the region.

■ **1818** The Illinois Territory is admitted to statehood.

■ **1833** The town of Chicago is officially incorporated.

■ **1850** Chicago has a population of roughly 30,000.

■ **1856** Chicago is the chief railroad center in the U.S.

■ **1860** The Republican National Convention in Chicago nominates Abraham Lincoln for the presidency.

▶

Dateline

- 1865 The Chicago Stockyards are founded.
- 1870 The city's population numbers almost 300,000, making it perhaps the fastest-growing metropolis in history.
- 1871 The Great Chicago Fire burns large sections of the city; rebuilding begins while the ashes are still warm.
- 1886 A dynamite bomb explodes during a political rally near Haymarket Square, killing eight policemen and wounding 65 others.
- 1893 Chicago has completely recovered from the fire and hosts the World Columbian Exposition.
- 1894 The workers of the Pullman Car Company plant join the American Railway Union in a general strike; President Cleveland sends federal troops to Chicago.
- 1896 William Jennings Bryan delivers his "Cross of Gold" speech before the delegates of the Democratic National Convention.

➤

Between the time of DuSable and 1833, when Chicago was officially founded, the land at the lip of the Chicago River served as a military outpost that guarded the strategic passage and provided security for a few trappers and a trading post. The military base, Fort Dearborn, which stood at the present site of the Michigan Avenue Bridge, was first garrisoned in 1803 under the command of Capt. John Whistler, grandfather of the famous painter. At first the settlement grew slowly as the result of continued Native American efforts to drive the new Americans from the Illinois Territory. During the War of 1812, Fort Dearborn was abandoned, and many of the settlement's military and civilian inhabitants were slain during the evacuation. Before long the trappers drifted back, and by 1816 the military, too, returned.

Conflict with the Native Americans diminished after that, but even as a civil engineer plotted the building lots of the early town as late as 1830, periodic raids continued, and only ceased with the defeat of Chief Black Hawk in 1832. A year later, the small settlement of 300-plus inhabitants was officially incorporated under the name Chicago, said to derive from a Native American word referring to the powerful natural odors of the wild vegetation that grew abundantly in the marshlands surrounding the riverbanks.

COMMERCE & INDUSTRY Land speculation began immediately, as Chicago was carved piecemeal and sold off to finance the Illinois and Michigan Canal that would eliminate the narrow land portage and fulfill the long-standing vision of connecting the two great waterways, linking the domesticated East to the pioneer West, with Chicago at midpoint, directing the flow of commerce in both directions. The commercial activity was not long delayed: In two to three years, local farmers in the outlying areas were already producing a surplus. Chicago grew in size and wealth, transshipping grain and livestock to the eastern markets and lumber to the treeless prairies of the West. Ironically, by the time the Illinois and Michigan Canal was completed in 1848, the railroad had arrived, and the water route that gave Chicago its raison d'être was rapidly supplanted by boxcars as the principal carriers for transported goods throughout the region. The combination of the railroad, the setting up of local manufacturing, and later, the Civil War caused Chicago to grow wildly.

The most revolutionary product of the era sprang from the mind of a Chicago inventor, Cyrus McCormick, whose reaper filled in for the farmhands who now labored on the nation's battlefields. Local merchants not only thrived on the contraband trade in cotton, but they also secured lucrative contracts from the federal government to provide the army with tents, uniforms, saddles, harnesses, lumber, bread, and meat. By 1870 Chicago had a population of 300,000, an increase of 1,000% in the brief interval of 37 years since the city's incorporation.

THE GREAT FIRE A year later the city lay in ashes. The Great Chicago Fire of 1871 began somewhere on the southwest side of the city on October 8, jumped the river, and continued northward through the night of the following day, when it was checked by the use of gunpowder on the south side and rainfall to the north and west, just before spreading to the prairie. In its wake, the fire destroyed 18,000 buildings and left 90,000 homeless, miraculously taking a toll of only 300 lives.

One thing the fire could not destroy was Chicago's strategic location, and on that solid geographic footing the city began to rebuild as soon as the rubble was cleared. By chance, Chicago's railroad infrastructure—manufactories, grain warehouses, and lumberyards—was also spared, being located beyond the circle of fire on the southern periphery of the city. By 1873 the city's downtown business and financial district was already rebuilt, and two decades later Chicago had suf-ficiently recovered to host the 1893 World Columbian

Dateline

- **1903** Theodore Roosevelt is nominated by the Republican National Convention.
- **1905** The Wobblies, Industrial Workers of the World (IWW), is founded in Chicago.
- **1919** The "Black Sox" bribery scandal stuns baseball.
- **1919–33** During Prohibition, Chicago becomes a "wide open town," as rival mobs battle violently throughout the city for control of the distribution and sale of illegal alcohol.
- **1932** Franklin Delano Roosevelt is nominated by the Democratic National Convention.
- **1955** Richard J. Daley is first elected mayor, he is widely regarded as the "last of the big-city bosses."
- **1968** Anti-Vietnam War protests in conjunction with the Democratic National Convention end in police riot.
- **1983** Harold Washington be-comes the first African-American mayor of Chicago.
- **1992** A retaining wall collapses, and the Loop is flooded by water from the Chicago River.

Exposition commemorating the 400th anniversary of the discovery of America.

AN AMERICAN ATHENS   The Great Fire gave an unprecedented boost to the professional and artistic development of many of the nation's architects, who either grew up in Chicago or were drawn there in droves by the unlimited opportunities to build. Chicago's deserved reputation as an American Athens, packed with monumental and decorative buildings, is a direct by-product of the disastrous conflagration that nearly brought the city to ruin. In the meantime, Chicago's population continued to grow as some immigrants bound for the uncultivated farmland of the prairie chose to remain townfolk, adding to the labor pool in the city. Chicago still shipped meat and agricultural commodities around the nation and the world, but the city itself was rapidly becoming a mighty industrial center in its own right, creating finished goods, particularly for the markets of the ever-expanding western settlements.

THE CRADLE OF TRADE UNIONISM   Like an adolescent who shoots up in gangly spurts, Chicago never seemed to outgrow its frontier rawness. Greed, profiteering, exploitation, and corruption were as critical to the growth of Chicago as hard work, ingenuity, and civic pride. The spirit of reform arose most powerfully from the ranks of the working classes, whose lives, despite the city's prosperity, were plagued by poverty and disease. When the sleeping giant of labor finally awakened in Chicago, it did so with a militancy and commitment that was to inspire the union movement throughout the nation.

By the 1890s many of Chicago's workers were already organized into the American Federation of Labor. The Pullman Strike of 1894 united black and white railway workers for the first time in common struggle for higher wages and workplace rights. The Industrial Workers of the World, the Wobblies, who embraced for a time so many great voices of American labor—Eugene V. Debs, Big Bill Haywood, Helen Gurley Flynn—was founded in Chicago in 1905.

POLITICS & RACE   Chicago was becoming not only a center of industry, transportation, and finance, and a beacon of labor reform, but the city—again by virtue of its location—was also becoming a powerhouse in national politics. Between 1860 and 1968 Chicago was the site of 14 Republican and 10 Democratic presidential nominating conventions. The first gave the country one of its most admired leaders, Abraham Lincoln, while the last was witness to the so-called Days of Rage, a police riot against demonstrators who had camped out in Grant Park to protest the Vietnam War.

IMPRESSIONS

I have struck a city—a real city—and they call it Chicago. The other places don't count. Having seen it, I urgently desire never to see it again. It is inhabited by savages.
—Rudyard Kipling, *From Sea To Sea* (1889)

The frontier spirit in Chicago finally expired sometime around the repeal of Prohibition, when the tommy-gun–toting gangsters were finally brought to heel. The major change in Chicago in the 20th century, however, stems from the enormous growth of the city's African-American population. The cultural and social differences that segregate blacks and whites in Chicago have begun to be mitigated through the same local political processes that other immigrant groups traditionally used to advance their interests. And so once again, this time in the critical area of race relations, Chicago continues to experience the conflict and compromise that has characterized the growth of this city from its inception.

2 Art, Architecture & Cultural Life

ART   In the world of art, Chicago has traditionally been more of a collector than a producer, at least until the current generation. The local nobility has tended to deflect charges of midwestern provincialism by accumulating great works and by building many museums to house them in. As a result, Chicago is a museumgoer's delight, where every epoch and specialty—ancient, classical, impressionist, abstract, contemporary, folk, Native American, Slavic, Jewish, and so forth—has its repository. Since the sixties, however, some portion of the city's youthful energy has been redirected toward the local creation of art for art's sake. There is an art scene in Pilsen, where painters seem more concerned with originality than with demands of the corporate or decorator markets. Hyde Park has also been hospitable to various movements within the plastic arts for several generations.

Public art, in the form of monumental sculpture created by some of the 20th century's biggest names—Picasso, Calder, Oldenburg, Moore, Chagall, and Miró—adorns many of the Loop's major commercial buildings.

ARCHITECTURE   As for Chicago's contribution to architecture, the list of names itself speaks volumes: Sullivan, Burnham, Adler, Shaw, Richardson, Wright, Mies van der Rohe, Goldberg, Johnson, and Jahn being the most recognizable names among many other worthy designers of buildings located throughout the city. A great visual bonus awaits any visitor to Chicago who likes to stroll along city streets and look at stately, majestic buildings.

CULTURAL LIFE   In the performing arts, Chicago can boast some of the finest institutions of high culture of any city in the world,

IMPRESSIONS
Hog Butcher for the World,
Tool Maker, Stacker of Wheat,
Player with Railroads and the Nation's Freight Handler;
Stormy, husky, brawling,
City of the Big Shoulders.
—Carl Sandburg, Part of "Chicago," from *Chicago Poems* (1916)

including the renowned Chicago Symphony. The theater is alive in Chicago like perhaps no other city in the United States, including New York. Beyond the Broadway-style mega-productions—which are certainly not alien to this city—Chicago possesses more than 100 small, highly professional theaters, with one located in practically every neighborhood.

3 Famous Chicagoans

Jane Addams (1860–1935)   Founder of Hull House and the leading spirit behind the American Settlement House Movement.

Nelson Algren (1909–81)   The novelist who penned *The Man with the Golden Arm* and *Chicago: City on the Make.*

L. Frank Baum (1856–1919)   He wrote *The Wizard of Oz* while living in Chicago.

Al Capone (1899–1947)   The most famous mobster of them all, he will be forever linked with Chicago and the dark days of Prohibition.

Nat "King" Cole (1919–65)   He was the crooner par excellence, with such hits as "Unforgettable," "Mona Lisa," and "Straighten Up and Fly Right."

Richard J. Daley (1902–76)   The father of the current mayor, he was one of the most powerful political bosses in the United States during his own reign as Chicago's mayor.

Clarence Darrow (1857–1938)   The brilliant defense attorney best known for squaring off against perennial presidential candidate William Jennings Bryan during the famous Scopes Monkey Trial.

Walt Disney (1901–66)   The film producer learned to draw cartoons in Chicago.

Ernest Hemingway (1899–1961)   The great American novelist and Nobel laureate grew up in the Chicago suburb of Oak Park.

Mahalia Jackson (1911–72)   A household name even among those not considered great fans of American gospel music.

Cyrus McCormick (1809–84)   He was the inventor of the reaper; his dying words were "Work! Work!"

Potter Palmer (1826–1902)   The famous department store magnate was also founder of the Palmer House Hotel.

Hyman Rickover (1900–86)   The father of the nuclear submarine.

Carl Sandburg (1878–1967)   Leading American poet and Lincoln's biographer.

Theodore Thomas (1835–1905)   Founder of the Chicago Symphony.

Muddy Waters (1915–83)   The king of Chicago blues.

Johnny Weissmuller (1904–84)   He overcame childhood polio to become a champion Olympic swimmer and Hollywood's most famous Tarzan.

Florenz Ziegfeld (1869–1932)   Theatrical producer and founder of the Ziegfeld Follies.

4   Recommended Books, Films & Recordings

Books

So many great American writers have either come from Chicago, lived here during their productive years, or set their work within the city's confines, that it is not easy to recommend a single book that captures Chicago in its essence. Each of these literary chroniclers provides an intriguing detail of the whole, a captivating aspect of the city that rings true, without pretending to provide the entire melody of the place. To know Chicago in that way, studying its history plus all those impressionistic sightings recorded by its novelists, you'd have to read so many books that you might never leave your armchair.

James T. Farrell's trilogy *Studs Lonigan,* published in the thirties, is one place to start if you want to understand the power of ethnic and neighborhood identity in Chicago. Certain works of novelists Theodore Dreiser (*Sister Carrie*) and Upton Sinclair (*The Jungle*) and journalist, sports columnist, and short-story writer Ring Lardner also reveal Chicago's social classes.

Other books set (in full or in part) within the city are Clancy Sigal's *Going Away,* John Dos Passos's *USA,* Philip Roth's *Letting Go,* and Saul Bellow's *The Adventures of Augie March* and *Humboldt's Gift.* Richard Wright spent time in Chicago and wrote about it in *Native Son* and *Cooley High.* Hemingway was a native son (Oak Park), though he didn't write much about the city. Chicago has had several fabled poets, including Carl Sandburg and Vachel Lindsay, and the brilliant troubador and popular novelist Nelson Algren wrote *Chicago: City on the Make,* a work of literary beauty. Even Bertolt Brecht set a play, *Saint Joan of the Stockyards,* in Chicago.

And, of course, no one has given a voice to the people of Chicago as has Studs Terkel—in *Division Street America, Hard Times,* and *Working.* These books as well as his own paean to the city, *Chicago,* reveal much about the city he adopted as his own.

Films

The Blues Brothers (1980), with Dan Akroyd, John Belushi, and John Candy.
Risky Business (1983), with Tom Cruise and Rebecca De Mornay.
About Last Night (1986), with Rob Lowe and Demi Moore.
The Color of Money (1986), with Tom Cruise, Mary Elizabeth Mastrantonio, and Paul Newman.

Ferris Bueller's Day Off (1986), with Matthew Broderick and Jennifer Grey.
Running Scared (1986), with Billy Crystal and Gregory Hines.
The Untouchables (1987), with Sean Connery, Kevin Costner, and Robert DeNiro.
Red Heat (1988), with James Belushi and Arnold Schwarzenegger.
Home Alone (1990), with Macaulay Culkin, Joe Pesci, and Daniel Stern.
Backdraft (1991), with William Baldwin, Robert DeNiro, Scott Glenn, and Kurt Russell.
The Babe (1992), with John Goodman and Kelly McGillis.
A League of Their Own (1992), with Geena Davis, Tom Hanks, and Madonna.
Prelude to a Kiss (1992), with Alec Baldwin, Kathy Bates, Ned Beatty, Patty Duke, Meg Ryan, and Sidney Walker.
The Fugitive (1993), with Harrison Ford and Tommy Lee Jones.

Recordings

CHICAGO SONGS

"Chicago That Toddling Town"; words and music by Fred Fisher, made famous by Fred Astaire and Ginger Rogers in the movie *The Story of Vernon and Irene Castle*. Later recorded by Count Basie, Tony Bennett, Benny Goodman, and Jimmy Dorsey, among others.
"Sweet Home Chicago"; recorded and written by Robert Johnson, 1925; later recorded by the Blues Brothers, 1979.
"My Kind of Town"; words by Sammy Cahn and music by James Van Heusen, 1964. Made famous by Frank Sinatra and later recorded by Count Basie and Guy Lombardo.
"Lake Shore Drive"; Aliotta, Haynes, & Jeremiah, 1974.
"Go Cubs Go"; music and words by Steve Goodman, 1984.

CHICAGO RECORDINGS

Chuck Berry, Chess Recording Studio, 5150 S. Michigan Ave., 1950s.
The Rolling Stones, *It's All Over Now,* Chess Recording Studio, 1965.
The Buckinghams, *Kind of a Drag,* Chess Recording Studio, 1966.

2

Planning a Trip to Chicago

AFTER DECIDING WHERE TO TRAVEL, MOST PEOPLE HAVE TWO
fundamental questions: What will it cost? and How do I get there?
This chapter will answer both of these questions and also will resolve
other important issues—such as when to go and where to obtain more
information about Chicago.

The calendar of events will help you plan for (or avoid) festivals,
shows, and parades, and the temperature and precipitation chart will
help you decide which jacket to bring. If you are disabled, a senior
citizen, single, traveling with your family, or a student, you will find
special tips and names of organizations that cater to your needs in
this chapter as well.

1 Information & Money

Sources Of Information

The **Chicago Office of Tourism,** Chicago Cultural Center, 78 E.
Washington St., Chicago, IL 60602 (**☎ 312/744-2400,** or toll free
800/ITS-CHGO), will mail you a packet of material, including
up-to-date calendars that survey special events at four-month intervals.

Chicago has several independent neighborhood associations, and
each can provide visitors with additional information on specific areas
of town. Such resources are listed where these neighborhoods are
highlighted in the text.

Another excellent source of free information is your local travel
agent, who can give you up-to-date information on bargain airline
fares and package land arrangements that often mean additional sav-
ings for you.

Money

In addition to paying close attention to the details below, foreign
visitors should also see Chapter 3 for monetary descriptions and
currency-exchange information.

U.S. dollar traveler's checks are the safest, most negotiable way to
carry currency. These are accepted by most restaurants, hotels, and
shops, and can generally be exchanged for cash at any bank. However, once you get away from downtown and outside the more affluent neighborhoods, smaller restaurants and shops may be reluctant
to accept traveler's checks. American Express offices are open Monday through Friday from 9am to 5pm, and one office is also open on
Saturday from 10am to 3pm. See "Fast Facts: Chicago" in Chapter
4 for office locations.

Most banks offer Automated Teller Machines (ATMs), which
accept cards connected to particular networks. Before your trip, ask
your bank for a directory to the banks connected to its network to
find out which (if any) Chicago ATMs you can use.

What Things Cost in Chicago	U.S.$
Taxi from airport to city center	25.00–30.00
Bus fare to any destination within the city	1.20
Double room at the Drake hotel (very expensive)	205.00–310.00
Double room at the Allerton hotel (moderate)	119.00–129.00
Double room at the City Suites Hotel (budget)	75.00
Lunch for one at the Frontera Grill (moderate)	15.00
Lunch for one at Ed Debevic's (budget)	7.00
Dinner for one, without wine, at the Everest Room (very expensive)	75.00
Dinner for one, without wine, at Zum Deutschen Eck (moderate)	25.00
Dinner for one at Mity Nice (budget)	15.00
Glass of beer	2.00
Coca-Cola	1.00
Cup of coffee	1.00
Admission to top of Sears Tower	6.00
Movie ticket	7.00
Theater ticket	10.00–40.00

2   When to Go—Climate & Events

Climate

If you hate the cold or want to avoid hot weather, the ideal time to visit is early autumn, when the days are most likely to be consistently pleasant.

Much of Chicago's weather seems to be strongly influenced by the proximity of Lake Michigan. At its most humane, the lake cools the city with gentle breezes, particularly welcome during those hours of sweltering humidity that often accompany the dog days of summer. When that same offshore breeze strengthens to the force of a biting wind and blows across the lakefront streets during late fall and throughout the long winter, you may justifiably wonder if any other American city suffers so miserably from the cold as Chicago does. Speaking as a resident of Maine, I think Chicago's winter cold is much maligned (those occasional punishing gale-force winds off Lake Michigan notwithstanding), and need not seem daunting if you dress properly and pay particular attention to insulating hands, feet, and ears. A wintertime visit to Chicago should not be ruled out automatically by the visitor who enjoys the outdoors in all seasons. Any city as big as Chicago has to be considered a four-season destination. After all, the city does not curl up and hibernate just because the mercury drops below zero. As an added incentive to "off-season" travelers, keep in mind that during the winter, hotel rates are rock-bottom.

Chicago's Average Temperatures and Precipitation

	Jan	Feb	Mar	Apr	May	June	July	Aug	Sept	Oct	Nov	Dec
High °F	20.2	33.9	44.3	58.8	70.0	79.4	85.3	82.1	75.5	64.1	48.2	35.0
Low °F	13.6	18.1	27.6	38.8	48.1	57.7	62.7	61.7	53.9	42.0	31.4	20.3
Precipitation (inches)	1.60	1.31	2.59	3.66	3.15	4.08	3.63	3.53	3.35	2.28	2.06	2.10

Chicago Calendar of Events

The best way to stay on top of the city's current crop of special events is to ask the **Chicago Office of Tourism** (☎ 312/744-2400, or toll free 800/ITS-CHGO) to mail you a copy of their quarterly publication, the *Chicago Illinois Calendar,* plus the latest materials produced by the **Mayor's Office of Special Events** (☎ 312/744-3315, or the Events Hotline 312/744-3370) with information on Chicago neighborhood festivals. Or you can opt for spontaneity and simply take potluck when you arrive. The one thing you can count on, whether or not you choose to inform yourself in advance, is that there will be a slew of these events to tempt your participation, whatever the duration of your stay and regardless of what month you visit Chicago.

Of the annual events, the most lively and unpredictable tend to revolve around the national parades and the street celebrations staged by many of Chicago's numerous ethnic groups. There are also food, music, art, and flower fairs that each have their special niches in the city's yearly schedule.

Remember that new events may be added to this list every year, and that occasionally special events are discontinued. So to avoid disappointment, be sure to telephone in advance to either the sponsoring organization, the Chicago Office of Tourism, or the Mayor's Office of Special Events to verify dates, times, and locations. Some events charge an admission fee or request a donation.

January
- **Chicago Boat, Sports, and RV Show,** McCormick Place, 2300 S. Lake Shore Dr. (☎ 567-8500). This extravaganza with big-time entertainment usually takes place immediately following New Year's.
- **Sports Fishing, Travel, and Outdoor Show,** O'Hare Expo Center, 9291 W. Bryn Mawr Ave. (☎ 692-2220). Generally held toward the end of the month.

February
- **Chicago Cubs Fan Convention** (☎ 951-CUBS). This annual confab for Cubbies' fans offers a chance to talk baseball with players and coaches.

- **Azalea Flower Show,** Lincoln Park Conservatory, 2400 N. Stockton Dr. (☎ **294-4770**), and also a **Camellia Flower Show** at the Garfield Park Conservatory (☎ **533-1281**). Both are held all month long.
- **Chinese New Year Parade,** on Wentworth and Cermak Streets (☎ **326-5320**). Join in as the sacred dragon whirls down the boulevard and restaurateurs pass out small envelopes of money to their regular customers. Call to verify the date, which varies from year to year.
- **Chicago Auto Show,** McCormick Place, 2300 S. Lake Shore Dr. (☎ **692-2220**). Hundreds of cars and trucks, domestic and foreign, current and futuristic, on display.
- **University of Chicago Folk Festival,** on campus at Mandel Hall, 57th and University Avenues. Call **702-9793** for more information.
- **Black History Month.** It's celebrated with special events at the Chicago Cultural Center, the Museum of Science and Industry, and the DuSable Museum.

★ The Medinah Shrine Circus

This is the Shriners' annual big-top event to benefit charity.
Where: Medinah Temple, 600 N. Wabash (☎ **266-5050**). **When:** Spread over three weeks between late February and early March. **How:** Tickets may be purchased through Ticketron or ordered directly from the Shriners' through the telephone number listed above.

March

★ St. Patrick's Day Parade

Expect the usual enthusiasm and an occasional donnybrook. The Chicago River is dyed kelly green for the occasion.
Where: Along Dearborn Street from Wacker Drive to Van Buren. **When:** March 17. **How:** Free. The best place to view the parade is around Wacker and Dearborn.

April

- **Opening Day.** For the Cubs, call **404-CUBS;** for the White Sox, call **924-1000.**
- **Spring and Easter Flower Show,** Lincoln Park Conservatory, 2400 N. Stockton Dr. Call **294-4700** for more information.
- **International Kennel Dog Show,** McCormick Place, 2300 S. Lake Shore Dr. (☎ **237-5100**). This event is for all breeds during the first week of April.
- **Hyde Park House,** University of Chicago, 969 E. 60th St. (☎ **667-3932**). Featuring the latest in restoration and renovation concepts and materials. Generally held the second weekend in April.

May

- **Buckingham Fountain Color Light Show,** in Grant Park, at Congress and Lake Shore Drive. Runs from May 1 to October 1 daily from 9 to 11pm.
- **Polish Constitution Day Parade,** along Clark Street from Wacker Drive to Congress (☎ 744-3315). Early May.
- **Annual Art & Crafts Exposition,** American Indian Center. Call 275-5871 for more information.
- **Chicago International Art Exposition,** Navy Pier, 600 E. Grand Ave. (☎ 787-6858). This five-day event involves the participation of 160 Chicago art galleries and exhibits the work of more than 1,500 artists.
- **Greek-American Parade,** south on Michigan Avenue from Wacker Drive to Congress (☎ 744-3315). May 14.
- **Armed Forces Day Parade,** south on LaSalle Street from Wacker Drive to Congress (☎ 926-2258). May 20.
- **Wright Plus Tour.** An annual tour of Frank Lloyd Wright's home and studio in Oak Park (☎ 708/848-1500). The second or third week in May.
- **Beverly Housewalk.** An organized tour of this South Side neighborhood (☎ 233-3100) starts at 2153 W. 111th St. in late May.
- **International Theater Festival of Chicago.** Various theaters participate; call 664-3370 for more information. Held biennially in even-numbered years.

June

⭐ **Ravinia Festival**

Ravinia is the summer home of the Chicago Symphony and venue of many other first-rate visiting orchestras, chamber ensembles, pop artists, and so forth.
Where: Ravinia Park, Highland Park. **When:** June through September. **How:** Call 728-4642 for ticket reservations.

- **Neighborhood Festivals.** Many begin this month at various city locations. Call 744-3315 for more information.

⭐ **Chicago Blues Festival**

This is a much-awaited and heavily attended event.
Where: Petrillo Music Shell, at Jackson and Columbus Drives in Grant Park (☎ 744-3315). **When:** Usually staged the second weekend of June. **How:** Free; get there in the afternoon to get a good spot on the lawn for the evening show.

- **Asparagus Fest,** on Lincoln, Lawrence, and Western Avenues. This local food festival near Lincoln Square occurs in early June. Call 878-7331 for more information.

⭐ **Gospel Festival**

This festival features the flip side of the blues.
Where: Petrillo Music Shell, at Jackson and Columbus
Drives in Grant Park (☎ 744-3315). **When:** Second or
third weekend in June. **How:** Free; just turn up.

- **Puerto Rican Day Parade,** along Clark Street from
  Wacker Drive to Congress (☎ 744-3315). Another of
  Chicago's animated Latino street celebrations. First
  Saturday in June.
- **Wells Street Art Fair,** 1900 N. Lincoln Ave. This Chicago
  tradition is always held in Old Town the second weekend
  in June (☎ 337-1938).
- **Filipino American Council Parade,** along Clark Street
  from Wacker Drive to Congress. June 12.
- **Celebrate State Street,** along State Street from Jackson to
  the lake (☎ 782-9160). Outdoor festivities are geared to
  the commercial resuscitation of "that great street."
- **Andersonville Midsommerfest,** along Clark Street from
  Foster to Catalpa (☎ 728-2995). This event recalls the
  heyday of this neighborhood as Chicago's principal Swedish
  community. Third weekend in June.
- **Printer's Row Book Fair,** on Dearborn Street from
  Harrison to Polk (☎ 987-1980). An outdoor book fair.
  Third weekend of June.
- **Grant Park Concerts,** Petrillo Music Shell, at Jackson
  and Columbus Drives in Grant Park (☎ 294-2920)
  The seasonal outdoor musical concerts in the park begin
  the last week in June.

⭐ **Gay and Lesbian Pride Week Parade**

The parade is the colorful culmination of a week of
activities by Chicago's gay and lesbian community.
Where: Halsted Street, from Belmont Avenue to
Broadway, south to Diversey Parkway, and east to Sheridan
Road. **When:** First Sunday in June at 2pm. **How:** Free;
take up a spot on Broadway for the best view. Call
348-8243 for information.

July

⭐ **Taste of Chicago**

Scores of Chicago's restaurants cart their fare to foodstands
set up throughout the park.
Where: In Grant Park. **When:** Eight days of street feasting,
in late June, and the first week of July. **How:** Free
admittance; you pay for the sampling, of course. Call
744-3315 for information.

- **The Fourth of July.** The holiday is celebrated in Chicago on the third of July: Concerts, fireworks, and a parade are the highlights of the celebration in Grant Park.
- **Annual Old-Fashioned Fourth of July Celebration,** Chicago Historical Society grounds, Clark Street and North Avenue (☎ 642-4600).
- **Gallery 37.** The outdoor art extravaganza (☎ 744-8925) of the Chicago Cultural Center, along State Street between Washington and Randolph. Early July.
- **Annual American Spanish Dance Festival,** put on by the Ensemble Español Spanish Dance Theater at Northeastern Illinois University, 5500 N. St. Louis (☎ 583-4050, ext. 3015). This free event is held over a two-week period in mid-July.
- **Chicago-Mackinac Island Boat Race,** with the starting line at the Monroe Street Harbor (☎ 861-7777). The grandest of the inland water races is scheduled toward the end of July.

August

- **Taste of River North,** on Superior between Franklin and Wells. Call **645-1047** for more information on this neighborhood festival.
- **Medieval Faire In Oz Park,** at Webster, Larabee, and Lincoln (☎ 880-5200). This event features troubadours, jugglers, acrobats, and other market-day entertainments inspired by the Middle Ages. First weekend of August.
- **Illinois State Fair,** in Springfield (☎ 217/782-6661). Middle of the month.
- **Venetian Night,** from Monroe Harbor to the planetarium (☎ 744-3315). The boat carnival on the lake is complete with fireworks.
- **Bud Billiken Parade and Picnic.** An African-American celebration (☎ 225-2400). The parade route follows 39th Street and King Drive to 55th Street and Washington Park. Second Saturday in August, beginning at 10am.

★ **Air & Water Show**

You'll enjoy this popular perennial aquatic and aerial spectacular.
Where: North Avenue Beach. **When:** Scheduled each summer toward the end of August. **How:** Free. An alternative viewing spot is Oak Street Beach, along the Gold Coast. Call **708/498-5071** for details.

September

★ **Jazz Festival**

The Jazz Festival is Chicago style, and plenty steamy.
Where: Petrillo Music Shell, Jackson and Columbus Drives in Grant Park. **When:** First week of September; almost

always over Labor Day weekend. **How:** Free; come early and stay late. Call **744-3370** for information.

- **"Viva! Chicago" Latin Music Festival.** The Latin beat in all its dynamic and sultry variations from mariachi to mambo, at the Petrillo Music Shell, Grant Park, Jackson Boulevard and Columbus Drive. Second weekend in September (☎ **744-3340**).

- **Berghoff Octoberfest,** Adams Street between Dearborn and State Streets (☎ **427-3170**). A popular three-day beerfest at one of Chicago's oldest and best-loved restaurants, right down in the Loop. Usually held in mid-September.

- **Mexican Independence Day Parade,** along Michigan Avenue between Wacker Drive and Congress. Call **744-3315** for more information.

- **Chicago Federation of Labor Parade,** along Dearborn between Wacker Drive and Van Buren Street. Call **744-3315** for more information; early in the month.

October

- **Columbus Day Parade,** Dearborn Street from Wacker Drive to Congress (☎ **828-0010**). Italian-American Day by any other name. The closest Monday to October 12.

- **Chicago International Antique Show,** Navy Pier (☎ **787-6858**). The show takes place at mid-month over a four-day period; it's not a flea market.

- **Chicago International Film Festival** (☎ **644-3400**). It's held the last week of October or the first week of November at various theaters.

- **The Big Top.** This is the month that Ringling Brothers, Barnum & Bailey comes to Chicago and sets up in the Chicago Stadium, 1800 W. Madison (☎ **733-5300**).

November

- **Christmas Around the World,** at the Museum of Science and Industry, 57th Street and Lake Shore Drive (☎ **684-1414**). The traditional Christmas exhibit opens in late November and stays open until New Year's.

- **Chrysanthemum Show,** Garfield Park Conservatory, 300 N. Central Park Ave. (☎ **826-3175**), and Lincoln Park Conservatory, at Fullerton and Stockton (☎ **294-2493**). The show lasts for two weeks in mid-November.

- **Veterans' Day Parade,** in the Loop (☎ **744-3515**).

- **Christmas Tree Lighting,** Daley Center Plaza, in the Loop (☎ **744-3315**). Toward the end of the month.

⭐ **Michigan Avenue Holiday Lights Festival**

Beginning at dusk, a procession of horse-drawn carriages works its way south along Michigan Avenue, with lights being illuminated block by block as the procession passes. Carolers, elves, and minstrels appear with Santa along the

avenue throughout the day and into the evening.
Where: Michigan Avenue from Oak Street to the Chicago River. **When:** Toward the end of November; call **642-3570** for the exact date and scheduling.

December

- *A Christmas Carol,* performed at the Goodman Theatre, 200 S. Columbus Dr. Call **443-3800** for information and tickets.
- **Nutcracker ballet,** at the Arie Crown Theater, McCormick Place, 23rd Street and Lake Shore Drive (☎ **791-6000**). This charity event is sponsored every year for two weeks during mid-December by the *Chicago Tribune.*
- **Caroling to the Animals,** Lincoln Park Zoo, 2200 N. Cannon Dr. (☎ **935-6700**). Call for the precise date of this mid-month event, which is of special interest to preschoolers.
- **Christmas Flower Show,** at the Lincoln Park Conservatory, at Fullerton and Stockton (☎ **294-2493**), and at Garfield Park Conservatory, 300 N. Central Park Ave. (☎ **826-3175**). The show begins the last week of December and continues through the holidays into January.

---

3 Insurance & Safety

Before you leave on your trip, be sure you are protected with adequate health insurance coverage.

INSURANCE Most travel agents sell low-cost health, loss, and trip-cancellation insurance to their vacationing clients. Rates for these short-term policies are generally reasonable, and these policies allow you to supplement existing coverage with a minimum of complications. Other forms of travel-related insurance are also available, including coverage for lost or damaged baggage. Often a single policy provided by your travel agent will protect you in all of these areas and will also provide supplementary medical coverage.

SAFETY Depending on where you travel in Chicago and what time of day it is, you are very unlikely to be a victim of a mugging or other violent crime. One place to be particularly careful is on the subway; avoid subway travel during the off-hours of early morning or late at night. There is no magic antidote to street crime; sometimes in a big city, you can simply be in the right place at the wrong time. But as most urban dwellers know, nothing protects you more from crimes

---

IMPRESSIONS

It rained and fogged in Chicago and muddy-flowing people oozed thick in the canyon-beds of the streets. Yet it seemed to me more alive and more real than New York.

—D. H. Lawrence, Letter To Mrs. Bessie Freeman, August 1923

of opportunity than a good dose of street smarts—maintain a state of alertness to place and circumstances at all times, but especially in remote areas and after dark.

4   What to Pack

Chicago is a city located in a four-season climate. That means you bundle up in the winter, strip down in the summer, and encounter sweater or light-jacket weather during the autumn and spring. Naturally, the local climate isn't always going to conform to this schematic rule. But the point is to come prepared for the worst. If, for example, you visit Chicago in the depth of winter, you may be treated to a balmy thaw for a week or so—but don't count on it. The opposite is true for Chicago sweltering summers; the only time you'll need a sweater or a wrap is when you don't bring one.

You don't necessarily have to travel with an umbrella; if it does rain, you can always purchase a cheap umbrella in a drugstore or from a curbside vendor. Also, don't forget to pack your medications and valid prescriptions for refills in case you run out during your stay.

5   Tips for the Disabled, Seniors, Singles, Families & Students

FOR THE DISABLED   Most of Chicago's sidewalks, as well as major museums and tourist attractions, are fitted with wheelchair ramps to accommodate physically challenged visitors. More and more hotels are also providing special accommodations and services for wheelchair-bound visitors. These include large bathrooms, ramps, and telecommunications devices for the hearing impaired.

For specific information on facilities for people with disabilities who are traveling in Chicago, call or write the **Mayor's Office for People with Disabilities,** located at 510 N. Peshtigo Court, Room 405B, Chicago, IL 60611 (☎ **312/744-6673** for voice; **312/744-4964** for TT/TDD), and staffed from 8:30am to 4:30pm Monday through Friday.

Also, the **Society for the Advancement of Travel for the Handicapped,** 347 Fifth Ave., Suite 610, New York, NY 10016 (☎ **212/447-SATH**), may offer some support.

FOR SENIORS   In Chicago, the term "seniors" usually refers to men and women age 65 and older. Seniors regularly receive discounts at museums and attractions, but seniors may also seek discounts at hotels and restaurants, many of which are willing to offer reduced prices, though they may not advertise the fact. Airlines also will sometimes offer senior discounts, but first compare these fares with any available promotional tickets.

One excellent source of travel information for seniors is the **American Association of Retired Persons (AARP),** 601 E. St. NW, Washington, DC 20049 (☎ **202/434-2277**). Members are offered discounts on car rentals, hotels, airfares, and even sightseeing. AARP travel arrangements are handled by American Express.

FOR SINGLES **Jens Jurgen, Travel Companion,** P.O. Box P-833, Amityville, NY 11701 (☎ **516/454-0880**), attempts to match single travelers with like-minded companions, and it is now the largest such company in the United States. New applicants fill out a form stating their preferences and needs; in reply, they receive a list of potential partners. **Grand Circle Travel,** 347 Congress St., Boston, MA 02210 (☎ **617/350-7500,** or toll free **800/221-2610**) offers escorted tours and cruises for retired persons, including singles.

FOR FAMILIES Traveling with infants and small children requires some additional planning. Don't forget the children's aspirin, thermometer, Band-Aids, and similar supplies; also bring along items of personal security, such as favorite blankets and stuffed animals.

Airlines will provide special children's meals with 24 hours' notice, but not baby food, which you must supply.

Most hotels maintain an active list of reliable babysitters.

For special tips on how to travel successfully with children, you might consider a subscription to *Family Travel Times,* a newsletter put out by the organization **TWYCH (Travel with Your Children),** 80 Eighth Ave., New York, NY 10011 (☎ **212/206-0688**). Subscribers may also call with questions between 10am and noon, eastern standard time.

FOR STUDENTS Students will find that their valid high school or college ID means discounts on travel, theater, and museum tickets, and at some nightspots.

6   Getting There

By Plane

Chicago's **O'Hare International Airport** has been—and to my knowledge still is—the world's busiest airport. A good travel agent is your best source of information on flights to Chicago. Best of all, timely bookings through a travel agency cost you nothing, and indeed, often save you money.

THE MAJOR AIRLINES Domestic carriers that fly regularly to Chicago include **American** (toll free **800/433-7300**), **Continental** (☎ toll free **800/525-0280**), **Delta** (☎ toll free

IMPRESSIONS

> *This Chicago is huge,* infinite *(of potential size and form, and even of actual) black, smoky,* old-*looking, very like some preternaturally boomed Manchester or Glasgow lying beside a colossal lake (Michigan) of hard pale green jade, and putting forth railway antennae of maddening complexity and gigantic length.*
> —Henry James, Letter to Edward Warren, March 19, 1905

800/241-4141), **Kiwi** (☎ toll free **800/221-2500**), **Northwest** (☎ toll free **800/225-2525**), **Southwest** (☎ toll free **800/435-9792**), **Tower** (☎ toll free **800/538-5494**), **TWA** (☎ toll free **800/221-2000**), **United** (☎ toll free **800/241-6522**), and **USAir** (☎ toll free **800/428-4322**). Commuter service is also provided by several regional airlines. International service to Chicago is also extensive via such operators as Aer Lingus (☎ toll free **800/223-6537**), Air Canada (☎ toll free **800/426-7000**), Air France, (☎ toll free **800/237-2747**), Alitalia, (☎ toll free **800/223-5730**), British Airways (☎ toll free **800/247-9297**), Japan Air Lines (☎ toll free **800/565-7000**), KLM (☎ toll free **800/777-5553**), Lufthansa (☎ toll free **800/645-3880**), Swissair (☎ toll free **800/221-6644**), and Mexicana (☎ toll free **800/531-7921**). The toll-free numbers listed are for the United States only.

REGULAR AIRFARES   The easiest, but not necessarily the cheapest, way to purchase an airline ticket is through your local travel agent. A travel agent is a convenience that doesn't cost you anything, but don't expect your travel agent to spend an inordinate amount of time trying to find you the cheapest ticket available—doing so will not only take up his or her time, but lead to a smaller commission from the airline as well.

To get the lowest possible fare, you will probably have to do some spade work yourself. First call several carriers that fly to Chicago. Ask them to quote you the lowest fare available. Airlines have sales and fare wars all the time so shop around before you make your decision, but remember, in general, the lower the fare, the more restrictions and penalties apply for changing dates and itineraries.

The lowest fare is referred to as **economy class,** and it often requires that you travel during the week; sometimes there are other

---

Frommer's Smart Traveler: Airfares

1. Check with all the airlines that fly to your destination before deciding on a carrier. Their fares are seldom uniform.

2. Don't use airline jargon, such as "super APEX" or "discount," when talking to a ticket agent; simply ask for the lowest available fare and the conditions that attach to it.

3. Keep checking with airlines; between yesterday's call and today's, an airline is capable of lowering the fare by an astounding amount.

4. For convenience and reliability, make your reservations and ground arrangements through a travel agent; for economy with a certain degree of risk attached, shop around the consolidators, discount travel agents, and charter companies.

5. Fares are usually lowest at midweek, so plan to travel then if possible.

Chicago and Vicinity

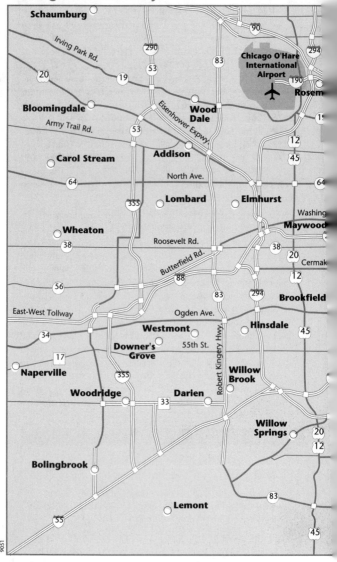

conditions that the airline ticket agent won't necessarily tell you unless you ask. Keep in mind that airfares fluctuate widely. At the time of this writing, round-trip fares from New York to Chicago were $149; from Los Angeles, $348; and from Atlanta, $218.

The next lowest fares are called **coach,** and the round-trip fare from New York to Chicago was listed as $219, while the **first-class** fare for the same itinerary was $776.

OTHER GOOD-VALUE CHOICES Many travelers in recent years have opted to act as their own travel agents, seeking out the lowest possible airfares offered by consolidators, charters, and even courier services.

Consolidators (also called **bucket shops**) buy blocks of tickets directly from the airlines. In a sense, they speculate in air-passage futures, and they can sell their "buckets" at prices that are often far below official rates. There are many well-known and legitimate bucket shops, and a number of fly-by-night operations as well. If you have any doubts about a particular company, consult your local branch of the Better Business Bureau.

Charter companies generally offer onetime flights to specific destinations. Charter flights can be an inexpensive means of traveling to a far-away destination, but generally they do not operate in the Chicago market. The same tends to be true for **courier** flights; you are more likely to arrange a courier flight to Hong Kong, or perhaps from coast to coast in the United States than to Chicago. News paper travel supplements and the yellow pages are good sources for information on the offerings or whereabouts of consolidators, charter companies, and courier services.

By Train

Travel by passenger train is definitely on the upswing in the United States, following years of decline due to the rapid growth of both air and automobile travel. Rail passenger service, while it may never approach the grandeur of its heyday, has made enormous advances in service, comfort, and efficiency since the creation of Amtrak in 1971. As in the past, but on a reduced scale, Chicago remains the hub of the national passenger rail system. Traveling great distances by train is certainly not the quickest way to go, nor always the most convenient. But train travel has its unique advantages over flying and driving. You have something of the pace of car travel, a feeling of security—real or imagined—that some travelers find impossible while flying, and the space to move about that neither cars nor planes can provide.

Consult your travel agent or call **Amtrak** (☎ toll free **800/USA-RAIL**). Ask the reservations agent to send you Amtrak's useful travel planner with information on train accommodations and package tours. For Amtrak information in Chicago, call **312/558-1075**. Some Chicago-bound intercity "name trains," with their principal stops, are:

Lake Shore Limited   Links New York and Boston with Chicago through Albany, Syracuse, Rochester, Buffalo, Cleveland, Toledo, and South Bend (with connecting service from Detroit).

Broadway Limited   Travels between New York and Chicago by way of Trenton, Philadelphia, Harrisburg, Pittsburgh, and Fort Wayne.

Capitol Limited   Connects Washington, D.C., and Chicago through Harper's Ferry, Pittsburgh, Canton, and Fort Wayne.

Cardinal   Links New York and Chicago via Philadelphia, Baltimore, Washington, D.C., Charlottesville, Charleston, Cincinnati, and Indianapolis.

City of New Orleans   Travels from New Orleans to Chicago stopping at Champaign, Memphis, Jackson, and several smaller Mississippi River cities.

Eagle   Travels between San Antonio and Chicago via Austin, Fort Worth, Dallas, Little Rock, and St. Louis.

Southwest Chief   Connects Los Angeles and Chicago through Flagstaff, Albuquerque, and Kansas City.

California Zephyr   Connects San Francisco and Chicago through Sacramento, Reno, Salt Lake City, Glenwood Springs, Winter Park, Denver, and Omaha.

Empire Builder   Links Seattle and Chicago by way of Spokane, Glacier National Park, Minneapolis, and Milwaukee.

By Bus

The bus is still the most convenient and economical mode of intercity travel for those who don't own or operate automobiles. Call your local **Greyhound** terminal for information nationwide on routes, schedules, and fares. Greyhound in Chicago (and Trailways, with which the company has consolidated) is located at 630 W. Harrison (☎ toll free **800/231-2222**).

By Car

Chicago is serviced by interstate highways from all major points on the compass. I-80 and I-90 approach from the east, crossing the northern sector of Illinois, with I-90 splitting off and emptying into Chicago via the Skyway and the Dan Ryan Expressway. From here I-90 runs through Wisconsin following a northern route to and from Seattle. I-55 snakes up the Mississippi Valley from the vicinity of New Orleans and enters Chicago from the west along the Stevenson Expressway, and in the opposite direction provides an outlet to the Southwest. I-57 originates in southern Illinois and forms part of the interstate linkage to Florida nad the South, connecting within Chicago on the west leg of the Dan Ryan. I-94 links Detroit with Chicago, arriving on the Calumet Expressway and leaving the city via the Kennedy Expressway en route to the Northwest.

Here are a few approximate driving distances in miles to Chicago: from Milwaukee, 90; from St. Louis, 290; from Detroit, 279; from Albuquerque, 1,293; from Phoenix, 1,729; from Wahington, D.C., 695; from New York City, 840; and from Los Angeles, 2,112.

IMPRESSIONS

At a literary conference at Notre Dame, I . . . ran into a poet who is noted for his verse celebrating the ecology, née Nature. He lives in a dramatic house nailed together completely from uncut pieces of hickory driftwood, perched on a bluff overlooking the crashing ocean. . . . I remarked that this must be the ideal setting in which to write about the ecological wonders. "I wouldn't know," he said. "I do all my writing in O'Hare."
—Tom Wolfe, "The Intelligent Coed's Guide to America," in *Mauve Gloves And Madmen, Clutter And Vine*, 1976

3

For Foreign Visitors

Aᴌᴛʜᴏᴜɢʜ Aᴍᴇʀɪᴄᴀɴ ꜰᴀᴅꜱ ᴀɴᴅ ꜰᴀꜱʜɪᴏɴꜱ ʜᴀᴠᴇ ꜱᴘʀᴇᴀᴅ ᴀᴄʀᴏꜱꜱ Eᴜʀᴏᴘᴇ and other parts of the world so that America may seem like familiar territory before your arrival, there are still many peculiarities and uniquely American situations that any foreign visitor will encounter.

1   Preparing for Your Trip

Entry Requirements

DOCUMENT REGULATIONS   Canadian citizens may enter the United States without visas; they need only proof of residence.

Citizens of the United Kingdom, New Zealand, Japan, and most western European countries traveling on valid passports may not need a visa for fewer than 90 days of holiday or business travel to the United States, providing that they hold a round-trip or return ticket and enter the United States on an airline or cruise line participating in the visa waiver program.

(Note that citizens of these visa-exempt countries who first enter the United States may then visit Mexico, Canada, Bermuda, and/or the Caribbean islands and then reenter the United States by any mode of transportation, without needing a visa. Further information is available from any United States embassy or consulate.)

Citizens of countries other than those stipulated above, including citizens of Australia, must have two documents: a valid passport, with an expiration date at least six months later than the scheduled end of the visit to the United States, and a tourist visa, available without charge from the nearest United States consulate.

To obtain a visa, the traveler must submit a completed application form (either in person or by mail) with a $1^1/_2$-inch square photo and demonstrate binding ties to a residence abroad. Usually you can obtain a visa at once or within 24 hours, but it may take longer during the summer rush from June to August. If you cannot go in person, contact the nearest U.S. embassy or consulate for directions on applying by mail. Your travel agent or airline office may also be able to provide you with visa applications and instructions. The U.S. consulate or embassy that issues your visa will determine whether you will be issued a multiple- or single-entry visa and any restrictions regarding the length of your stay.

MEDICAL REQUIREMENTS   No inoculations are needed to enter the United States unless you are coming from, or have stopped over in, areas known to be suffering from epidemics, particularly cholera or yellow fever.

If you have a disease requiring treatment with medications containing narcotics or with drugs requiring a syringe, carry a valid signed prescription from your physician to allay any suspicions that you are smuggling drugs.

CUSTOMS REQUIREMENTS   Every adult visitor may bring in, free of duty: 1 liter of wine or hard liquor; 200 cigarettes or 100 cigars (but no cigars from Cuba) or 3 pounds of smoking tobacco; and $100 worth of gifts. These exemptions are offered to travelers who spend at least 72 hours in the United States and who have not claimed them within the preceding six months. It is altogether forbidden to bring into the country foodstuffs (particularly cheese, fruit, cooked meats, and canned goods) and plants (vegetables, seeds, tropical plants, and so on). Foreign tourists may bring in or take out up to $10,000 in United States or foreign currency with no formalities; larger sums must be declared to Customs on entering or leaving.

Insurance

Unlike most other countries, there is no national health system in the United States. Because the cost of medical care is extremely high, we strongly advise every traveler to secure health coverage before setting out.

You may want to take out a comprehensive travel policy that covers (for a relatively low premium) sickness or injury costs (medical, surgical, and hospital); loss of, or theft of your baggage; trip-cancellation costs; guarantee of bail in case you are arrested; and costs of accident, repatriation, or death. Such packages (for example, "Europe Assistance" in Europe) are sold by automobile clubs at attractive rates, as well as by insurance companies and travel agencies.

Money

CURRENCY & EXCHANGE   The U.S. monetary system has a decimal base: one American **dollar** ($1) = 100 **cents** (100¢).

Dollar bills commonly come in $1 ("a buck"), $5, $10, $20, $50, and $100 denominations (the last two are not welcome when paying for small purchases and are not accepted in taxis or at subway ticket booths). There are also $2 bills (seldom encountered).

There are six denominations of coins: 1¢ (one cent or a "penny"), 5¢ (five cents or a "nickel"), 10¢ (ten cents or a "dime"), 25¢ (twenty-five cents or a "quarter"), 50¢ (fifty cents or a "half dollar"), and the rare $1 piece.

The foreign-exchange bureaus so common in Europe are rare even at airports in the United States and nonexistent outside major cities. Try to avoid having to change foreign money, or traveler's checks denominated other than in U.S. dollars, at a small-town bank, or even a branch in a big city. In fact, leave any currency other than U.S. dollars at home—it may prove more nuisance to you than it's worth.

TRAVELER'S CHECKS   Traveler's checks denominated in U.S. dollars are readily accepted at most hotels, motels, restaurants, and large stores. But the best place to change traveler's checks is at a bank. Do not bring traveler's checks denominated in other currencies.

CREDIT CARDS   The method of payment most widely used is the credit card: VISA (BarclayCard in Britain), MasterCard

(EuroCard in Europe, Access in Britain, Chargex in Canada), American Express, Diners Club, Discover, and Carte Blanche. You can save yourself trouble by using "plastic money" rather than cash or traveler's checks in most hotels, motels, restaurants, and retail stores (a growing number of food and liquor stores now accept credit cards). You must have a credit card to rent a car. It can also be used as proof of identity (often carrying more weight than a passport), or as a "cash card," enabling you to draw money from banks that accept them.

Safety

GENERAL   While tourist areas are generally safe, crime is on the increase everywhere, and U.S. urban areas tend to be less safe than those in Europe or Japan. This is particularly true of large U.S. cities. Visitors should always stay alert. It is wise to ask the city's or area's tourist office if you're in doubt about which neighborhoods are safe. Avoid deserted areas, especially at night. Don't go into any city park at night unless there is an event that attracts crowds—for example, New York City's concerts in the parks. Generally speaking, you can feel safe in areas where there are many people, and many open establishments.

Avoid carrying valuables with you on the street, and don't display expensive cameras or electronic equipment. Hold on to your pocketbook, and place your billfold in an inside pocket. In theaters, restaurants, and other public places, keep your possessions in sight.

Remember also that hotels are open to the public, and in a large hotel, security may not be able to screen everyone entering. Always lock your room door—don't assume that once inside your hotel you are automatically safe and no longer need be aware of your surroundings.

DRIVING   Safety while driving is particularly important. Question your rental agency about personal safety, or ask for a brochure of traveler safety tips when you pick up your car. Obtain from the agency written directions, or a map with the route marked in red, showing how to get to your destination. And, if possible, arrive and depart during daylight hours.

Recently more and more crime has involved cars and drivers. If you drive off a highway into a doubtful neighborhood, leave the area as quickly as possible. If you have an accident, even on the highway, stay in your car with the doors locked until you assess the situation or until the police arrive. If you are bumped from behind on the street or are involved in a minor accident with no injuries and the situation appears to be suspicious, motion to the other driver to follow you. *Never* get out of your car in such situations. You can also keep a pre-made sign in your car which reads: PLEASE FOLLOW THIS VEHICLE TO REPORT THE ACCIDENT. Show the sign to the other driver and go directly to the nearest police precinct, well-lighted service station, or all-night store.

If you see someone on the road who indicates a need for help, do *not* stop. Take note of the location, drive on to a well-lighted area, and telephone the police by dialing **911.**

Park in well-lighted, well-traveled areas if possible. Always keep your car doors locked, whether attended or unattended. Look around you before you get out of your car, and never leave any packages or valuables in sight. If someone attempts to rob you or steal your car, do *not* try to resist the thief/carjacker—report the incident to the police department immediately.

2   Getting to the U.S.

Travelers from overseas can take advantage of the **APEX (Advance Purchase Excursion) fares** offers by all the major U.S. and European carriers.

British Airways (☎ toll free **800/247-9297** in the U.S., or **081/897-4000** in the U.K.) offers direct flights from London's Heathrow Airport to Chicago. Their fares range from U.S. $734 round-trip during the summer high season to U.S. $519 during the low-traffic winter months. **Virgin Atlantic** (☎ toll free **800/862-8621** in the U.S., or **02/937-4774** in the U.K.) offers competitive (and frequently lower) fares from London's Gatwick Airport to Chicago.

Some large American airlines (for example, TWA, American, Northwest, United, and Delta) offer travelers on their transatlantic or transpacific flights special discount tickets under the name **Visit USA,** allowing travel between any United States destinations at minimum rates. They are not for sale in the United States, and must, therefore, be purchased before you leave your foreign point of departure. This system is the best, easiest, and fastest way to see the United States at low cost. You should obtain information well in advance from your travel agent or the office of the airline concerned, since the conditions attached to these discount tickets can be changed without advance notice.

The visitor arriving by air, no matter what the port of entry, should cultivate patience and resignation before setting foot on United States soil. Getting through immigration control may take as long as two hours on some days, especially summer weekends. Add the time it takes to clear Customs and you will see that you should make very generous allowance for delay in planning connections between international and domestic flights—an average of two to three hours at least.

In contrast, for the traveler arriving by car or by rail from Canada, the border-crossing formalities have been streamlined to the

IMPRESSIONS

Chicago . . . perhaps the most typically American place in America.
—James Bryce, *The American Commonwealth,* 1888

vanishing point. And for the traveler by air from Canada, Bermuda, and some places in the Caribbean, you can sometimes go through Customs and Immigration at the point of departure, which is much quicker and less painful.

For further information about travel to and arriving in Chicago, see "Getting There" in Chapter 2, and "Arriving" in Chapter 4, Section 1.

3 Getting Around the U.S.

Flying is the fastest, and most expensive, mode of domestic travel in the U.S. For a list of the major carriers that service Chicago from within the U.S., see Section 6, "Getting There" in Chapter 2.

Travel by car (or perhaps bicycle) is perhaps the best way to see the U.S. if you have the time to really wander. After all, the U.S. is an automobile culture, so the roads here are excellent. But the real adventure is off the interstates, and onto the "blue" highways, the secondary roads, along which the small towns of America are strung like beads on a wire.

International visitors can also buy a **USA Railpass,** good for 15 or 30 days of unlimited travel on Amtrak. The pass is available through many foreign travel agents. Prices in 1994 for a 15-day pass are $208 off-peak, $308 peak; a 30-day pass costs $309 off-peak, $389 peak. (With a foreign passport, you can also buy passes at some Amtrak offices in the U.S., including locations in San Francisco, Los Angeles, Chicago, New York, Miami, Boston, and Washington, D.C.) Reservations are generally required and should be made for each part of your trip as early as possible.

Visitors should also be aware of the limitations of long-distance rail travel in the U.S. With a few notable exceptions (for instance, the Northeast Corridor line between Boston and Washington, D.C.), service is rarely up to European standards: delays are common, routes are limited and often infrequently served, and fares are rarely significantly lower than discount airfares. Thus, cross-country train travel should be approached with caution.

The cheapest way to travel the U.S. is by **bus.** Greyhound, the nation's nationwide bus line, offers an **Ameripass** for unlimited travel for 7 days (for $250), 15 days (for $350), and 30 days (for $450). However, bus travel in the U.S. can be both slow and uncomfortable, so this option is not for everyone.

Fast Facts: For the Foreign Traveler

Automobile Organizations   Auto clubs will supply maps, suggested routes, guidebooks, accident and bail-bond insurance, and emergency road service. The major auto club in the United States, with 955 offices nationwide, is the **American Automobile Association (AAA).** Members of some foreign auto clubs have reciprocal arrangements with the AAA and enjoy its services at no charge. If you belong to an auto club, inquire about AAA reciprocity before you leave. The AAA can provide you with an **International Driving Permit** validating your foreign license. You may be able to join the AAA even if you are not a member of a reciprocal club. To inquire, call toll free **800/336-4357.** In addition, some automobile rental agencies now provide these services, so you should inquire about their availability when you rent your car.

Automobile Rentals   To rent a car you need a major credit card. A valid driver's license is required, and you usually need to be at least 25. Some companies do rent to younger people but add a daily surcharge. Be sure to return your car with the same amount of gas you started out with; rental companies charge excessive prices for gasoline.

Business Hours   Banks are open weekdays from 9am to 3 or 4pm, although there's 24-hour access to the automatic tellers (ATMs) at most banks and other outlets. Generally, offices are open weekdays from 9am to 5pm. Stores are open six days a week, with many open on Sunday, too; department stores usually stay open until 9pm at least one day a week.

Climate   See "When to Go" in Chapter 2.

Currency   See "Money" in "Preparing for Your Trip," earlier in this chapter.

Currency Exchange   You will find currency exchange services in major airports with international service. Elsewhere, they may be quite difficult to come by. Thomas Cook Currency Services offers a wide variety of services: more than 100 currencies; commission-free traveler's checks, drafts, and wire transfers; check collections; and precious metal bars and coins. Rates are competitive and service excellent. Call toll free **800/582-4496** for information. Many hotels will exchange currency if you are a registered guest.

Note: The "foreign-exchange bureaus" so common in Europe are rare even at airports in the U.S. and nonexistent outside major cities. Try to avoid having to change foreign money, or traveler's checks denominated other than in U.S. dollars, at small-town banks or even at branches in a big city; in fact, leave any currency other than U.S. dollars at home—it may prove more nuisance to you than it's worth.

However, if you do need such a service, the Chicago consumer Yellow Pages lists names and numbers of foreign-exchange groups under the heading "Foreign Exchange Brokers." In the Loop, try **World Money Exchange, Inc.,** 6 E. Randolph, Suite 204 (☎ **641-2151,** or toll free **800/441-9634**).

Drinking Laws   The legal drinking age in Chicago is 21. Depending on the nature of their license and the day of the week, bars may remain open until anywhere from 2 to 5am.

Electric Current   The U.S. uses 110–120 volts, 60 cycles, compared to 220–240 volts, 50 cycles, as in most of Europe. Small appliances of non-American manufacture, such as hairdryers or shavers, will require both a 100-volt converter and a plug adapter with two flat parallel pins.

Embassies and Consulates   All embassies are located in the national capital, Washington, D.C.; some consulates are located in Chicago, and most nations have a mission to the United Nations in New York City.

Listed here are the embassies (all in Washington, D.C.) and the Chicago consulates of the major English-speaking countries. Travelers from other countries can get telephone numbers for their embassies and consulates by calling "Information" in Washington, D.C. (☎ **202/555-1212**).

The **Australian embassy** is at 1601 Massachusetts Ave. NW, Washington, DC 20036 (☎ **202/797-3000**). There is no consulate in Chicago.

The **Canadian embassy** is at 501 Pennsylvania Ave. NW, Washington, DC 20001 (☎ **202/682-1740**). The **consulate** in Chicago is located at 180 N. Stetson Ave., Suite 2400, Chicago, IL 60601 (☎ **312/616-1870**).

The **Irish embassy** is at 2234 Massachusetts Ave. NW, Washington, DC 20008 (☎ **202/462-3939**). The **consulate** in Chicago is located at 400 N. Michigan Ave., Room 911, Chicago, IL 60611 (☎ **312/337-1868**).

The **New Zealand embassy** is at 37 Observatory Circle NW, Washington, DC 20008 (☎ **202/328-4800**). The **consulate** in Los Angeles is located at 10960 Wilshire Blvd., Suite 1530, Los Angeles, CA 90024 (☎ **213/477-8241**). There is no consulate in Chicago.

The **British embassy** is at 3100 Massachusetts Ave. NW, Washington, DC 20008 (☎ **202/462-1340**). The **consulate** in Chicago is located at 33 N. Dearborn St., Chicago, IL 60602 (☎ **312/346-1810**).

Emergencies   Call **911** for fire, police, and ambulance. If you encounter such traveler's problems as sickness, accident, or lost or stolen baggage, call **Traveler's and Immigrant's Aid** (☎ **312/629-4500**), an organization that specializes in helping distressed travelers, whether American or foreign.

Gasoline [Petrol]   One U.S. gallon equals 3.75 liters, while 1.2 U.S. gallons equals one Imperial gallon. You'll notice there are several grades (and price levels) of gasoline available at most gas stations. And you'll also notice that their names change from company to company. The unleaded ones with the highest octane are the most expensive (most rental cars take the least expensive "regular" unleaded), and leaded gas is the least expensive. Only older cars can take leaded gas anymore, so check if you're not sure.

Holidays On the following national legal holidays, banks, government offices, post offices, and many stores, restaurants, and museums are closed: January 1 (New Year's Day); third Monday in January (Martin Luther King Day); third Monday in February (Presidents' Day); last Monday in May (Memorial Day); July 4, (Independence Day); first Monday in September (Labor Day); second Monday in October (Columbus Day); November 11 (Veteran's Day/Armistice Day); last Thursday in November (Thanksgiving Day); and December 25 (Christmas Day).

The Tuesday following the first Monday in November, Election Day, is a legal holiday in presidential-election years.

Information Before British visitors leave home, they can obtain information on Chicago from the United States Travel and Tourism Administration. P.O. Box 1EN, London W1A 1EN (☎ 071/495-4466).

A multilingual information desk operates in Terminal 3 at O'Hare airport (☎ 686-2304). The Chicago Office of Tourism distributes a "Chicago Welcomes" brochure in five languages—English, Spanish, French, German, and Japanese. A section of the excellent CTA map is written in Spanish.

Languages The Chicago Tour Guides Institute, 101 N. Wacker, Suite CM 285, Chicago, IL 60606 (☎ 276-6683), organizes tours in many languages; some 24 different languages are listed on their brochure, including Tagalog.

Finally, many hotels have concierges who are multilingual.

Legal Aid The foreign tourist, unless positively identified as a member of the Mafia or of a drug ring, will probably never become involved with the American legal system. If you are pulled over for a minor infraction (for example, of the highway code), never attempt to pay the fine directly to a police officer or you may wind up arrested on the much more serious charge of attempted bribery. Pay fines by mail, or directly into the hands of the clerk of the court. If accused of a more serious offense, it's wise to say and do nothing before consulting a lawyer. Under U.S. law, an arrested person is allowed one telephone call to a party of his or her choice. Call your embassy or consulate.

Mail If you want your mail to follow you on your vacation and you aren't sure of your address, your mail can be sent to you, in your name, **c/o General Delivery** at the main post office of the city or region where you expect to be. The addressee must pick it up in person and produce proof of identity (driver's license, credit card, passport, etc.).

Generally to be found at intersections, mailboxes are blue with a red-and-white stripe and carry the inscription U.S. MAIL. If your mail is addressed to a U.S. destination, don't forget to add the five-figure postal code, or ZIP (Zone Improvement Plan) Code, after the two-letter abbreviation of the state to which the mail is addressed (CA for California, FL for Florida, NY for New York, and so on).

Newspapers/Magazines   National newspapers include the *New York Times, USA Today,* and the *Wall Street Journal.* National news weeklies include *Newsweek, Time,* and *U.S. News & World Report.*

Radio and Television   Audiovisual media, with four coast-to-coast networks—ABC, CBS, NBC, and Fox—along with the Public Broadcasting System (PBS) and the cable network CNN, play a major part in American life. In big cities, televiewers have a choice of about a dozen channels (including the UHF channels), most of them transmitting 24 hours a day, without counting the pay-TV channels showing recent movies or sports events. All options are usually indicated on your hotel TV set. You'll also find a wide choice of local radio stations, each broadcasting particular kinds of talk shows and/or music—classical, country, jazz, pop, gospel—punctuated by news broadcasts and frequent commercials.

Safety   See "Safety" in "Preparing for Your Trip," above.

Taxes   In the United States there is no VAT (Value-Added Tax) or other indirect tax at a national level. Every state, and each city in it, has the right to levy its own local tax on all purchases, including hotel and restaurant checks, airline tickets, and so on. Chicago sales tax is 8.75%.

Telephone, Telegraph, Telex   The telephone system in the U.S. is run by private corporations, so rates, especially for long distance service, can vary widely—even on calls made from public telephones. Local calls in the U.S. usually cost 25¢.

Generally, hotel surcharges on long-distance and local calls are astronomical. You are usually better off using a **public pay telephone,** which you will find clearly marked in most public buildings and private establishments as well as on the street. Outside metropolitan areas, public telephones are more difficult to find. Stores and gas stations are your best bet.

Most **long-distance** and **international** calls can be dialed directly from any phone. For calls to Canada and other parts of the U.S., dial 1 followed by the area code and the seven-digit number. For international calls, dial **011** followed by the country code, city code, and the telephone number of the person you wish to call.

For **reversed-charge or collect calls,** and for **person-to-person calls,** dial **0** (zero, *not* the letter "O") followed by the area code and number you want; an operator will then come on the line, and you should specify that you are calling collect, or person-to-person, or both. If your operator-assisted call is international, ask for the overseas operator.

For local **directory assistance** ("information"), dial **411;** for **long-distance information,** dial **1,** then the appropriate area code and **555-1212.**

Like the telephone system, **telegraph** and **telex** services are provided by private corporations like ITT, MCI, and above all, Western Union, the most important. You can bring your telegram to the nearest Western Union office (there are hundreds across the country), or dictate it over the phone (a toll-free call, **800/325-6000**). You can also telegraph money, or have it telegraphed to you, very quickly over the Western Union system.

Telephone Directory There are two kinds of telephone directories available to you. The general directory is the so-called **White Pages,** in which private and business subscribers are listed in alphabetical order. The inside front cover lists the emergency number for police, fire, and ambulance, and other vital numbers (like the Coast Guard, poison-control center, crime-victims hotline, and so on). The first few pages are devoted to community-service numbers, including a guide to long-distance and international calling, complete with country codes and area codes.

The second directory, printed on yellow paper (hence its name, **Yellow Pages**), lists all local services, businesses, and industries by type of activity, with an index at the back. The listings cover not only such obvious items as automobile repairs by make of car, or drugstores (pharmacies), often by geographical location, but also restaurants by type of cuisine and geographical location, bookstores by special subject and/or language, places of worship by religious denomination, and other information that the tourist might otherwise not readily find. The Yellow Pages also include city plans or detailed area maps, often showing postal ZIP Codes and public transportation routes.

Time The United States is divided into four **time zones** (six, if Alaska and Hawaii are included). From east to west, these are: eastern standard time (EST), central standard time (CST), mountain standard time (MST), Pacific standard time (PST), Alaska standard time (AST), and Hawaii standard time (HST). Always keep changing time zones in mind if you are traveling (or even telephoning) long distances in the United States. For example, noon in New York City (EST) is 11am in Chicago (CST), 10am in Denver (MST), 9am in Los Angeles (PST), 8am in Anchorage (AST), and 7am in Honolulu (HST).

Chicago is on central standard time. **Daylight saving time** is in effect from the last Sunday in April through the last Saturday in October (actually, the change is made at 2am on Sunday) except in Arizona, Hawaii, part of Indiana, and Puerto Rico. Daylight saving time moves the clock one hour ahead of standard time.

Tipping The standard rates for tipping are 15% (before tax) to waiters for a well-served meal; 15% of the fare for a cab ride; $1 to the bellhop for carrying one or two bags ($1 per additional bag); and a couple of dollars for maid service when you check out.

Toilets Often euphemistically referred to as "restrooms," public toilets are nonexistent on the streets of Chicago. They can be found, though, in bars, restaurants, hotel lobbies, museums, department stores, and service stations—and will probably be clean (although ones in the last-mentioned sometimes leave much to be desired). Note, however, that some restaurants and bars display a notice that "Toilets are for use of patrons only." You can ignore this sign, or better yet, avoid arguments by paying for a cup of coffee or soft drink, which will qualify you as a patron. The cleanliness of toilets at railroad stations and bus depots may be questionable; some public places are equipped with pay toilets that require you to insert one or two dimes (10¢) or a quarter (25¢) into a slot on the door before it will open. In restrooms with attendants, leaving at least a 25¢ tip is customary.

The American System of Measurements

Length

1 inch (in.)	=	2.54cm			
1 foot (ft.)	=	12 in.	=	30.48cm	=	.305m
1 yard (yd.)	=	3 ft.	=	.915m	
1 mile	=	5,280 ft.	=	1.609km	

To convert miles to kilometers, multiply the number of miles by 1.61. Also use to convert speeds from miles per hour (m.p.h.) to kilometers per hour (kmph).

To convert kilometers to miles, multiply the number of kilometers by .62. Also use to convert kmph to m.p.h.

Capacity

1 fluid ounce (fl. oz.)	=	.03 liters			
1 pint	=	16 fl. oz.	=	.47 liters	
1 quart	=	2 pints	=	.94 liters	
1 gallon (gal.)	=	4 quarts	=	3.79 liters	=	.83 Imperial gal.

To convert U.S. gallons to liters, multiply the number of gallons by 3.79.

To convert liters to U.S. gallons, multiply the number of liters by .26.

To convert U.S. gallons to Imperial gallons, multiply the number of U.S. gallons by .83.

To convert Imperial gallons to U.S. gallons, multiply the number of Imperial gallons by 1.2.

Weight

1 ounce (oz.)	=	28.35g				
1 pound (lb.)	=	16 oz.	=	453.6g	=	.45kg
1 ton	=	2,000 lb.	=	907kg	=	.91 metric tons

To convert pounds to kilograms, multiply the number of pounds by .45.

To convert kilograms to pounds, multiply the number of kilograms by 2.2.

Area

1 acre	=	.41ha				
1 square mile	=	640 acres	=	259ha	=	2.6km²

To convert acres to hectares, multiply the number of acres by .41.

To convert hectares to acres, multiply the number of hectares by 2.47.

To convert square miles to square kilometers, multiply the number of square miles by 2.6.

To convert square kilometers to square miles, multiply the number of square kilometers by .39.

Temperature

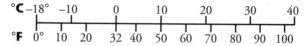

To convert degrees Fahrenheit to degrees Celsius, subtract 32 from °F, multiply by 5, then divide by 9 (example: 85°F – 32 × $^5/_9$ = 29.4°C).

To convert degrees Celsius to degrees Fahrenheit, multiply °C by 9, divide by 5, and add 32 (example: 20°C × $^9/_5$ + 32 = 68°F).

4

Getting to Know Chicago

THE ORDERLY CONFIGURATION OF CHICAGO'S STREETS AND THE EXCELLENT system of public transportation make this city more accessible than perhaps any other large city in the world. As the central urban oasis between the east and west coasts, Chicago is also one of the easiest places to visit from anywhere in the United States and, at least where the major Western European countries are concerned, from abroad as well.

1 Orientation

Arriving

BY PLANE   Chicago's initial attraction is quite simply the ease of access to and from **O'Hare International Airport** by rapid transit. A train running on all three levels—surface, elevated, and underground—links Passenger Terminal 4 (connected to the other terminals via moving walkways, through high-tech and neon-studded corridors and tunnels) with the heart of downtown, the Dearborn Street subway stop, in only 35 minutes. All this for $1.50; add 30¢ if you want a transfer good for a connecting train or bus. Cabs to downtown Chicago cost $25 to $30.

Five information booths are distributed throughout the airport to service the needs of foreign visitors. Multilingual staff are conversant in a wide variety of world tongues—from French, Spanish, German, and Italian to Russian, Japanese, Cantonese, and Tagalog, to name just a few. The information booths are open daily from 8am to 8pm.

Many frequent fliers to Chicago swear by the smaller **Midway Airport,** located 11 miles from downtown in the city's southwest quadrant. It's less glitzy than O'Hare by a long shot, but it's even closer to the city. Since Midway Airlines went out of business, Southwest Airlines has taken over most of its routes. Limo services from Midway have a fixed route of hotel stops.

Meigs Field is an in-town airstrip for private planes, located just south of the downtown Loop on a spit of land that seems to float in Lake Michigan like an aircraft carrier at its slip.

Continental Air Transport (☎ 454-7800) services most first-class hotels in Chicago; check with your bell captain. The cost is $14.75 one-way ($25.50 round-trip) to O'Hare, and $10.75 one-way ($19 round-trip) to Midway.

For limo service from either O'Hare or Midway airport, call **Carey of Chicago, Inc.** (☎ 663-1220), or **Chicago Limousine Service** (☎ 726-1035). Cost, with tax and tip, comes to approximately $75.

BY TRAIN   **Union Station** is located at Adams and Canal Streets (☎ 312/558-1075, or toll free 800/872-7245). Bus nos. 1, 60, 151, and 156 all stop at the station, and the nearest subway/el stop is at Congress and Clinton (on the O'Hare/Congress/Douglas line), which is a fair walk away.

BY BUS   The **Greyhound Bus Station** recently relocated to 630 W. Harrison (☎ toll free **800/231-2222**) on the Near West Side of Chicago, not far from Union train station. The nearest subway stop is Clinton/Congress on the O'Hare-Douglas line, and the no. 61 Blue Island bus passes in front of the terminal building.

Tourist Information

The Chicago Office of Tourism staffs a **visitor information desk,** located in the lobby of the Water Tower Pumping Station, 163 E. Pearson, at the corner of North Michigan Avenue (☎ 312/280-5740, or toll free **800/ITS-CHGO**). It is the only information center in Chicago open seven days a week, from 9:30am to 5pm. The Pumping Station also houses a multimedia show called *Here's Chicago!* and a hospitality center, offering among its amenities clean restrooms and a bank of pay telephones nestled in a quiet corner.

The **Illinois Office of Tourism,** 310 S. Michigan Ave. (☎ 312/793-2094), operates a drop-in center very convenient to anyone wandering or lodged within the Loop. They also staff an **information booth** in the State of Illinois Center, 100 W. Randolph St. (☎ toll free **800/223-0121** for an information packet or toll free **800/822-0292** to speak directly with a vacation counselor), in the Helmut Jahn building located in the Loop near the main branch of the Chicago River. The office of tourism can provide general and specific information covering the entire state of Illinois. Other state-run information centers are located in the Sears Tower (entrance on South Wacker Drive between Jackson and Adams) and at O'Hare and Midway Airports. The information centers are open Monday through Friday from 8:30am to 5pm (except the information booth in the State of Illinois Center, which opens at 9am).

Local merchants in the State Street Mall (on State Street, closed to auto traffic) staff an **information center** at the corner of State Street and Madison Avenue, open Monday through Saturday from 9am to 5pm.

INFORMATION BY TELEPHONE   The **Events Hotline** (☎ 312/744-3370) is a recorded hotline listing current special events occurring throughout the city.

The city of Chicago maintains a 24-hour **information line for the hearing impaired** who have TDD equipment. Call **312/744-8599.**

IMPRESSIONS

> *This is the greatest and most typically American of all cities. New York is bigger and more spectacular and can outmatch it in other superlatives, but it is a "world" city, more European in some respects than American. Chicago ... gives above all the sense that America and the Middle West are beating upon it from all sides.*
> —John Gunther, *Inside U.S.A.,* 1947

> *Chicago is as full of crooks as a saw with teeth.*
> —Ibid.

The **Chicago Architecture Foundation** maintains a telephone line giving information on the group's numerous tour offerings (☎ 312/922-TOUR).

PUBLICATIONS   For a brochure listing more than 80 neighborhood festivals, contact the **Mayor's Office of Special Events,** 121 N. LaSalle St., Room 703, Chicago, IL 60602 (☎ **312/744-3315,** or toll free **800/ITS-CHGO**).

Chicago's major daily newspapers are the *Sun-Times* and the *Tribune.* Both have daily cultural listings including movies, theaters, and live music, not to mention reviews of the latest crop of restaurants that are sure to have appeared in the city since this guidebook went to press. The Friday edition of the *Tribune* contains a special "Weekend" section with more detailed information on special events occurring over Saturday and Sunday.

In a class by itself is the *Chicago Reader,* a thick weekly that is free and an invaluable source of entertainment listings, classifieds, and well-written articles on contemporary issues of interest in Chicago. Published after 1pm every Thursday (except the last week of December), the weekly has a wide distribution downtown and on the North Side, and is available in many retail stores, building lobbies, and at the paper's offices, 11 E. Illinois St. (☎ **828-0350**).

Most Chicago hotels stock their rooms with at least one informational magazine, such as *Where? Chicago,* that reviews the city's entertainment, shopping, and dining locales.

City Layout

Bridges are everywhere as you drive the periphery of downtown Chicago, because the Chicago River forms a Y that divides the city into its three geographic zones—North Side, South Side, and West Side. A tight cluster of tall buildings is in a downtown canyon called the Loop. Along an expanse of roadway called the Magnificent Mile, dozens of skyscrapers, the most modern in the city, are spaciously arranged. Above and below this downtown zone, the city stretches out along 29 miles of Lake Michigan shorefront that is, by and large, free of commercial development, reserved for public usage as green space and parkland from one end of town to the other. Chicago today has about three million inhabitants living in an area about two-thirds the size of New York City; another four million make the suburbs their home. But the real trademark of Chicago is found between the suburbs and the hub of the city where scores of neighborhoods give the city a character all its own.

FINDING AN ADDRESS   Chicago's streets are laid out in a grid system, as if at the city's creation a giant piece of graph paper lined with symmetrical squares had been superimposed over its virgin topography. From this original rectangular overlay, the city's actual, somewhat stubby and elongated dimensions seem to have been cut out haphazardly, in the manner of a young child first learning to manipulate a pair of scissors. The resulting shape may be irregular, but the graphic pattern remains, and the streets continue to run true, up and down, side to side. The great exceptions are the city's half dozen or so major diagonal thoroughfares. Street numbering, moreover, does not originate at the city's geographical midpoint, but nearer to Chicago's historic and commercial center, more north than south, and so far east as almost to border Lake Michigan.

Point zero is located at the downtown intersection of **State** and **Madison Streets;** State divides east and west addresses and Madison divides north and south addresses. From here, Chicago's highly predictable addressing system begins. Making use of this grid, it is relatively easy to plot the distance in miles between any two points in the city.

Virtually all of Chicago's principal north-south and east-west arteries are spaced by increments of 400 in the addressing system— regardless of the number of smaller streets nestled between them. And each addition or subtraction of 400 numbers to an address is equivalent to a half mile. Thus, starting at point zero on Madison Street, and traveling north along State Street for one mile, you will come to 800 N. State, which intersects Chicago Avenue. Continue uptown for another half mile and you arrive at the 1200 block of North State at Division Street. And so it goes right to the city line, with suburban Evanston located at the 7600 block north, $9^1/_2$ miles from this arbitrary center.

The same rule applies when traveling south or east to west. Thus, heading west from State Street along Madison, Halsted Street—at 800 W. Madison—is a mile's distance, while Racine, at the 1200 block of West Madison, is $1^1/_2$ miles from the center. Madison then continues westward to Chicago's boundary along Austin Avenue, with the near suburb of Oak Park, which at 6000 W. Madison is approximately $7^1/_2$ miles from point zero.

The key to understanding the grid is that the side of any square formed by the principal avenues (noted in dark or red ink on most maps) represents a distance of half a mile in any direction. Understanding how Chicago's grid system works is of particular importance to those visitors who wish to do a lot of walking in the city's many neighborhoods, and who want to plot in advance the distances involved in trekking from one locale to another.

STREET MAPS   A suitably detailed map of Chicago is published by Rand McNally, available at most newstands for $2.95.

NEIGHBORHOODS IN BRIEF

THE LOOP & VICINITY   "Downtown," in the case of Chicago, means the Loop. The Loop refers literally to a core of commercial, cultural, and residential buildings contained within a corral of elevated

IMPRESSIONS

The city that works.
—Quoted in *The Economist,* March 3–9, 1979, as "Recently Traditional," without source

subway tracks, but greater downtown Chicago overflows these confines and is bounded by the Chicago River to the north and west, by Lake Michigan to the east, and by Roosevelt Avenue to the south. The Loop and vicinity contain many of Chicago's most important cultural and tourist attractions.

NORTH SIDE NEIGHBORHOODS • The Magnificent Mile and River North

North Michigan Avenue, known as the Magnificent Mile, is Chicago at its most elegant. On and around North Michigan, many of the city's best hotels, shops, and restaurants are to be found. Adjacent to this zone of high life and sophistication is an old warehouse district called River North, increasingly gentrified and filled with great eateries, nightspots, and art galleries. The southern and western borders of these two neighborhoods are two branches of the Chicago River. Lake Michigan is the eastern boundary, and Oak and Division Streets cap the neighborhoods to the north.

• **Old Town and the Gold Coast** Some of Chicago's most desirable real estate and historic architecture is found along Lake Shore Drive and its adjacent side streets of the Gold Coast. This neighborhood is also home to the famous Pump Room in the Omni Ambassador East Hotel. West of Dearborn, principally on North Wells between Division and North Avenue, is the nightlife district of Old Town, where many comedy clubs, such as Second City, have served up the lighter side of life to Chicagoans for over a generation.

• **Lincoln Park** This fashionable residential neighborhood is north of Armitage and bordered by the huge park of the same name as far north as Diversey. The triangle formed by Lincoln Avenue, Halsted Street, and Armitage, where many of Chicago's in-spot bars and restaurants are located, is explored in detail in Chapter 8, "Strolling Around Chicago."

• **New Town and Wrigleyville** Midway up the city's North Side is the semigentrified/bohemian quarter called New Town, which has become the neighborhood of preference for many gays and lesbians, artists, and urban homesteaders. The main thoroughfare is Belmont, between Broadway and Sheffield. Wrigleyville designates the onetime blue-collar neighborhood in the vicinity of Wrigley Field—home of the Chicago Cubs—at Sheffield and Addison. Many homesteaders have moved into this area in recent years, and a slew of nightclubs and restaurants have followed in their wake.

• **Uptown and Andersonville** Uptown, along the lake and about as far north as Foster, is where the latest wave of immigrants—including internal migrants from Appalachia and the Native American reservations—has sought fulfillment of the American dream within Chicago's city limits. The "New Chinatown" is here, around Broadway and Argyle. Slightly to the north and west is the old Scandinavian neighborhood of Andersonville, whose main drag is Clark Street, between Foster and Bryn Mawr.

• **Lincoln Square**   West of Andersonville, and slightly to the south, where Lincoln, Western, and Lawrence Avenues intersect, is Lincoln Square, the only identifiable remains of Chicago's once vast German-American community. The neighborhood hosts a big outdoor party on German American Day in the fall. Lincoln Square now also has a distinctly Greek flavor, with several restaurants of that nationality to boot.

• **The Gaza Strip and Rogers Park**   Gaza Strip is what witty Chicagoans have dubbed Devon Avenue, on the northern fringes of the city. The blend here is Orthodox Jewish and East Indians; and the food ranges from bagels and lox to tandoori. Above Devon begins the appealing neighborhood of Rogers Park, a quiet corner of the city bordering suburban Evanston, with several interesting shops and restaurants to visit.

THE WEST SIDE • Near West   On the Near West Side, just across the Chicago River from the Loop, on Halsted between Adams and Monroe, is Chicago's old "Greek Town," and still the Greek culinary center of the city. Much of the old Italian neighborhood in this vicinity was the victim of urban renewal, but remnants still survive on Taylor Street; the same is true for a few old delis and shops on Maxwell Street, dating from when a large Jewish community lived in the area around the turn of the century.

• **The Milwaukee Avenue Corridor**   A rich variety of neighborhoods can be found stretched along Milwaukee Avenue from Racine to Diversey. Wicker Park is one of Chicago's hot spots of upward mobility and cultural development. There are Mexican/Central American enclaves between Western and California, and a still traditional Polish neighborhood, with several great restaurants, around Logan Square.

THE SOUTH SIDE • Pilsen   This old Bohemian neighborhood, centered around Halsted and 18th Street, is now an artists' colony within a wider community that is largely Chicano.

• **Bridgeport and Canaryville**   Bridgeport, whose main crossroads is 35th and Halsted, is Mayor Daley's old neighborhood. After Comiskey Park was torn down, the Chicago White Sox didn't move from Bridgeport, but instead recently inaugurated their new stadium here. Nearby Canaryville, just south and west, is typical of the "back of the yard" blue-collar neighborhoods that once surrounded the Chicago Stockyards.

IMPRESSIONS

Chicago is stupefying ... an Olympian freak, a fable, an allegory, an incomprehensible phenomenon ... monstrous, multifarious, unnatural, indomitable, puissant, preposterous, transcendent ... throw the dictionary at it!
—Julian Street, *Abroad At Home*, 1914

• **Hyde Park**   Hyde Park is like an independent village within the confines of Chicago, right off Lake Michigan, and roughly a 30-minute subway ride from the Loop. Fifty-seventh Street is the main drag, and the University of Chicago—with all its attendant shops and restaurants—is the neighborhood's principal tenant. Hyde Park's main attraction, however, is the world-famous Museum of Science and Industry.

• **Pullman**   Pullman is the historic district on Chicago's Southeast Side, site of the former planned community—now preserved as a living museum—of the Pullman Palace Car Company.

2 Getting Around

By Public Transportation

The **Chicago Transit Authority (CTA)** operates an extensive system of trains and buses throughout the city of Chicago. The sturdy system carries more than two million passengers a day. Subways and elevated trains are generally safe and reliable, though it's advisable to avoid long rides through unfamiliar neighborhoods late at night.

Fares are $1.50, with an additional 30¢ for a transfer that must be used within two hours of receipt. A package of 10 tokens may be purchased for $12.50 at Jewel and Dominick supermarkets and at some token booths. Children under 7 ride for free, while those between the ages of 7 and 11 pay 90¢ (15¢ for transfers), as do senior citizens over 65 (call 814-0700 to obtain appropriate ID).

Buses are now equipped with machinery that accepts $1 bills. Fares are $1.25, 25¢ for a transfer, and $1.50 during rush hour (Monday through Friday from 6 to 10am and from 3 to 7pm).

CTA INFORMATION   The CTA operates a useful **telephone information service** (☎ 836-7000) that functions daily from 4:45am to 1am. When you wish to know how to get from where you are to where you want to go, call the CTA. Make sure you specify any conditions you might require—the fastest route, for example, or the simplest (the route with the fewest transfers or least amount of walking), and so forth.

An excellent **CTA Map** is available at subway or El fare booths, or by calling 836-7000.

BY THE EL & THE SUBWAY   The rapid transit system operates four major lines, north-south, west-south, west-northwest (the O'Hare train), and a zigzag northern route called the Ravenswood line. A separate express line services Evanston, while a smaller, local line in Skokie is linked to the north-south train. Skokie and Evanston are adjacent suburbs on Chicago's northern boundary.

Study your CTA map carefully before boarding any train. During the working day (6am to 7pm) A and B trains on all lines make alternate stops. However, major stations, including all downtown stations (except State/Harrison), are combined AB stops throughout the day. While most trains run around the clock, decreasing in frequency in the off-peak and overnight hours, some stations close after work hours (as early as 8:30pm) and remain closed on Saturday, Sunday, and holidays. Other stops will remain open on weekends and holidays despite the fact that their fare booths are closed. Simply climb to the platform and board the train; a conductor will collect your fare and provide necessary transfers on the train itself. Please note that you may not use your transfer on the line where you first obtained it.

BY BUS   Add to Chicago's gridlike layout a comprehensive system of public buses, and there is virtually no place in the city that isn't within close walking distance of a bus stop. Other than on foot, the best way to get around Chicago's warren of neighborhoods—the best way to actually see what's around you—is while riding a public bus. (The view from the elevated trains can be pretty dramatic too; the difference is that on the trains you get the backyards, while on the bus you see the buildings' facades and the street life.)

PACE buses (☎ 836-7000) service the suburban zones that surround Chicago. They run every 20 to 30 minutes during rush hour, operating until mid-evening Monday through Friday, and early evening on weekends. Suburban bus routes are marked nos. 208 and above, and vehicles may be flagged down at intersections since few of the lines have bus stops that are marked.

By Train

The **Metra commuter railroad** (☎ 322-6777 Monday to Friday 8am to 5pm; at other times call RTA at **836-7000**) which services the suburban zones that surround Chicago, has terminals at several downtown locations, including Union Station at Adams and Canal, LaSalle Street Station at LaSalle and Van Buren, Northwestern Station at Madison and Canal, and Randolph Street Station at Randolph and Michigan. To visit some of the most affluent suburbs in the country, take the Northwestern train and select from among the following destinations: Kenilworth, Winnetka, Glencoe, Highland Park, and the créme de la créme, Lake Forest (where the real millionaires live). The Illinois Central–Gulf Railroad, known locally as the IC, runs close to Lake Michigan on track that occupies some of the most valuable real estate in Chicago, and will take you to Hyde Park and Pullman, both of which are described in this guidebook. Commuter trains have graduated fare schedules based on the distance you ride.

IMPRESSIONS

I say God's Chicago, for who else will own it, complete it, and gather it to be the perfect city upon earth? Chicago has all the possibilities of becoming the earth's final city, the Babylon of the Plains.
—Shane Leslie, *American Wonderland,* 1936

Chicago Transit System

Lake Street/Dan Ryan Route

LAKE STREET

Stop	Station
AB	Harlem
AB	Oak Park
AB	Ridgeland
AB	Austin
AB	Central
AB	Laramie
AB	Cicero
AB	Pulaski
B	Homan
A	Kedzie
A	Ashland
B	Halsted
AB	Clinton

(see Downtown Stations map)

Stop	Station
B	Cermak/Chinatown
AB	Sox/35th St.
A	47th St.
B	Garfield
A	63rd St.
AB	69th St.
AB	79th St.
AB	87th St.
AB	95th St.

DAN RYAN

O'Hare/Congress/Douglas Route

O'HARE

Stop	Station
AB	O'Hare
AB	River Road
AB	Cumberland
AB	Harlem
AB	Jefferson Park
A	Montrose
AB	Irving Park
B	Addison
AB	Belmont
AB	Logan Square
A	California
B	Western
AB	Damen
AB	Division
AB	Chicago
B	Grand

LEGEND:
- A — A Train stop
- B — B Train stop
- AB — A & B Trains stop

(see Downtown Stations map)

Stop	Station
AB	Clinton
AB	Halsted/U of I
AB	Racine

Polk B   18th St. B

Stop	Station (Congress)	Stop	Station (Douglas)
A	Medical Center	B	Hoyne
A	Western	B	Western
A	Kedzie/Homan	B	California
A	Pulaski	B	Kedzie
A	Cicero	B	Central Park
A	Austin	B	Pulaski
A	Oak Park	B	Kildare
A	Harlem	B	Cicero
A	DesPlaines	B	54/Cermak

CONGRESS   **DOUGLAS**

9052

By Taxi

Taxis are very affordable for getting around Chicago on short runs—moving around the downtown area, for example—or for excursions to Near North Side neighborhoods of Old Town or Lincoln Park or to Greektown on the Near West Side. Beyond that, as in any large city, a cab ride is not economical. Even budget travelers, or those not

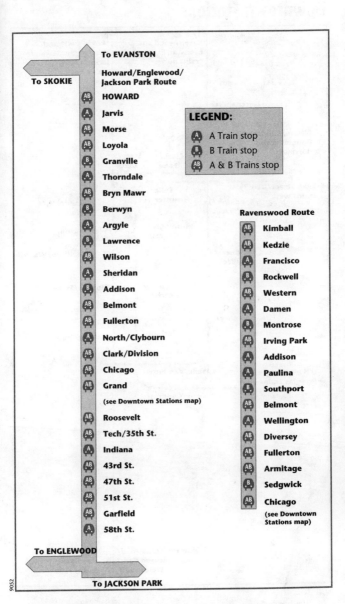

To EVANSTON

To SKOKIE

Howard/Englewood/Jackson Park Route

- **HOWARD**
- Jarvis
- Morse
- Loyola
- Granville
- Thorndale
- Bryn Mawr
- Berwyn
- Argyle
- Lawrence
- Wilson
- Sheridan
- Addison
- Belmont
- Fullerton
- North/Clybourn
- Clark/Division
- Chicago
- Grand

(see Downtown Stations map)

- Roosevelt
- Tech/35th St.
- Indiana
- 43rd St.
- 47th St.
- 51st St.
- Garfield
- 58th St.

To ENGLEWOOD

To JACKSON PARK

LEGEND:
- A Train stop
- B Train stop
- A & B Trains stop

Ravenswood Route

- Kimball
- Kedzie
- Francisco
- Rockwell
- Western
- Damen
- Montrose
- Irving Park
- Addison
- Paulina
- Southport
- Belmont
- Wellington
- Diversey
- Fullerton
- Armitage
- Sedgwick
- Chicago

(see Downtown Stations map)

9052

blessed with generous expense accounts, will find taxis a viable transportation option for the short runs, however.

At this writing, the flag drops at $1.20 in Chicago cabs, increasing by $1.50 for each added mile, with a 50¢ surcharge for each additional rider.

Some cab companies are **American** (☎ 248-7600), **Flash** (☎ 561-1444), and **Yellow/Checker** (☎ 829-4222).

Downtown Stations

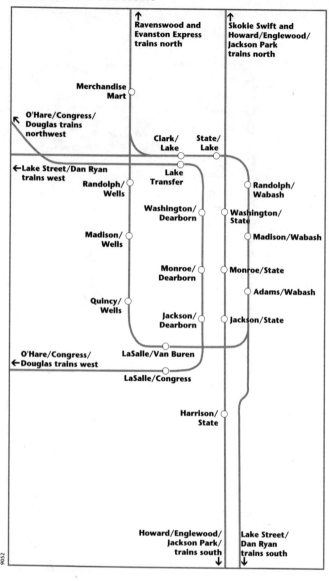

↑ Ravenswood and Evanston Express trains north

↑ Skokie Swift and Howard/Englewood/ Jackson Park trains north

Merchandise Mart

← O'Hare/Congress/ Douglas trains northwest

Clark/ Lake

State/ Lake

← Lake Street/Dan Ryan trains west

Lake Transfer

Randolph/ Wells

Randolph/ Wabash

Washington/ Dearborn

Washington/ State

Madison/ Wells

Madison/Wabash

Monroe/ Dearborn

Monroe/State

Adams/Wabash

Quincy/ Wells

Jackson/ Dearborn

Jackson/State

O'Hare/Congress/ ← Douglas trains west

LaSalle/Van Buren

LaSalle/Congress

Harrison/ State

Howard/Englewood/ Jackson Park/ trains south ↓

Lake Street/ Dan Ryan trains south ↓

By Car

Chicago is spread out so logically that even for a visitor, driving around the city is relatively easy. Rush-hour traffic jams are not as daunting in Chicago as in other U.S. cities. Traffic seems to run fairly smoothly at most times of the day. The combination of wide streets and strategically spaced expressways running in all directions makes for generally easy riding (although construction on the Dan Ryan over the past several years is said to have slowed things down a bit on that particular roadway, with no end in sight).

The great diagonal corridors violate the grid pattern at key points in the city, and shorten many a trip that would otherwise be tedious on the checkerboard surface of the Chicago streets. Lake Shore Drive (also known as the Outer Drive) has to be one of the most scenic and useful urban thoroughfares to be found anywhere. You can travel the length of the city (and beyond), never far from the great sea-lake that is certainly Chicago's most awesome natural feature.

RENTALS   Hertz (☎ toll free **800/654-3131**) has an office downtown at 9 W. Kinzie (☎ **372-7600**); at O'Hare Airport (☎ **686-7272**); and at Midway Airport (☎ **735-7272**). **Avis** (☎ toll free **800/831-2847**) has an office downtown at 214 N. Clark (☎ **782-6825**); at O'Hare Airport (☎ **694-5600**); and at Midway Airport (☎ **471-4495**). **National** (☎ toll free **800/227-7368**) has an office downtown at 203 N. LaSalle (☎ **236-2581**); at O'Hare Airport (☎ **694-4640**); and at Midway Airport (☎ **471-3450**). **Budget** (☎ toll free **800/527-0700**) has an office downtown at 1025 N. Clark (☎ **708/968-6661** for reservations); at O'Hare Airport; and at Midway Airport (☎ **686-6780**).

DRIVING RULES   One bizarre anomaly in the organization of Chicago's traffic is the absence of signal lights off the principal avenues. Thus, a block east or west of the Magnificent Mile (North Michigan Avenue)—one of the most traveled streets in the city—you will in some cases encounter only stop signs to control the flow of traffic. Once you've become accustomed to the system, it works very smoothly, with everyone—pedestrians and motorists alike—advancing in their proper turn. A right turn on red is allowed unless otherwise posted.

PARKING   Parking regulations are vigorously enforced throughout the city of Chicago. There are few urban experiences more discouraging than having to retrieve your impounded car from the police tow-away lot. To avoid unpleasantness, be sure to check parking signs at curbside, and if you run out of luck, find a parking lot and pay the premium prices as you would in any metropolitan area.

Public parking lots are available at the following locations: **Grant Park Parking,** Michigan Avenue at Congress, and Michigan at Monroe (☎ **294-2437**); **MAP Parking,** 350 N. Orleans (☎ **986-6822**); **McCormick Place Parking,** 2301 S. Lake Shore Dr. (☎ **294-4600**); **Midcontinental Plaza Garage,** 55 E. Monroe (☎ **986-6821**); and **Navy Pier Parking,** 601 E. Grand (☎ **791-7437**).

By Boat

A shuttle boat operates daily from April through October between a dock adjacent to the Michigan Avenue bridge and Northwestern Station, a suburban train station across the river from downtown. The ride, which costs $1.25 each way and takes about 10 minutes, is popular with both visitors and commuters. The service operates in the morning from 7:45 to 8:45am from the station, and in the afternoon from 4:45 to 5:27pm from the bridge.

By Bicycle

Turin Bicycle Shop, 435 E. Illinois (☎ **923-0100**), on conveniently located North Pier, offers 21-speed mountain bikes at a rate of $10 per hour, $40 maximum for the day. Renters must leave a $350 deposit on their VISA, MasterCard, or Discover cards; helmets and locks are provided at no additional charge. Open Monday to Thursday 10am to 9pm, Friday and Saturday 10am to 10pm, Sunday noon to 6pm.

On the Far North Side of the city, **Arnold's Adventure Travel,** 6318 N. Winthrop Ave. (☎ **262-4808**), rents bikes for $8 an hour. Arnold manages the youth hostel near the Loyola University campus (see Chapter 5, "Chicago Accommodations").

On Foot

The real spice of Chicago can only be savored by walking its streets. You cannot truly claim to have gotten to know a city that you haven't crisscrossed by foot. While this may not be everyone's idea of a leisure activity, many will find Chicago fertile ground for long excursions on foot. Skyscrapers give way to green spaces, which in turn yield to industrial wastelands and riverscapes (the Chicago River seems to be everywhere in the city). But mostly Chicago is like a necklace whose every bead is a unique residential quarter, some defined by income and social status, others by ethnic uniformity. Are there areas where you ought not to wander, that might not be safe? Undoubtedly. I suggest that you use your own instincts coupled with local information from hotel desks and the tourist office.

Fast Facts: Chicago

Airports   See "Orientation" in this chapter.

American Express   Travel service offices are located at the following locations: 34 N. Clark (☎ **263-6617**); 122 S. Michigan (☎ **435-2595**); 230 S. Clark (☎ **629-0685**); and 625 N. Michigan (☎ **435-2570**). All are open Monday through Friday from 9am to 5pm, and the office at 625 N. Michigan is also open on Saturday from 10am to 3pm.

Area Codes   For Chicago, it's 312; for the suburbs, it's 708.

Babysitters   Check with the concierge or desk staff at your hotel, who are likely to maintain a list of reliable sitters that they have worked with in the past.

Business Hours   Shops generally keep normal business hours, opening around 10am and closing by 6pm Monday through Saturday. These days, however, most stores generally stay open late at least one evening a week. And certain businesses, such as bookstores, are almost always open during the evening hours all week long. More and more shops are now open on Sunday as well, usually for half a day, during the afternoon. Malls, including Water Tower Place at 835 N. Michigan Ave., are generally open until 8pm, and are open Sunday as well.

Banking hours in Chicago are normally from 9am (8am in some cases) to 3pm Monday through Friday, with select banks remaining open later on specified afternoons and evenings.

Car Rentals   See "Getting Around" in this chapter.

Climate   See "When to Go—Climate and Events" in Chapter 2.

Currency Exchange   The Chicago consumer Yellow Pages list the names and numbers of groups offering this service under the heading "Foreign Exchange Brokers."

In the Loop, try the World Money Exchange, Inc., 6 E. Randolph, Suite 204 (☎ **641-2151**, or toll free **800/441-9634**).

Dentists   Chicago's Dental Emergency Service number is 836-7300; this service can refer you to an area dentist.

Doctors   In the event of a medical emergency, your best bet—unless you have friends who can recommend a doctor—is to rely on your hotel physician or go to the nearest hospital emergency room.

Driving Rules   See "Getting Around" in this chapter.

Drugstores   Walgreen's, 757 N. Michigan Ave. (☎ **664-8686**), is open 24 hours. Osco Drugs has a toll-free number (☎ **800/654-6726**) that you can call to locate their 24-hour pharmacy nearest to you.

Embassies and Consulates   See "Fast Facts: For the Foreign Traveler" in Chapter 3.

Emergencies   The city of Chicago proclaims the following policy: "In emergency dial 911 and a city ambulance will respond free of charge to the patient. The ambulance will take the patient to the nearest emergency room according to geographic location."

If you desire a specific, nonpublic ambulance, call the Vandenberg Ambulance Service (☎ **248-2712**).

Eyeglasses   Pearle Vision Center, 134 N. LaSalle (☎ **372-3204**), offers one-hour service in many cases. Glasses Ltd. has two locations downtown: 49 E. Oak (☎ **944-6876**) and 900 N. Michigan (☎ **751-0073**).

Hairdressers and Barbers   Deluxe and first-class hotels for the most part maintain the tradition of in-house beauty salons. You might also try Supercuts, at 745 N. Wabash (☎ **649-0234**), and at 1628 N. Wells (☎ **944-7778**).

Hospitals   By consensus, the best emergency room in Chicago is at **Northwestern Memorial Hospital,** 233 E. Superior (☎ **908-2000**), right off the Magnificent Mile.

Hotlines   For help with alcoholism, call **577-1919.** The drug-abuse hotline in Chicago is **278-5015.** There are also two crisis hotlines in Chicago: **769-6200** or **908-8100;** the latter number is the Institute of Psychiatry, which accepts referrals and walk-ins.

Information   See "Tourist Information," earlier in this chapter.

Laundry and Dry Cleaning   If you want to pay the premium, you may make use of the services provided by your hotel. Otherwise, find the neighborhood Laundromat and dry cleaner and make like a local.

Libraries   The Chicago Public Library's main branch is in the Harold Washington Library Center at 400 S. State (☎ **747-4300**).

Liquor Laws   Most bars and taverns have a 2am license, allowing them to stay open until 3am on Sunday ("Saturday night"); some have a 4am license and may remain open until 5am on Sunday.

Lost Property   There is a lost-and-found service at O'Hare International Airport (☎ **686-2201**).

Luggage Storage and Lockers   These may be found in limited numbers at O'Hare and Midway Airports, at Union Train Station, and at the Greyhound Bus Station.

Money   See "Information and Money" in Chapter 2.

Newspapers and Magazines   The *Chicago Tribune* (☎ **222-3232**) and the *Chicago Sun-Times* (☎ **321-3000**) are the two major dailies. The *Chicago Reader* (☎ **828-0350**) is an excellent free weekly, with informative articles of local interest and all current entertainment and restaurant listings.

Photographic Needs   Central Camera, 232 S. Wabash (☎ **427-5580**), has been a Chicago institution since 1899. Local photographers speak highly of the Darkroom Aids Company, 3449 N. Lincoln (☎ **248-4301**).

Police   For emergencies, call **911.**

Post Office   The main post office is at 433 W. Van Buren (☎ **765-4357**); a convenient branch is at 540 N. Dearborn (☎ **644-7603**).

Radio   WBEZ (91.5 FM) is the local National Public Radio station. WFMT (98.7 FM) specializes in talk radio and classical music, and for years has been the home of Studs Terkel's syndicated interview show. WLUP (97.9 FM and 1000AM) and WXRT (93 FM) play rock.

Religious Services   Times are usually posted outside the houses of worship. Consult your hotel staff or a telephone directory for the nearest location of the denomination or religion of your choice.

Restrooms   There is a clean restroom in the visitor information center located in the lobby of the Water Tower Pumping Station, 163 E. Pearson, at the corner of Michigan Avenue. The Chicago

Historical Society at Clark Street at North Avenue has a restroom downstairs accessible without entering the museum itself.

Safety   Whenever you're traveling in an unfamiliar city or country, stay alert. Be aware of your immediate surroundings. Wear a moneybelt and keep a close eye on your possessions. Be particularly careful with cameras, purses, and wallets, all favorite targets of thieves and pickpockets. In Chicago, be careful of where you walk alone at night; consult your hotel concierge or personnel if in doubt.

Shoe Repairs   Sam the Shoe Doctor has 11 locations, including one in the Sears Tower (☎ 876-9001), and will do repairs while you wait.

Taxes   The local sales tax is 8.75%. Be sure to calculate the tax when you are budgeting for accommodations and meals.

Telephone, Telex, and Fax   Hotel lobbies are excellent places from which to make pay phone calls. A telex or fax can also be sent from your hotel. Kinko's Copies is a copy center with a fax service and has several locations throughout the city, including 843 W. Van Buren (☎ 421-7373), 444 N. Wells (☎ 670-4460), and 2451 N. Lincoln (☎ 327-7770).

Time   All of Illinois, including Chicago, is located in the central time zone, so clocks are set one hour earlier than those on the East Coast and two hours later than those on the West Coast. Chicago switches to daylight saving time in early April, and back to standard time on the last Sunday in October.

Useful Numbers   For directory assistance, dial **411;** for the time, dial **976-1616.**

Weather   For the weather, dial **976-1212.**

---

3   Networks & Resources

A nationwide nonprofit service organization whose mission is to assist travelers in distress, **Traveler's and Immigrant's Aid** (☎ 312/629-4500) can provide food and shelter for those who are stranded, reunite family members who have become separated, locate lost luggage, and even furnish crisis counseling. In case of emergency after business hours (Monday through Friday 8:30am to 5pm), call **222-0265.**

FOR STUDENTS   There are many fine colleges and universities located throughout Chicago, all of which are centers of student life and study. The **University of Chicago** (☎ 702-1234) is in Hyde Park; the **University of Illinois at Chicago** (☎ 996-3000) is near the Loop on the Near West Side; **Loyola of Chicago** (☎ 274-3000) is on Sheridan Road in Rogers Park; and **Northwestern University** (☎ 491-7271) is in the northern suburb of Evanston.

FOR GAY MEN & LESBIANS   Gay and Lesbian Pride Week is a major event on the Chicago calendar each June, highlighted by an animated parade on the North Side. A good resource for access to various gay and lesbian networks is the **Gay and Lesbian Pride Week Planning Committee** (☎ 348-8243), which functions year round. **Horizon Community Services** (☎ 879-CARE) provides referrals daily from 7am to 10pm.

FOR WOMEN   The **Women and Children First Bookstore,** 5233 N. Clark (☎ 769-9299), is an excellent source of information for women, as is the **Community Information and Referral Service** (☎ 876-0010).

FOR SENIORS   There are many resources available in Chicago for seniors, including discounted fares for public transportation, discounted admissions for museums and other attractions, and citywide programs; call the **Chicago Park District** at **294-2309** for specific information.

5

Chicago Accommodations

Chicago's hotels are among the finest in the world. The hotel scene here caters first and foremost to the business traveler. During the week, Monday through Friday, Chicago's robust convention trade fills hotels to capacity with conventioneers. Individual corporate travelers, the rich and famous in town for a fling, and a small minority of actual tourists make up the rest of Chicago's hotel roll call most of the year. If Chicago has a slow season for hotels, it's during the deepest part of winter, or the stickiest days of summer, when most people seem to find the charms of any large city least appealing.

But weekends year-round are a different story entirely. These same fine hotels that often boast near 100% occupancy during the week have plenty of room on the weekends after the conventioneers have left for home. The same room or suite that costs $200 a night during the week can be had for about half price on most weekends during the year, and can include such promotional amenities as complimentary breakfast, free parking, even theater tickets. Travelers on modest budgets can come to Chicago practically any weekend of the year and experience the very best lodgings the city has to offer (and I repeat, in hotel comfort and luxury, Chicago is second to none) without spending a fortune.

Since you'll need at least a week to really experience what Chicago has to offer as a destination, you can find cheaper accommodations during the business week and move into your swell digs for the weekend finale. Fortunately Chicago still offers some moderately priced accommodations fairly near the commercial, cultural, and transportation center of the city. The really inexpensive hotels and motels tend to be on the city outskirts. Even with weekend bargains, though, you must expect to spend at least $60 per night for a single and $70 for a double, if you wish to be lodged in or near the center city. The traveler whose budget will not allow such extravagance can find inexpensive motels along the interstates that feed Chicago.

RESERVE IN ADVANCE   Whatever hotel or hotels you choose, regardless of season, be sure to make your reservations sufficiently in advance to ensure not only getting the lodging of your choice but the best rate available as well. Remember also that most hotels expect you to arrive sometime between 3 and 6 pm; if for any reason you are going to be delayed, call ahead and reconfirm your reservation, which might otherwise be canceled.

CORPORATE DISCOUNTS   Most hotels offer a discount of roughly 10% to individuals who are visiting Chicago on business. To qualify for this rate, your corporation or company must have an account on file at the hotel, or you may only be required to present some perfunctory proof of your commercial status, like a business card or an official letterhead.

A BED-&-BREAKFAST RESERVATIONS SERVICE   A centralized reservations service called **bed & breakfast/chicago,** P.O.

Box 14088, Chicago, IL 60614 (☎ 312/951-0085), can place you in someone's spare bedroom, or provide the keys to an unhosted apartment, in private houses and apartment buildings located in downtown Chicago or in select neighborhoods throughout the city as well. The minimum reservation accepted is for two nights if you choose someone's home, host included, or three nights in a self-contained but otherwise uninhabited apartment. Breakfast is self-service, continental style, if you elect the latter option; otherwise your host provides the fare, usually a full meal in the typical B&B tradition. Rates ranges from $55 to $85 a night, though there are several accommodations offered that are considerably more pricey.

1 The Loop

Strictly speaking, "downtown" in Chicago means the Loop, the central business district, a six- by eight-block rectangle enveloped by elevated tracks on all four sides. An outer circle beyond this literal loop of tracks is bounded by the Chicago River and its south branch, forming an elbow on two sides, by Michigan Avenue running along the edge of Grant Park to the east, and by the Congress Expressway to the south. Within these confines are the city's financial institutions, the trading markets, municipal government, and the major venues of the high culture, music, theater, and the arts. And you will also find an interesting selection of old Chicago hotels, no longer in the first rank perhaps, but with plenty of charm and character, and of undeniable convenience for those who prefer to be at the center of the city.

Very Expensive

⭐ **Stouffer Riviere Hotel,** One West Wacker Dr., Chicago, IL 60601. ☎ 312/372-7200, or toll free **800/HOTELS-1.** Fax 312/372-0093. 565 rms. A/C MINIBAR TV TEL

Rates: $230 deluxe single or double; $250 Club Level single or double; from $550–$2,500 suite. Weekend rates $149 double. AE, DC, DISC, MC, V. **Parking:** $19 valet.

Beginning with this edition, I must add another hotel to my small list of Chicago favorites. Comfort, service, style, scenic river view, amenities, convenient location—the Stouffer Riviere has it all. For that special weekend, you might even say the Stouffer Riviere is a bargain, especially for those visitors who are coming to Chicago for some serious museum hopping, restaurant sampling, or for strolling amid the city's innumerable architectural wonders—they could not be more perfectly situated between the Loop and the Magnificent Mile than in this hotel.

But let's go back to service for a moment. From the front desk to the bellmen, from the waitstaff to the chambermaids, the staff exhibits a totally natural friendliness and helpfulness, nothing forced

Chicago Accommodations

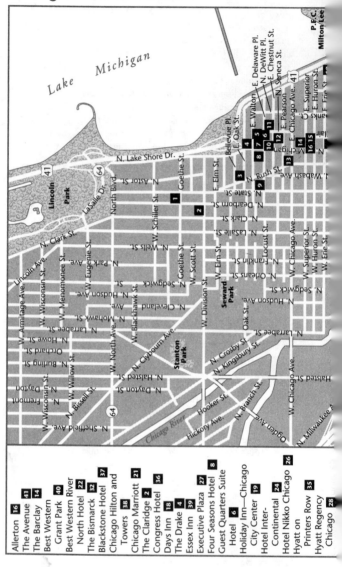

or officious. You really do get the sense that it is their pleasure to serve you.

The rooms are also above the norm in size, decor, and furnishings, and, with their views of the river and the cityscape surroundings, provide a very pleasant environment. Terrycloth robes and hairdryers are in every bathroom, along with the usual lotions and

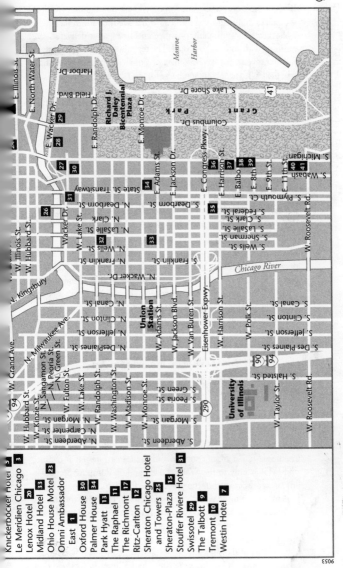

Knickerbocker Hotel **2**
Le Meridien Chicago **3**
Lenox Hotel **20**
Midland Hotel **33**
Ohio House Motel **23**
Omni Ambassador East **1**
Oxford House **30**
Palmer House **34**
Park Hyatt **13**
The Raphael **11**
The Richmont **17**
Ritz-Carlton **12**
Sheraton Chicago Hotel and Towers **25**
Sheraton-Plaza **15**
Stouffer Riviere Hotel **31**
Swissotel **29**
The Talbott **9**
Tremont **10**
Westin Hotel **7**

fine soaps. For a relatively minor increase in the nightly rate, you can enjoy the privileges of the Club Level rooms, including a sumptuous continental breakfast in a private lounge, and complimentary hors d'oeuvres in the evening.

Dining/Entertainment: The Great Street Restaurant and Bar, with its contemporary American menu and view over the Chicago

River, is the hotel's main dining room. Another restaurant, Cuisines, specializes in lunches and dinners with a Mediterranean flavor.

Services: Complimentary coffee and newspaper delivered each morning with your wake-up call. The management has also thoughtfully removed what has become a perennial annoyance at most hotels: there is no telephone surcharge for toll free, collect, or credit-card calls or for incoming faxes.

Facilities: Indoor swimming pool with skylights, plus a fully equipped health club, including sauna and whirlpool with complimentary chilled water, juices, and fresh fruit.

Expensive

Executive Plaza, 71 E. Wacker Dr., Chicago, IL 60601.
☎ **312/346-7100,** or toll free **800/2-RAMADA** outside Illinois.
Fax 312/346-1721. 417 rms. A/C MINIBAR TV TEL
Rates: $185 single or double. Weekend rates $85–$129. AE, CB, DC, DISC, MC, V. **Parking:** $18 per day, with 24-hour in/out privileges.

This Ramada-owned hotel is very modern, with a fabulous location on the river, facing the northern downtown zone centered around the Magnificent Mile. The rooms are furnished in tasteful contemporary detail. Tariffs for these rooms are higher than those at comparable Loop hotels, but at the Executive Plaza you are paying extra for the favored location and, perhaps, room spaciousness as well. The rooms have either a city or a river view. Club-floor rooms, where guests have access to a private lounge, are priced slightly higher.

★ **Hyatt on Printers Row,** 500 S. Dearborn St., Chicago, IL 60605. ☎ **312/986-1234,** or toll free **800/233-1234.**
Fax 312/939-2468. 161 rms. A/C MINIBAR TV TEL
Rates: $129 single; $154 double. Weekend rates (available Fri–Sun) $89 double. AE, CB, DC, DISC, ER, JCB, MC, V. **Parking:** $9.50 self, $12 valet on weekends, $18 valet on weekdays (all with 24-hour in/out privileges).

South of the Congress Expressway are many of Chicago's oldest buildings. These are not survivors of the Great Fire—that distinction belongs only to the Water Tower and its Pumping Station—but structures erected in the years immediately following the disaster, among them the world's first skyscrapers. In one of the smaller of these historic landmarks, you will find this fine small hotel.

The discreet and tasteful lobby announces your arrival at the one hotel in Chicago that can truly claim a certain sensibility usually found only at a handful of fine European establishments. But what could be more American at the same time than a hotel in Chicago that outfits each of its very fashionably decorated rooms—all renovated in 1992—with two (count 'em, two) color TVs and a videocassette player?

Dining/Entertainment: Not only will you be comfortable, and in a great neighborhood for browsing old buildings, but you'll also dine well at the Prairie restaurant, one of my favorite eateries in Chicago (see Chapter 6).

Services: Complimentary coffee or tea daily, free daily newspaper.

Facilities: Access to the City Club, a complete health/fitness club.

Midland Hotel, 172 W. Adams St. (at LaSalle), Chicago, IL 60603. ☎ **312/332-1200,** or toll free **800/621-2360.** Fax 312/332-5909. 257 rms. A/C TV TEL

Rates (including buffet breakfast and complimentary cocktail hour): $160–$220 single; $175–$240 double; from $350 suite. Weekend package $89–$119 per night. AE, DC, DISC, MC, V. **Parking:** $6 credit toward nearby parking on Fri–Sat nights.

If you arrive in Chicago by train and are traveling light, you could easily walk to the Midland Hotel, a few short blocks across the river from Union Station. You'll think you're in an American Venice, because the river here is such a dominant feature of the landscape, and because of the half dozen or so of Chicago's more than 50 bridges that you can glimpse as you cross over one of them, the Adams Street Bridge.

In truth, the Midland, once a private men's club, is a business hotel, though it's also a perfect base for visitors who wish to concentrate their attentions on the many attractions and distractions of the Loop. The hotel's lobby is narrow but grandiose within its restricted dimensions, designed primarily to speed guests to their rooms or to the public spaces. A number of deluxe rooms with large seating areas and king-size beds are available.

Dining/Entertainment: There are two restaurants. Breakfast is served in the Exchange, a miniature beaux arts eating gallery mounted, continental style, in a mezzanine above the lobby.

Services: Guests receive complimentary copies of the *Wall Street Journal* and have use of the hotel's unique limo—an authentic English Austin taxi. The Midland offers its regular business clients membership in a corporate travel program called the Lion's Share, which allows members to upgrade their rooms at no added cost (depending on availability) and entitles them to special rates.

Facilities: The Midland's meeting facilities are legitimate curios in their own right, worth a detour; each meeting room is designed in the manner of some famous Chicago architect, Wright, Sullivan, and Adler among them.

Palmer House, 17 E. Monroe St., Chicago, IL 60690. ☎ **312/726-7500,** or toll free **800/HILTONS.** Fax 312/263-2558. 1,696 rms. A/C MINIBAR TV TEL

Rates: $125–$205 single; $145–$230 double. Weekend rates (including continental breakfast) $89–$119. AE, DC, DISC, MC, V. **Parking:** $15.25 on weekdays, $12.25 on weekends.

Not long before the Great Chicago Fire of 1871, a local merchant named Potter Palmer, who had profited handsomely in cotton speculation during the Civil War, purchased land along State Street. The area was still peripheral to the city's commercial district at that time. At opposite ends of this strip of wood-framed residences, which he had acquired to recast as a major merchandising district, Palmer erected two fine buildings, one to house Field and Leiter, a retail and wholesale dry goods company (predecessor of Marshall Field & Co.), and the other, a fine hotel called the Palmer House. Both buildings were consumed by the fire. A second, even more splendid, hotel was constructed soon thereafter, and this in turn was replaced in 1925 by the current Palmer House. The "third" coming of the Palmer House was a considerable enlargement over its original namesakes, a palatial full-service hotel in every sense.

Guests enter the Palmer House at street level from either Monroe or State Street. The approach in both directions takes you into the hotel's ground floor of arcade shops and entrances to the more public restaurants, including Trader Vic's. In the center of this area stand several banks of escalators to carry you to the second-floor lobby, an absolutely cavernous room, gilded in a way that modern architects can only dream about, but never re-create. Among the seven restaurants under the single roof of the Palmer House, the Empire Room is said to hold its own as one of the most fashionable luncheon spots in the city.

Rooms are large, bright, and well furnished, but not special in the manner of the deluxe hotels. The hotel's top two floors, called the Palmer House Towers, are a private executive area where rooms cost slightly more. Amenities for guests of the Towers include private elevators, an exercise room with both steam and sauna compartments, and complimentary movies.

Moderate

The Bismarck, 171 W. Randolph St., Chicago, IL 60601. ☎ **312/236-0123,** or toll free **800/643-1500.** Fax 312/236-3711. 500 rms. A/C TV TEL

Rates: $110 single; $130 double. Weekend package available. AE, DC, MC, V. **Parking:** $16.50, valet with in/out privileges.

The Bismarck, located smack-dab in the middle of Chicago's financial quarter, celebrated its 100th birthday in 1994. The hotel boasts newly furnished and tastefully decorated rooms and is within walking distance of all the Loop's centers of trade and culture. Guests have access to a number of fine specialty shops and restaurants within the hotel, and they may use the indoor pool and fitness facilities at a private club across the street. As with many of the Loop's other business-oriented hotels, the Bismarck offers a range of promotional packages to attract weekend visitors. A courtesy van transports guests to various stops within a four-mile radius of the hotel.

$ **Oxford House,** 225 N. Wabash Ave. (at Wacker Dr.), Chicago, IL 60601. ☎ **312/346-6585,** or toll free **800/344-4111.** Fax 312/346-7742. 175 rms. A/C MINIBAR TV TEL

Rates: $79–$89 single; $89–$99 double; $175 one-bedroom suite; $200 two-bedroom suite. Weekend rates $55 double; weekend package $80 per person for three days. Monthly rates start at $960 for one. Children under 16 stay free in parents' room. AE, DC, DISC, MC, V. **Parking:** $10.25 per 24 hours (with no in/out privileges).

Another well-situated hotel, but one considerably less pricey than the Bismarck, is the Oxford House. Regular rooms come with two double beds and a kitchenette, underscoring the hotel's attractiveness to those in Chicago for temporary assignment who wish to set up at least the semblance of housekeeping. "Executive Kings" have king-size beds and a seating area with a convertible sofa. One- and two-bedroom suites are available. Monthly rates in regular kitchenette-equipped efficiencies are available. And when you're not eating in, try the Oxford's Café Angelo, a restaurant of good repute located on the premises. The weekend splurge at the Oxford House ought to be within the budget possibilities of many travelers.

2 The Magnificent Mile

The stretch of Michigan Avenue running north of the Chicago River to Walton Street is known as the Magnificent Mile.

Very Expensive

Chicago Marriott, 540 N. Michigan Ave., Chicago, IL 60611. ☎ **312/836-0100,** or toll free **800/228-9290.** Fax 312/836-6139. 1,173 rms and suites. A/C MINIBAR TV TEL

Rates: $164 single; $194 double; $480 suite. Weekend rates $109–$129. AE, DC, DISC, MC, V. **Parking:** $20 valet.

A number of awards by convention trade magazines indicate that the Chicago Marriott, the only convention hotel on North Michigan Avenue, is indeed a popular venue for many professional groups. The spacious rooms are decorated in soft colors that complement the maple woodwork and the colonial-style furnishings.

Dining/Entertainment: Three in-house restaurants and an entertainment lounge with nightly dancing add to the hotel's self-contained environment.

Services: Room service (6:30am to 3am), same-day valet cleaning.

Facilities: Four outdoor platform tennis courts, indoor swimming pool with whirlpool and exercise facilities, sun deck, rooftop putting green.

★ **The Drake,** 140 E. Walton Place (at Michigan Ave.), Chicago, IL 60611. ☎ **312/787-2200,** or toll free **800/HILTONS.** Fax 312/787-1431. Telex 270278. 535 rms and suites. A/C MINIBAR TV TEL

Rates: $194–$280 single; $205–$310 double; $595 suite. Weekend rates start at $159 ($170 with continental breakfast) single or double.

AE, CB, DC, DISC, ER, JCB, MC, V. **Parking:** $21.50 valet per day with in/out privileges.

Formally opened on New Year's Eve in 1920, the Drake has reigned alone as "Chicago's hotel" for more than 70 years. The 13-story landmark building, constructed of Bedford limestone in a design inspired by the Italian palaces of the High Renaissance, also fronts Lake Shore Drive, the hotel's secondary entrance. The Drake looks over a quiet vest-pocket park beyond which—and very much in view—are the sands of Oak Street Beach, washed by Lake Michigan.

From the lobby and other public spaces, through the corridors and on to the guest rooms, you sense that you are lodged in a special place, where unusual care and sensitivity have contributed to every design decision. The effect of the rich carpeting and polished woodwork; the subtle arrangements everywhere of art or artifact; the aristocratic, almost wasteful spaciousness might at first seem old-fashioned, too out of pace with the high-tech pulse of the times. Take a closer look though and you will observe how every design is also utterly modern in line, color, and texture.

A room at the Drake is not cheap; but the Drake has the best $205 room (for two) in the city. The typical bedroom is generously large, lit with five table lamps, and furnished to perfection. The furnishings include a king-size bed; a seating area with a well-stuffed settee, armchair, and coffee table; a writing desk with a separate chair; and an attractive bathroom stocked with bathrobes, complimentary toiletries, and a wicker laundry hamper.

A slightly more expensive "executive top floor" reserves 38 rooms and five suites that provide guests with such additional amenities as personalized stationery, a continental breakfast in a private 10th-floor "panorama lounge," free cocktails and hors d'oeuvres, plus a daily newspaper and valet assistance for polishing shoes, packing and unpacking, and securing theater tickets. The "concierge floors" (fourth and fifth) have some rooms with extra baths, plus a lounge open from 6:30am to midnight, where snacks, soft drinks, and fresh-brewed coffee are available without charge. The Drake has five immense boardroom suites, a bargain for the corporate set at $550 per night, each with separate conference room and bedroom, kitchen, and a spacious living area.

Dining/Entertainment: Public areas at the Drake are enticing enough to make you temporarily abandon the privileged comfort of your room. First, stop at the Palm Court off the lobby, an enormous room softened by yards of fine draperies, antique Oriental screens pinned to the walls, and a dramatic recessed ceiling lined with mirrors. Potted greenery and well-spaced seating clusters surround an ornate bubbling fountain, creating an ideal retreat for private teas or intimate cocktails. Within the Drake are two fine dining restaurants, the Oak Terrace and the Cape Cod Room, long local favorites for business lunches and family dinners.

Services: All rooms are provided with fresh fruit, flowers, Swiss chocolates at turn-down, and newspapers each morning.

Facilities: Exercise facility with state-of-the-art equipment; convention and business facilities.

⭐ **Four Seasons Hotel,** 120 E. Delaware Place, Chicago, IL 60611. ☎ 312/280-8800, or toll free **800/332-3442.** Fax 312/280-8800. 346 rms. A/C MINIBAR TV TEL

Rates: $260–$325 single; $290–$355 double. Weekend rates $185–$195 AE, CB, DC, DISC, MC, V. **Parking:** $15 self, $22 valet.

The swank new Four Seasons Hotel occupies floors 30 through 46 of the 900 North Michigan Avenue building, Chicago's newest upscale vertical mall. The Four Seasons, Chicago's only five-star, five-diamond hotel, was specifically designed to reflect the feeling that you are a guest in someone's home—someone rather well-off, it need hardly be noted. The interior design is classically traditional, and includes such noteworthy elements as a winding staircase uniting the lobby with the public spaces on the floor above and an antique Italian marble fireplace (the only wood-burning fireplace in any Chicago hotel).

Guest rooms have richly upholstered English furnishings, custom-woven carpets and tapestries, and armoires. In each room there are three two-line phones and windows that open to let in the fresh air. Each bathroom is equipped with a hairdryer, a lighted makeup mirror, oversize bath and bath towels, and other indulgences from cotton balls to terry robes.

Dining/Entertainment: An 18-foot white marble fountain marks the entrance to the opulent Seasons Restaurant, which serves elegantly presented American and continental fare.

Services: Your newspaper is delivered with your coffee each morning.

Facilities: The hotel's health spa was designed for pure enjoyment and features a 50-foot pool with Roman columns, a skylight, and a Jacuzzi that accommodates 20 people. There is also a sun deck and outdoor jogging track in addition to all the normal health-club services.

Guest Quarters Suite Hotel, 198 E. Delaware Place, Chicago, IL 60611. ☎ 312/664-1100, or toll free **800/424-2900.** Fax 312/664-9881. 345 suites. A/C MINIBAR TV TEL

Rates: $178 single suite; $235 double suite. Weekend and summer promotional rates start at $119; a weekend rate of $159 includes breakfast and parking. Children under 18 stay free in parents' room. AE, CB, DC, DISC, MC, V. **Parking:** $20 valet per day with in/out privileges.

The Guest Quarters, just up the block from the Four Seasons, is a full-service all-suite hotel spread over 25 floors. Each suite features a separate living room and bedroom, deluxe bath, refrigerator, two telephones, and two remote-control color TVs. The prices of the suites depend on bed size, floor, and furnishings.

Dining/Entertainment: The Grille 98 serves breakfast and dinner, and the Cityside Bistro and Bar serves lunch and dinner. The hotel also has live entertainment most nights featuring jazz and contemporary music.

Services: Each guest receives daily a complimentary coffee or tea and newspaper.

Facilities: The hotel has a rooftop health club with a pool.

Hotel Inter-Continental, 505 N. Michigan Ave. Chicago, IL 60611. ☎ **312/944-4100,** or toll free **800/33-AGAIN.** Fax 312/944-1320. 337 rms. A/C MINIBAR TV TEL

Rates: $109 single; $229 double. AE, CB, DC, DISC, MC, V. **Parking:** $20 per night for cars, $25 for vans.

Rivaling the best hotels in Chicago, the brand-new Hotel Inter-Continental has been installed with great elegance in a landmark building at the foot of the Magnificent Mile. Located in an old tower of pre-Depression vintage, it sports a timeless classical motif in its interior decor. There is little in the hotel's appearance to suggest that the Inter-Continental has not occupied this favored spot for many years. Truly, the designers have executed a *coup de trompe-l'oeil* worthy of our admiration.

Spacious, well furnished, and decorated in muted earth tones, each of the plush rooms is equipped with a refrigerator, three dual-line phones, a thick terry robe, and a large desk.

Dining/Entertainment: The public spaces, in particular the Lobby Lounge—prosaic in name only—the Alhambra Boardroom, the Grand Ballroom, and the Gourmet Restaurant, recall the best in the tradition of continental charm. Rounding out the hotel's facilities is a fine restaurant with service in cut crystal and polished silver.

Services: Special amenities include twice-daily maid service, weekday newspaper, and complimentary overnight shoeshine.

Facilities: The hotel has a health club on the premises, featuring an all-tile junior Olympic-size indoor pool, a gymnasium, aerobics room, saunas, whirlpools, and steam and massage rooms.

⭐ **Hotel Nikko Chicago,** 320 N. Dearborn St., Chicago, IL 60610. ☎ **312/744-1900,** or toll free **800/NIKKO-US**; reservations also through Japan Air Lines offices. Fax 312/527–2664. 425 rms. A/C MINIBAR TV TEL

Rates: $205 single; $225 double; $240–$260 river-view room: from $300 suite. Weekend rate $135 per night based on two-night stay. Other packages available. AE, DC, DISC, JCB, MC, V. **Parking:** $21 valet with in/out privileges.

At the end of the Magnificent Mile, the Hotel Nikko Chicago sets its own standard of luxury. The key to the Nikko, beyond the elegant simplicity of its sleek design and its riverfront location, is the hotel's relative smallness.

Guests enter the 20-story Nikko from Dearborn Street west of Michigan Avenue. The main lobby is small, but incorporates the spacious and sunken Hana Lounge, the whole affair trimmed in the most subtle and graceful of natural materials, polished granite, Japanese ash, and African mahogany. A small private Japanese garden separates the lobby from a walkway along the river that crosses through the Nikko's Riverfront Park, a 300-foot-long landscaped strip between Dearborn and Clark Streets.

A suite on the 19th floor will tempt those few who can splurge on such extravagances as three enormous rooms including a huge marble bathroom, black-leather couches in the living room, and a large window offering a side view of the river.

A very tony place, the Nikko is faithful to the tradition of Japanese taste at its most impeccable and discriminating.

Dining/Entertainment: In addition to the Hana Lounge, open for lunch and drinks, the Nikko's other public facilities include the Les Célébrités and Benkay restaurants.

Every Sunday from 11am to 2pm, the Nikko plays host to an elaborate brunch in Les Célébrités that has become the rage of Chicago. The $32 per person cost ($19 for children ages 5 to 12) includes a lavish spread of cold cuts, sausages, cheeses, breads, pastries, fruits, salmon and other seafoods, and hot and cold breakfast treats served from steaming chafing dishes. Also included in the price is a full menu of made-to-order dishes, like eggs Benedict, three-pepper omelettes, vanilla flapjacks, stir-fry chicken and shrimp, and so forth, along with all the fresh-squeezed juices and cappuccino or caffe latte you desire to wash it all down. Twice monthly, radio station WNUA broadcasts its smooth jazz format live from its head table among the Nikko's well-stuffed and well-satisfied Sunday brunchers. Afternoon tea is served as well.

Services: Free daily newspaper and shoeshine.

Facilities: There's an executive health club/cardio-fitness center that costs $10 per session, which includes shorts, shirts, socks, plus free fruit and juices.

Park Hyatt, 800 N. Michigan Ave. (off Water Tower Sq.), Chicago, IL 60611. ☎ **312/280-2222,** or toll free **800/228-9000** outside Illinois. Fax 312/280-1963. 216 rms. A/C MINIBAR TV TEL
Rates: $220–$250 single or double. Weekend rates $139–$155. AE, CB, DC, DISC, MC, V. **Parking:** $24 overnight with in/out privileges.

Water Tower Square is not only the site of the Chicago landmark tower that survived the Great Fire of 1871, but it is also the current headquarters of the Chicago Office of Tourism and the starting point for the horse-drawn carriage rides that tour the surrounding streets. The Park Hyatt, another gem among Chicago's small elegant hotels, is set back from Michigan Avenue opposite this pleasant, tree-shaded square, and the hotel's entrance is actually on a side street called Chicago Avenue. A marble floor adorns the two-story, cathedral-ceilinged lobby, which is long, narrow, and well appointed.

The rooms are on a par with those of the hotel's competitors, with such extras as small TVs in the bathrooms. "Our trademark is service," I was told by an assistant manager, who added, "We try to go that extra portion."

Dining/Entertainment: Open for breakfast, lunch, and dinner, Jaxx is a regional American restaurant with a British accent. Boasting magnificent views of the Water Tower, it tempts diners with offerings such as Dover sole meunière or grilled shrimp with leaf spinach and tomato salsa. There's a "Cuisine Naturelle" menu with several low-fat, health-conscious items, and light fare is offered throughout the day. Save room for dessert—there's English trifle, rhubarb crumble, a white chocolate brownie, and a concoction called "chocolate oblivion." A pianist entertains every night from 6 to 10pm, and on weekends, a jazz trio takes the reins. High tea is served in Jaxx Lobby Bar each afternoon.

Services: A Mercedes can often be seen parked at the entrance to the Park Hyatt, which guests may use without charge, on a first-come, first-served basis, for short local trips to restaurants, museums, and so forth. There's also maid service three times daily, complimentary shoeshine, and assistance in unpacking your bags. An Exercycle or rowing machine can be brought directly to your room on request. Complimentary coffee and tea service is available for guests in the lobby until 9am daily.

Facilities: For $10, guests have access to a nearby full-service health club.

Ritz-Carlton, 160 E. Pearson St., Chicago, IL 60611.
☎ **312/266-1000,** or toll free **800/621-6906.** Fax 312/266-1194. 431 rms, 82 suites. A/C MINIBAR TV TEL
Rates: $240–$325 single; $270–$355 double. Weekend rates $185–$250. **Parking:** $22.50 valet.

Catercorner from Water Tower Square is Water Tower Place, one of North Michigan Avenue's premier addresses, an immense and shiny skyscraper housing a vertical mall, elegant condominiums, and the upscale Ritz-Carlton, a favorite roost for the Grateful Dead when the group plays Chicago. On Water Tower's bottom floors, you will find more than a hundred shops and arcades surrounding a central atrium. The plush digs of the Ritz-Carlton begin at the 10th level. Guests deliver their luggage to waiting bellmen on the ground level and ride elevators to the 12-floor lobby to register. Your first glance at the fountain-centered lobby is likely to provide more than a pleasant surprise. Stretched out before you over one entire floor of the enormous building are a variety of sparkling restaurants, meeting rooms, and boutiques designed to delight the eye. Without a doubt, the most dramatic is a roomy cocktail restaurant of greenhouse design, glass roof and all, that seems to jut out over the city.

Standard rooms are large, with high ceilings, and are traditional in their appointments, including antique wall prints, cherrywood armories, and king or twin beds with down quilts. Rooms are equipped with VCRs and two-line telephones. Complimentary coffee is served in the lobby from 5:30am to 8am, and complimentary newspapers are available on request.

Dining/Entertainment: The Dining Room is one of the better hotel restaurants in Chicago, serving French cuisine in an atmosphere of elegance.

Services: One-hour pressing, overnight dry cleaning, overnight shoeshine, 24-hour business services including in-room fax machines.

Facilities: Skylighted indoor pool, private sun deck, complete health and exercise facility.

★ **Sheraton Chicago Hotel And Towers,** 301 E. North Water St., Chicago, IL 60611. ☎ **312/464-1000.** Fax 312/464-9140. 1,200 rms. A/C MINIBAR TV TEL

Rates: $175–$210 single; $195–$230 double. Tower rates $168–$220 single; $168–$240 double. Weekend rates start at $119. AE, DC, DISC, MC, V. **Parking:** $19 valet with in/out privileges.

Chicago's newest entry in the luxury-hotel category is the stunning Sheraton Chicago, a major convention center during the workweek, and a full-service leisure hotel on the weekends, one block east of North Michigan Avenue right along the Chicago River. Enormous only begins to define the spacious Sheraton, which now anchors two acres of land in the reconstructed downtown neighborhood once known as Sreeterville. It stands amid many lovely architectural rivals, including the gorgeous NBC building.

Separate registration desks process conventioneers and individual guests in the Sheraton's cavernous lobby, and many of the hotel's public spaces, including restaurants, shops, and lounges, are to be found on the fringes of this space. The 34-story building has 96 tower rooms in addition to its thoroughly modern standard accommodations, where amenities include in-room individual voice mail. Guests in the tower rooms have access to a courtesy lounge, where a complimentary continental breakfast is served daily.

Dining/Entertainment: The flagship restaurant at the Chicago Sheraton is the Streeterville Grille, featuring steaks and seafood with an Italian flavor, and already very popular with local Chicagoans as well as hotel guests. The Riverside Café offers a more informal dining option, and the Spectator Sports Bar provides a club atmosphere for sports fans. At ground level, along the river promenade both inside and out is the Esplanade Express Café.

Services: Handicapped-accessible rooms are available, and all guests are provided with a daily newspaper of their choice free of charge. There is a concierge to facilitate entertainment and dining arrangements.

Facilities: A complete business center with all services, a fully equipped health club and pool, boat-docking facilities.

Sheraton-Plaza, 160 E. Huron St., Chicago, IL 60611. ☎ **312/787-2900,** or toll free **800/325-3535.** Fax 312/787-5758. 334 rms. A/C MINIBAR TV TEL

Rates: $155 single; $175 double. Corporate rates $160–$185 single or double. Weekend package starts at $100–$145. AE, CB, DC, DISC, ER, JCB, MC, V. **Parking:** $19 overnight.

The Sheraton-Plaza is located roughly at midpoint along the Magnificent Mile, which means that the hotel is within walking distance of many attractions located in the Loop. Rooms are priced in five categories, depending on such factors as view or size of bed. The Sheraton's most expensive accommodations are the "top-floor" rooms, and prices get progressively cheaper as you descend toward street level.

The Sheraton-Plaza also offers year-round weekend packages and special summer rates. Inquire to see what's being offered during your visit.

Dining/Entertainment: Guests enjoy the Bentley restaurant for full dining, Tiff's for cocktails, and the Terrace Café, which overlooks the lake.

Services: Concierge, room service.

Facilities: The Sheraton has a very appealing penthouse pool and a library off the lobby.

Westin Hotel, 909 N. Michigan Ave., Chicago, IL 60611.
☎ **312/943-7200**, or toll free **800/228-3000.** Fax 312/943-4509. Telex 206593. 742 rms. A/C MINIBAR TV TEL

Rates: $155–$170 single; $180–$195 double; $225–$1,800 suite. Weekend rates $385 double for Fri and Sat. AE, DC, JCB, MC, V. **Parking:** $18.95 per day with in/out privileges.

The Westin's lobby is an animated spot most anytime of day, as you might expect at one of Chicago's larger hotels. Its size and stylish accommodations make the Westin a favorite among groups and conventioneers who are seeking a full-service hotel that doesn't scrimp on service or surroundings. Rooms are spacious and nicely decorated, and all have free CNN and ESPN cable-TV channels. Rooms on the private Executive Level floors include such amenities as breakfast. A number of weekend packages offering reduced rates are available as well, so be sure to inquire about special offerings when you reserve.

The Westin is on the corner of Delaware Place, close to some of Michigan Avenue's finest shopping, with "Bloomie's" practically across the street, in no. 900.

Dining/Entertainment: Chelsea is the hotel's restaurant.

Services: Concierge, valet service, 24-hour room service.

Facilities: Health club (free to guests).

Expensive

⭐ **The Barclay**, 166 E. Superior St., Chicago, IL 60611.
☎ **312/787-6000**, or toll free **800/621-8004.**
Fax 312/751-0370. 120 suites. A/C MINIBAR TV TEL

Rates (including continental breakfast): $99 junior suite; $109 "Executive Parlour"; $119 one-bedroom suite. AE, DISC, MC, V. **Parking:** $17 valet (with no in/out privileges).

What the Barclay lacks in grand public spaces it makes up for in coziness, room size, and one or two other intrinsic features. First of all, the "rooms" at the Barclay are actually suites. The 29-story hotel offers suites of four sizes, limiting the number of accommodations per floor to six.

One-bedroom suites offer living room, separate sleeping room, and full kitchen. The mini and junior suites, and the "Executive Parlour" units combine sleeping and living areas within a single large space. The "Executive Parlour" suites also include full kitchens and dressing rooms.

The one-bedroom suites, which are the Barclay's pattern accommodations, are in some ways the hotel's best bargain. The foyer rests on a platform that is large enough for both a writing desk and small dining table with several chairs, in effect, a totally separate alcove. A small but fully equipped kitchen is off to one side, with a service counter that opens to the large, comfortably furnished living room, sunken below the level of the entryway. A narrow passageway opens into a small dressing area, and leads to the bathroom and separate bedroom.

Service at the Barclay also merits a nod. The lobby is small but the staff is efficient and attentive. Breakfast is served in the Barclay Club, a private dining establishment operating for more than 40 years on the hotel's premises, which is also open to the hotel's guests. Also available in the lobby each morning free of charge are coffee and a variety of daily newspapers, including the *Wall Street Journal* and the two Chicago papers. Another thoughtful touch is a basket of fresh fruit on the reception counter from which guests may help themselves. A stairwell from the lobby leads to the very appealing Bookmark Lounge, open from noon to midnight, where complimentary hors d'oeuvres are served during the cocktail hours. An unexpected plus at the Barclay is the small rooftop pool and sun deck. Another one of the hotel's conveniences is its location, only a block from Water Tower Place.

Holiday Inn-Chicago City Center, 300 E. Ohio St., Chicago, IL 60611. ☎ **312/787-6100,** or toll free **800/HOLIDAY.** Fax 312/787-6238. 500 rms. A/C MINIBAR TV TEL
   Rates: $145–$170 single; $161–$186 double. Weekend rates $89–$119. AE, CB, DC, DISC, MC, V. **Parking:** $14.

Another hotel favored by conventioneers, north of the Chicago River, is the Holiday Inn, located in an area east of the Magnificent Mile that is being called City Center. Right next door to the hotel is the McClurg Court Sports Complex, where guests may enjoy the facilities free of charge. With its own fifth-floor outdoor pool and sun deck, and the hotel's proximity to such attractions as the new entertainment mall on nearby North Pier, and the Navy Pier—site of dozens of special events and open-air festivals—the Holiday Inn would make an excellent choice for summer visitors to Chicago.

Knickerbocker Hotel, 163 E. Walton St., Chicago, IL 60611.
   ☎ **312/751-8100,** or toll free **800/621-8140.** Fax 312/751-0370. 256 rms. A/C MINIBAR TV TEL

Rates: $105–$165 single; $165–$265 double; from $225 suite. Weekend rates $99 double; Royal Weekend package $164; Getaway Weekend package $139. AE, DC, DISC, MC, V. **Parking:** $19 per day with full in/out privileges.

Near the corner of North Michigan Avenue and directly across from the Drake, the Knickerbocker is hard to classify. While slightly shy of genuine deluxe status, it ranks among Chicago's fine traditional hotels. For a time the hotel was expropriated by Hugh Hefner's Chicago empire and rechristened the Playboy Towers. Now restored to its former name and renovated a few years ago, the hotel offers several interesting weekend options. The Royal Weekend, for example, includes suite accommodations and dinner at the Knickerbocker's Prince of Wales restaurant.

★ **The Talbott,** 20 E. Delaware Place, Chicago, IL 60611. ☎ **312/944-4970,** or toll free **800/621-8506.** Fax 312/944-7241. 98 rms, 50 suites. A/C MINIBAR TV TEL

Rates (including continental breakfast): $155 single junior suite; $175 double junior suite; $255–$275 one-bedroom suite. Weekend packages from $99–$109 per night. AE, DC, MC, V. **Parking:** $11 across the street in a lot.

The Talbott is another one of those small, European-style gems that abound in Chicago and seem to thrive here, despite the city's reputation as a convention town. About one-third of the units here are full suites; all rooms contain either kitchenettes or actual kitchens. The hotel's standard room is called a junior suite because of the spacious seating area in each room. One-bedroom suites have separate sleeping rooms. Breakfast is served in the Talbott's Delaware Room, a fine restaurant with an ambitious and always-intriguing menu, serving nouvelle cuisine. Be sure to inquire about weekend packages.

Tremont, 100 E. Chestnut St., Chicago, IL 60611. ☎ **312/751-1900,** or toll free **800/621-8133** outside Illinois. Fax 312/280-1304. 137 rms and suites. A/C MINIBAR TV TEL

Rates: $190–$210 single or double; $450 one-bedroom suite; $600–$800 penthouse suite. Corporate rate $155. Weekend rates start at $99. AE, DC, DISC, MC, V. **Parking:** $19.50 per day (with no in/out privileges).

The Tremont has been described as the first small luxury European-style hotel in Chicago. The hotel, which opened its doors in 1976, was formerly an apartment building. Thus, one of the Tremont's unique attractions is that no two accommodations are exactly the same.

All rooms at the Tremont are decorated in manorial, English country–house style. The reception area is narrow and utilitarian, but a warm, inviting common room is just off the lobby. The privacy of celebrities and businesswomen traveling alone is well guarded—though it is hard to fathom how the presence of Elizabeth Taylor, said to favor the Tremont when visiting Chicago, could be sufficiently muffled in such intimate surroundings as these.

Attached to the Tremont is Cricket's bar and restaurant, a Chicago meeting place similar in tradition to New York's 21 Club. A very protective bartender at Cricket's is said to ensure that the bar remains a comfortable place for unaccompanied women, who are among its regular patrons. Services at the hotel include a concierge, 24-hour room service, and complimentary shoeshines.

Moderate

 Allerton, 701 N. Michigan Ave., Chicago, IL 60611.
☎ **312/440-1500,** or toll free **800/621-8311, 800/572-7839** in Illinois. Fax 312/440-1819. 450 rms. A/C TV TEL

Rates: $109–$119 single; $119–$129 double. Weekend rates $79 room, $89 suite. AE, JCB, MC, V. **Parking:** Next door for $19 for 24 hours with in/out privileges.

The sturdy, timeless Allerton is one of Chicago's real hotel bargains, considering its privileged location. While the lobby entrance is actually around the corner on Huron Street, along this strip of towering glass-and-steel newcomers, there is no building that is more characteristic of "old" Chicago than the Allerton. The rooms and suites have been comfortably decorated and are large, light, and well scrubbed, but by no means palatial. The hotel offers several attractive promotional packages, so be sure to inquire when you reserve your room. Avanzare, one of my favorite Chicago restaurants, is located near the Allerton on Huron (see Chapter 6 for details).

$ Days Inn, 644 N. Lake Shore Dr., Chicago, IL 60611.
☎ **312/943-9200,** or toll free **800/325-2525.** Fax 312/649-5580. 578 rms. A/C TV TEL

Rates: $95–$110 single; $110–$120 double. Weekend rates $95. AE, DC, DISC, ER, MC, V. **Parking:** $10 per day.

The lakefront location of Chicago's Days Inn sets it apart from all the city's other hotels, especially those in the moderate price range. The Days Inn is large, on the scale of a resort hotel. In fact, with a bit of imagination, you could almost consider the Days Inn as Chicago's beach hotel, since it has an outdoor swimming pool and the walk to nearby Oak Street Beach is not overly taxing. The more expensive rooms overlook the lake. For dining, there is the Lake Shore Cafe, and for Sunday brunch, the Pinnacle, Chicago's only revolving hospitality room. There is also a newly developed complex of eateries on nearby North Pier. The Days Inn has a complete fitness center.

Lenox Hotel, 616 N. Rush St. (at E. Ontario St.), Chicago, IL 60611.
☎ **312/337-1000,** or toll free **800/44-LENOX** outside Illinois. Fax 312/337-7217. 300 rms. A/C MINIBAR TV TEL

Rates: $109–$129 single studio; $154–$164 double in large one-bedroom. Weekend rates $79–$109. Monthly rates on request. AE, CB, DC, DISC, MC, V.

The Lenox is within walking distance or a short cab ride of the city's principal corporate and financial zones in the Loop. So the hotel is largely geared toward the transient corporate worker who is in Chicago on temporary assignment and who needs more spacious digs than the average hotel can reasonably provide. Most of the accommodations at the Lenox, therefore, are suites. Even the Executive Studios are equipped with kitchenettes and queen-size Murphy beds that swing up to vertical storage in wall cabinets. Rooms are decorated with attractive rugs and fabrics, and have large couches, plus round dining tables with accompanying chairs. Extended-stay rates are also available. There is no parking.

★ **The Raphael,** 201 E. Delaware Place, Chicago, IL 60611.
☎ **312/943-5000,** or toll free **800/821-5343.** Fax 312/943-9483.
175 rms and suites. A/C MINIBAR TV TEL

Rates: $120–$140 single; $140–$160 double. Weekend rates $105–$125. AE, CB, DC, DISC, MC, V. **Parking:** $19 with unlimited in/out privileges.

When a hotel looks and feels like a classy private residence or club, set off in some exclusive part of town, you know it must be a special place. Such are the appearances that recommend the Raphael. The lobby is small but inviting. Service at the reception desk is crisp and good-natured. Off the lobby are a small continental restaurant and the very chummy Raphael bar and lounge. Decor varies in the hotel's rooms and suites from contemporary styling to the ornate. And suites at the Raphael cost less than some comparable hotels charge for their rooms.

★ **The Richmont,** 162 E. Ontario St., Chicago, IL 60611.
☎ **312/787-3580,** or toll free **800/621-8055.** Fax 312/787-1299.
191 rms. A/C MINIBAR TV TEL

Rates (including continental breakfast): $114–$144 single or double; $124–$154 single or double suite. Weekend spa package $120, including wine tasting, room upgrade, deluxe continental breakfast, and $25 credit at Victor's European Spa. AE, CB, DC, DISC, MC, V. **Parking:** $17.50 valet; $12.50 self parking.

The Richmont is a charming, European-style hotel just east of North Michigan Avenue. The service is warm and highly personalized, and regular guests are sure to get themselves on the Richmont's quarterly newsletter mailing list. The rooms are on the small side, but very comfortable, and the continental breakfast consists of croissant, bran muffins, coffee, and orange juice. A bistro on the premises, called the Rue St. Clair, serves food with a French accent. Ask about good-value weekend packages when you reserve your room.

3 River North

The name River North is a relatively new designation for a vast area parallel to the swank North Michigan Avenue zone, bounded by the river to the west and south, by Clark Street to the east, and by Division Street to the north. The earthy red-brick buildings that characterize the area were once warehouses of various kinds, and today form the core of Chicago's new art gallery district. The Chicago art district is strictly a commercial development, not a center of artists' lofts and studios. Still, River North is fertile visual ground for the amateur urban archeologist, who will enjoy taking in the forms of the buildings and streets themselves, the ubiquitous (and, to my eye, quite charming) Chicago riverscapes, and the handful of commercial services, some new wave, but many of a decidedly downscale variety.

Moderate

$ Best Western River North Hotel, 125 W. Ohio St. (at the corner of LaSalle), Chicago, IL 60610. ☎ **312/467-0800,** or toll free **800/528-1234.** Fax 312/467-1665. 150 rms. A/C TV TEL
Rates: $79–$159 single; $79–$175 double. Weekend and holiday packages featured for $89 the first night, $79 for the second, and $69 for the third. AE, DC, DISC, JCB, MC, V. **Parking:** Free for guests.

This hotel is one of few that are right in the midst of some of the trendiest nightspots and restaurants in the city today. Harry Caray's and Ed Debevic's (see Chapter 6), and the original rock-and-roll McDonald's, at 600 N. Clark St. (☎ **664-7940**), are all within easy walking distance, as are a number of interesting shops located along nearby Wells Street. The hotel also has an all-season rooftop pool and a ground-floor restaurant called Great Plains. Rooms are designer-modern, large, and tastefully decorated.

$ Ohio House Motel, 600 N. La Salle St., Chicago, IL 60610. ☎ **312/943-6000.** 76 rms and suites. A/C TV TEL
Rates: $54 single; $61 double; $66 triple; $86 suite. AE, DC, DISC, MC, V. **Parking:** Free.

The Ohio House Motel is one of the best bargains in all Chicago, especially for the younger set, when you consider its location in the heart of the hottest entertainment and restaurant district in Chicago. This is a motel, folks—clean and well maintained, but without the frills you'll find in the fancier places just east of here. The breakfast at the Ohio House Coffee Shop, served all day, is on the grand scale, however: two eggs, two strips of bacon, two sausages, and two pancakes for $2.95.

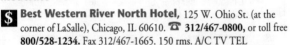

4   Near North

Don't confuse "Near North" with "River North"; the two areas couldn't be less similar. River North is a former industrial area, cheek-by-jowl with the city's center, now being reclaimed for trendy commercial and residential purposes. "Near North" refers to a neighborhood beginning above Division Street, bounded by Clark Street to the west and by North Avenue to the north, that embraces Chicago's fabled Gold Coast—a short strip of the city's priciest real

Frommer's Smart Traveler: Hotels

1. The cheapest hotel rates in Chicago are available on the weekends—they are normally about half the weekly rates—and amenities, such as free parking, are often included.

2. Promotional packages at reduced rates are also available for weekday stays, as are corporate rates if you qualify. Check with your travel agent, or inquire directly from the hotel.

3. Never be afraid of asking for a discount any time of year. The hotel would rather offer you a reduced rate than have the room remain empty for the night.

4. Beware of using your hotel phone too frequently. Service charges even for local calls can run to $1 or more.

estate along Lake Shore Drive. From the standpoint of social status, the streets clustered here are the finest addresses in Chicago. There are bona fide "architectural sights" scattered among the inventory of graceful town houses; the several lavish mansions that remain as relics from an even-glitzier past; and the usual modern, luxury high-rise apartment buildings.

Very Expensive

Le Meridien Chicago, 21 E. Bellevue Place, Chicago, IL 60611.
☎ **312/266-2100,** or toll free **800/543-4300.** Fax 312/266-2141.
247 rms. A/C MINIBAR TV TEL
Rates: $210 single; $230 double; $275 Junior Suite for one or two. Weekend rate (including breakfast and valet parking) $149 double. AE, DC, DISC, MC, V. **Parking:** $20.

This luxury hotel stands in the midst of what was formerly the Rush Street entertainment zone, sandwiched between the Gold Coast and the Magnificent Mile, an area currently undergoing total gentrification. Le Meridien Chicago opened in June 1988 under the name Hotel 21 East. Since then, the Meridien group has obtained the property, but has otherwise changed little about this glitzy gem. Well-heeled travelers would choose this particular deluxe hotel because each of its guest rooms is equipped with a VCR, a CD player, and three two-line speaker phones. Other amenities abound in the form of upscale furnishings, quilts, and bathrooms that have a stall shower and a separate deep-soaking tub.

I had an enjoyable experience when I spent a night in a Junior Suite at Le Meridien. The elongated corner room was light and spacious, and very pleasantly decorated. Some sample CDs are provided, mostly classical music.

Dining/Entertainment: There is a lobby restaurant and an outdoor cafe.

Services: In the morning you get your choice of morning papers from among the *New York Times, Chicago Tribune, Wall Street Journal,* or *USA Today.* Guests can zip around town in the hotel's BMW limo, which is at their disposal. As for the VCR in your room, the bellman will bring you the movie of your choice, secured from the video outlet next door, for a service fee of $5.

Facilities: Health-club facilities are available at the Downtown Sports Club and McClurg Court at discounted rates.

Omni Ambassador East, 1301 N. State Pkwy., Chicago, IL 60610. ☎ 312/787-7200, or toll free **800/843-6664.** Fax 312/787-4760. 275 rms and suites. A/C MINIBAR TV TEL

Rates: $185 single; $215 double; $210–$230 executive suite. Weekend rates $99 room, $135 suite. AE, CB, DC, DISC, MC, V. **Parking:** $20 per day (with in/out privileges).

The Omni Ambassador East occupies, with the Drake, the first rank among Chicago's deluxe traditional establishments. The building housing the Ambassador East, with its staid Georgian overtones, blends in discreetly on the tree-shaded corner of State Parkway and Goethe Street in this quiet, residential neighborhood over which the nearby Chicago skyline looms. Owned in its early days by Ernie Byfield, a great showman/hotelman who first attracted luminaries and stars to the Pump Room, the Ambassador East, following a decline throughout the sixties and seventies, once again caters to the carriage trade. The lobby in the Ambassador East is voluminous and tasteful, if a little underdefined in the sense of being either a useful space or a monumental statement of design.

As for the rooms, you will find no better in the city of Chicago. The executive suite, in fact, is out of this world. This enormous single space (not subtracting for the generous entry foyer and walk-in closet) is designed and furnished for intimacy, like a French boudoir. It is no small task for any hotel to provide home comfort and to achieve an ideal suitable to the fancy at the same time. And while rooms with unobstructed views of the nearby city skyline are rare at the Ambassador East, the four large windows evenly spaced along the street wall literally bathe the room in light of varying intensity, both morning and afternoon.

As you may imagine, there are the usual amenities, the terry cloth robes and a valet stand, for example. The weekend rate makes this suite at the Ambassador East my first choice in Chicago for a splurge overnight. Standard rooms, also very attractive and not small by any means, contain king- or queen-size beds.

Dining/Entertainment: For the past 50 years, celebrities who have come to mingle with Chicago's Gold Coast society have done so most publicly from a designated booth in the Pump Room (see Chapter 6).

Services: A telephone extension connects you immediately to a troubleshooter if there is any problem with your room or service, and at turn-down, you'll find a bottle of Perrier with a bucket of ice, and a small bell jar of tasty Tollhouse cookies.

Facilities: A health-club facility five minutes away by cab costs around $10.

Moderate

$ The Claridge, 1244 N. Dearborn Pkwy., Chicago, IL 60610. ☎ **312/787-4980,** or toll free **800/245-1258** outside Illinois. Fax 312/266-0978. 175 rms. A/C MINIBAR TV TEL

Rates (including continental breakfast): $115–$145 single or double. Weekend rates $78–$93, AE, DC, DISC, MC, V. **Parking:** $16, valet.

The only other "tourist quality" hotel in the Near North, the Claridge is a block farther west than the Omni Ambassador East, but still only a brief stroll to the lakefront outer drive and the Oak Street Beach, and even closer to the north end of the Magnificent Mile, just across Division and east of Rush Street.

The Claridge is a small hotel; the lobby, which is not large, is meant only as a funnel to the rooms or to the restaurant, JP's Eating Place, in the rear of the building. Thanks to the excellent and friendly desk staff, what could be a terrible bottleneck functions fluidly.

Some new rooms have a sitting area in what were formally the hotel's small, one-guest-only Club rooms. Three executive suites on the 14th floor have working fireplaces. All guests receive a complimentary morning newspaper. Rooms are priced in three categories with a single rate for one or two persons. Standards on the lower floors have queen-size beds, superiors with either king- or queen-size beds are on the upper floors, and deluxe accommodations have king-size beds and seating areas.

---

5   The North Side

Above the Lincoln Park/DePaul neighborhoods stretches the spacious North Side of Chicago. The area has many interesting nooks and corners of its own, including the New Town entertainment zone, Wrigleyville—home of the Cubs, the German and Greek communities around Lincoln Square, and quiet, comfortable Rogers Park. Finally, someone has opened up a few small, affordable hotels beyond the city center, in New Town, only minutes from downtown on the Howard Line train. And students will also find an inexpensive bed for the night in the city's only youth hostel, on the Far North Side campus of Loyola University.

In addition to the two hotels listed below, there's now a third option for visitors looking for moderately priced accommodations away from the downtown area. Brand-new in 1994, the **Park Brompton Hotel,** 528 W. Brompton (☎ **312/404-3499**), offers 29 rooms, each air-conditioned and offering a TV. Singles or doubles run $65, and suites, all with kitchenettes, are $79 per night. There are golf and tennis facilities nearby. I haven't checked this one out yet personally, so if you stay there, please drop me a line and tell me what you think.

Inexpensive

 City Suites Hotel, 933 W. Belmont Ave., Chicago IL 60657.
☎ **312/404-3400.** Fax 312/528-8483. 13 rms. A/C TV TEL
Subway/El: Howard St. line to Belmont station.

Rates: $75 single or double; $89 suite. Sun rates are discounted 50%
if you stay Fri–Sat. AE, DISC, MC, V. **Parking:** $5 in nearby lot.

Two or three doors down from the elevated train stop on Belmont
Avenue, not far from the corner of Sheffield, an enterprising team
has remodeled a transient dive called the Wilmont and turned it into
a charming small hotel, with overtones of a friendly urban bed and
breakfast.

Most of the rooms here are suites, with separate sitting rooms and
bedrooms, all furnished with first-rate pieces and decorated in a
homey and comfortable style. A bonus, or drawback, depending on
your point of view, is the hotel's neighborhood setting—very nineties and youthful—combining this generation's extremes, from
yuppie preppydom to punks in full regalia. Blues bars, nightclubs,
and restaurants abound hereabouts, making the City Suites a find
for the bargain-minded and adventuresome. Room service is available from the nearby Rocky Mountain Bagel, during the shop's hours.
The hotel is a $5 cab ride from the Belmont stop of the
O'Hare-Douglas line from the airport.

 The Surf Hotel, 555 W. Surf St., Chicago IL 60657.
☎ **312/528-8400.** Fax 312/528-8483. 20 rms. A/C TV TEL
Bus: No. 151 from anywhere on Michigan Ave.; get off at Sheridan
and Surf and walk one block west.

Rates: $69 single; $79–$85 double. Sun rates are discounted 50% if
you stay Fri–Sat. AE, DISC, MC, V. **Parking:** $5.

Owned by the same group as the City Suites Hotel, and possessed of
a similar history, the Surf was once an SRO building and is gradually being converted into a neighborhood hotel. The company behind the hotel is purchasing a residential building to rehouse former
tenants of the hotel who lived there for many years.

In contrast to the City Suites, the Surf Hotel occupies a site on a
quiet, tree-lined street several blocks east of its sibling, and relatively
close to Lake Michigan. Most of the building's vintage 1920 architectural details are being preserved and restored, and the rooms—
slightly more hotellike than those at City Suites—are equally modern and comfortable.

Budget

 Chicago International Hostel, 6318 N. Winthrop Ave.,
Chicago, IL 60660. ☎ **312/262-1011. Subway/El:** Howard St. line
north to Loyola station; use Sheridan Rd. exit.

Rates (payable in cash or money order): $13. Length of stay at discre-
tion of manager. No credit cards.

Hosteling is alive and well at the Chicago International Hostel. There
are dormitories for men and women, and some rooms are available

for couples and disabled persons—the hostel is accessible to handi-capped guests. All prices include tax and linen; you must provide your own blanket or sleeping bag. Locked storage is available at $1 per day. The hostel is open from 7 to 10am, it's closed from 10am to 4pm, and check-in is from 4pm to midnight. Midnight is the cur-few. Parking is not available. From the subway, enter the Loyola campus, following the path to the right half a block south.

6   The East Side

The term *East Side,* in the case of this high-rise/high-rent dist-rict, which is undergoing rapid development, reflects marketing nomenclature over local usage. Traditionally, Chicago's only "East Side" is far to the south, where the shoreline bulges into Lake Michi-gan, creating the only geographical landmass of any volume east of State Street. You are far more likely to hear Chicagoans talk about the North Side, the South Side, and the West Side. So in the sense of a designated neighborhood, the "East Side" moniker was up for grabs. This new East Side, therefore, is not so much a neighborhood as a developer's concept.

South of the river and stretching along Wacker Drive as far as Lake Michigan, the district is confined by Randolph Street to its south (which is also the upper boundary of Grant Park), and is hedged on the west by a short strip of Michigan Avenue between Randolph and the river. The area (or at least a complex of buildings near the Hyatt Regency hotel) also goes by the name of Illinois Center. Most na-tives, however, don't seem to have any name for the area at all. Un-like the nearby Loop, there is no organic streetlife here, no storefronts to browse, a fact no doubt explained by the district's radical meta-morphosis from virtual wasteland to elite residential/commercial zone over the last generation. The East Side is definitely a luxury "privacy zone," and the hotels here make the most of that mandate.

Very Expensive

Hyatt Regency Chicago, 151 E. Wacker Dr., Chicago, IL 60601. ☎ **312/565-1234,** or toll free **800/228-9000.** Fax 312/565-2966. Telex 256237. 2,033 rms. A/C MINIBAR TV TEL

Rates: $195–$230 single; $220–$255 double; $230–$260 Regency Club single or double. Weekend rates start at $109. AE, DC, DISC, MC, V. **Parking:** Valet with in/out privileges $19 Sun–Thurs, $10 Fri–Sat.

Dean of the East Side's luxury establishments is the Hyatt Regency, which occupies two tall modern towers connected by a glass-enclosed skyway over a small side street. The lobby, in the east tower, covers half an acre and rises four stories beneath a greenhouse roof. It's a virtual theme park, with a lagoon surrounded by foliage as its centerpiece. There is no reason to venture onto the streets at night when lodged at the Hyatt Regency; some version of everything you might need is to be found within.

With its considerable meeting facilities, high-tech check-in, and other streamlined services, the hotel caters heavily to exhibitions and conventions. A new "Business Plan" creates a workstation in the actual guest room, including a desk, a telephone line with no extra access charge that is also PC compatible, and an in-room fax machine.

This is not to suggest that the Hyatt Regency Chicago is without its share of fancy digs on the premises. On the top two floors of the west tower, 45 rooms are reserved for the Regency Club, with its private lounge where guests are served a complimentary continental breakfast in the morning and cocktails at the end of the workday. If you really want to scale the heights of personal comfort, book a penthouse Monarch Suite some winter night and stretch out near the fireplace before the 1,600-square-foot parlor space (rates available on request).

Dining/Entertainment: Restaurants and cafes occupy three different levels, all connected by walkways. A pianist, on prominent display atop a raised platform near the center of things, plays softly on a dramatic, white grand piano.

Services: 24-hour room service, kosher meals available Sunday to Friday.

Facilities: Sports club a half-block away (with a $10 fee for adults, $7 for children under 12) with Olympic-size swimming pool.

Expensive

Swissotel, 323 E. Wacker Dr., Chicago, IL 60601. ☎ **312/565-0565,** or toll free **800/654-7263.** Fax 312/565-0540. 630 rms. A/C TV TEL

Rates: $135–$195 single; $135–$215 double. Weekend rates $109–$139 double; weekend package $170 double. AE, CB, DC, DISC, JCB, MC, V. **Parking:** $18.

This hotel seems to consciously pursue the discerning business executive who wants a city-centered luxury hotel with a tradition of European service and a restaurant on the premises serving haute cuisine. In the striking glass-and-steel tower, rooms are elegant, but also organized for homework or business meetings, with oversize writing desks, separate seating areas, two-line telephones, and TV monitors with access to financial markets. The "corner kings," the long, narrow corner rooms with lakefront views, are the ones to reserve.

There are four other room categories: standard, moderate, superior, and deluxe, distinguished from one another by location, size, and view. One facility giving the hotel a unique edge over many rivals is an in-house Executive Fitness Center on its penthouse level, with a heated indoor pool among other facilities. There's also a full-service business center. As for fine dining, there's Le Prince restaurant. Be sure to inquire about weekend packages. S'Weekend starts at $109 per night and features a room with a panoramic view. The Bed 'N' Breakfast package costs $139 per night and includes tax, gratuities, a breakfast buffet in Café Suisse or a room service breakfast.

7   Along South Michigan Avenue

If North Michigan Avenue rates the sobriquet "magnificent," then the avenue's extension below the river, running the length of Grant Park, could be described as solid and cosmopolitan. The word *boulevard* also comes to mind, because South Michigan Avenue is a very likely place to take a long city stroll, especially on a Sunday. This single stretch of avenue has it all—the greenery, grounds, and statuary of a park; museums, outstanding architecture, symphonic hall, and stage shows; and a range of lodging possibilities to fit all budgets. As for shoppers and window gazers, they have only to walk the two blocks to parallel State Street, now a mall closed to auto traffic and Chicago's number two retailing district.

Expensive

Chicago Hilton and Towers, 730 S. Michigan Ave., Chicago, IL 60605. ☎ **312/922-4400,** or toll free **800/HILTONS.** Fax 312/922-5240. 1,620 rms. A/C MINIBAR TV TEL

Rates: $105–$205 single; $130–$230 double. Weekend rates start at $109 double, $149 for a Tower room. AE, CB, DC, DISC, JCB, MC. V.
Parking: $19 per day valet, $16 self-parking.

The mammoth Chicago Hilton and Towers actually divides its rooms between a majority of first-class, tourist-quality accommodations and a smaller selection of luxury rooms. Judging by its lobby alone, however, when you first enter the Chicago Hilton you'd think that you're in one of the city's most deluxe lodging establishments. There is a scale of grandeur here. Rooms are both light and beautifully decorated, appointed with cherrywood furnishings.

Five different restaurants provide culinary options, from prime aged steaks at Buckingham's to snacks and sandwiches at the Fast

---

Frommer's Cool for Kids: Hotels

Children will probably feel most comfortable staying at one of the large hotels on or near South Michigan Avenue. Grant Park is right across the street, and other kid-oriented attractions, such as the Field Museum, the Shedd Aquarium, and the Adler Planetarium, are only a short distance away. The large hotels, including the **Chicago Hilton** (on this page), the **Palmer House** (see p. 67), and the **Congress Hotel** (see p. 90), are cavernous, and they allow kids plenty of room to explore; they also have a variety of options for hanging out, including game rooms and coffee shops. The advantage for parents at these (as well as most other hotels in Chicago) is that children under 18 housed in the same room as their parents stay free.

Lane Deli. A fully equipped health club boasts a pool and indoor track among its more typical accoutrements of exercise equipment and saunas. For shoppers, the hotel provides complimentary transportation to the stores of the Magnificent Mile.

Moderate

Best Western Grant Park, 1000 S. Michigan Ave., Chicago, IL 60605. ☎ **312/922-2900,** or toll free **800/528-1234.** 172 rms. A/C TV TEL

Rates: $89–$96 room with a queen-size bed; $96–$106 room with a king-size bed; $116 room with two beds. Weekend rates $55–$65. AE, DC, DISC, ER, JCB, MC, V. **Parking:** $7 per day.

Until 1994, the Best Western Grant Park was known as the Ascot. Major renovations preceded the hotel's name change by several years, and the hotel is no longer the bargain it was during its years as a dive on the downtown fringe. Still, rates are reasonable given the location, and the rooms today are up to mid-range tourist standards. There's an outdoor swimming pool, and health club facilities are also available. The Shopper's Special weekend package costs $59 a night and includes use of the fitness center and complimentary coffee and morning newspaper.

★ **Blackstone Hotel,** 636 S. Michigan Ave., Chicago, IL 60605. ☎ and fax **312/427-4300,** or ☎ toll free **800/622-6330.** Telex 721507. 305 rms. A/C TV TEL

Rates (including continental breakfast): $109–$149 single; $119–$159 double. Weekend rates $69–$99 double. AE, DC, DISC, JCB, MC, V. **Parking:** $16 valet.

When a suitable location was needed for the banquet scene in the movie *The Untouchables,* there really could not have been any other choice these days in Chicago but the Blackstone Hotel. Al Capone once actually holed up at the old Metropole Hotel, a mile or so farther south, but the Blackstone is a good match in the style of the period. A reference or two to the Blackstone may also be culled from literary sources. The Blackstone, for example, is the setting for a New Year's party in James T. Farrell's novel *Studs Lonigan,* a trilogy about the lives of the Chicago Irish during the early years of this century.

Today the genteel Blackstone holds its own among the hotels of this quarter, like a fading beauty among the newer and brighter faces on the rise. But the Blackstone offers more than merely past glory. A few of the hotel's more immediate enticements include a genuine jazz club, Joe Segal's Jazz Showcase. This is the real stuff, folks. Most of the greats, now departed, have played here, and durable headliners, such as Phil Woods, still make the scene. Add to this a smashing Victorian lobby and a room with a great lakefront view, and a mushy-minded jazz lover (like me) might easily find the Blackstone a very appealing harbor for a night or two in Chicago.

Most of the rooms are large and comfortable enough, and some are relatively inexpensive. From mine on the eighth floor I could see the Navy Pier and the harbor lighthouse to the north, the park with its fountain and gardens in front, and the Field Museum and Chicago's aquarium and planetarium, the latter two occupying a promontory that juts out into the lake. The Blackstone provides guests with a simple continental breakfast each morning, a good excuse for hanging about the lobby and appreciating its rich details: the highly worked plaster ceiling, the dark hardwood wall paneling trimmed in gold-leafed molding, giant brass wall sconces, a grand black marble fireplace set off by empire mirrors, crystal chandeliers, black-and-white marble floors, and an imposing central staircase leading to the Mayfair Theater and banquet rooms. The Blackstone also boasts a new game-and-billiards room, and a health club available to guests at $10 a day.

$ Congress Hotel, 520 S. Michigan Ave., Chicago, IL 60605. ☎ **312/427-3800,** or toll free **800/635-1666.** Fax 312/427-7264. 850 rms. A/C MINIBAR TV TEL

Rates: $105–$145 single; $135–$165 double. Weekend rates start at $69 single or double; weekend package $79 double per night. AE, CB, DC, DISC, MC, V. **Parking:** $10 per day.

Operating since the days of the World Columbian Exposition, which opened near Hyde Park in 1893, the Congress Hotel has a colorful tradition all its own. The hotel was once a favorite venue for presidential political conventions, at least among candidates named Roosevelt. TR opened his Bull Moose convention at the Congress in 1912, and cousin FDR accepted the Democratic nomination here in 1932. Other notables who slept at the Congress made their own journeys along divergent paths—Dempsey, Edison, Caruso, and the Red Hot Mama herself, Sophie Tucker. For some years the Congress has been undergoing a steady modernization, no longer attracting celebrity guests, but a steady flow of convention travelers.

The hotel offers five distinct restaurants, and the rooms at the Congress are quite spacious, attractively furnished, and reasonably priced. The hotel also offers good-value weekend packages.

Essex Inn, 800 S. Michigan Ave. (at 8th St.), Chicago, IL 60605. ☎ **312/791-1901,** or toll free **800/621-6909.** Fax 312/939-1605. 225 rms. A/C MINIBAR TV TEL

Rates: $102 single; $112 double. Weekend rates start at $59. AE, CB, DC, DISC, MC, V. **Parking:** $6.

The Essex is nothing fancy, but a very good medium-priced choice, well managed and accommodating. The Essex, however, is particularly imaginative in its appeal to weekend visitors, offering special packages that are subject to availability from May to September. The deluxe package for two nights includes breakfast both days in the hotel's New York–style 8th Street Deli, welcoming cocktails, parking, and a two-hour bus tour of Chicago's sights, including admission at the Museum of Science and Industry. Minibars are available on request.

Budget

The final hotel choice along the South Michigan Avenue strip is in the budget range, so don't expect the Ritz. It's well located: While still on the periphery, it remains within the city's downtown orbit. At the same time, it is within easy striking range of Chicago's South Side neighborhoods, including McCormick Place.

The Avenue, 1154 S. Michigan Ave., Chicago, IL 60605.
☎ **312/427-8200,** or toll free **800/621-4196** outside Illinois. 78 rms. A/C TV TEL
Rates: $50 single; $55 double. AE, DC, DISC, MC, V. **Parking:** Free.

The Avenue, on the corner of Roosevelt Street, is a genuine motel. From any front or side window of the motel, you can see the tracks of the old Illinois Central (few cities ever delivered such prized real estate into the hands of a railroad) and Soldier Field (the old football stadium), and the troika of museums—the Field for natural history, the Shedd for marine life, the Adler for the heavens—that anchor this southern boundary of Grant Park. Other attractions include a heated outdoor swimming pool and a restaurant.

8   The South Side

Ramada Inn Lakeshore, 4900 S. Lakeshore Dr., Chicago, IL 60615.
☎ **312/288-5800,** or toll free **800/228-2828.** Fax 312/288-5745. 330 rms. A/C TV TEL
Rates: $79–$99 single; $89–$105 double. Weekend rates $69–$79. AE, DC, MC, V. **Parking:** Free.

A city within a city is how Hyde Park has often been described, and quite accurately so. Site of the Columbian Exposition of 1893 and the birthplace of both nuclear fission and urban renewal, it's home to the Museum of Science and Industry, the Afro-American DuSable Museum, the architecture of Frank Lloyd Wright, and the culture-packed campus of the lovely and elite University of Chicago, not to mention fine food and specialty shops. A guidebook just for this neighborhood alone could almost be justified.

Hyde Park is a 20-minute train ride from downtown (half an hour by express bus), so a stay at the Ramada does not put you beyond the city by any means. There is also a complimentary hourly shuttle bus to the North Michigan Avenue shopping and dining district. Bright and very modern, the Ramada has many of the appearances of a resort hotel, including a large outdoor swimming pool and sun patio. There's also a restaurant with a great view of the Chicago skyline and the lake; the scene is most dramatic on a starlit night. The hotel's rooms have received a recent facelift.

9   Near O'Hare Airport

Chicago's urban sprawl is duplicated twice over on the vast tracts of suburbia that surround the city and ripple outward to the borders of the nation's heartland. With more and more suburbanites finding employment among the many corporations that have moved to their communities, the Chicago suburbs are undergoing a subtle transformation. The former commuters no longer visit downtown Chicago regularly—they want the very same conveniences where they work as well as live. Because of the growth of their local economies, the suburbs are becoming municipal entities, more like independent towns and less dependent on the "city" to provide their only cultural and culinary outlets.

Moreover, there are many business travelers who deplane at O'Hare and never go anywhere near the city. Everything they require in lodgings, food, and entertainment is available within a small radius of the airport itself. In fact, the hotels in the immediate vicinity of the O'Hare airport contain more than 2,500 rooms. In addition to the hotels listed below, there are representations of the Embassy Suites, Hilton, Hyatt, Marriott, Radisson, and Ramada chains near the airports; reservations for any of these hotels can be made through the chains' nationwide toll-free numbers.

Very close to the airport, throughout the neighboring suburbs you will encounter the familiar names of Howard Johnson, Holiday Inn, Ramada, Quality Inn, and TraveLodge, to name the most prominent. These and many less expensive establishments line the access roads that approach Chicago. They cater to the road traffic, to people passing through, not to the visitor who has come to get a close-up view of Chicago and is better served by securing lodgings much closer to the center of the city.

Expensive

Hotel Sofitel, 5550 N. River Rd., Rosemont, IL 60018.
☎ **708/678-4488,** or toll free **800/233-5959.** Fax 708/678-4422. 363 rms. A/C MINIBAR TV TEL
Rates: $165 single; $185 double. Weekend rate $89. AE, DC, MC, V. **Parking:** Free.

Linked by a heated tunnel to the O'Hare Exposition Center, the Hotel Sofitel is part of a French-owned chain now making its appearance in the American market. Touches in the hotel's decor suggest inspiration from the era of Louis XIV. The lobby suggests the monumental, with its marble floor, muraled walls, and bubbling fountain. Among the hotel's facilities are two restaurants, a bakery, and a health club with a swimming pool.

Westin Hotel, O'Hare, 6100 N. River Rd., Rosemont, IL 60018.
☎ **708/698-6000,** or toll free **800/228-3000.** Fax 708/698-4591. Telex 280325. 525 rms. A/C MINIBAR TV TEL
Rates: $180 single; $208 double. Weekend rate $91.50. AE, CB, DC, DISC, JCB, MC, V. **Parking:** Free.

In addition to the chain's downtown branch, there is a Westin Hotel directly adjacent to O'Hare. In decorous, sleek surroundings, guests are offered such distractions as aerobics classes, racquetball courts, Nautilus equipment, and a swimming pool. Each guest room is spacious, with an oversize desk, two telephones, two TVs with free cable (one is in the bathroom), and an alarm clock. The Westin's Bakery Café restaurant, specializing in chicken pot pie, is said to actually attract diners from the city. Other facilities include an additional restaurant and two bars.

6

Chicago Dining

THE ONLY PROBLEM WITH FINDING A GOOD RESTAURANT IN CHICAGO IS
being overwhelmed by too many choices. It also helps to bring money,
but not all the city's best restaurants are beyond the reach of the average pocketbook. Ethnic and neighborhood restaurants abound and
offer the tasty fare of many countries at reasonable prices. When you
consider that Chicago has something like 77 separate neighborhoods,
the potential for culinary adventures becomes literally endless.

As with the city's hotels, all restaurants in this guidebook are listed
in neighborhood clusters, beginning with those located off the Magnificent Mile and in the Loop, because these are the most accessible
to the great majority of visitors from out of town. From this center
of fine dining, we fan out into Chicago's more remote corners, taking you into neighborhoods you may not have thought of visiting.

1   Downtown

The Loop

See "Specialty Dining," below, for restaurants in the Sears Tower and
for restaurants that are open for breakfast.

VERY EXPENSIVE

Everest, 440 S. La Salle St. ☎ **663-8920.**

> **Cuisine:** ALSATIAN. **Reservations:** Required.
>
> **Prices:** Appetizers $14.50–$19.50; soups and salads $7.50–$9.50; main
> courses $26.50–$32.50; fixed-price meal from $69 per person. AE, DC,
> DISC, MC, V.
>
> **Open:** Tues–Thurs 5:30–8:30pm; Fri–Sat 5:30–10pm.

On a recent evening, I ascended by elevator some forty stories above
the Chicago Stock Exchange to the elite La Salle Club. There, I took
up my position in the lovely dining room of Everest, with its windows overlooking the shimmering nightscape of downtown Chicago,
and I ate one of the finest meals of my life. Chef (and owner) Jean
Joho, a baker in his youth in Strasbourg, France, suggested the *menu
dégustation* and *tout de suite,* a parade of dishes began their march
from the nearby kitchen to the spacious table where I was seated.

Chef Joho's early training as a baker, his earthy appreciation of
the home-style cookery of the Rhine country, and his near obsession
with the procurement of North American foodstuffs for his menu
combine with a rare delicacy of touch and imagination. My first
appetizer was an unusual but successful mixture of cauliflower and
caviar, and was followed by an exotic plate of chilled barnacles from
British Columbia, bathed in a vegetable vinaigrette. The napoleon
of razor clams and the strudel of marinated cabbage paid further
homage to the lofty agility of the kitchen. A more-than-credible foie
gras from New York State was served next on a bed of marinated
turnips, and this gave way to the seafood entrée, a rich Maine

lobster roasted with ginger in a brine of Gerwurtztraminer wine. The pièce de résistance was the Texas-bred saddle of venison with wild huckleberries and gray shallots, sweet, tender, and gamy as if it had come directly from the larder of a superior huntsman.

From the root cellar, the peasant's pantry, the rangeland, and the craggy sea bottom, Chef Joho spun his turnips, cauliflower, sauerkraut, clams, barnacles, and game into a most extraordinary and memorable culinary event. The assortment of desserts was more traditional, but equally sublime, and the whole extravaganza was accompanied by a variety of fine American and Alsatian wines. One may dine at Everest from the set menu or à la carte. In addition, there is a lighter but elegant three-course pre-theater dinner for $39 per person, which includes complimentary parking.

EXPENSIVE

Exchange Restaurant, in the Midland Hotel, 172 W. Adams.
☎ **332-1200.**
Cuisine: CONTINENTAL. **Reservations:** Required.
Prices: Appetizers $5.95–$7.95; main courses $16.95–$23.95. AE, DC, DISC, MC, V.
Open: Lunch Mon–Fri 11:30am–2pm; dinner Mon–Fri 5–9pm. Private dinner parties can be arranged through the hotel's sales department.

There are many fine restaurants in the Loop that are traditional favorites for business lunches. Gaining in reputation among the noon-hour corporate set is the diminutive Exchange Restaurant, which occupies one wing of the atrium mezzanine above the lobby of the Midland Hotel. This location, owing to the quiet rumblings in the lobby below, actually provides a variation on the "trading floor" ambience. But the analogy is largely spatial, since there is none of the din or frenzy typical of the real exchange. On its beautifully decorated perch, the clublike Exchange is suitably removed, above the fray, so to speak.

The decor is very beaux arts, despite the Midland's initial creation as a private men's club in 1929, a period when deco styling pointed the way to a future unencumbered by old-world sentiment. The interior of the Exchange, of course, is of more recent installation, and the architect is said to have been heavily influenced by European designs.

In this relatively tiny space, seating perhaps two dozen patrons, a different menu is provided for each season. Typical of the offerings at the Exchange are the smoked chicken salad, the seafood stir-fry, chilled poached salmon, and boiled whitefish with lemon and dill. Among the more exotic appetizers is the plate of New Zealand green-tipped mussels with garlic sauce. The dessert tray carries many tempting, freshly baked sweets, including a creamy carrot cake, topped with fresh raspberries. In all, a very satisfactory lunch, in very pleasant surroundings, for a reasonable price.

INEXPENSIVE

⭐ **Berghoff's,** 17 W. Adams. ☎ **427-3170.**
Cuisine: GERMAN/INTERNATIONAL. **Reservations:** Recommended.
💲 **Prices:** Appetizers $1.50–$5.75; main courses $6.50–$9.95 at lunch, $8.75–$13.95 at dinner. AE, MC, V.
Open: Mon–Thurs 11am–9:30pm, Fri–Sat 11am–10pm.

Berghoff's has been a Chicago institution for 90 years, occupying its current quarters since 1905. It's housed in one of the first buildings constructed in the Loop after the Chicago Fire, and one of the only remaining buildings in the city with a cast-iron facade. The restaurant, covering the first floor and the lower level, is immense and can seat 700 people.

In addition to the typically heavy, carbohydrate-rich dishes, the menu also includes many lighter international selections and salads. However, to my mind, ordering anything but the scrumptious German specialties that Berghoff's has to offer is somewhat pointless. The menu of Berghoff's is rotated eight times a year, depending on the availability of various game (such as elk, venison, and wild duck) and of vegetables and fruits. The food is terrific, but the price is downright unbeatable, making Berghoff's one of the best restaurant values in Chicago.

To start the meal, you might want to order a shot of apricot schnapps, and to accompany the food, try Berghoff's own brand of dark beer, brewed especially for the restaurant in nearby Wisconsin. Your appetizer might be a plate of knockwurst and bratwurst with potato salad and sauerkraut. You might request a side order of mashed potatoes with your sauerbraten—normally served with a potato pancake and creamed spinach—to have just the right side dish to soak up that delicious vinegary gravy. Dessert could be a Black Forest cake. In all, the meal is a little gem.

South Loop

The so-called South Loop, below Congress, looks and feels like New York's SoHo. Both SoHo and the South Loop were built roughly a century ago and many of the buildings dating from this period have been preserved within the two areas. But while art is the focus in SoHo, the buildings themselves claim attention in Chicago's South Loop, officially renamed Burnham Park by the city to honor one of the old neighborhood's principal architectural creators, Daniel Burnham. Many of the landmarks, formerly commercial structures, have been converted into medium- to high-income co-ops and apartments in recent years, engendering a residential revival in the area and attracting two particularly good local restaurants.

MODERATE

⭐ **Prairie,** in the Hyatt on Printers Row, 500 S. Dearborn.
☎ **663-1143.**
Cuisine: HEARTLAND. **Reservations:** Required.
Prices: Appetizers $5–$8.50; main courses $13.50–$21.50; Sun brunch $15. AE, CB, DC, MC, V.

Chicago Dining

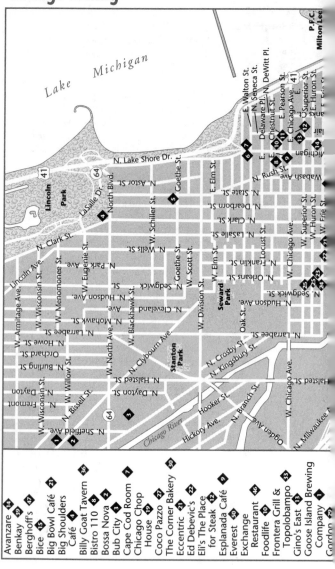

Avanzare 🔷 14
Benkay 🔷 39
Berghoff's 🔷 45
Bice 🔷 18
Big Bowl Café 🔷 36
Big Shoulders Café 🔷 4
Billy Goat Tavern 🔷 21
Bistro 110 🔷 8
Bossa Nova 🔷 2
Bub City 🔷 1
Cape Cod Room 🔷 7
Chicago Chop House 🔷 29
Coco Pazzo 🔷 27
The Corner Bakery 🔷 30
Eccentric 🔷 3
Ed Debevic's 🔷 22
Eli's The Place for Steak 🔷 12
Esplanada Café 🔷 9
Everest 🔷 50
Exchange Restaurant 🔷 46
Foodlife 🔷 10
Frontera Grill & Topolobampo 🔷 33
Gino's East 🔷 13
Goose Island Brewing Company 🔷 1
Gordon 🔷

Open: Mon–Fri 6:30am–10pm, Sat 7am–11pm, Sun 8am–11pm.

The inside of the restaurant on the ground floor of the Hyatt on Printers Row is designed after a Frank Lloyd Wright interior, the colors and wood trim forming patterns like those on a Native American blanket. As the name implies, Prairie is meant to self-consciously celebrate the culinary traditions and food products of the Midwest,

- Greek Islands
- Green Door Tavern
- Hard Rock Cafe
- Harry Caray's
- Hat Dance
- Lou Mitchell's
- Maggiano's
- Mambo Grill
- Marché
- Michael Jordan's
- Mity Nice
- Mr. Beef
- Mrs. Levy's
- The Original A-1
- Papagus Greek Taverna
- Parthenon
- Pizzeria Due
- Planet Hollywood
- Prairie
- Printer's Row
- Pump Room
- The Saloon
- Scoozi
- Shaw's Crab House and Blue Crab Lounge
- Spiaggia
- Tucci Milan
- Vivo
- Zinfandel

and in principle, all ingredients used to prepare the meals here come from the 14 midwestern states, including the wines. There is also an emphasis on seasonal specialties.

Don't expect, however, that anything arriving at the table will look homespun and plain. Paramount to Prairie's success is that the food tastes even better than it looks. For starters, there is a multitoned tomato soup, in swirls of yellow, red, and green, with sour cream and sturgeon caviar floating in the center. The tarragon-smoked chicken soup is a very healthy and tasteful brew. The grilled, beer-braised Sheboygan bratwurst embodies the Teutonic ideal of the great sausage. Among the main courses, the must-sample is the buffalo steak, served in its natural juices. For dessert, have a great hot-fudge sundae with real bittersweet chocolate, or a slice of mom's apple pie.

Printer's Row, 550 S. Dearborn. ☎ 461-0780.

> **Cuisine:** AMERICAN. **Reservations:** Required.
> **Prices:** Appetizers $4.50–$9.50; main courses $13.50–$24.50. AE, CB, DC, DISC, MC, OPTIMA, V.
> **Open:** Lunch daily 11:30am–2:30pm; dinner Mon–Thurs 5–10pm, Fri–Sat 5–10:30pm.

Printer's Row is another citadel of new wave American cuisine catering to the hip clientele who now live in buildings where Chicago's publishing industry was once centered. But if the neighborhood has lost its ink-stained commercial character, the Loop in general has gained by the return of inner-city dwellers, and the creation of some interesting and innovative restaurants.

Printer's Row has built a solid reputation over the past few years, mostly through chef Michael Foley's imaginative cooking. Among the chef's novelties are the preparation of New York State foie gras in a variety of ways. Venison, the chef's signature dish, is also regularly featured on the menu, as are tasty fish and poultry dishes, and all meals are accompanied by a healthy assortment of fresh vegetables. The game, incidentally, is New Zealand farm-raised, and may be accompanied by a sun-dried blueberry-and-brandy sauce, or by a sauce of honey-glazed wheatberries and lemon-rosemary. Homemade desserts and ice creams are also reputed to be first-rate.

2   Market West District

Across the Chicago River from the northwest corner of the Loop is the old Randolph Street wholesale market district. In real estate lingo, the area has been tagged "River West," while one local food critic described it as a "honey-check-that-map-again neighborhood." Whatever name eventually sticks, the district is already home to several of the hottest restaurants and watering holes in Chicago.

Transportation to the market district is easy, by the way, about a $5 cab ride from Michigan Avenue, or a slightly longer hike by bus (nos. 8 or 9) or subway, with stops at Halsted and Lake, a block from the restaurant. The walk from the Loop is very pleasant, and totally secure in the daytime.

Expensive ─────────────────────────────

Marche, 833 W. Randolph St. ☎ 226-8399.

> **Cuisine:** FRENCH BISTRO. **Reservations:** Recommended.
> **Prices:** Appetizers $4–$9; main courses $9–$16. AE, DC, DISC, MC, V.
> **Open:** Breakfast and lunch Mon–Fri 8am–2:30pm; dinner Mon–Wed 5pm–midnight, Thurs–Sat 5pm–2am.

The basic idea behind Marche is derivative of the popular and cavernous Paris café. The menu, naturally, is also a by-product of French inspiration. But the execution at Marche is pure Americana. Co-owner and furniture designer Jerry Kleiner created the interior and everything in it. It's the kind of visual potpourri that favors the eclectic, the postmodern, and the outrageous. Ten thousand square feet of warehouse space have been converted into an anarchic cultural event where people mingle, and food and beverages are served. Multilevel seating enhances the effect and suggests a perpetual fiesta, perhaps inside a vast spacecraft, speeding toward nowhere in particular. The decor is likewise all mixed-media and mixed materials—from wrought iron to mahogany. It's all a mishmash of the fine and the crude, all self-consciously conceived and not as easy to pull off as it might appear.

To ensure that Marche will outlast the impact of its perishable aesthetic, Michael Kornick, a dynamic young chef with some impressive power credits already notched on his resume (Gordon in Chicago, Four Seasons in Boston) was brought in to create the menu and supervise the kitchen—which, incidently, is visible to diners from behind a glass barrier along one corner of the building. Whatever the idiom, the ordinary or the exotic, Chef Kornick seems to handle each extreme with equal ease and grace. There's still nothing like a steaming bowl of good onion soup ($5) to remove that inner chill on a blustery day. The coriander-crusted tuna with horseradish and arugula ($8) is as delicious as it is original, and ditto the seasonal offering of spring morels served with wild leeks ($8).

The entrées the night I dined at Marche were divided almost equally between meat and fish, plus a couscous of grilled vegetables ($9) and two pasta dishes for vegetarians. My grilled veal chop ($19) was delicate yet hearty, and my companion chose that old bistro standby, steak with pommes frites ($16). After sating our respective sweet tooths with a chocolate pot de crème ($3) and a scoop of vanilla-bean ice cream doused with a compote of rhubarb ($4), we rolled off into the rainy night, leaving Marche to party on, no doubt for some time to come.

Vivo, 838 W. Randolph. ☎ 226-2555.

Cuisine: SOUTHERN ITALIAN **Reservations:** Accepted.
Prices: Appetizers $3.50–$6.50; pasta $8.95–$13.95; main courses $12.95–$17.95. AE, CB, DC, MC, V.
Open: Lunch Mon–Fri 11:30am–2:30pm; dinner Mon–Thurs 5pm–midnight, Fri–Sat 5pm–1am; Sun 4:30–11pm.

Before there was Marche, there was Vivo, pioneer and prototype of the genre, half the size, and hot, hot, hot since the day it opened. Vivo's mock-market ambience is enhanced by fragments of the old warehouse that are allowed to peek through the artsy decor.

I suspect Vivo's kitchen has been somewhat underrated by the local food mavens in the glare of publicity that has surrounded the place since its opening in the fall of 1991. I lunched there, and perhaps the pressure was off, but the meal was excellent and the atmosphere very laid back—no office-worker hustle-bustle, or "look at me, please, I'm at Vivo's" vibes whatsoever.

For starters, I tried the portobella alla griglia ($5.50) and the antipasta della casa ($4.25), both positively first-rate. I then sampled several pasta dishes, each of which could hold its head high in any of Chicago's fine Italian restaurants.

3 The Magnificent Mile

See "Specialty Dining," below, for the restaurants in the Water Tower Place and in the 900 North Michigan Avenue Building.

Very Expensive

⭐ **Eli's the Place for Steak,** 215 E. Chicago Ave. ☎ **642-1393.**
Cuisine: STEAK/CHOPS. **Reservations:** Recommended.
Prices: Appetizers $3.50–$9.25; main courses $17.95–$29.95. AE, DC, DISC, MC, V.
Open: Lunch Mon–Fri 11am–2:30pm; dinner Sun–Thurs 4–10:30pm, Fri–Sat 4–11pm.

Every big town has its short list of restaurant institutions; Eli's is definitely on Chicago's. But Eli's is much more that a traditional steak joint where an occasional big name celebrity shows up for a meal and a photo session. The restaurant has some deep roots of its own. The potato pancakes, the sautéed liver-and-onions, and the chicken fricassee (chicken in the pot, $18.95) are variations on the comfort foods of Central European origin that have found their way here by way of a neighborhood delicatessen—where the late Eli Schulman got his start in Chicago fifty years ago. Add to this solid pedigree an element of friendly formality, a commitment to quality in the food and its preparation, and generous servings that will almost ensure that you have something left for tomorrow's lunch, and you have in a nutshell the formula that has kept Eli's at the forefront of Chicago eateries since 1966.

At Eli's the meal begins with a scoop of delicate chopped liver, accompanied by diced eggs and onions, a colorful crudité of fresh vegetables, and a basket of various breads and rolls, all included with the meal. The restaurant's signature appetizer is the shrimp de jonghe, baked to succulent perfection with garlic and bread crumbs ($9.25, but also available as an entree for $22.95). Now about those steaks. I've always had a preference for T-bones, and Eli's does not disappoint. The 20-ounce T-bone ($29.95) is perfect—full-flavored, juicy, and not too rich. And liver connoisseurs will appreciate the calf's liver Eli, a truly delicate and palate-pleasing selection.

Be sure to save some room for a slice of Eli's famous cheesecake, rapidly becoming a superstar dessert retailed throughout the country. A dozen or so of the fifty varieties are always available at the restaurant at $3.95 a slice. For something on the lighter side try the pumpkin, or go for broke with the mud pie, a creamy chocolate concoction. The only problem is how to choose just one!

Expensive

Benkay, in the Hotel Nikko, 320 N. Dearborn St. ☎ 836-5490.

Cuisine: JAPANESE. **Reservations:** Required.
Prices: Appetizers $3.50–$10.50; main courses $10–$38; full meals
$45–$100. AE, CB, DC, DISC, MC, V.
Open: Lunch Mon–Fri 11:30am–2pm; dinner daily 5:30–10pm.

Benkay is a fine Japanese restaurant named for a legendary
warrior-monk, whose life provides the tale of a 15th-century romance
entitled *Gikeiki*. We are rarely exposed to the range of Japanese cuisine in America, apart from the sushi bar. At the Nikko's Benkay, if
such familiar plates as teriyaki and sukiyaki are even listed, they are
buried among the dozens of other specialties that appear on the extensive menu.

I had my meal at the Benkay in a traditional room with the table
at floor height, surrounded by straw mats (called *tatami*) on which
diners normally sit cross-legged at their meals. To accommodate the
more stiff-jointed Westerners among us, there is a cutaway under the
table where the legs may be stretched. The small room is sparse, containing only an ebony-stained table, some flowers, and an art scroll
hung on walls painted in subdued winter tones. The single window,
shuttered with sliding rice-paper panels, overlooks the Chicago River
and frames a close-up view of Helmut Jahn's controversial State of
Illinois Building.

Begin with a glass of ozeki (hot sake), the proper cocktail before
eating Japanese food. For appetizers, the menu lists soups—fish and
miso—along with platters, such as beef sashimi, or a "combination"
of Japanese specialties that varies with the season. Main courses are
listed by type: nimono (the stewed dishes), yakimono (from the grill),
agemono (fried specialties), and sunomono (the vinaigrettes). The
sushi, with tuna, eel, and those seaweed-wrapped cylinders of rice,
are also filled with Japanese cucumber, avocado, and roe from the
flying fish. There's also a shokado bento for lunch, a partitioned
bamboo box each of whose small compartments contains an item of
traditional Japanese cooking, all fish or vegetables, including tempura,
baked yellowtail, sashimi, and many condiments. To drink, there's
a very dry cold sake, called *otokoyama*, that is quite potent. Brown
tea is served throughout the meal. Dessert can be a Japanese confec-
tion, ice cream, or fruit, and green tea is served with the check.

Bice, 158 E. Ontario St. ☎ 664-1474.

Cuisine: NORTHERN ITALIAN. **Reservations:** Required.
Prices: Appetizers $5.95–$9.95 at lunch, $7.95–$12.95 at dinner; main
courses $10–$17 at lunch, $13–$23 at dinner. AE, DC, MC, V.
Open: Lunch Mon–Sat 11:30am–2:30pm; dinner Sun–Thurs 5:30–
10:30pm, Fri–Sat 5:30–11:30pm.

Direct from Milan comes Bice, which first opened its doors in 1926
as a small *contadina*, a workingman's restaurant, and now has fashionable affiliates in New York and Beverly Hills, where it continues
to be one of the hottest luncheon spots in town. Bice occupies a lovely

two-story building just minutes from North Michigan Avenue, and seating options follow the style of a continental cafe, beginning with open-air tables on the street level and moving through a series of raised platforms to the more or less formal interior dining room. The Bice menu, which changes daily, is chosen from a core of 70 traditional dishes, emphasizing northern Italian tastes.

During a recent lunch at Bice, I first sampled the insalata d'aragosta, a lobster salad with arugula, Belgian endive, and hearts of palm. A unique and intriguing appetizer is carpaccio of either tuna or swordfish. I was very satisfied with my misto di pasta della casa main course, a selection of four exquisitely prepared pastas, and likewise the simple scaloppine di vitello, veal scaloppine sautéed with roasted peppers, oregano, and basil. Desserts are a special item at Bice, all made on the premises, including the ice cream. Highly recommended is the tiramisù della Bice, ladyfingers with mascarpone cheese flavored with espresso and Kahlúa.

⭐ **Cape Cod Room,** in the Drake Hotel, 140 E. Walton Place. ☎ 787-2200.

Cuisine: SEAFOOD **Reservations:** Required.
Prices: Appetizers $7.50–$10.50; main courses $16.75–$31. AE, CB, DC, DISC, ER, JCB, MC, V.
Open: Daily noon–11pm. **Closed:** Christmas Day.

The Cape Cod Room is usually filled to capacity even during the middle of the week, underscoring the perennial popularity of the restaurant. The large, multilevel room, with tables and booths covered in red-and-white checkerboard cloths, is wood-beamed and stuffed with nautical paraphernalia. Since the fresh seafood catch from Lake Michigan and nearby rivers is minimal, the Dover sole I ordered—the dish favored by Paul Newman, who is said to dine here often when in Chicago—is flown in fresh every two days from its native Channel waters off the coast of England. The sole had been broiled to a light crusty golden brown and was served in a superb almond meunière sauce. My waiter performed the delicate surgery of deboning the fish at tableside. Served in four delectable strips, the sole was accompanied by au gratin potatoes and a mixed salad—the iceberg lettuce a reminder that there is nothing nouvelle about the Cape Cod Room.

For starters, you can begin with the praised Bookbinder red snapper soup—very hearty and chewy, flavored to taste by dry sherry brought to the table. Or you might order a mixed seafood appetizer of shrimp, bay scallops, salmon, and lobster in a creamy tarragon sauce. Other appetizer choices include clams on the half shell (either cherrystones or littlenecks), and clams casino and oysters Rockefeller. As for the other finny varieties among the main courses, you may choose from pike, Wisconsin largemouth (freshwater) bass, turbot from the coast of France, pompano from Florida, Gulf swordfish, and Pacific salmon. Shellfish include bay and sea scallops, shrimp, and Maine lobster. And if you want the works, try the bouillabaisse. The menu also offers a small selection of prime meat cuts, steaks, and chops. All main courses at the Cape Cod Room are à la carte. For dessert, try a simple bowl of fresh red raspberries and cream.

The Saloon, 200 E. Chestnut St. ☎ 280-5454.
   Cuisine: STEAK. **Reservations:** Recommended.
   Prices: Appetizers $4.95–$7.95; main courses $9.95–$26.95. AE, MC, V.
   Open: Mon–Sat 11am–midnight; Sun brunch 11am–3pm.

Forget the prosaic name. The Saloon is no diamond in the rough. Its setting, a few steps below sidewalk level in one of the neighborhood's most elegant apartment buildings, is all tone; the food, superb. You wouldn't think there are many more spins you could give to a meal of honest meat and potatoes. But The Saloon has managed to turn a corner or two as it lives up to its claim to be a "steakhouse for the nineties." The Kansas City Bone-in Strip ($18.95), served "black 'n blue," was a knockout, rich as butter under its outside crust, and just as tender. The Saloon's bargain taste treat is a thick slab of smokey barbecued meat loaf ($8.95). There is also a wide selection of nonbeef and seafood dishes on the menu. And let's not forget those potatoes, six varieties from mashed to hashed, all $1.95 as sides when they don't accompany a given entrée. Standouts for me were the puffy cottage fries, and always, the mashed potatoes blended with scallions and bacon. Within a year of its opening, The Saloon had already managed to climb into the city's top ten steakhouses on the list of one prominent Chicago food critic. Lunch here, incidentally, is popular and quite reasonable.

★ **Spiaggia,** 980 N. Michigan Ave. ☎ 280-2750.
   Cuisine: ITALIAN. **Reservations:** Required.
   Prices: Appetizers $7.95–$13; main courses $9.95–$18 at lunch, $26–$29 at dinner. AE, CB, DC, DISC, MC, V.
   Open: Lunch Mon–Sat 11:30am–2pm; dinner Mon–Thurs 5:30–9:30pm, Fri–Sat 5:30–10:30pm, Sun 5:30–9pm.

Picture a long, narrow room, with a ceiling two stories high, decorated in soft desert pastels, and contoured in sharply defined shapes, a melding of deco sleekness and the sparse abstract designs of the Aztecs. Against the outer wall, a curtain of tall, segmented windows gives the illusion that the entire room is curved, and in motion. This is Spiaggia, a restaurant across from the Drake, whose boldness and novelty of design matches its innovative cuisine. A pianist provides nightly entertainment.

Spiaggia recognizes that pizza is a suitable appetizer, no matter how elegant the restaurant, if the dough is treated as pastry, carefully baked (in the restaurant's wood-fired ovens), and the toppings finely chosen. The small pizza margherita with fresh tomato sauce, basil, and mozzarella is thin, crisp, and delicious. It's not unreasonable to make a lunch at the Spiaggia exclusively from side dishes, adding to the pizza, say, an order of tender carpaccio (sun-dried beef), zuppa di gamberi e fagioli (shrimp and white bean soup), and the insalata normale. Unequivocally, this is the best salad I have eaten in any

Chicago restaurant—an interesting variety of leaves, well-dressed with a light coating of herb vinegar and olive oil.

But why stop at mere appetizers with such a choice of tempting main courses before you? Among the many pasta dishes are pappardelle con salsiccia e pollo (wide pasta with Italian sausage, chicken, mushrooms, tomatoes, and herbs), and agnolotti di vitello (veal-filled pasta crescents with tomato-basil sauce). Or if fish appeals, you might select the mista griglia di pesce (mixed seafood grill).

Lovers of sweets unite, and confront your finest struggle at Spiaggia! Try the hot zabaglione with seasonal fruits; the cannoli, an almond cone filled with ricotta/chocolate-chip gelato, and covered with orange and pistachio sauces; or the cioccolato bianco e nere, semisweet chocolate layers filled with white-chocolate mousse and seasonal fruits. Such a feast demands a finale, an apéritif from Spiaggia's list of fine grappas (grappa is a fortified wine, like cognac, distilled from the fermented dregs of the best Italian wines). The Nonino Grappa is as smooth as velvet.

Adjacent to the restaurant in another narrow, window-dominated space is the **Café Spiaggia** (☎ **280-2764**), a more informal but equally spiffy trattoria serving pizzas, pastas, and antipasti.

Moderate

Many of my personal favorites are included in the listings below. These restaurants are less pricey than the gourmet restaurants described above, and very popular with Chicagoans for excellent food and ambience.

★ **Avanzare**, 161 E. Huron. ☎ **337-8056.**
Cuisine: NORTHERN ITALIAN. **Reservations:** Required.
Prices: Appetizers $3.75–$9.75; main courses $10.50–$17.25 at lunch, $10.75–$27.75 at dinner. AE, DC, DISC, MC, V.
Open: Lunch Mon–Fri 11:30am–2pm; dinner Mon–Thurs 5:30–10pm, Fri–Sat 5–11pm, Sun 5–9:30pm.

Avanzare is one of those hangar-size continental-style cafes with wraparound windows overlooking the street. The space at ground level is fitted out with banquettes, trimmed in hardwood and padded with green-leather cushions. But the chandeliers are quite unusual, enormous box-shaped ensembles of white leaded glass. On an upper-level balcony there are a small number of individual, linen-covered tables for more private dining. But on most days during the lunch and dinner hours, downstairs is like a public square on a Saturday night in summer. Reasonable prices ensure a crowd of regulars.

I recommend the pollo al rosemarino (breast of chicken in rosemary sauce with mushrooms), the tortellini di pollo affumicato (smoked chicken-filled pasta with a sauce of provolone and spinach), and the spiedini di manzo con aglio (a skewer of sirloin tips rubbed with garlic)—all of gourmet quality. The linguine with shrimp sautéed in garlic, basil, and chiles is merely "good."

With one of the restaurant's tasty sweets or pastries for dessert, plus drink or beverage, the bill probably won't come to more than $45 for two—not cheap, but a fair exchange at Avanzare.

Bistro 110, 110 E. Pearson St. ☎ 266-3110.

    Cuisine: CONTINENTAL. **Reservations:** Accepted for lunch; not accepted for dinner.

    Prices: Appetizers $5.95–$9.95; main courses $9.95–$21.95. AE, CB, DC, DISC, MC, V.

    Open: Mon–Thurs 11:30am–midnight, Fri–Sat 11:30am–1am, Sun 11:30am–11pm.

One of the few restaurants in Chicago with a year-round sidewalk cafe, al fresco during the warm season and enclosed the rest of the year, is half a block west of North Michigan Avenue. Here, patrons sitting outdoors have a close-up view of Chicago's historic water tower, the spindly edifice of yellow stone that miraculously escaped destruction despite being directly in the path of the Great Fire. Inside, Bistro 110 is divided into several environments—the sidewalk enclosure, a bar area, and a large back room where most diners are seated. An activities chalkboard covers one whole side wall near the front of the restaurant, listing such bulletins as the daily news headlines, weather forecasts, movie and theater information, market quotations, and sports results. Neighborhood cronies tend to congregate here, drawn by the familiar faces and the reasonably priced daily specials.

A sample dinner might begin with half a dozen raw oysters or a novel baked Brie with sliced apples; move on to classic main courses like steak au poivre or filet of salmon, served with a whole squadron of veggies, a wedge of orange bell pepper, a plum tomato, new potatoes, a section of corn on the cob, carrots, and asparagus; and for dessert try the crème brûlée, fresh fruit, cream custard of caramelized sugar flavored with Tahitian vanilla beans, or a white-chocolate terrine, a creamy white-chocolate mousse with a fresh raspberry sauce.

Esplanada Cafe, 840 N. Michigan Ave. ☎ 751-2121.

    Cuisine: BISTRO. **Reservations:** Required.

    Prices: Appetizers $4; main courses $9–$14. AE, MC, V.

    Open: Mon–Sat 11am–5:30pm.

On the top floor of a four-story building occupied exclusively by the Plaza Esplanada Boutique, a small cafe enjoys a very privileged view over North Michigan Avenue. The food was quite good when I ate there with a female companion one midday not long ago. Our lunch began well with the yellow pepper soup ($4), after which I chose the lemon chicken Caesar salad ($12), and my friend the gratin of crab with fricassee ($14). Several ladies also stopped here, not for lunch, but to pause over a pot of tea and "something sweet" before moving on about their business.

★ **Harry Caray's,** 33 W. Kinzie. ☎ 312/HOLY-COW.

    Cuisine: ITALIAN. **Reservations:** Not accepted.

    Prices: Appetizers $4.95–$10.95; main courses $8–$26.95. AE, DC, DISC, MC, V.

Open: Lunch Mon–Fri 11:30am–3pm; dinner Mon–Thurs 5:30–10:30pm, Fri–Sat 5pm–midnight, Sun 4–10pm.

When I first entered Harry Caray's, I was thinking "sports bar" or perhaps "singles bar," but not "fine restaurant." Harry, of course, is the dean of baseball's play-by-play announcers. I was expecting a good boutique burger, or at best a nice cut of beef, not tongue-tingling fancy Italian food.

But Harry Caray's *is* a sports bar. It even looks exactly the way an "in" sports bar ought to look, housed in a brick building, located on a quiet, quasi-commercial back street. The interior is surprisingly large, divided between a huge barroom with a giant screen TV, and a separate dining room downstairs, with private dining rooms upstairs. Every available piece of wall space on both levels is covered with baseball memorabilia.

Try Harry's own brand of potato chips, made on the premises, and dubbed—what else?—"cow chips." (They're also sold by the bag for munching at home in the event you get hooked.) Start with a few appetizers, or just make a meal of them if you like. Choose from succulent beef carpaccio, roasted red peppers in olive oil with anchovies, or toasted meat ravioli. Main courses range from ravioli and meat sauce to a 22-ounce porterhouse steak. A "must" is the chicken Vesuvio, delicately spiced white meat accompanied by baked potato wedges. The zabaglione with fresh strawberries and blueberries is a fitting finale to a great meal. At midnight the waiters and patrons (led by Harry himself, if in attendance) join together in a chorus of "Take Me Out to the Ballgame." The bar sometimes remains open as late as 3am, depending on the crowd.

Mity Nice, 835 N. Michigan Ave. ☎ 335-4575.

> **Cuisine:** AMERICAN. **Reservations:** Not required.
> **Prices:** Appetizers $3.95–$6.50; main courses $7.95–$18.95. AE, DC, DISC, MC, V.
> **Open:** Mon–Thurs 11am–10pm; Fri–Sat 11am–11pm; Sun noon–9pm.

Ensconced in the mezzanine of the busy vertical shopping mall at Water Tower Place, Mity Nice is not just a place to go for a consolation meal while you've rushed during a frenzied bout of shop hopping. Mity Nice is worth a digression, even when shopping is the furthest thing from your mind. This is a good restaurant, period; the food is excellent, plentiful, and reasonably priced. Most dinner entrées are in the $10 to $14 range, and the hot lunches rarely exceed $9. One lunchtime treat not on the dinner menu is the grilled lemon chicken with capers ($8.95), a large and lightly breaded filet of chicken breast. On both menus is the house specialty, a generous slice of meat loaf served with mashed potatoes and green beans ($8.95 at lunch, $10.95 at dinner). Among the Italian specialties, the toasted macaroni and cheese ($7.95), made with penne instead of egg noodles, is about the best I've ever tasted—better by leaps and bounds than the "m and c" offering at Michael Jordan's.

Shaw's Crab House and Blue Crab Lounge, 21 E. Hubbard.
☎ 527-2722.

Cuisine: SEAFOOD. **Reservations:** Not accepted.
Prices: Appetizers $4.95–$9.95; main courses $12.95–$18.95. AE, CB, DC, DISC, MC, V.
Open: Lunch Mon–Thurs 11:30am–5pm; dinner Sun–Thurs 5–10pm, Fri–Sat 5–11pm.

This is a moderate to high-priced fish house, organized continental style, with plush red banquettes along the walls and linen-covered tables in the center. As a favorite spot for business lunches, Shaw's is right up there in popularity with any of its downtown rivals. For starters, if you're in luck, there are fresh oysters (based on availability at market prices). Other appetizers include baked oysters Alexander, blue crab fingers, and popcorn shrimp; and for soup there is a house gumbo by the bowl or the cup. Shaw's menu offers a number of side dishes, both traditional and exotic, like broccoli and asparagus, both topped with hollandaise, or Cajun-style four-grain wild rice. Main courses include dishes such as Calico Bay scallops and a pound of fresh Texas stone crab claws. Other popular specials are crab cakes and french-fried shrimp. If there is a theme at Shaw's it is layered on ever so lightly, the idea of Key West and Papa Hemingway suggested subtly by the restaurant's trademark dessert, key lime pie, and by the suave strains of such thirties tunes as "Begin the Beguine" playing in the background.

Inexpensive ────────────────────────────

foodlife, 835 N. Michigan Ave. ☎ 878-7340.

Cuisine: VARIED. **Reservations.** Not accepted.
Prices: Most items $4.50–$8. AE, DISC, DC, MC, V.
Open: Mon–Sat juice, espresso, and corner bakery 7:45am–10pm, Sun 7:45am–9pm; all other kiosks Mon–Sat 11am–10pm; Sun 11am–9pm.

foodlife is a festive and imaginative food court—a dozen or so kiosks offering many ordinary and exotic specialties—located on the mezzanine of Water Tower Place, just outside the entrance of the Mity Nice restaurant. Four hundred seats are spread out cafe style in a very pleasant environment under realistic boughs of artificial trees festooned with strings of lights in the shapes of grapes and other fruits. This could be an inexpensive place to have lunch or a snack, if you can avoid the temptation of wanting to taste everything! And there is much to tempt you, beginning with the Miracle Juice Bar with its spectacular fresh orange juice and raspberry fruit smoothy. From among the kiosks, you can choose vegetarian and grain dishes, south-of-the-border specialties, an assortment of pan-Asian dishes, salads galore, or a charcoal-broiled hamburger and an order of fries. Healthy and/or gooey desserts are not in short supply, and a booth called Sacred Grounds serves up various espresso-based beverages, plus an array of fine chocolates.

The Original A-1, 401 E. Illinois St., North Pier. ☎ 644-0300.

Cuisine: TEXAS BARBECUE/MEXICAN. **Reservations:** Not required.
Prices: Appetizers $2.95–$6.95; sandwiches $5.25–$6.50; main courses $6.95–$14.95. AE, DC, DISC, MC, V.
Open: Mon–Thurs 11:30am–10pm, Fri–Sat 11:30am–midnight.

If you happen to find yourself at North Pier for one reason or another (bike rental, river architectural tour, shop hopping), you could look on a meal at the Original A-1 as an unexpected bonus. I recommend heartily the tender, tasty, baby back ribs ($9.95); the jalapeño mashed potatoes (rivaling Oprah's horseradish variety of the same species at the Eccentric); and the lethal frozen margaritas ($3.75). If all that doesn't fill you up, a chuck wagon circulates offering barbecue beans and various salads at no additional cost.

Budget

★ **Billy Goat Tavern,** 430 N. Michigan Ave. ☎ 222-1525.
Cuisine: BREAKFAST/BURGERS. **Reservations:** Not accepted.
$ **Prices:** Menu items $3–$6. No credit cards.
Open: Mon–Sat 7am–3am, Sun 7am–11pm.

"Cheesborger, Cheeseborger —No Coke . . . Pepsi." Viewers of the original "Saturday Night Live" will certainly remember the classic John Belushi routine, a moment in the life of a crabby Greek short-order cook. The comic got his material from the Billy Goat Tavern, located under North Michigan Avenue near the bridge that crosses to the Loop. Just "butt in anytime," says the sign on the red door with the picture of the billy goat on it. The tavern is a hangout for the newspaper workers and writers who occupy the nearby Tribune Tower and Sun-Times Building. Offering beer and greasy food, in the kind of atmosphere journalists love to haunt, it's a good place to watch a game, chitchat at the bar, and down a few beers. Or come here for a cheap breakfast, perhaps two eggs, toast, and hash browns; a cheese omelet; or steak and eggs. Breakfast is not served on weekends.

$ **Gino's East,** 160 E. Superior. ☎ 943-1124.
Cuisine: PIZZA. **Reservations:** Not required.
Prices: Pizza $6.95–$17.40. After 9pm a 15% gratuity is added to all checks. AE, CB, DC, DISC, MC, V.
Open: Mon–Thurs 11:30am–11pm (10pm in winter), Fri–Sat 10:30am–midnight, Sun 3–10pm.

At Gino's East you may actually have to wait on line, especially in the summertime, before being seated. This is the place *People* magazine once called the "pizza de résistance." The doorman at the Barclay Hotel, two doors down from Gino's, says that the line often snakes past him on its way down the block. Considering that Gino's can seat about 600 patrons, this is indeed astounding.

From the outside Gino's looks like a condemned building. Inside is even worse. But the prerenovation look is purposeful, a studied part of Gino's rathskeller ambience. Diners sit in dark-stained booths, surrounded by paneled walls covered with graffiti. Each of these effects is craftily fashioned as a form of construction art, so well done in some cases that you don't realize they are all around you unless you look closely. As for the graffiti, you are allowed to indulge, but "if it isn't clean," the earnest young manager confided, "we don't allow it."

As for the pizza, it's elaborate and tasty, "a banquet served on a lush, amber bed of dough," or so one critic described it in a burst of rhapsodic prose. A small cheese pizza is enough for two unless you're binging. A better bet for a satisfactory dinner is the small supreme, with layers of cheese, sausage, onions, green pepper, and mushrooms; or the vegetarian, with cheese, onions, peppers, asparagus, summer squash, zucchini, and eggplant.

Next to the restaurant is Gino's carryout, with its own telephone number (☎ **988-4200**); pizzas take 30 to 40 minutes' cooking time.

---

4   River North

The River North gallery area, west of Michigan Avenue and paralleling the north branch of the Chicago River as far as Division Street, although still quasi-industrial, is the setting for a number of very fashionable restaurants.

Expensive

⭐ **Coco Pazzo,** 300 W. Hubbard. ☎ **836-0900.**
Cuisine: NORTHERN ITALIAN. **Reservations:** Accepted.
Prices: Appetizers $5–$6.75 at lunch, $5.50–$7.75 at dinner; main courses $10–$14 at lunch, $12.50–$26 at dinner. AE, DC, MC, V.
Open: Lunch daily 11:30am–3pm; dinner Mon–Thurs 5:30–11pm; Fri–Sat 5:30–11:30pm; Sun 5–10:30pm.

From Milano to Chicago by way of New York, the Coco Pazzo reputation has traveled well. Northern Italian food has become something of a rage in the nineties, so one must be careful to single out the few select sheep from the more numerous goats among the eateries specializing in this cuisine. Coco Pazzo can certainly be counted among the select. At its best, the food of northern Italy is simple, and allows the ingredients to shine through. So much depends on the deft touch of the cook staff and the quality of their ingredients. Coco Pazzo wins high marks on both accounts.

Coco Pazzo's menu, naturally, undergoes periodic changes, but there is always a risotto del giorno, and at lunchtime, a focaccia, a thin-crust pizza filled with delectables, in addition to a tempting list of pastas, pizzas, seafood, veal, and chicken dishes. At my lunch, I began with a fresh vegetable antipasto ($5), and sampled as well the excellent grilled portobello mushrooms ($6.60). The manager was very helpful in introducing the house wines, sold by the glass, one Barbera red ($6) being particularly memorable. There was a selection of tasty breads on the table, and the absolutely best virgin olive oil for dipping, which went especially well with alternating swallows of the rich and robust wines.

The meal's high point was the focaccia alla gene, a thin-crust white pizza filled with prosciutto, fontina cheese, and fresh tomatoes ($11). My companion would demur; for her the highpoint followed the entrées, so let's call it a draw. The desserts were indeed special. We feasted on the crostata, a tart filled with fresh raspberries that day and topped with a dreamy, champagne-spiked zabaglione ($5.50), and we were both bowled over by the fondente ciocolato, a flourless chocolate cake with a warm mousse center, chocolate sauce, and cappuccino ice cream ($6). Coco Pazzo is located deep within the River North neighborhood, an easy cab ride from downtown Chicago; but anyone housed in a hotel on or near Michigan Avenue might find the stroll along Hubbard Street a pleasant way to arrive there as well.

★ **Gordon,** 500 N. Clark St. ☎ 467-9780.

Cuisine: AMERICAN/INTERNATIONAL. **Reservations:** Required.
Prices: Appetizers $4.95–$8.50; main courses $17.95–$25.95; chef's five-course tasting menu $48.95. AE, DC, DISC, JCB, MC, V.
Open: Lunch Mon–Fri 11:30am–2pm; dinner Sun–Thurs 5:30–9:30pm, Fri–Sat 5:30pm–12:30am; brunch Sun 11am–2pm.

Gordon's "Americanized international cuisine" epitomizes a blending of continental flare and sophistication with the quality control and freshness of the American kitchen. The roast loin of lamb with orange couscous, for example, hints of Moorish Europe, but the accompanying onion marmalade and asparagus bring the platter back to the heartland. Presentations of the meals at Gordon, moreover, are as artful as the food is delicious.

You can drop a bundle for dinner here, the quintessential Gordon experience, or sample the same fare under more mundane conditions at lunch for roughly half the price. I enjoyed the restaurant's signature appetizer, the superb artichoke fritters, went on to a very palatable sirloin plate, and ended with a trio of crèmes brûlées. Weekend diners can come to dance Friday and Saturday nights from 8:30pm to midnight. And the Sunday brunch ($19.95) consists of a drink and several courses. Another Gordon trademark is the nightly wine tasting, three 5-ounce samples of selected wines ($10 to $13).

Michael Jordan's, 500 N. La Salle St. ☎ 644-DUNK.

Cuisine: AMERICAN. **Reservations:** Not accepted.
Prices: Appetizers $4.95–$7.95; main courses $6–$12.50 at lunch, $12–$22 at dinner. AE, CB, DC, DISC, MC, V.
Open: Sun–Thurs 11:30am–10:30pm; Fri–Sat 11:30am–midnight.

At ten to noon, within twenty minutes of opening on a fall Saturday, Michael Jordan's was already filling up rapidly. This was months after Mike's bombshell announcement that he was retiring from basketball. Such is the Jordan aura that the young people lunching there that day—mostly in the company of adults, but representing some three-quarters of the clientele—sat, ate, and acted as respectfully as if they were at table in their girl- or boyfriend's home for the very first time. This is in marked contrast to the high-energy behavior encouraged at other places popular with children and teens, like the Hard Rock or Planet Hollywood. Perhaps, on the longshot chance that Mike himself might suddenly make an appearance, none of the kids wanted to seem like an ill-mannered jerk in the eyes of their idol. It was, to this parent of a teenager, a phenomenon.

I don't mean to imply, however, that Michael Jordan's is not a restaurant that would also appeal to a more mature crowd, primarily at night, I suppose. I myself found the food surprisingly good, and very affordable at lunchtime, from a family point of view. I began with a soup of the day, a very tasty chicken gumbo ($2.75), which was so thick with big chunks of meat, it was a satisfying meal in itself. Next I sampled a side dish of Juanita's macaroni and cheese ($3.50), a traditional preparation, followed by a super-size grilled chicken breast sandwich on herb focaccia with melted provolone ($7.95). There is also a very economical children's menu with items priced from $3.50 to $4.95. It was a comforting feeling that despite the restaurant's mass popularity (you might have to wait on line for some time to be seated), the owners have not exploited Mike's fame to the point of making Michael Jordan's inaccessible to those families whose budgets don't normally allow for dining in expensive, fashionable eateries.

★ **Zinfandel,** 59 W. Grand St. ☎ 727-1818.
Cuisine: AMERICAN. **Reservations:** Accepted.
Prices: Appetizers $4.95–$6.95; main courses $12.50–$17.95. AE, DC, MC, V.
Open: Lunch Tues–Fri 11:30am–2:30pm; Sat noon–2:30pm; dinner Tues–Thurs 5:30–10pm, Fri–Sat 5:30–11pm.

As well as I dined in other establishments while researching this edition of *Frommer's Chicago*, Zinfandel was, hands down, the best of the current harvest. When a chef can make someone who eats out professionally and frequently feel really excited about the menu, and instill a sense of anticipation from one course to the next, she's really accomplished something. In this respect, Susan Goss, chef/co-owner of Zinfandel, has, in the realm of natural foods, advanced the culinary wheel forward one full revolution.

The food at Zinfandel is at once totally familiar and totally unique. Using many of her grandmother's "basic" recipes as a starting point, Ms. Goss crafts such home-comfort standbys as buttermilk biscuits ($2.25). Sound prosaic enough? Heavenly is more like it; cooking each batch to order in a hot iron skillet is the trick, she says. Two other starters I can happily recommend are the cheese sampler with marinated salads and grilled farmhouse bread ($5.25), and the "wilted" field greens, with strips of Smithfield ham, Stewart pecans, sweet red onions, and a warm maple dressing ($3.96 small; $6.95 large).

I can almost guarantee that you've never tasted cornbread as grainy and delicious as her crispy hazelnut corn cakes ($5.25), listed with the main dishes on the lunch menu, and served with a tangy relish of woodland mushrooms, dried cherries, and maple sugar. The smoky roast chicken breast, with cheesy corn grits, braised greens, and roasted chile relish ($9.50), presented with all the artsy flourish of the nouvelle-style kitchen, is a masterpiece of juices, tastes, and textures. And on and on go the variations on Zinfandel's inspired menu.

Two other features recommend Zinfandel, as if the food were not enough. The design and atmosphere of the restaurant are as comforting and stirring as the menu, where overtones of Asian serenity in the woodwork and screen hangings are juxtaposed with avant-garde artworks of the nineties. And the natural food store/deli you first encounter upon entering offers one-of-a-kind specialty items gathered from the four corners of North America, plus great sandwiches and other fresh preparations for takeout.

Moderate

⭐ **Eccentric,** 159 W. Erie St. (at the corner of Wells). ☎ 787-8390.
Cuisine: AMERICAN. **Reservations:** Not accepted.
$ **Prices:** Appetizers $3.95–$7.95; main courses $7.95–$19.95. AE, DC, DISC, MC, V.
Open: Lunch Mon–Fri 11:30am–2pm; dinner Mon–Thurs 5:30–10pm, Fri–Sat 5:30–11pm, Sun 5–9pm.

The Eccentric, opened by Oprah Winfrey, daytime talk show host extraordinaire, is an attractive place, laid out in the manner of a brasserie, but with eclectic wall art. Not only have Oprah's partners in the kitchen managed to add dimensions of genuine subtlety to such old-time stick-to-the-ribs favorites as mashed potatoes and pepper steak, but they routinely turn out some of the most refined and fattening dessert creations in the city, all for a surprisingly reasonable price.

Quality, quantity, and economy are the formulas that make the restaurant one of the most popular luncheon spots in town. This is also *the* place for steak tartare, the chopped sirloin and veal specialty served in all its raw and capered splendor. The Pepper Steak à la Fritizel is truly one of the tastiest (and most filling) dishes to be found in all Chicago. On the sandwich side, the monster-size Unclubbable filled with chicken, bacon, tomatoes, and greens is also an unbeatable bargain. The side dish here not to be missed is Potatoes Oprah, whipped with horseradish. For dessert you must sample the Banana & Chocolate in a United State, a melt-in-your-mouth banana crème brûlée, and Three Puffs on a Plate.

READERS RECOMMEND

The Chicago Chop House, 60 W. Ontario St. (☎ 229-2356). *"You must not be quite the steak lover I am. You fail to mention one of the most famous steakhouses in Chicago. The Chicago Chop House is the best steakhouse I've ever been to. Easily. Anywhere. It's not that cheap. My last visit came to $115 for dinner for two, with a $30 bottle of Bordeaux included."*—Tom Kieltyka, Lisle, IL

A popular evening event at the Eccentric, Monday through Friday from 4:30 to 7pm, is the Grand Brasserie Buffet happy hour, featuring such complimentary platters as roasted fish and pasta with mustard sauce. Valet parking is available for $4. For parties of five or more, a 16% gratuity will be added to the bill.

⭐ **Frontera Grill & Topolobampo,** 445 N. Clark St.
☎ 661-1434.

Cuisine: MEXICAN/MESOAMERICAN. **Reservations:** Not accepted at Frontera Grill; accepted at Topolobampo.
Prices: Appetizers $4–$5.95; main courses $8.95–$19.50. AE, DC, DISC, MC, V.
Open: Lunch Tues–Fri 11:30am–2pm, Sat 10:30am–2:30pm; dinner Tues–Thurs 5:30–10pm, Fri–Sat 5–11pm.

For several years now, despite its no-reservation policy, Frontera Grill has been one of Chicago's most popular restaurants. Perhaps this is because owners Rick and Deann Groen Bayless have dared to introduce American diners to the fine dining tradition most Mexican restaurants north of the Rio Grande seem to ignore. To reinforce this element of their mission, the Baylesses recently expanded their enterprise, adding Topolobampo under the same roof, a more formal version of Frontera, with a menu all its own.

Typical of the Frontera Grill's fare are the *tacos al carbón* ($7.50 to $8.50), a generous portion of grilled beef, pork, duck, or catfish, folded into hot corn tortillas by the customer to prevent the shells from becoming soggy. On the lighter side are the Mexico City–style *quesadillas,* corn turnovers filled with melted cheese, and accompanied by fried black beans (a southern Mexican specialty) and guacamole ($5.25).

From the Topolobampo menu, the *sopa de hongos y nopales* ($4), wild mushrooms and cactus paddles, is very subtle, and for the main course you may choose from a number of intriguing dishes, including grilled, marinated, free-range, baby chicken with salsa ($10.50), and Amish duck, a breast and a roasted drumstick, served with red chili mole ($18.50). Another option is the *ensaladas surtidas,* a tasting plate of salads ($7) with many exotic ingredients.

⭐ **Maggiano's,** 516 N. Clark St. ☎ 644-8100.
Cuisine: CLASSIC ITALIAN. **Reservations:** Recommended.
Prices: Appetizers $3.95–$7.95; main courses $7.50–$13.95 at lunch, $8.50–$26.95 at dinner. AE, DC, DISC, MC, V.
Open: Lunch Mon–Fri 11:30am–2pm; dinner Mon–Thurs 5:30–10pm, Fri–Sat 5pm–midnight, Sun 4–9pm.

The benchmark at Maggiano's is large portions, served family style, a protocol that has now spread through several of Chicago's newest and best Italian restaurants. The other novelty is tradition; there has been a simultaneous turning away citywide from the skimpy, lighter fare of north Italy, in favor of the full-belly classic food many Italian families still get at Mama's for Sunday dinner. The key to Maggiano's success, of course, is that its kitchen also manages to maintain Mama's high standards of preparation and taste.

Two outstanding appetizers at Maggiano's are the zuppa di mussels, and the baked shrimp oreganata served with sliced tomato, mozzarella, and peppers. The pasta dishes and some main courses on the dinner menu come in two sizes, the larger of which usually satisfies at least two persons. Favorites among the pastas are the spaghetti with meat ragù. ($9.25 to $11.25), the fettuccine Alfredo with broccoli ($10.95 to $12.95), and the garlic shrimp with shells ($11.50 to $14.50). The whole roast chicken, with peppers and onions ($12.95), will certainly go around the table several times, while the smothered New York steak ($25.95), cooked Maggiano style, is a house specialty.

Mambo Grill, 412 N. Clark St. ☎ 467-9797.

Cuisine: LATIN AMERICAN. **Reservations:** Accepted for parties of five or more only.
Prices: Appetizers $3.95–$5.95; main courses $8.95–$14.95. AE, DC, DISC, MC, V.
Open: Mon–Sat 11am–1am.

If you want to see how the other half eats (other half of the western hemisphere, that is), check out this bright, colorful River North storefront eatery with its pan-Latino menu. What are listed as appetizers might better be viewed as tapas, perfect for small-platter midnight grazing. You can make a meal of these treats without ever getting near the list of the more substantial *entradas.*

You could, moreover, go Cubano and Brasileiro, simultaneously, with *mojitos* ($4) and *caipirinhas* ($4) to quench your thirsty demons, and *tiritas* (potato-crusted calamari with dipping sauces for $4.75) and *tostones* (plantain chips with black bean dip) to tease the palate. Linger in the Caribbean for some Puerto Rican *pasteles* (tamales filled with shredded duck criollo wrapped in banana leaves for $4.95) then rumba 'round to Bogotá for some Colombian-style *arepas* (cornmeal cakes filled with sautéed mushrooms and manchego cheese for $4.95). After that, if you just can't resist that cauldron of steaming, spicy Latin bouillabaisse, go for the *zarzuela de mariscos* (Cuban-style seafood stew priced at $13.95.) Dessert at Mambo Grill can only mean the pumpkin flan ($3.50).

Papagus Greek Taverna, 620 N. State St. (on the ground floor of the Embassy Suites Hotel). ☎ 642-8450.

Cuisine: GREEK. **Reservations:** Recommended for dinner on weekends.
Prices: Appetizers $1.95–$8.50; main courses $4.75–$13.95. AE, DC, DISC, MC, V.
Open: Mon–Thurs 11:30am–10pm, Fri–Sat noon–midnight, Sun noon–10pm.

Papagus is a sprawling and attractive restaurant attached to the Embassy Suites Hotel, decorated with the colorful artifacts typical of a Greek tavern or cafe. And as with an authentic Greek tavern, at Papagus you don't have to go near the main courses to sample a wide range of dishes and flavors and come away satisfied; you can make a meal—especially lunch—from a combination of delicious hot and cold appetizers.

Every table is equipped with a stack of small plates, which you use to sample each of the items you have selected. From the list of cold appetizers, you might enjoy the whipped feta cheese ($3.95), or the roasted eggplant ($3.95), both of which can be spread on the excellent, crusty house bread.

Most of the hot appetizers come in two sizes—the small serving is more than adequate for two persons who are sampling various dishes. Among the choices are a tasty moussaka, ground beef layered with lamb, eggplant, and squash ($3.95), and an exceptional pastitsio, baked macaroni with ground meat wrapped in phyllo pastry ($3.75). The spinach pie ($3.95) is a must, and the spicy lamb-and-beef meatballs ($3.95) possess a uniquely Greek flavoring. Finish off the meal with a shot of ouzo, a cup of espresso (or thick Greek coffee if you dare), and a slice of Papagus's divine baklava.

Planet Hollywood, 633 N. Wells. ☎ 266-9850.
Cuisine: AMERICAN. **Reservations:** Not accepted.
Prices: Appetizers $3.25–$8.95; main courses $6.50–$17.95. AE, DC, DISC, MC, V.
Open: Sun–Fri 11am–2am; Sat 11am–3am.

It's clearly not for this curmudgeon. It's loud, frenetic, crowded, and the food left much to be desired. I don't think even the kids are going to be taken in by this brainless "concept" for very long.

★ **Scoozi,** 410 W. Huron. ☎ 943-5900.
Cuisine: ITALIAN. **Reservations:** Required.
Prices: Appetizers $4.95–$5.95 at lunch, $4.95–$7.95 at dinner; pasta $6.95–$8.50 at lunch, $7.95–$11.00 at dinner; main courses $8.95–$14.95 at lunch, $9.95–$15.95 at dinner. AE, DC, DISC, MC, V.
Open: Lunch Mon–Fri 11:30am–2pm: dinner Mon–Thurs 5–10:30pm, Fri–Sat 5–11:30pm, Sun 5–9pm.

Scoozi has been one of the most popular watering holes in this city since opening in December 1986. You can opt for a relatively calm luncheon at Scoozi or the madcap people-scene at night, but on the weekends there is often a wait of up to two hours before being seated. The management, however, distributes pizza and beverages among the waiting masses.

For cafe decor and atmosphere, Scoozi is without peer in Chicago. With its lively strains of classical music buzzing in the background, no other cafe in town can transport you—in spirit—to Europe with quite the same élan as Scoozi. And the food is of exceptional quality.

For an appetizer, you might begin with a pizza smothered with asparagus, mushrooms, and three types of cheese. Next you might try salmaccio, smoked salmon with melon and chives, and then panzanella, antipasto salad on friselle bread. Main courses include pollo stephano, chicken breast with steamed vegetables; tricolored mezzaluna bandiera, cheese-filled pasta with separate pesto, tomato, and Alfredo sauces; and mastaccioli al formaggio, with broccoli, walnuts, and a sauce of four cheeses. Finish your meal with tiramisù, a bing cherry tart, or the granita—chipped ice flavored with cantaloupe.

The dinner menu at Scoozi is twice as long as the lunch menu, and prices are slightly more expensive.

Inexpensive

Hard Rock Cafe, 63 W. Ontario. ☎ 943-2252.

Cuisine: AMERICAN. **Reservations:** Not accepted.
Prices: Appetizers $3.95–$5.95; main courses $5.95–$12.95. AE, MC, V.
Open: Sun–Fri 11am–2am, Sat 11am–3am.

Around the corner from Ed Debevic's (see below) is another establishment, replicated by franchise in various cities, here and abroad, the Hard Rock Cafe. This version of the temple of Rock looks more like a branch of the public library, except for the trademark globe twirling over the portico. It offers shakes, burgers, and fries to all who might dig the memorabilia and the loud rock soundtrack that typifies the Hard Rock style, regardless of location. If you don't binge, you can get away with $10 to $15 per person.

Hat Dance, 325 W. Huron. ☎ 649-0066.

Cuisine: MEXICAN/JAPANESE. **Reservations:** Required.
Prices: Appetizers $3.50–$6.50; main courses $7.95–$15.95. AE, DC, DISC, MC, V.
Open: Lunch Mon–Fri 11:30am–2pm, Sat 11:30am–3:30pm; dinner Mon–Thurs 5–10pm, Fri–Sat 5–11:30pm, Sun 5:30–9pm.

Hat Dance is billed as a Mexican-Japanese restaurant, and only a few of the dishes I sampled rise above the ordinary. Most memorable are the simpler items: an appetizer called *un ostión*, a single oyster in a shot glass filled with salsa; the sirloin tartare, neither Mexican nor Japanese; a cob of roasted corn smothered in hot-and-sour sauce; and a fresh corn tamale filled with shredded chicken and coated with mole poblano. All of which points to a positive outcome: You can make the scene at Hat Dance and not spend a fortune if you avoid the pricey main courses.

Tucci Milan, 6 W. Hubbard. ☎ 222-0044.

Cuisine: ITALIAN. **Reservations:** Required.
Prices: Appetizers $4.75–$8.95; main courses $4.95–$20. AE, DC, DISC, MC, V.
Open: Mon–Thurs 11:30am–10pm, Fri–Sat 11:30am–11pm, Sun 5–9pm.

You might say that Tucci Milan is the city cousin of its country kin, Tucci Benucch (see "Dining Clusters/Complexes" under "Specialty Dining," below), several notches less homey, but a good deal more sophisticated. On the level of decor, the difference is that of high-tech versus high-schlock. Tucci Milan has a ceiling, for example, where hundreds of tiny white Christmas-tree bulbs are strung among the yards of industrial conduit, creating a kind of planetarium-in-the-boiler-room effect, which is actually quite attractive. The layout of tables and banquettes is that of a traditional Italian trattoria. Tucci Milan has a better-than-average kitchen.

For a light snack, I recommend a pizza monte napoleone, a very tasty item said to be a favorite low-calorie lunch choice among Milan's high-fashion models. The crust is very thin with the consistency of matzoh, and topped in this case with arugula, black olives, and thin strips of mozzarella. For dessert, try the espresso tiramisù cake, consisting of layers of chocolate mousse and an Italian cream cheese filling; the incredibly delicious bread pudding with caramel sauce; or the zuccotto, a mixed-layer cake of crushed hazelnuts and white-chocolate mousse. The lunch and dinner menus at Tucci Milan are the same, and offer the usual selection of antipasto, salads, and pastas.

Budget

⭐ **Ed Debevic's,** 640 N. Wells (at Ontario). ☎ **664-1707.**
$ **Cuisine:** AMERICAN. **Reservations:** Not accepted
Prices: Menu items $2.80–$6.25. No credit cards.
Open: Mon–Thurs 11am–midnight, Fri 11am–1am, Sat 10am–1am, Sun 10am–11pm.

Another of entrepreneur Rich Melman's theme-park restaurants, Ed Debevic's is a temple to America's hometown lunch-counter culture. The whole idea behind Ed's is to put you on. The waitresses play the parts of gum-chewing toughies with hearts of gold who could hail from Anywhere, USA. Most are very consciously costumed to fit the image. It's all a performance—but it works.

A more basic reason for Ed's success is that the food is kept simple and reasonably priced. In addition to the basic dinner staples, there's chili and Chicago hot dogs, and daily blue-plate specials, from meat loaf to turkey with dressing and gravy. Ed's also serves as a cocktail lounge. Wherever you sit you are surrounded by fifties nostalgia, while tunes like "Duke of Earl" or other vintage goldies fill the air.

Green Door Tavern, 678 N. Orleans. ☎ **664-5496.**
Cuisine: BURGERS. **Reservations:** Not accepted.
Prices: Appetizers $2.95–$4.95; main courses $4.95–$7.95. AE, DC, MC, V.
Open: Dinner only, daily 5pm–midnight.

Across the street from Hat Dance (see above) is the Green Door Tavern, looking for all the world like an old off-campus hangout. The old wood-frame building was put up temporarily (and presumably illegally) after the 1871 fire, when such construction was banned inside the newly designated "fire zone." Apparently the original framing crew went light on the bracing timbers in a few places, because the whole building lists to the right. Typical of the items on the sandwich menu are the Bearnaiseburger, triple-decker grilled cheese, and the Steve Dahlburger (Dahl is a local radio personality and part owner of the neighboring Hat Dance). Dinner specials are also posted daily and are served after 5pm.

120

$ Mr. Beef, 666 N. Orleans. ☎ 337-8500.
Cuisine: ITALIAN BEEF SUBS.
Prices: Sandwiches from $3.40. No credit cards.
Open: Mon–Sat 9am–6pm.

Something the Midwest can boast of (or maybe it's only Chicago?) that is lacking on either coast is Italian beef sandwiches. Italian beef is thinly shredded slices of roast beef marinated in a tasty brine and distributed to both food stands and the public in two-gallon jars. "Want good Italian beef? Go to Mr. Beef" is the common wisdom. What could be better than a juicy sandwich for $3.40?

Pizzeria Due, 619 N. Wabash (at the corner of Ontario).
☎ 943-2400.
Cuisine: PIZZA. **Reservations:** Not accepted.
Prices: Pizza $3.35–$11.85. AE, CB, DC, DISC, MC, V.
Open: Mon–Thurs 11:30am–1:30am, Fri 11:30am–2:30am, Sat 4pm–2:30am, Sun 4pm–11:30pm.

Two of Chicago's gourmet pizza restaurants, **Pizzeria Uno,** at 29 E. Ohio, at the corner of Wabash (☎ 321-1000), and Pizzeria Due, are jointly owned and located a block from one another. Uno was so successful, but lacking in room for expansion, that Due had to be opened in a lovely, gray-brick Victorian town house on a nearby corner. You can't miss it. The ornate trim is smartly painted in deep green, which makes the building a real standout on the block. You may eat in the restaurant itself on the basement level or, weather permitting, in the outdoor patio right off the sidewalk. One popular feature at Due is the express lunch, a choice of soup or salad, and a personal-size pizza, all served up within five minutes for $4.95. Daily pizza specials for the same price are also featured, with any topping you choose. Salads, sandwiches, and a house minestrone are also available.

5   Near North

Near North, as the area is referred to by Chicagoans, begins more or less above Oak Street. But like so many of Chicago's neighborhoods, there is little agreement among local denizens about the exact boundaries. Traditionally, Near North began at the river, just beyond the Loop, incorporating Streeterville and the Magnificent Mile, as well as the Gold Coast, Old Town, and Lincoln Park. The restaurants described in this section, however, are found within the more restricted zone that begins immediately above the Magnificent Mile and goes up to North Avenue.

The Gold Coast

EXPENSIVE

Pump Room, in the Omni Ambassador East Hotel, 1301 N. State Pkwy. ☎ 266-0360.
Cuisine: AMERICAN. **Reservations:** Required.

Prices: Appetizers $6–$13.50 (beluga caviar $65); main courses $16.50–$26. AE, DC, DISC, MC, V.
Open: Mon–Thurs 7am–10pm, Fri–Sat 7am–midnight. Sun 10:30am–2:30pm (brunch) and 5–10pm.

There was a time in the thirties and forties when celebrities on their transcontinental crossings by train between Hollywood and New York stopped to court the Chicago press from a booth at the Pump Room. Booth One, in those days, had high visibility in the gossip columns. Publicists worked Booth One for its endless bounty of photo opportunities and guaranteed exposure, and for some reason it was a place where a whole lot of celebrities felt comfortable. Ernie Byfield, who died in 1950, owned the Ambassador East during that period and was the creator of the Pump Room. He seems to have had a knack for befriending big-name movie stars. Some of the stars, like Bogart, were even Ernie's friends in return. And Ernie ran a classy hotel, classy enough for the very particular Alfred Hitchcock, who shot some scenes for his masterpiece *North by Northwest* here.

I have some suggestions for meals in today's version of the Pump Room, which under Richard Melman's stewardship is currently trying to recapture its former prominence as a celebrity showcase. If you go looking for the Pump Room Experience at 9 on a Sunday morning, you will be sorely disappointed. The place screams "nightclub," not breakfast. Go in the evening to savor the experience of a graceful and decorous nightspot where you may soak up the fanciful atmosphere and dine well in the bargain.

The selection on the dinner menu is limited to four appetizers—two of which are soups—a seafood salad, and three main courses: two varieties of grilled fish and a sautéed filet of beef. Presumably for someone finding the selection too narrow, an alternative dish

---

Frommer's Smart Traveler: Restaurants

1. Your best bet for an inexpensive meal is an ethnic restaurant outside the city's central tourist hub.

2. Go for lunch rather than dinner at that fancy in-spot you simply refuse to leave Chicago without going to. Lunch menus are normally 10% to 15% cheaper than dinner menus.

3. Even small, ethnic restaurants offer lunchtime specials; several all-you-can-eat buffets are listed in this chapter.

4. Watch your bar bill; this can add up quickly and can easily double the amount you were planning to spend.

5. Reservations are essential at the most fashionable and fine dining restaurants.

6. Like the poet said, "A loaf of bread, a jug of wine . . ." Season permitting, take-out and picnic fare are alternatives to the high cost of restaurants. And Chicago is filled with beautiful green spaces where you can spread your meal under a shady bough.

might be prepared in the kitchen. Five very potable wines are also offered on the menu. My roast eggplant soup, with basil and red pepper, and twin filets of beef with wild mushrooms in bourbon sauce, were superb. My companion was well pleased with her fried calamari with roast garlic-tartare sauce, but indifferent to her main course of Florida red snapper. Some droll wag conceived the dessert I chose, the world's smallest hot-fudge sundae, the ingredients for which were served in individual shot glasses.

An evening at the Pump Room isn't merely intended as a culinary experience; it is also a stop on the circuit of Chicago's nightlife culture. This is not to slight the cuisine, but simply to emphasize that the food here is not "the" event the way it is in places featuring "new cuisine."

The Clybourn Corridor

One of Chicago's shorter diagonal thoroughfares, Clybourn Avenue, running between Division and Belmont Streets, has undergone a radical transformation in recent years. Warehouses and manufactories along this former light industrial corridor have been either razed or converted for other uses. In lots formerly occupied by old, red-brick mills, a succession of elongated mini-malls have sprung up, set back from the street behind ample parking lots, giving the Clybourn Corridor a suburban look. Anchoring the corridor at its southern end, however, are several isolated pockets of genuinely urban attractions, including the following restaurants.

MODERATE

Bossa Nova, 1960 N. Clybourn Ave. ☎ **248-4800.**

> **Cuisine:** TAPAS. **Reservations:** Recommended on weekends.
> **Prices:** Tapas $3.95–$6.95; main courses $9.95–$14.95. CB, DC, DISC, MC, V.
> **Open:** Sun–Thurs 6–10pm; Fri 6pm–2am; Sat 5pm–3am.

You're in the mood for some hip Afro-Latino music, maybe a little dancing, but you're also hungry. If Chicago were Toon Town, you'd see a neon sign from miles away, with a rounded cartoon finger flashing above the entrance to Bossa Nova, proclaiming, "This is the place!" Bossa Nova, in reality, is everybody's fantasy of a sophisticated supper club brought to life. The neighborhood is a bit off the track, like you're headed for a Prohibition-era speakeasy, but you're dressed to the nines. You enter the old industrial building from a side door, descend a flight of stairs, and whammo!—you step into the kind of clublike atmosphere you'd think only Hollywood could imagine or create. It's spacious, yet the seating is intimate; and it's warm, with soft pinpoint lighting, a decor in fine woods and earth tones, and drapery of black velvet.

Then comes supper; there must be over a hundred items to choose from, including more than fifty different appetizer-sized servings called tapas, both hot and cold. You try a few dishes. They're excellent. So you try a few more, and wonder how the kitchen can maintain such high standards when there is so much variety and so many exotic ingredients to contend with. There's grilled Jamaican jerk chicken ($3.95); shrimp, chorizo, and sweet peppers spiced with cumin ($4.95); a sesame-crusted tuna medallion ($5.95); and mashed potato pie with shredded chicken and chilies ($3.95). The daredevil gourmands among you might want to dazzle the more timid souls by calling for a plate of "pasta from hell" ($4.95), marked with three chilies on the jalapeño scale for "seriously hot." A nice thing about tapas is that you can keep it simple or go for broke—if you've got your plastic in tow and a healthy credit line.

At ten, the live music begins, and the party shifts gears, moving onto the dance floor. Reggae, salsa, samba, sounds of the Ivory Coast, what have you—the rhythms are irresistible, music you surrender to, but not at your table. From time to time, of course, you must replenish your lost fluids with a little wine perhaps: something from Bossa Nova's eclectic, international list, or maybe a bit of homegrown, like the Oregon offering called Grateful Red ($22 a bottle)! Bossa Nova definitely is the place for a night out to remember.

★ **Bub City,** 901 W. Weed St. ☎ **266-1200.**

Cuisine: CREOLE/TEX-MEX. **Reservations:** Not accepted.
Prices: Appetizers $3.95–$10.95; main courses $9.95–$19.95. AE, DC, DISC, MC, V.
Open: Lunch Mon–Fri 11:30am–4pm; dinner Mon–Thurs 5–11pm, Fri–Sat 5pm–midnight, Sun 4–10pm.

At the tip of the Clybourn Corridor, just south of North Avenue, the Melman restaurant chain has installed Bub City.

When I entered the bar, Club Bub, I was amazed at how successfully the ambience of a barnlike, edge-of-town roadhouse has been reproduced, right down to the rowdy, foot-stomping crowd scene.

The restaurant is not fancier but is less noisy by several dozen decibels. The food is terrific. There is a superior gumbo, followed by a medley of appetizers, each one tastier—and more finger-licking—than the one before. There are Texas torpedoes—fried jalapeños; a mumbo-jumbo combo of oysters, shrimp, crab claws, and blue crab fingers; Ralphy Boy baked oysters; hot and spicy shrimp; and mushrooms stuffed with crab and shrimp in lemon-butter sauce.

Here you might stop, sated and well satisfied. But noooo. . . . Instead plunge with abandon into the main courses, such as the salmon barbecue, or the mixed grill with salsa pepino, consisting of blackened lamb chop, chicken breast, and boneless pork chop with pepper jelly. Or you might try the huge platter of linguine loaded with home-smoked shrimp and scallops and smothered in a sauce of fresh tarragon, tomatoes, yellow peppers, and scallions in lemon butter. Texas beer (Rattlesnake and Lone Star) and Muther Margaritas prove the ideal beverages to wash down your feast. Don't forget the house specialty, bread pudding, for dessert. When the waitress was asked if they had espresso, she replied, "No, but we have really old coffee." It's that kind of place. On Friday and Saturday, the bar is open until 2am.

⭐ **Goose Island Brewing Company,** 1800 N. Clybourn Ave. ☎ 915-0071.

Cuisine: AMERICAN. **Reservations:** Accepted only for parties of eight or more.

Prices: Appetizers $1.95–$6.95; sandwiches $5.25–$7.50; main courses $7.95–$13.95. AE, DISC, MC, V.

Open: Mon–Thurs 11am–1am; Fri–Sat 11am–2am; Sun 11am–midnight; kitchen closes two hours before the bar.

The best beer in Chicago—hell, some of the best brew in the world—is manufactured at this modest microbrewery on the Clybourn corridor. Don't take my word for it. An impressive cast of professional beer mavens and critics have arrived at the same conclusion. In the course of a year, Goose Island brewmeister Greg Hall (whose dad John is the pub/brewery's owner) mixes up some thirty different varieties of lagers, ales, stouts, pilsners, and porters that change with the seasons. Normally a pint costs $3.25, but a 6-oz. sampler glass is only $1. A friend and I lined up half a dozen sampler brews on the bar in front of us and were hard pressed to choose a winner. I tended toward the bitters, he toward the lagers; or was it the other way around?

The only thing I remember for sure was that we had to be pried from our stools by another companion in order to honor a dinner reservation we'd made elsewhere that same evening. We did manage to get a head start on our meal at the Goose Island Brewery, however, sampling a delicious cup of jalapeño chicken soup and some corn chowder (both $1.95), plus an order of very tangy and delicate fresh mussels, drenched in garlic butter ($6.95). I used to think that Harry Caray's served the best "made-on-the-premises" potato chips in Chicago. Sorry, Harry, it's Goose Island by a head. Goose Island goes through 3,000 lbs. of spuds a week, and the only problem (as at Harry's, to be fair) is that you have to muster some self-control—the chips are free!

6   Lincoln Park

Near The Park

VERY EXPENSIVE

⭐ **Ambria,** 2300 Lincoln Park North, ☎ 472-0076.

Cuisine: FRENCH. **Reservations:** Required.

Prices: Appetizers. $6.50–$10.25; main courses $19.50–$29.95 fixed-price meals $42–$55. AE, DC, DISC, MC, V.

Open: Dinner only, Mon–Thurs 6–9:30pm, Fri–Sat 6–10:30pm.

Near Lincoln Park Conservatory and housed in the impressive former Belden Stratford Hotel, Ambria is ensconced in several large rooms off the old lobby. The hotel's name very conveniently contains both the cross street of its address—Belden—and the birthplace of the great bard, suggesting one obvious explanation for the placement of his statue across the road.

Ambria is, quite simply, one of Chicago's finest restaurants. The dimly lit, wood-paneled interior is refined and intimate, almost clublike, and eminently civilized. On one national survey after another honoring the nation's finest restaurants, the name Ambria appears time and again. There is not much room at the top, but Ambria maintains its position with grace and consistency.

The menu changes frequently, of course, so the dishes described here are simply examples of the style of the preparations you will encounter while dining at Ambria. On one recent occasion, my companion and I began our meal with a flaky, mouthwatering napoleon of lobster, bacalhao, and crispy potato ($11.95), and a pastry stuffed with escargot and summer vegetables ($8.95) that was equally successful. This was followed by an imaginative salad comprised of tender squab with red cabbage, endive, and bacon ($11.95). For our main courses, we chose a roasted rack of lamb with stuffed baby eggplant, couscous, and artichoke chips, served in the lamb's herb-scented natural juices ($28.50); and the roasted medallions of New Zealand venison with wild rice pancakes, caramelized rhubarb, and root vegetables, accompanied by a blackberry sauce. Both dishes were superb.

The wine steward had provided us with an excellent recommendation, a California cabernet, one of those wonderful private cellar selections the Napa Valley is justly famous for. We chose our desserts first from the daily pastry creations ($8), a concoction rich with cream and dark chocolate, then exercised a bit more discretion in our second selection, the bowl of firm and sweet fresh red raspberries ($9).

INEXPENSIVE

⭐ **Big Shoulders Cafe,** Clark Street and North Ave. at the Chicago Historical Society. ☎ **642-4600.**
Cuisine: CAFE FARE. **Reservations:** Accepted.
Prices: Appetizers $2.95–$4.50; salads and sandwiches $2.95–$7.95; main courses $6.95–$7.95. AE, DC, MC, V.
Open: Mon–Fri 11:30am–8pm; Sat 11am–8pm; Sun 10:30am–8pm.

Here's an option for a nice light meal, whether or not you are tying the occasion into a swing through the Chicago Historical Society, which occupies the bulk of these quarters. The Big Shoulders is not just a cafeteria serving the needs of the museum traffic, but a popular restaurant in its own right, which has recently expanded its hours and is now open even when the Historical Society is closed.

Soon after you are seated in Big Shoulders, your waiter will appear with a plate of owner Jerome Kliejunas's trademark cornbread, generously sprinkled with flecks of jalapeño and millet. This is a truly tasty and original treat. A very nice luncheon or supper can then be made of the Caesar salad with grilled chicken breast or strips of sirloin ($7.95). Much sought after as well is the double Sheboygan bratwurst with grilled onions, roasted potatoes, and a small vegetable salad ($6.95). Those who wish to drop in for coffee or tea and dessert are also welcome. Occasionally the cafe is closed for private parties during the dinner hours, so it is best to call ahead if that is the time frame you have in mind.

$ R. J. Grunts, 2056 Lincoln Park West. ☎ **929-5363.**

Cuisine: AMERICAN. **Reservations:** Not accepted. $4.95–$13.95
Prices: Appetizers 75¢–$4.50: sandwiches and main courses. AE, DC, DISC, MC, V.
Open: Mon–Thurs 11:30am–11pm (10pm in winter), Fri–Sat 11:30am–midnight (11 pm in winter), Sun 10am–2:30pm (brunch) and 3:30–10pm.

For Richard Melman and his Lettuce Entertain You restaurant empire, it all began in relative modesty at R. J. Grunts. Grunts is one of those restaurant/bars that somehow manages to be all things to all people. The neighborhood crowd hangs out there, it's popular with the young college-age set, and even the cops on the beat go for the modified P. J. Clarke's atmosphere. One big draw at Grunts, which began as a salad and veggies eatery at the dawn of the health-food movement, is the Sunday brunch, an all-you-can-eat feast from the salad bar, plus such side dishes as omelets or eggs Benedict. Be advised there can be a long wait for the brunch. The menu otherwise features many types of burgers, chicken and vegetarian dishes, and steaks and chops. Grunts is located at the corner of Dickens Street, just north of Armitage, directly across from Lincoln Park, and incidentally, right near a highly regarded small museum, the Chicago Academy of Sciences.

On or Near Armitage

VERY EXPENSIVE

Charlie Trotter's, 816 W. Armitage. ☎ **248-6228.**

Cuisine: NOUVELLE. **Reservations:** Required.
Prices: Fixed-price dinners $55, $75, and $85. AE, DC, MC, V.
Open: Dinner only, Tues–Sat 5:30–9:30pm.

The grand menu dégustation, $75 a person for a minimum party of two, is the perfect introduction to the innovative creations of the owner/chef who has given his name to this critically acclaimed palace of nouvelle cuisine. Mr. Trotter's "tasting" menu consists of many courses and changes frequently (there is no à la carte menu). The evening I dined here, the meal began with a terrine lightheartedly dubbed the amuse bouche. Next followed a very colorful serving of striped artichoke cannelloni cooked in a saffron oil of roasted garlic and aged chèvre, and then a seafood course, smoked sea scallops with a timbale of lobster. The greens were a sheaf of shredded Belgian endive accompanied by bits of Stilton cheese, apricot, watercress, and almond slivers. A dish of seared salmon in a sesame crust preceded a selection of flavored granita (chipped ices), which was followed by a meat course of spit-roasted free-range veal with zucchini. Dessert was a chocolate mousse with bananas in a caramel-rum sauce, and an assortment of petits fours, accompanied by coffee freshly brewed at tableside. The wine was a 1979 BV Burgundy Reserve, a superior California selection.

The waiter boasted that 80% of the produce used at Charlie Trotter's was grown organically, and most of the meat is pasture-raised. The restaurant further recycles all plastics and paper generated in their operation. A vegetable dégustation menu ($55) is also available and no doubt represents a similar lush parade of highly stylized presentations as that of the big production to which I was so happily treated.

EXPENSIVE

⭐ **Geja's,** 340 W. Armitage, ☎ **281-9101.**
Cuisine: FONDUE. **Reservations:** Required.
Prices: Appetizers $7.25; main courses $18.50–$26.50. AE, CB, DC, DISC, MC, V.
Open: Dinner only, Mon–Thurs 5–10:30pm, Fri 5pm–midnight, Sat 5pm–12:30am, Sun 4:30–10pm.

Geja's (pronounced "*Gay*-haz") was the first wine bar in Chicago, opened in 1963 by John Davis, who is very active in this Lincoln Park community. The specialty here is fondue, a culinary anachronism that was nonetheless quite fashionable a quarter century ago. Fortunately, Mr. Davis has preserved single-handedly in Chicago the fondue experience, which is both fun and a welcome break from the ordinary mode of dining.

If there are at least two in your party (all main courses are served for two or more), choose the connoisseur fondue dinner, the best Geja's has to offer. The meal begins with a cheese fondue appetizer, a dish of imported Gruyère and kirsch, kept melted over a burner at your table, into which you dip apple wedges and chunks of dark bread; the flavorful Gruyère is the key to the tastiness of this delicious dish. Next, a huge platter arrives, brimming with squares of beef tenderloin, lobster tails, and jumbo shrimp—all raw—and a caldron of boiling oil to cook them in. These delicacies are accompanied by a variety of raw vegetables, such as green pepper, mushroom, broccoli, and small potatoes, which are also softened in the oil. And when the flaming chocolate fondue arrives for dessert, with fresh fruit and pound cake for dipping, you want to beg for mercy. As an added incentive, Geja's usually has a flamenco or classical Spanish guitarist to provide the background music.

MODERATE

Four Farthings, 2060 N. Cleveland. ☎ **935-2060.**
Cuisine: CONTINENTAL. **Reservations:** Not accepted.
Prices: Appetizers $3.95–$6.95; main courses $10.95–$17.95 AE, CB, DC, DISC, MC, V.
Open: Mon–Thurs 11:30am–2am, Fri–Sat 11:30am–3am, Sun 11am–2am (brunch 11am–3pm).

Several blocks in from the park along Dickens (at a triangle formed by Lincoln and Cleveland Avenues) is a tavern and a restaurant owned by Bill and John Nordhem that has been a Lincoln Park institution for many years. At the Four Farthings, the restaurant and the bar clientele are completely different, the former catering to a somewhat upscale gourmet set, the latter to a sports crowd who like to gather for Bears and Cubs games. A delicious shrimp Caesar salad and an equally tasty appetizer of smoked-salmon ravioli might start your meal. Four Farthings's menu features seafood main courses. The restaurant's wine selection is also quite extensive, with many excellent varieties sold by the glass.

The Four Farthings is excellent for an after-theater supper, or just dessert and cognac. The restaurant also has an outdoor cafe in season.

North Halsted Street Restaurant Row

North Halsted Street's Restaurant Row is a strip of fancy shops and restaurants of recent vintage running from Armitage to Fullerton.

MODERATE

Café Ba-Ba-Reeba!, 2024 N. Halsted. ☎ 935-5000.

Cuisine: SPANISH. **Reservations:** Recommended, especially on weekends.
Prices: Tapas $1.95–$7.50; main courses $8.95–$11.95. AE, DC, MC, V.
Open: Lunch Tues–Fri 11:30am–2:30pm, Sat 11:30am–3:30pm; dinner Mon–Thurs 5:30–11pm, Fri–Sat 5:30pm–midnight, Sun 5–10:30pm.

Located at the southern end of Restaurant Row, near Armitage, is Café Ba-Ba-Reeba!, marked by a neon sign announcing *tapas*. Café Ba-Ba-Reeba! is a valiant attempt to popularize the merits of this unique Iberian snack tradition with a selection of some 26 hot and cold tapas of the restaurant's own creation.

Inside, the café includes a covered patio, two bars, and several dining rooms. The bright acrylic and oil paintings, mostly pop portraiture and other representations, are some of the most delightful you will see gathered in one room anywhere in Chicago.

The *plato de la casa* is a plate of very satisfactory traditional meats and cheeses. The queso con albahaca, slices of fresh mozzarella on plum tomato topped with fresh basil leaf, was excellent. Among the hot tapas, the pincho de pollo y chorizo, chicken and chorizo sausage brochettes with a dip of garlic-cumin mayonnaise, was economical and very tasty. Be careful and keep track of what you're ordering—those tapas quickly add up.

For dessert you might try the tarta de frambuesa, a delicious raspberry-custard tart, or a chocolate concoction served with ice cream called profiteroles de chocolate.

Café Bernard, 2100 N. Halsted. ☎ 871-2100.

Cuisine: FRENCH. **Reservations:** Recommended.
Prices: Appetizers $3.50–$6.50; main courses $12–$25. AE, DC, MC, V.
Open: Dinner only, Sun–Thurs 5–10:30pm, Fri–Sat 5–11:30pm.

The Café Bernard features *cuisine du pays français* at moderate prices—many dishes are in the $12 to $14 range. This little French restaurant on the corner, incidentally, has the authentic look of a Parisian back-street bistro.

⭐ **Carlucci,** 2215 N. Halsted. ☎ **281-1220.**
Cuisine: ITALIAN. **Reservations:** Required.
Prices: Appetizers $4.95–$7.50; main courses $10.95–$22.95. AE, CB, DC, MC, V.
Open: Dinner only, Mon–Thurs 5:30–10:30pm, Fri–Sat 5:30–11:30pm, Sun 5–10pm.

Located at the far-northern end of this strip is Carlucci, conceivably the best Italian restaurant in Chicago. What appears a simple aw-ninged storefront from the street, is in fact a deceptively large, multi-environment restaurant, including an interior open-air court-yard. During your dinner, try a glass of Spanna, a dry red wine squeezed from the nebbiolo grape in Italy's Piemonte region.

Crusty, soft-centered bread to dip in a puddle of virgin olive oil spiked with hot chili peppers is served with each meal at Carlucci. The many antipasti on the menu include several varieties of pizza. I chose an insalata quattro colori of radish, arugula, endive, and tiny yellow pear tomatoes, flavored with walnuts and Gorgonzola, and dressed with lemon juice and olive oil—a superb combination. Half orders are permitted, so you can sample both a pasta and a meat main course. The linguine della nonna, served with thin vertical slices of zucchini, is soaked lightly in olive oil seasoned with roasted garlic, and topped with raw tomatoes and toasted breadcrumbs. The paillard di vitello ai ferri consists of scaloppine of veal, seasoned with lemon sage and grilled to tender perfection.

Oo La La! 3335 N. Halsted St. ☎ **935-7708.**
Cuisine: FRENCH/ITALIAN. **Reservations:** Accepted.
Prices: Appetizers $4.25–$6.95; main courses $8.95–$15.95. AE, MC, V.
Open: Dinner daily 5:30–11pm; Sun brunch 10am–3pm.

It happens sometimes in big cities where there's a surplus of both creativity and storefronts. A strange and exciting synthesis can oc-cur; wait-on-line restaurants spring up in modest spaces that, in a prior existence, might have housed the neighborhood dry cleaner or the corner hardware store. In such a space, Oo La La!—a border bistro—provides both scene and substance for some sixty lucky pa-trons at a time, who squeeze into its swank and chummy confines on a given night.

Border bistro? The term refers to the bi-national inspiration of Chef Jill Dietz-Rosenthall's dishes, which may be traced to the typical workaday Parisian bistro or Roman trattoria, but which have been modified and pampered to satisfy the more demanding palates of those who dine out frequently. So, at Oo La La!, you may have your grilled chicken ($10.95) or roasted lamb shank ($12.95), and eat it too, so to speak, not only with gusto but with pleasure. The pasta dishes, on the other hand, have evolved somewhat farther from the steamtables of the homeland trattorias. But pasta is like that, be-cause nine-tenths of the challenge is in the sauce, and Chef Jill's al-chemy in this medium is on a par with the best Chicago has to offer. Here again, however, her emphasis is on simplicity and preparation, rather than novelty for its own sake. Take the penne with smoked eggplant in a tomato and basil sauce with goat cheese ($9.95); the pasta is embraced, not smothered. Even the outrageous tomato pumpkin ravioli—tomato pasta stuffed with pumpkin in a sage cream sauce ($11.95)—however arch, is food first and foremost. Oo La La!, just north of Belmont, about an $8 cab ride from downtown, is definitely in, definitely fun, and definitely good.

INEXPENSIVE

P.S. Bangkok 2, 2521 N. Halsted. ☎ **348-0072.**

> **Cuisine:** THAI. **Reservations:** Not accepted.
> **Prices:** Appetizers $2.50–$6.95; main courses $3.50–$12.95. AE, DC, DISC, MC, V.
> **Open:** Mon–Thurs 11:30am–10pm, Fri–Sat 11:30am–11:30pm, Sun 4:30–10pm.

This is a Thai restaurant with oodles of dishes, mostly in the $5 to $8 range. With a menu of 20 appetizers, 10 soups, and more than 24 main courses, you ought to be able to find something to tempt your palate—though for many of us, practically any Thai platter is a tasty treat.

BUDGET

Edwardo's, 2120 N. Halsted. ☎ **871-3400.**

> **Cuisine:** PIZZA. **Reservations:** Not accepted. **Subway/El:** From the Fullerton stop of the Ravenswood or Howard line, walk south on Halsted; from the Armitage stop on the Ravenswood line, walk north on Halsted.
> **Prices:** Pizzas $9.50–$22; all-you-can-eat pizza and salad Mon–Sat 11:30am–3pm $4.95. AE, MC, V.
> **Open:** Mon–Thurs 11am–midnight, Fri–Sat 11am–1am, Sun 11am–11:30pm.

Some locals claim that Edwardo's has the best pizza in Chicago. The chain has several locations, and the all-you-can-eat special is unique in Chicago.

$ Grants, 2138 N. Halsted. ☎ **348-3665.**

> **Cuisine:** AMERICAN. **Reservations:** Not accepted.
> **Prices:** Menu items $2.50–$7.50. AE, CB, DC, MC, V.
> **Open:** Sun–Thurs 11am–11pm, Fri–Sat 11:30am–midnight.

Grants has windows that open onto the street and designates itself with a sign in one of them as "a neighborhood tavern," a plausible enough claim judging from the comfortable informality of the place. The menu includes omelets and sandwiches. On Tuesday drinks are $2, and on Friday meals are half price.

$ Nookies, Too, 2114 N. Halsted. ☎ **327-1400.**

> **Cuisine:** AMERICAN
> **Prices:** Menu items $1.95–$8.95. CB, DC, MC, V.
> **Open:** Mon–Thurs 6:30am–11pm, Fri–Sat 24 hours, Sun 12:01am–9pm.

Nookies, Too is open for breakfast, lunch, and dinner, serving hash and eggs, eggs Benedict, omelets (over a dozen varieties), blintzes, pancakes, burgers, sandwiches, and blue-plate specials. Cheery, well-lighted, and with its big counter, it's an appealing place for a good, solid, everyday meal.

Lincoln Avenue

INEXPENSIVE

Jada, 1909 N. Lincoln. ☎ **280-2326.**

Cuisine: THAI. **Reservations:** Not accepted.
Prices: Appetizers $2.95–$6.95; main courses $3.95–$7.95. AE, DC, MC, V.
Open: Dinner only, Mon 5–10pm, Tues–Sat 5–11pm, Sun 4–10pm.

Jada is a Thai restaurant offering such standards as *nam tok* (stir-fried spicy marinated beef) and chicken satay appetizers, lemongrass soup, and numerous traditional dishes like chili chicken and tomato squid.

Lindo Mexico, 2642 N. Lincoln. ☎ **871-4832.**

Cuisine: MEXICAN. **Reservations:** Not accepted.
Prices: Appetizers $3.95–$8.50; main courses $7.25–$12.95. AE, DC, MC, V.
Open: Sun–Thurs 11am–2am, Fri–Sat 11am–5am.

According to a resident of Lincoln Park, the Lindo Mexico serves authentic Mexican dishes. The place is immense, with many rooms, and is usually packed, an undeniable indication of its popularity.

Ranalli's Pizzeria, Libations & Collectibles, 1925 N. Lincoln. ☎ 642-4700.

Cuisine: ITALIAN/PIZZA. **Reservations:** Not accepted.
Prices: Appetizers $2.95–$5.50; main courses $6.50–$12.95. AE, CB, DC, DISC, MC, V.
Open: Sun–Fri 11am–2am, Sat 11am–3am.

On the east side of the street is Lincoln on the Mall, where this outdoor cafe and bar has some three-score tables spread out on its patio under the sky. Acres of memorabilia (the "collectibles") line the walls of the adjoining indoor restaurant and bar, though in the proper weather the festive potential of the open-air setting far outshines the cavelike atmosphere inside and under cover (unless you're a sports fan glued to the big game). Thin crust (as opposed to "Chicago" deep-dish) pizza is the specialty, along with Philadelphia-style "hoagie" sandwiches, salads, pasta, ribs, and steak.

7   The Mid-North Side

In Chicago, where so many Germans settled, particularly in the Mid-North Side area, there remain several German bakeries, delis, and eateries. Most of these are located along Lincoln Avenue, including **Kuhn's Delicatessen,** 3053 N. Lincoln (☎ 525-9019); the **Meyer Import Delicatessen,** 3306 N. Lincoln (☎ 281-8979); **Dinkel's Bakery,** 3329 N. Lincoln (☎ 281-7300); and the **Paulina Market,** 3501 N. Lincoln (☎ 248-6272).

In addition to Zum Deutschen Eck (see below), **Schulien's Restaurant and Saloon,** at 2100 W. Irving Park Rd. (☎ 478-2100), preserves the old German traditions of the neighborhood and is a favorite Mid-North Side landmark from the turn of the century.

German and Eastern European–style sausages are the specialty at **Joe's Homemade Sausage House,** 452 N. Western (☎ **478-5443**). The pastry delights of Eastern Europe are featured at **Tomas Bakery,** 4054 N. Lincoln (☎ **472-6401**), including lots of gooey whipped-cream concoctions. Strictly for bread, including all the German favorites like pumpernickel, Bauernbrot, and Kommissbrot, try the **North Star Bakery,** 4545 N. Lincoln (☎ **561-9858**).

Another of the neighborhood's reliable German-style restaurants is **Heidelberger Fass,** 4300 N. Lincoln (☎ **478-2486**).

Moderate

Bella Vista, 1001 W. Belmont Ave. ☎ **404-0111.**
  Cuisine: ITALIAN. **Reservations:** Recommended for dinner on weekends. **Subway/El:** Go to the Belmont stop on the Howard line.
  Prices: Appetizers $4.95–$6.95; main courses $9.25–$17.95. AE, DC, MC, V.
  Open: Mon–Thurs 11:30am–midnight, Fri–Sat 11:30am–2am, Sun 5–10pm.

Near the corner of Sheffield, the Bella Vista was installed in an old bank building, where the former financial institution's glorious and ornate interior decor of columns, painted plaster, and marble—not to mention a skylight covering virtually the entire ceiling of one room—have been totally preserved.

The food at Bella Vista—the in-spot along the Belmont entertainment strip—is classic Italian, with a slightly nouvelle accentuation. Among the appealing selections are the antipasti di giorno ($6.95), with seven different items daily; the pasta del mare ($17.95), black-pepper linguine with prawns, clams, mussels, and roasted peppers; and the bisteca griglia ($17.95), strip steak with garlic and portobello mushrooms and potato ravioli.

Moti Mahal, 1033 W. Belmont (at the corner of Kenmore St.).
  ☎ **348-4392.**
  Cuisine: INDIAN. **Reservations:** Not accepted.
  Prices: Appetizers $3.50–$8; main courses $8–$18. AE, DC, MC, V.
  Open: Daily 11am–10pm.

Moti Mahal is a simple, moderately priced Indian restaurant that hosts a lively dinner crowd, serving the usual wide selection of curries, kormas, biryanis, and so forth.

Vinny's, 2901 N. Sheffield Ave. ☎ **871-0990.**
  Cuisine: CLASSIC ITALIAN. **Reservations:** Recommended, especially for dinner on Fri–Sat. **Subway/El:** Take the Ravenswood line to the Diversey stop and walk north on Sheffield.
  Prices: Appetizers $2.50–$11.95; main courses $7.95–$22.95. AE, DC, MC, V.
  Open: Mon–Thurs 5:30–11pm (midnight for pizzas and salads), Fri–Sat 5:30–midnight (1am for pizzas and salads), Sun 5–10pm.

Vinny's is in! An old warehouse has been converted into a family restaurant on the scale of a continental cafe, and as enormous as the space is with its two hall-size separate rooms, you will still have to wait for a table during peak dinner hours. How to explain Vinny's success? The time-honored formula of quality…and quantity.

Vinny's has locked step with the new Chicago "tradition" of serving family-style portions that can easily stretch for three or four people. For starters, try spicy broccoli ($3.95), or a generous platter of fried calamari ($5.95). The Goomba chicken plate ($11.95), with sausage, peppers, onions, and roasted potatoes, is certainly big enough to share; the platter ($21.95) would serve a small army. Don't miss the Aunt Tessie's rum cake for dessert, or the homemade lemon ice if you're in the mood for something lighter.

Zum Deutschen Eck, 2924 N. Southport. ☎ 525-8389.

Cuisine: GERMAN. **Reservations:** Recommended. **Bus:** Take the Lincoln Ave. bus no. 11 to Diversey, and walk west to Southport.

Prices: Appetizers $2.50–$6.95; cold and hot appetizers serving two to four persons $13.95–$18.95; main courses $11.95–$18.95. AE, DC, MC, V.

Open: Mon–Thurs 11am–midnight, Fri noon–2am, Sat noon–3am, Sun noon–midnight.

Zum Deutschen Eck translates as "The German Corner," a restaurant housed in a large Bavarian-style chalet just north of Diversey and west of Lincoln Avenue, where the menu features the best of German and continental cooking.

After munching on the fresh rolls and breadsticks served at the beginning of each meal, try liver-dumpling consommé ($2.50), accompanied by a crisp cucumber salad ($1.95). Owner Al Wirth, Jr., whose father opened Zum Deutschen Eck in the late fifties, suggests the *Ochsenmaul* ($3.95), which literally means calves' cheeks, and tastes something like a sweeter, more tender version of prosciutto. I ordered the German Schlact Platte ($14.95), a selection of German wursts and smoked pork loin, served with parsley potatoes and sauerkraut; never have I sampled a more delicious knackwurst or Thueringer bratwurst, which it turns out are procured from local butchers and contain no filler, but only pure meat. Dinners here include soup, appetizer, and salad. You can drink draft Dortmunder lager during your meal, and for dessert, there's a small but scrumptious Black Forest devil's food cake with fresh whipped cream.

Ample parking is available at Zum Deutschen Eck, and the music—sing-along and schmaltzy of course—never stops, as a duo of accordion and drums bang out one familiar beer-drinking song after another, alternating between German and English.

Inexpensive

In addition to the following, **Mongolian House,** at 3410 N. Clark (☎ 935-1100), has maintained its reputation for many years as a reliable neighborhood restaurant specializing in northern Chinese food.

Ann Sather's, 929 W. Belmont. ☎ 348-2378.

Cuisine: SWEDISH. **Reservations:** Not accepted.
Prices: Appetizers $1–$7; main courses $6.95–$11.95. MC, V.
Open: Daily 7am–11pm.

A sign hanging by the door marks Ann Sather's with the following inscription: "Once one of many neighborhood Swedish restaurants, Ann Sather's is the only one that remains." It's a real Chicago institution, where you can enjoy Swedish meatballs with buttered noodles and brown gravy, or the Swedish sampler of duck breast with lingonberry glaze, meatball, potato-sausage dumpling, sauerkraut, and brown beans. All meals are full dinners, including appetizer, entree, vegetable, potato, and dessert. On Monday nights there are live performances upstairs at Ann Sather's in a cabaret setting. There is another branch at 5207 N. Clark (☎ 271-6677).

★ **Barry's Spot,** 5759 N. Broadway. ☎ 769-2900.

Cuisine: PIZZA. **Reservations:** Not accepted.
Prices: Appetizers and soups $1.95–$4.95; pasta dishes and sandwiches $3.95–$6.95; pizza $5.70–$17.95. AE, CB, DC, DISC, JCB, MC, V.
Open: Mon–Thurs 4pm–1am, Fri–Sat 4pm–2am, Sun 4pm–midnight.

Great-tasting pizza is the specialty here—thin, pan, or stuffed varieties with homemade sausage, fresh mushrooms, zucchini, eggplant, or sliced tomatoes. Barry's also has freshly baked lasagne, and vegetable-and-spaghetti parmigiana (eggplant, zucchini, and mushrooms with meat sauce), each complete with a healthy serving of salad and French bread. All main courses are served with minestrone soup as well. Owners Barry and Barbara Bernsen take the time to greet customers, and if you are an out-of-towner, they'll be happy to give you directions.

8 Neighborhoods & Ethnic Areas

Wicker Park

MODERATE

★ **Club Lucky,** 1824 W. Warbansia (at the corner of Honore, near North and Damen). ☎ 227-2300.

Cuisine: ITALIAN AMERICAN. **Reservations:** Recommended.
Subway/El: Take the O'Hare line to Damen, then walk northwest (consult map).
Prices: Appetizers $4.95–$9.95; main courses $5.95–$18.95. MC, V.
Open: Mon–Thurs 5–11pm, Fri–Sat 5pm–midnight, Sun 4–10pm.

Club Lucky is one of the hottest spots in Chicago, in one of the city's most up-and-coming neighborhoods, near the home court of the Chicago Bulls. The scene here is youngish, and very dress-up; expect to wait for a seating.

Club Lucky seems to have been carved from a local fifties-era corner tavern with a catering business in the back room. In fact, the place was designed to look like that, with plenty of Naugahyde banquettes, a Formica-topped bar and tables, and Captain Video ceiling fixtures.

You may or may not take to the scene, but the food does not disappoint. Prices overall are moderate, and the portions generous.

Take the large calamari appetizer ($7.95)—"for two," the menu says—my friend and I nibbled calamari out of the take-out container at home for the next two days. The menu offers real Italian home-style cooking, such as *pasta e fagioli* (thick macaroni-and-bean soup—really a kind of stew). You might also order the rigatoni with veal meatballs, served with steamed escarole and melted slabs of mozzarella ($10.95); or the spicy, grilled boneless pork chops served with sour peppers ($12.95).

⭐ **Mareva's,** 1200 N. Milwaukee Ave. ☎ **227-4000.**
Cuisine: POLISH. **Reservations:** Required.
Prices: Appetizers $3.50–$9.95; main courses $8–21.95. AE, DC, MC, V.
Open: Lunch Sat–Sun 11:30am–3pm; dinner Fri–Sat 5pm–midnight, Sun 5–10pm.

A very fine Polish restaurant is located on the fringes of Wicker Park. Before they opened the restaurant, Stanley and Irene Idzik had managed the family catering business part-time. When their children grew up, Irene was able to launch the restaurant of her dreams, Mareva's.

Mareva's reminds us of sophistication and continental charm, celebrating the best of Polish culture and cookery with considerable dignity. Wednesday through Sunday a pianist plays Chopin and other classical pieces at both lunch and dinner.

In Slavic fashion, you might begin your dinner with shots of frozen vodka, then follow with your choice of pirogi. There is one stuffed with a chicken mousse flavored with cognac, leeks, and cream; and another with a mousse of swordfish and sole, served with homemade yogurt, dill, and pear sauce. The traditional pirogi filled with veal, potato, and cabbage, served with sour cream, is also on the menu. Next, try one of the borschts, the clear beet or the Ukrainian, both of which are savory and salutary. Follow this with a perfect Caesar salad. From the game dishes, you might choose the lean duck breast that is first grilled and then baked in a juice of oranges and champagne, or the venison in a sauce of mushrooms and herbs over a bed of wild rice. For dessert, you might choose the fruit compote à la polonaise, fresh fruit served hot over vanilla ice cream with a dash of brandy; or one of several pastries.

The luncheon menu at Mareva's is more modestly priced, which makes the restaurant a bargain as well as a culinary standout. And from the banqueting side of the operation, which still hosts and caters weddings and other social functions on the upper stories of the same building, there is a unique carryout service. The main intention of this service is to provide a Polish meal for home-catered parties, but individuals giving a day's notice may also take out this well-packed "nine-course" special, which includes clear borscht or assorted pirogi, fresh green beans and carrots, salad, new potatoes with parsley, butter-fried chicken, roast beef in gravy, potato dumpling, Polish sausage and sauerkraut, rolls and butter, and pastries. Valet parking for 350 cars is available.

INEXPENSIVE

The Bongo Room, 1560 N. Damen. ☎ 489-0690.

Cuisine: BREAKFAST/LIGHT LUNCH. **Reservations:** Not required.
Prices: Most items $1.50–$6.
Open: Mon–Fri 6:30am–3pm; Sat–Sun 10am–2:30pm.

At about seven-thirty in the morning, the commuters are streaming by this little storefront oasis, racing to the station next door to catch the downtown El. A fair number of them pop in here first for take-out, or pause long enough to enjoy their large cup of cappuccino or caffe latte ($2) with perhaps a homebaked muffin ($1.50), while seated at one of the handful of tables that line the plate glass window. Buried behind their papers, they take in the rumbling of the trains through one ear, and the blaring arias that are the ambient music of the Bongo Room, through the other. Quiche and other good light fare is also served, all of it well prepared and reasonably priced.

Cafe Bolero, 2252 N. Western Ave. ☎ 227-9000.

Cuisine: CUBAN/YUGOSLAVIAN. **Reservations:** Not required.
Prices: Appetizers $1.95–$4.50; main courses $4.95–$11.95. AE, MC, V.
Open: Tues–Sun 9:30am–10pm.

This is perhaps a bit farther west than most visitors will want to travel. But the more adventurous among you will be rewarded if you do. The Cafe Bolero is the combined enterprise of a multicultural husband-and-wife team; he's Cuban, she's Serbian. The cafe was brand-spanking-new in 1994, very tastefully laid out, even possessing a touch of elegance—all the more noticeable in this lack-luster, lower-middle-class neighborhood. Most of the dishes lean toward the Caribbean; this is certainly one of the few restaurants west of the Appalachians where you can get a genuine Cuban sandwich, grilled pork and cheese on French-style bread ($3.50). They also have tostones (fried plantains), but these are very special, cupped on top and filled with ground beef picadillo ($4.50). One Slavic-style dish is the homemade grilled sausage, with feta cheese and marinated roasted peppers ($6.50 for one, $11.95 for two). And there's a daily entrée as well, like picadillo criollo ($4.95), or bifstec Palomilla ($7.95). Espresso coffee and cafe con leche are also available.

Hyde Park

In addition to the listings below, two restaurants to keep in mind are the **Piccolo Mondo Café,** 1642 E. 56th St. (☎ 643-1106), fea-turing gourmet Italian take-out, and the other **Medici** (☎ 667-4008) at Harper Court (between 52nd and 53rd Streets), a more formal, sit-down–style restaurant than its counterpart on 57th Street. Hyde Park also has a branch of **Starbucks** coffee shop at Harper and 53rd (☎ 324-1241).

INEXPENSIVE

Medici, 1327 E. 57th St. ☎ 667-7394.
> **Cuisine:** AMERICAN.
> **Prices:** Appetizers $2.50–$6.50; main courses $3.45–$8.95; pizzas $3.50–$18.95. MC, V.
> **Open:** Sun–Thurs 7am–12:30am, Fri–Sat 7am–1am.

One local community leader characterizes Medici's as "the most popular restaurant in Hyde Park." No doubt. Medici is the paradigm of the college hangout, serving the kind of survival food generations of college students know so well. The feature here is the "big" hamburger, a half-pound patty served on either black bread or a Kaiser roll. Another attraction is the restaurant's second-floor outdoor terrace.

University Gardens, 1373 E. 53rd St. ☎ 684-6660.
> **Cuisine:** MIDDLE EASTERN. **Reservations:** Not accepted.
> **Prices:** Appetizers $1.25–$3.25; main courses $5.95–$9.95. No credit cards.
> **Open:** Mon–Sat 11am–10pm, Sun 1–10pm.

When he lived here, Muhammad Ali's favorite restaurant was the University Gardens. It is one of those small (12 tables), intimate places, where the wall space is crowded with memorabilia that reflect an eccentric owner; best of the lot are the snapshots of Ali, flashing his angelic and genial smile. The fare includes homemade pita bread, hummus, felafel, lamb dishes—everything fresh, not frozen or from the can—and thick Turkish coffee.

BUDGET

Jimmy's Woodlawn Tap, 1172 E. 55th St. ☎ 643-5516.
> **Cuisine:** BURGERS/SANDWICHES.
> **Prices:** Menu items $2–$5. No credit cards.
> **Open:** Mon–Fri 11am–2am, Sat 11am–3am.

This is a popular U of C hangout and hamburger joint, and the only actual tavern within the confines of Hyde Park. With its three rooms, though, Jimmy's is big enough to accommodate the weekend crowds.

Valois, 1518 E. 53rd St. ☎ 667-0647.
> **Cuisine:** CAFETERIA.
> **Prices:** Menu items $1–$7. No credit cards.
> **Open:** Daily 6am–10pm.

Everybody's favorite greasy spoon in Hyde Park is the venerable Valois, where the slogan "see your food" emblazons the outdoor sign. A local bank president once threw a black-tie dinner here to celebrate his 40th birthday. It's a great place to start the day with a three-egg cheese omelet.

Bridgeport

This neighborhood is home of the Daley clan, including the current mayor, and also the White Sox, who moved to their new stadium in 1991.

BUDGET

$ Bridgeport Restaurant, 3500 S. Halsted (at the corner of 35th St.). ☎ 247-2826.

> **Cuisine:** COFFEE SHOP. **Reservations:** Not accepted. **Bus:** Take the Halsted St. bus no. 8 to 35th St.
> **Prices:** Menu items $3–$9.50. No credit cards.
> **Open:** Daily 6am–10pm.

The Bridgeport is one of the most congenial family-style restaurants in the entire city. They serve reasonably priced eats—witness my breakfast of hotcakes, sausage, stewed prunes, and coffee for $2.50. It's decorated in original fifties' glitz, with a large counter and vinyl booths, each with its individual jukebox.

Rogers Park

Rogers Park is a quiet, tree-shaded neighborhood bordering the northern suburb of Evanston.

INEXPENSIVE

★ Heartland Café, 7000 N. Glenwood. ☎ 465-8005.
$ Cuisine: HEALTH FOOD/VEGETARIAN. **Reservations:** Not required.
Subway/El: The Howard line to the Morse stop.

> **Prices:** Appetizers $2.25–$5.50; main courses $5.75–$12. AE, DC, MC, V.
> **Open:** Daily 9am–10:30pm (bar open later on weekends).

The Heartland Café is a bit of a shrine to the counterculture of the sixties. One of the owners had been a leader in a Chicago organization called Rising Up Angry, an antiwar group that was also trying to organize some of the poorer sections of Chicago around social issues. Sometime back in the seventies Michael James and a few of his colleagues decided that the way to reach the masses was through their stomachs, so they opened a health-food restaurant and co-op called the Heartland Café. Today no longer exclusively vegetarian, it has a reputation for good food at affordable prices. The cafe's Buffalo Bar is a popular meeting place, and there is also a general store selling dry goods and T-shirts and a studio offering a variety of classes, mostly for theater. It also publishes a newspaper, the *Heartland Journal,* espousing its political opinions and raising community issues. In the cafe, breakfast, lunch, and dinner are served. The menu features such regulars as eggs and omelets, turkey, and burgers made from lentils and farm-raised buffalo.

Poolgogi Steak House, 1366 W. Morse Ave. ☎ 761-1366.

> **Cuisine:** ASIAN. **Reservations:** Not accepted.
> **Prices:** Appetizers $2.50–$4.75; main courses $2.75–$8.95. DC, MC, V.
> **Open:** Tues–Fri 10am–9:30pm, Sat 9am–9:30pm, Sun 9am–8pm.

I looked in the Poolgogi, attracted by the strange juxtaposition of the restaurant's name with a menu that offered Korean, Chinese, Japanese, and American dishes. Most of the food, in fact, is Korean; the word *poolgogi* refers to the most popular Korean dish, marinated and barbecued beef. Teriyaki, chop suey, and "breakfast and sandwiches" are representative of the Japanese, Chinese, and American fare, respectively. No MSG is added to the food.

BUDGET

Café Ennui, 6781 N. Sheridan Rd. ☎ **973-2233.**

Cuisine: COFFEE SHOP. **Reservations:** Not accepted.
Subway/El: The Howard line to the Morse stop. **Bus:** No. 151 from Michigan Ave.
Prices: Menu items: $2.25–$3.89; No credit cards.
Open: Sun–Thurs 7:30am–10:30pm, Fri–Sat 8am–midnight.

Poets and cafe bohemians have long feared the power of ennui, or boredom, to dampen their inspiration. Perhaps it was to poke fun at this artistic fixation with despair that motivated the naming of the Café Ennui, where the atmosphere is lighthearted. In nice weather a few tables are placed outside on a patch of grass between the sidewalk and the street, where patrons can enjoy cappuccino or caffe latte.

Chinatown

Chicago's Chinatown, about 20 blocks south of the Loop and about two long blocks west of the McCormick convention complex, is expanding. For the moment, most of the commerce, which includes approximately 50 restaurants, plus several colorful food-and-vegetable markets and import houses, is strung along two thoroughfares, Cermak Road and Wentworth Avenue as far south as 24th Place. The Cermak stop on the Lake/Dan Ryan train is right on the edge of the Chinatown commercial district. Still under construction when this guide was being updated, just north of Cermak on Archer Avenue, is a new mixed commercial/residential block, which will almost certainly add more Asian-style restaurants to the Chinatown census. Many shops in Chinatown provide interesting browsing, especially the dry goods and fresh vegetable markets. You might also want to visit a Chinese bakery, such as **Keefer Bakery,** 249 W. Cermak. (☎ **326-2289**). Chinese baked goods are made with less sugar than is used in Western bakery products, and many pastries are filled with lotus or red-bean paste. The Keefer Bakery also has a line of dumplings, one filled with pork, another with ham and egg. The red-bean snowball is a typical pastry. As for the store's non–Chinese-sounding name, it comes from a street in Hong Kong! It's open daily from 8am to 6pm.

INEXPENSIVE

The Saigon Vietnamese Restaurant & Shabu Shabu, 232 W. Cermak. ☎ **808-1318.**

Cuisine: VIETNAMESE/CHINESE/MALAYSIAN. **Reservations:** Not required.
Prices: Appetizers $2.75–$4.95; soups $1.95–$12.95; main courses $4.95–$14.95. DISC, MC, V.
Open: Daily 11am–3am.

The food here is eclectic, and there aren't as many authentic Vietnamese dishes as one might wish. You can't blame the restaurant's owners, however; the American dining public simply has never acquired a taste for this very special cuisine. The spring rolls are Vietnamese style, though, and go down nicely with a bottle of Chinese beer. Shabu shabu is a kind of Chinese fondue where you construct a soup: to a steaming bowl of hot broth, you add the shrimp, fish, and veggies. Another soup, rice noodle, is a very generous serving for the price.

65 Seafood Restaurant, 2414 S. Wentworth. ☎ 225-7060.
Cuisine: CANTONESE SEAFOOD. **Reservations:** Not required.
Prices: Appetizers $1–$15; main courses $5.25–$17. AE, DC, MC, V.
Open: Sun–Thurs 10:30am–midnight. Fri–Sat 10:30am–1am.

There are two other branches of this restaurant in Chicago, one right across the street, the other on South Michigan Avenue. The restaurant's food—the menu includes 378 separate items—has been critically noticed by the Chicago media.

Three Happiness, 209 W. Cermak Rd. ☎ 842-1964.
Cuisine: CHINESE. **Reservations:** Not required.
Prices: Appetizers $1.50–$5.50; main courses $4.75–$12. AE, DC, MC, V.
Open: Sun–Thurs 11:30am–10pm; Fri–Sat 11:30am–11pm.

Three Happiness has enjoyed a reputation over many years of providing consistently reliable dishes from several regions of China. City residents come back to Three Happiness year after year during their once- or twice-annual visit to Chicago's traditional Chinatown. There are actually two locations in close proximity to one another, the second is at 2130 S. Wentworth (☎ 791-1228).

Won Kow, 237 S. Wentworth. ☎ 842-7500.
Cuisine: DIM SUM/CANTONESE. **Reservations:** Not required.
Prices: Appetizers $1.95–$4.95; main courses $5.95–$11.25. MC, V.
Open: Sun–Thurs 10am–11pm, Fri–Sat 10am–midnight.

A colorful marquee ushers diners to Won Kow's mezzanine-level dining room, where dim sum is served daily from 10am to 3pm. Most of the dumplings cost between $1.50 and $2 an order. Other house specialties include Mongolian Chicken, and 8 Treasure Duck with seafood.

Greek Town

In a building complex at 322 S. Halsted, between Van Buren Street and Gladys Avenue, you will find the **Athens Grocery** and the **Pan Hellenic Pastry Shop** (☎ 454-1886).

INEXPENSIVE

Greek Islands, 200 S. Halsted. ☎ 782-9855.
Cuisine: GREEK. **Reservations:** Not accepted.
Prices: Appetizers $2.25–$7.95; main courses $5.95–$18.95. AE, DC, DISC, MC, V.
Open: Sun–Thurs 11am–midnight, Fri–Sat 11am–1am.

Greek Islands is one of the block's most popular restaurants, with such daily specials as lamb and artichokes or Greek-style shrimp. There are some very touching snapshots of Anthony Quinn in the window.

Parthenon, 314 S. Halsted. ☎ **726-2407.**

Cuisine: GREEK. **Reservations:** Not accepted.
Prices: Appetizers $1.95–$7.25; main courses $4.25–$13.95. AE, DC, DISC, MC, V.
Open: Sun–Fri 11am–1am, Sat 11am–2am.

"We created flaming saganaki," proclaims the sign in the window at the Parthenon. Flaming saganaki? Wedges of fried Romano cheese, doused in brandy and served aflame at your table.

Logan Square

Orbis, 2860 N. Milwaukee Ave. (☎ **342-7800**), just beyond California Avenue, serves a platter brimming with kielbasa, meatballs, pirogi, potatoes, sauerkraut, and blintzes ($7.50). Open daily from 11am to 11pm.

Farther along is a nameless **deli,** at no. 2924, the window filled with Polish meats and cheeses, and all those wonderful goods in jars and boxes with their distinct Eastern European style of packaging. The **Senkowski Home Bakery and Delicatessen,** 2931 N. Milwaukee Ave. (☎ **252-3708**), is across the street on the corner of the quaint residential Gresham Avenue. Dry and baked goods occupy the bulk of the space inside, but there is a very informal and moderately priced restaurant in the back room as well. Several doors up the block is the **Zacopane Restaurant,** 2943 N. Milwaukee (☎ **342-1464**), the fanciest eatery on the avenue. Starters include meat dumplings, the beet dish of the day, and steak tartare. Main courses range from the Polish assortment to veal escalope. Open seven days a week from 10am to 10pm.

At the **Pasieka Home Quality Bakery,** 3056 N. Milwaukee Ave. (☎ **278-5190**), you'll find cookies, pastries (like Bismarcks, the Eastern/Central European term for jelly doughnuts), and "cakes for all occasions." Very little English is spoken in the neighborhood, testifying to the vitality of this Polish community in which people still converse in the language of the Old Country.

"New Chinatown"

Despite the feeling that the neighborhood is a way station, there is nothing transient-looking about the string of restaurants that have rooted themselves along Argyle.

$ **Mekong,** 4953 N. Broadway. ☎ **271-0206.**

Cuisine: VIETNAMESE/CHINESE. **Reservations:** Not accepted. **Subway/El:** Take the Howard line to the Argyle stop.
Prices: Appetizers $2.75–$8.95; main courses $3.25–$10.95. AE, DC, DISC, MC, V.
Open: Sun–Thurs 10am–10pm, Fri–Sat 10am–11pm.

The Mekong has achieved a certain status, having been listed by a Chicago food critic as one of his favorite restaurants in the entire city. A daily, all-you-can-eat, buffet lunch costs $4.95, and other luncheon specials are priced at $3.95, including soup, an egg roll, and fried rice.

Pilsen

Most of Pilsen's restaurants are Mexican, located along 18th Street a fair distance to the west of the art colony on Halsted.

In addition to the ones described below, two other favorite Pilsen eateries are the **Ostioneria Playa Azul,** at 1514 W. 18th St. (☎ 421-2552), a seafood restaurant; and **Bishop's Famous Chili,** at 1958 W. 18th St. (☎ 829-6345), a chili parlor serving Chicago for 50 years.

Nuevo León, 1515 W. 18th St. ☎ 421-1517.

> **Cuisine:** MEXICAN. **Reservations:** Not accepted. **Subway/El:** Take the B train on the O'Hare–Douglas line to 18th St. **Bus:** Take the Ashland bus to 18th St., then walk east.
> **Prices:** Appetizers $3.50–$6.50; main courses $3–$8. No credit cards.
> **Open:** Daily 8am–midnight.

There are many Hispanic faces among the diners at the Nuevo León, and the jukebox is pure Latino, from salsa to the mariachi favorites of Mexico. The refried beans are superb, and the tamales are excellent in every way, from their rough-ground cornmeal shells to the chunks of roasted pork within.

The Gaza Strip

For nosh Jewish style, there's **Kosher Karry,** on the corner of Devon and Mozart (☎ 973-4355), where you can pick up ready-made varieties of traditional edibles—kasha varniskes, blintzes, kreplach, and the like. Jewish baked goods, such as buttery challah bread, almond rings, and hamantashen (prepared during Passover), can be purchased at the **Tel Aviv Bakery,** at 2944 W. Devon (☎ 764-8877), open Sunday through Thursday from 6am to 6pm and on Friday from 6am to an hour before sundown.

INEXPENSIVE

Gandhi India, 2601 W. Devon. ☎ 761-8714.

> **Cuisine:** INDIAN. **Reservations:** Not accepted.
> **Prices:** Appetizers $1.50–$4.50; main courses $4–$9. AE, DC, DISC, MC, V.
> **Open:** Lunch daily 11:30am–3:30pm; dinner Sun–Thurs 5–10pm, Fri–Sat 5–11pm.

Gandhi India, at the corner of Rockwell, has gotten some favorable attention from Chicago's food critics. Among the specialties are the tandoori-style lamb or chicken roasted in earthen pots, as well as curries, appetizers, soups, and desserts. The line of customers waiting to be seated just inside the door indicates the restaurant's popularity. A luncheon buffet is served daily from 11:30am to 3:30pm; it's all-you-can-eat for $5.95. Indian beer is also available.

BUDGET

Annapurna Fast Foods, 2608 W. Devon. ☎ **764-1858.**
    Cuisine: INDIAN/CAFETERIA. **Reservations:** Not accepted.
    Prices: Appetizers 50¢–$2; main courses $1.50–$5. No credit cards.
    Open: Mon and Wed–Fri 11am–9pm, Sat–Sun 11am–10pm.

Annapurna serves curries, stuffed pastries, and breads—all vegetarian—cafeteria style. Mix and match your own feast from among the steaming trays of pilao, nan, raita, korta, samosa, puri, uttapam, and much, much more.

The Milwaukee Avenue Corridor/Ukrainian Village

The Ukrainian Village, centered around Chicago Avenue and Oakley Boulevard, south of Wicker Park, has two restaurants to keep an eye out for: **Sak's Ukrainian Village Restaurant,** 2301 W. Chicago Ave. (☎ **278-4445**); and **Galans Ukrainian Café,** 2210 W. Chicago (☎ **292-1000**). In either place, you will find such typical Ukrainian specialties as chicken Kiev, borscht, blintzes smothered in sour cream, and stuffed cabbage.

In addition to the White Palace Grill (see below), a popular Polish restaurant in this same vicinity is the moderately priced **Busy Bee,** 1546 N. Damen Ave. (☎ **772-4433**).

⭐ **White Palace Grill,** 711 N. Ashland Ave. ☎ **939-7167.**
    Cuisine: POLISH/AMERICAN.
💲 **Prices:** Menu items $1–$5. No credit cards.
    Open: Mon–Fri 5am–5pm, Sat 5am–4pm.

The White Palace Grill is a Polish-American–owned breakfast nook and luncheonette tucked away in this lower-southeastern corner of West Town. Owner Wally Rabenda holds forth at the grill, flipping burgers and crafting combo breakfasts that include the White Palace Trio (two eggs, two slices of bacon, two sausages, shredded hash browns, and toast), or Mom's Breakfast Special (scrambled eggs, Polish sausage, and trimmings). Customers during the day favor the house specialty called "gliders," tiny burgers for 45¢ apiece (55¢ with cheese), or choose from the list of old standby sandwiches like BLTs, grilled cheese, and Italian sausage. The White Palace is always filled with regular customers, who help themselves to the excellent coffee while Wally plays gin in the back booth. The restaurant is closed on Sunday so Wally can watch network golf.

Valkommen Andersonville

Many Swedish immigrants coming to the United States after 1840 in search of arable farm and dairy lands throughout the northern prairie states never went farther than Chicago. Andersonville—north to south from Foster to Bryn Mawr Avenues, and east to west from Clark Street to Broadway—is one of five Swedish neighborhoods within the Chicago area. The remnants of that culture remain in the form of several shops, bakeries, and a museum, all to be found along Clark Street. The Swedes themselves, like those of German background, have long been absorbed into the mainstream of American life. Today Andersonville, like so many similar neighborhoods in contemporary Chicago, is a bit like a sociological Noah's Ark—practically every group and type has its representation here.

The several-mile trek up Clark from Wrigley Field will bring you to the **Swedish Bakery,** 5348 N. Clark (☎ 561-8919), with its window full of pretty pastries.

The **North Shore Grill II,** at 5314 N. Clark (☎ 728-5415), is part Asian kitchen, part American diner. They offer yet-ca-mein, a noodle soup with sliced beef and boiled eggs, and akutagawa, three eggs mixed with chopped beef, bean sprouts, onion, and green pepper, and served with rice and gravy ($3.50). Another popular favorite showing the influence of the Appalachian South is biscuits and gravy for $1.95. They even serve meat loaf. Open from 7am to 8pm Tuesday through Saturday and from 8am to 8pm on Sunday.

Reza's, 5255 N. Clark (☎ 561-1898), is a Persian restaurant—which is to say Iranian—and is always crowded, offering good food, and plenty of it at low prices. Middle Eastern music will accompany your dinner on Tuesday and Wednesday nights. The menu emphasizes charbroiled meats, lamb kebabs, and stews, costing between $5 and $12.95 per main course. Open daily from 11:30am to midnight; reservations recommended.

Two Swedish-style delicatessens grace this block: **Erickson's,** at 5250 N. Clark (☎ 561-5634); and **Wikstrom's,** at 5247 N. Clark (☎ 275-6100), where the queen of Sweden made a purchase on her visit to Chicago a number of years back.

Ann Sather's, at 5207 N. Clark (☎ 271-6677), is the companion to its original on Belmont Avenue (listed in the "Mid-North" section, above), serving the same Scandinavian favorites, and is particularly popular with the breakfast crowd.

9 Specialty Dining

Local Favorites

The **Billy Goat Tavern,** at 430 N. Michigan Ave. (☎ 222-1525), is the tavern John Belushi made famous on *Saturday Night Live.* It's under North Michigan Avenue, near the bridge that crosses to the Loop. **Mr. Beef,** at 777 N. Orleans (☎ 337-8500), is a good spot to try an Italian beef sandwich. It's in the River North area. (Both are listed previously in this chapter.)

Hotel Dining

Some of Chicago's finest restaurants are located in the city's best hotels. Tops among them are **Jaxx,** in the Park Hyatt; the **Cape Cod Room,** in the Drake; the **Pump Room,** in the Omni Ambassador East; **Benkay,** in the Nikko; **Seasons Restaurant,** in the Four Seasons; the **Boulevard Restaurant,** in the Hotel Inter-Continental; and **Oak Terrace,** in the Drake. Also not to be overlooked are the **Prince**

Frommer's Cool for Kids: Restaurants

McDonald's in the Field Museum   This could get the kids to the museum; the interactive displays will win their interest.

Rock-and-Roll McDonald's   The original R&R McDonald's, located at 600 N. Clark St. (☎ 664-7940), in River North, is like a museum of fifties cultural artifacts and kitsch.

Mr. Beef   (see p. 120) This sub joint is popular with kids.

Gold Coast Dogs   (see p. 148) If your children like hot dogs, this is the place to go.

Ed Debevic's   (see p. 119) Like the R&R McDonald's, this is a crossover spot; nostalgia for the grown-ups, but the young actor staff and the home-style food make it hip from a kid's point of view as well.

The Hard Rock Café   (see p. 118) Also in River North, this is a perennial favorite with young people—for the vibes as well as the burgers.

Vinny's   (see p. 132) This informal pasta palace is one of the few restaurants that isn't a fast-food joint that the kids will probably like.

North Pier   (see p. 174) With lots of loud and casual eateries, North Pier has a kind of carnival scene that the kids will appreciate.

---

of Wales, in the Knickerbocker; **Cricket's,** in the Tremont; **In My Neighborhood,** in the Claridge; the **Raphael Restaurant,** in the Raphael; and **Café Angelo,** in Oxford House.

Dining with a View

Now that the Mayfair Hotel has closed, and with it, the rooftop Le Ciel Bleu overlooking Oak Street Beach, dining with a view has to be divided into the best place by day and the best place by night. **Everest** captures the starlight titles, and of course has the cuisine to rival the glamour of the downtown urban skyline. In the daytime, a hands-down winner has to be **Sounder's Restaurant** at water's edge overlooking Lake Michigan, open only for lunch. Sunday brunch at Days Inn puts you in the **Pinnacle,** a revolving top-floor lounge also with close-up view of the lake.

Dining Clusters/Complexes

WATER TOWER PLACE

Water Tower Place is the newish skyscraper at 845 N. Michigan Ave., with numerous shops off a central atrium on the lower floors and the Ritz-Carlton hotel tucked away on the upper stories. Among the boutiques are several good restaurants that cater primarily to mall shoppers and to the building's large population of office workers.

D. B. Kaplan's, on the 7th floor, Water Tower Place. ☎ **280-2700.**

> **Cuisine:** DELI. **Reservations:** Not accepted.
> **Prices:** Sandwiches from $6. AE, CB, DC, DISC, MC, V.
> **Open:** Mon–Thurs 10am–9:30pm, Fri–Sat 10am–11pm, Sun 11am–9pm.

D. B. Kaplan's isn't so much a delicatessen as a pre–Ed Debevic's sandwich shop (Ed Debevic's is discussed earlier in this chapter). All 148 sandwiches have cutesy names like Tongue Fu and Studs Turkey, are as extravagant as their names imply, and run about $6 apiece. D. B. Kaplan's prides itself on being set up so that you can get in and out quickly, if that is your agenda.

900 NORTH MICHIGAN AVENUE

Also known—much less widely, however—as the Avenue Atrium, Chicago's newest vertical mall on a grand scale and rival to Water Tower Place houses its fair share of restaurants and delis to relieve the hunger pangs of shoppers wishing to break for lunch or dinner without leaving the building.

Tucci Benucch, on the 5th floor, 900 N. Michigan Ave. ☎ **266-2500.**

> **Cuisine:** ITALIAN. **Reservations:** Not accepted.
> **Prices:** Appetizers $2.25–$3.50; pizza $5.95–$7.50; pasta $5.95–$9.50; main courses $8.95–$9.95. AE, DC, DISC, MC, V.
> **Open:** Mon–Thurs 11:30am–10pm, Fri–Sat 11:30am–11pm, Sun noon–9pm.

Tucci Benucch was created by the Rich Melman gang to resemble an Italian country villa. Each dining area is a stage-set replica of a typical room—kitchen, living room, sun room, and so forth—complete with all the domestic details, including garden plants and clothes on the line.

The inexpensive fare showcases different regions of Italy, and portions are generously large. For about $20 total, a couple can dine on any variety of thin-crust pizzas, delicately sauced pastas, or garlic roasted chicken, and that includes a glass of Chianti with the meal.

SEARS TOWER

The dark metallic Sears Tower, currently the world's tallest building, at 233 S. Wacker Dr., dominates the skyline of the Loop. The building's principal restaurant tenant is the Levy organization, with nine separate establishments. Via their Chef's Express service (☎ **842-LEVY**), you may order out selections from any of these nine eateries, including gourmet take-out, a doughnut shop, Mexican and Jewish cooking, and a "fine dining" Italian Restaurant called **Mia Torre.**

Mrs. Levy's, on the concourse level, Sears Tower. ☎ **993-0530.**

> **Cuisine:** DELI. **Reservations:** Not accepted.
> **Prices:** Sandwiches $4–$6.99. No credit cards.
> **Open:** Mon–Fri 6:30am–8pm.

To paraphrase the well-known slogan of rye-bread fame, "You don't have to be Jewish to like Mrs. Levy's," an eat-in delicatessen. It's all here at Mrs. Levy's in the Loop: matzoh-ball soup, bagels, lox and cream cheese, gefilte fish, latkes (potato pancakes), pastrami and corned beef, and much, much more. Despite the fancy location, there's nothing trendy about Mrs. Levy's—just good solid deli food, excellent, friendly service, and no pressure at all if you want to linger a bit over your meal.

Light, Casual & Fast Food

Practically any of the restaurants listed in this guide provide the option for "light" dining; you have to provide the self-discipline. Check "Frommer's Cool for Kids: Restaurants," "Pizza," "Hot Dogs," and so on. One new restaurant that opened recently in the River North district is uniquely suited to this category:

Big Bowl Café, 159¹/₂ W. Erie St. ☎ 787-8279.

Cuisine: CALIFORNIAN/ASIAN. **Reservations,** Not required.
Prices: Little bowls $1.95–$4.95; big bowls $4.95–$8.95. AE, DC, DISC, MC, V.
Open: Mon–Thurs 11:30am–10pm, Fri–Sat 11:30am–11pm, Sun 5–9pm.

The Big Bowl Café, attached to the Eccentric Restaurant (discussed earlier in this chapter) but a completely separate entity, is the ideal place for a light lunch or an after-show snack or supper. Set up like a long, narrow dining car along the sidewalk, there are large windows that lift to the ceiling, creating an open-air atmosphere when the weather permits. The food, prepared in the larger kitchen of the Eccentric, is steamed hot with each order. And although the presentation and the use of certain ingredients, such as fresh ginger, lend a definite Asian accent to the dishes, there is also an unmistakable link to the health-food and salad tradition of post-sixties California.

All dishes are served in bowls, large or small, and may be eaten with chopsticks if desired. One real bargain is a Big Bowl Chicken Salad, a generous order of shredded chicken combined with many fresh greens and vegetables. The Smokin' Shrimp is also an exotic and tasteful treat, with good-size, succulent butterfly shrimp served over a wild rice pilaf in a rich beef broth.

Pizza

To clear up any potential confusion, there's a fundamental difference between New York pizza and Chicago pizza. The standard in Chicago is not the thin, wedge-shaped slice available on practically any street corner in New York, but thick-crusted, deep-dish, knife-and-fork pizza—similar to what New Yorkers call "Sicilian." The pizza may be different in Chicago, but it's no less popular, and even fashionable, depending on where you go to eat it.

Two of Chicago's gourmet pizza restaurants, **Pizzeria Uno,** at 29 E. Ohio, at the corner of Wabash (☎ 321-1000), and **Pizzeria Due,** 619 N. Wabash, at the corner of Ontario (☎ 943-2400), are listed under the "River North" section of this chapter. **Gino's East,** 160

E. Superior (☎ 943-1124), is mentioned under the "Magnificent Mile."

Edwardo's is a pizza chain with several Chicago locations, including one at 2120 N. Halsted (☎ 871-3400), which is mentioned in the "Lincoln Park" section. Also in Lincoln Park is **Ranalli's Pizzeria, Libations & Collectibles,** 1925 N. Lincoln (☎ 642-4700).

In the Mid-North Side of Chicago is **Barry's Spot,** 5759 N. Broadway (☎ 769-2900), which has great-tasting pizza.

Hot Dogs

Chicagoans take as much pride in their hot dogs as they do in their pizza. It's not as if the hot dog is foreign to this city where Armour and Swift once located their sprawling packing plants down by the stockyards. The facades of Chicago's hot-dog stands, as if by some unwritten convention, are all very colorful, with bright signs of red and yellow, exaggerated lettering, and comic illustrations of the wieners and fries.

Naturally, Chicago is home to a few designer hot-dog shops, such as **Gold Coast Dogs,** 418 N. State St., at Hubbard (☎ 527-1222). These are the smarty-pants of hot-dog gastronomy in Chicago, selling healthy fast food. The setting of this storefront two blocks off North Michigan Avenue, just across the river from the Loop, is like that around nearby Harry Caray's (discussed earlier in this chapter), a mixture of residential and commercial blocks. At Gold Coast Dogs you can grab your food and run, or join the crowd on one of the stools around the counter. Choose your frank with hot peppers, celery salt, green relish, or veggies (someone from the store shops at Chicago's central market every day for fresh produce). Hot dogs start at $1.90, and burgers at $3.57. You can also have melted cheddar cheese on your french fries, and homemade brownies for dessert. It's open Monday through Friday from 7am to midnight, on Saturday from 8am to 8pm, and on Sunday from 11am to 8pm. A second branch of Gold Coast is located on the Near North Side, at 2100 N. Clark (☎ 327-8887).

A Brewery

In addition to the listing below, see also the review of the **Goose Island Brewing Company** in Section 5, "Near North," earlier in this chapter.

Chicago Brewing Company, 1830 N. Besly Court.
☎ 252-BREW.

As any beer lover knows by now, the microbrewery phenomenon is sweeping across the country. With years of foreign travel under our collective belts since World War II, Americans have tired of discovering that the rest of the world has better beer than we do, and our only option for drinking good brew was to buy the imported stuff when we got home. In recent years, American entrepreneurs have happily reintroduced the art of good beermaking on the homefront; the Chicago Brewing Co., only recently established, is part of that growing movement. One reader writes us that, "They produce Legacy

Lager, Legacy Red Ale, Heartland Wiess, and Big Shoulders Porter; possibly the best American brews available. They have a free tour on Saturdays at 2pm with free samples." The company's brew is available throughout the city, but the brewery is not easy to find: Call first for exact directions, even if you go there by cab.

Breakfast/Brunch

Chicago has breakfast spots for all occasions. Businesspeople staying in the Loop can get a good, and definitely upscale, breakfast at the **Savoy Bar & Grill,** 440 S. LaSalle, second floor (☎ 663-8800), right in the heart of the financial district. Someone referred to the Savoy as serving "trader fast food," and cocktails are served from 10am. Open Monday to Friday 10am to 2:30pm for lunch; the bar is open till 6:30pm.

You can also have brunch—called *almuerzo*—Mexican style every Saturday from 10:30am to 2:30pm at **Frontera Grill,** 445 N. Clark (☎ 661-1434), and order your *huevos* with all those great pre-Columbian ingredients.

You might also want to try **Ann Sather's,** at 929 W. Belmont (☎ 348-2378) and at 5207 N. Clark (☎ 271-6677), famous for their homemade cinnamon rolls and popular with the breakfast crowd. (See the "Mid-North Side" for the listing.)

The **Big Shoulders Cafe** at the Chicago Historical Society, Clark St. at North Ave. (☎ 642-4200) offers weekend breakfast specials, and **Oo La La!,** 3335 N. Halsted St. (☎ 935-7708), weighs in with a trendy brunch of its own, from 10am to 3pm, for those who want to wander north a bit on a Sunday morn. That walk up Halsted, from say, Armitage, would really get the day off to a pleasant start.

The **Ohio House Coffee Shop** (corner of Ohio and La Salle) has an old-fashioned breakfast special for $2.95: two strips of bacon, two sausage patties, two pancakes, and two eggs.

The Corner Bakery, 516 N. Clark St. ☎ 644-7700.
Cuisine: BREAKFAST/SANDWICHES.
Prices: Breakfast $2.50–$6; sandwiches $3–$7. AE, DC, DISC, MC, V.
Open: Mon–Fri 7am–2pm, Sat–Sun 8am–noon.

Sunday morning is a nice time to come to Chicago's River North neighborhood, especially if the weather is agreeable, and you could begin your day with a fine continental breakfast at the Corner Bakery, the honest-to-goodness bakery attached to Maggiano's Italian restaurant. The baked goods are exceptionally good, especially when accompanied by an oversized cup of creamy caffe latte. Many local office workers also come to the Corner Bakery during the week for their unique selection of sandwiches, most of which are gone by 2pm. And, of course, all Chicago—restaurants included—are starting to come to the Corner Bakery for their bread.

Lou Mitchell's, 625 W. Jackson. ☎ 939-3111.
Cuisine: AMERICAN/BREAKFAST. **Reservations:** Not accepted.
Prices: Breakfast items $1.50–$5.95. No credit cards.
Open: Mon–Fri 5:30am–4pm, Sat 5:30am–2:30pm. **Closed:** Holidays.

A favorite for breakfast among Chicagoans since 1923 is Lou Mitchell's, across the south branch of the Chicago River from the Loop, a block farther west than Union Station. A French food critic passing through Chicago rated Lou Mitchell's the number one breakfast spot in America, home of the "five-star breakfast." The owner greets you at the door with a basket of doughnut holes (milk duds for the ladies—don't ask), so you can nibble while waiting for a table. The wait is short, since turnover is continuous and service efficiently attentive. I had the best bowl of oatmeal I've ever eaten, deliciously creamy. An order of two double-yolk fried eggs with toasted homemade Greek bread, homemade orange marmalade, and hash browns is served at your table in the same skillet it was all cooked in. There are 14 different omelets, including one made with apples and cheddar cheese.

Afternoon Tea/Coffee

One of the nicest tea ceremonies—occidental style, that is—takes place in the **Mayfair Regent Hotel,** 181 E. Lake Shore Dr. (☎ 787-8500). The afternoon tea, including scones and finger sandwiches, is served daily off the lobby, and costs approximately $15.

A new breed of coffee shops has moved into Chicago and now virtually dominates the take-out market. Straight from Seattle is the chain called **Starbucks,** and many Chicagoans with gourmet palates shake their heads in disbelief that a chain can actually turn out a great cup of coffee or espresso. You will find Starbucks in the Loop at 150 N. Wacker (☎ 704-0655), on the Gold Coast at 948 N. Rush St. (☎ 337-0480), and in Hyde Park at 53rd and Harper (☎ 324-1241).

The snazzy competition is called **Coffee Chicago,** with their very fin-de-siècle interiors and equally excellent java. You'll find them off the Magnificent Mile at 801 N. Wabash (☎ 664-6415), and in the New Town section at 3323 N. Clark (☎ 477-3323).

Kava Kane, 1013 W. Webster (☎ 404-KAVA), caters to both a neighborhood crowd and a student crowd (De Paul University) slightly west of the Halsted strip. Settle in behind the Sunday paper for good vibes and good coffee.

Late Night/24 Hour

Late night isn't too hard in Chicago, but finding 24-hour joints isn't easy. **Nookie's Too,** 2114 N. Halsted (☎ 327-1400), in the Lincoln Park neighborhood, has a great all-day breakfast menu and stays open straight through from 6:30am on Friday to 9pm on Sunday.

Mexican and Chinese restaurants often stay open seven days a week until 3am or even later on weekends. For example, **Lindo Mexico,** 2642 N. Lincoln (☎ 871-4832), is often filled with an after-club/theater crowd at 3am, and stays open as late as 5am on the weekend. Most hotels offer room service until at least midnight, and sometimes later.

Picnic Fare & Where to Eat It

Some good places to buy your picnic fare are **Food Works,** 1002 W. Diversey (☎ 348-7800), near Sheffield; or **Treasure Island Imported Food,** 2121 N. Clybourn (☎ 880-8880)—"the closest thing in the city to Balducci's," says one Chicagoan who knows that New York mecca of nosh.

If you're near the Magnificent Mile, go get some of the varied fare offered by **foodlife** in Water Tower Place, 835 N. Michigan Ave. (☎ 335-FOOD), and carry it out to the Oak Street Beach. The **Corner Bakery** (see "Breakfast Brunch" earlier in this section) makes incredible sandwiches that are wildly popular among the local office workers, and sell out quickly on any given day. Superior sandwiches in the natural foods tradition, vegetarian or otherwise, are also a specialty at **Zinfandel,** 59 W. Grand (☎ 727-1818); gourmet salads and cheeses are also available from the deli case.

As for where to eat it? Consult your map and pick a park that appeals. The way of least resistance will lead you to Lincoln Park, the city's largest, following Lake Michigan from the Gold Coast to the Far North Side.

Ice Cream

There's a **Ben and Jerry's** at 338 W. Armitage on the Near North Side (☎ 281-5152). At the **Oak Terrace** in the Drake hotel, 140 E. Walton (☎ 787-2200), you can build your own sundae while enjoying the sweeping view of the lake. **D. B. Kaplan's,** on the mezzanine level of Water Tower Place, 845 N. Michigan (☎ 280-2700), offers a full fountain of sweet delights, as does **Mrs. Levy's** in the Sears Tower, 233 S. Wacker (☎ 993-0530).

7

What to See and Do in Chicago

WHAT ARE GENERALLY RECOGNIZED AS THE CITY'S TRADITIONAL SIGHTS— its principal boulevards, museums, parks, and buildings—are all located in downtown Chicago or close to it, all within walking distance of (or a short cab ride from) the city's principal hotels. The greatest concentration of these "must-see" sights is within the general vicinity of the Loop itself, Chicago's commercial and financial core, or on the main avenues along its periphery.

Suggested Itineraries

If You Have One Day

If you only have a day in Chicago, take to the streets. Either select one of the walking tours outlined in Chapter 8, or go exploring in a more remote neighborhood, such as Wicker Park on the West Side, Bridgeport on the South Side, or Rogers Park on the North Side. You might choose to tour the Loop (perhaps taking "Walking Tour 1" in Chapter 8), as this is the essential Chicago experience, where the highest concentration of traditional sights is to be found. These include the Sears Tower, the Art Institute, the Chicago Board of Trade, Printer's Row, and the many monumental sculptures by world-class artists scattered throughout the downtown area.

If You Have Two Days

On the first day, follow the Loop itinerary referred to above. On the second day, do another one or two of the other museums. Go to Hyde Park in the morning for the Museum of Science and Industry. Eat lunch, then return to South Michigan Avenue for the Field Museum, the Shedd Aquarium, or the Adler Planetarium. Other museum options include the Terra Art Museum on the Magnificent Mile (North Michigan Avenue), plus the Chicago Historical Society and the Chicago Academy of Sciences Museum, both of which are near Lincoln Park in the Gold Coast section of the Near North Side. An alternative for museum lovers would be to visit one of the smaller cultural and ethnic institutions, of which Chicago has a great selection, including the Smart Museum on the University of Chicago campus, the DuSable African American Museum, also in Hyde Park, and the Polish, Ukrainian, and Mexican museums on the Near West Side.

If You Have Three Days

Begin the third day with some leisurely shopping along the Magnificent Mile, making sure to stop at the great vertical shopping malls, Water Tower, Chicago Place, and 900 North Michigan Avenue. North Pier, along East Illinois, is another option for many unusual shops, or for an architectural tour of the city along the Chicago River (departing from Ogden Slip at North Pier).

After shopping, you could walk west of North Michigan Avenue to any number of great restaurants in the River North district.

154

At night, kick up your heels at a dance or blues club somewhere in the Lincoln Park neighborhood, or along Belmont Avenue and its vicinity. Or take in a drama or comedy show at one of Chicago's many fine theaters.

If You Have Five Days or More

You've still only scratched the surface. There are ball games to be seen at Wrigley Field or Comiskey Park; there's great music to hear at the Chicago Symphony. You can dine on Polish food north of Logan Square, German food on Lincoln Square, or Mexican food in Pilsen. You'll be able to visit an extra museum or two among all those mentioned above under "If You Have 2 Days." And don't forget the possibilities for day and side trips. Suburban Oak Park, one half hour by subway from downtown, is a must for any fan of Frank Lloyd Wright's architecture, and Milwaukee—a very interesting midsize city with a culture all its own—is only an hour and a half away by car or train.

1 The Top Attractions

In & Around the Loop

Most of the Loop's major cultural draws are clustered around South Michigan Avenue and Grant Park, and offer both day- and nighttime activities, ranging from museum-hopping to evening concerts and theater. With the exception of one or two oases—usually a

Did You Know?

- The two blue bars on the Chicago flag represent the two branches of the Chicago River.
- Chicago has more large-scale, free outdoor concerts than any other city in the world.
- Historic Wrigley Field, home of the Chicago Cubs, is owned by the Tribune Company, also publisher of the city's largest-circulation newspaper.
- The Chicago Board of Trade is the world's largest futures and options exchange.
- Second City, the famous improvisational theater, launched the careers of Alan Alda, Dan Akroyd, John Belushi, Gilda Radner, and Joan Rivers.
- The Shedd Aquarium is the world's largest indoor marine mammal pavilion.
- Chicago has 29 miles of frontage along Lake Michigan.
- The yearly outdoor bash Taste of Chicago is the largest food and entertainment festival in the world.

restaurant or hotel of interest—the inner blocks of the Loop are occupied by office buildings. So after dark the streets are virtually empty, apart from a few square blocks where nightlife predominates. There are several residential pockets on the fringes of downtown, here and there a luxury apartment tower among the office buildings that stand along the river's edge, or the so-called South Loop, a reclaimed historic,

district around Printer's Row, where commercial buildings have been converted into condo apartments and living lofts. From the tourist's point of view, other than for those who choose an evening at the opera or at the Chicago Theater, the Loop's interior streets offer, in general, daytime activities only. The most common of these are walking tours—organized or informal—to view the architectural standouts or the city's famous outdoor sculpture collection; visits to the spectator galleries of the various financial exchanges or to a session of the city council; or an elevator ride 100 floors up to the observation deck of the world's tallest skyscraper, the Sears Tower.

★ **Art Institute of Chicago**, Michigan Ave. (at Adams St.). ☎ 443-3600.

Chicago's temple of art houses a major collection—from El Greco, Rembrandt, Cézanne, and Renoir to Rothko and all the modernists, plus a few signal paintings, including Grant Wood's *American Gothic* and Seurat's famous *Sunday Afternoon on the Island of la Grande Jatte*. In addition to the galleries of paintings, there are exhibits of photography, furnishings, prints and drawings, ceramics, and Chinese art. Another popular attraction is the original Trading Room of the old Chicago Stock Exchange, salvaged when the Adler and Sullivan Stock Exchange building was demolished in 1972.

Admission: $6.50 adults; $3.25 children, students, and seniors. Free admission on Tues.

Open: Mon and Wed–Fri 10:30am–4:30pm, Tues 10:30am–8pm, Sat 10am–5pm, Sun and holidays noon–5pm. **Bus:** No. 3, 4, 60, 145, 147, or 151. **Subway/El:** Take the Lake/Dan Ryan, Evanston, or Ravenswood line to Adams, or the Howard line to Monroe or Jackson. **Closed:** Thanksgiving Day, Christmas Day.

Sears Tower, 233 S. Wacker Dr. ☎ 875-9696.

The view from the world's tallest skyscraper (and second-most popular attraction in Chicago after the Museum of Science and Industry) is everything you'd expect it to be, a momentary suspension between earth and sky. The city is spread before you in a splendor both intimate and colossal. There are two observatory decks, one on the 100th floor, the other on the 103rd floor. The Sears Tower may be surpassed in height by twin towers scheduled to be erected in 1995 in Kuala Lumpur.

Admission: $6.50 adults, $4.75 seniors, $3.25 children ages 5–17, free for children under 5, $18 family (two adults and up to six children).

Open: Skydeck daily Mar–Sept 9am–11pm; Oct–Feb 9am–10pm. **Bus:** No. 7, 126, 151, or 156. **Subway/El:** Take the Ravenswood or Evanston line to Quincy.

Chicago Attractions

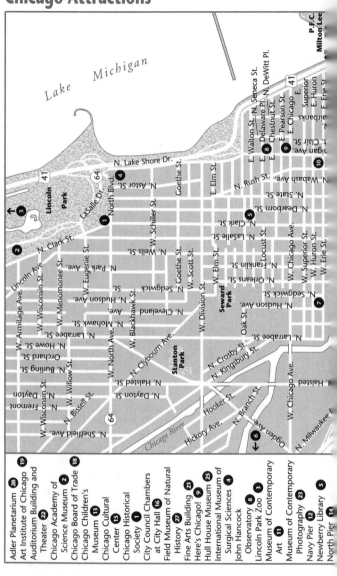

Terra Museum of American Art, 666 N. Michigan Ave.
☎ **664-3939.**

The Terra Museum of American Art houses the formerly private collection of industrialist Daniel J. Terra. Currently the museum has assembled some 400 pieces of 18th-, 19th-, and 20th-century American art.

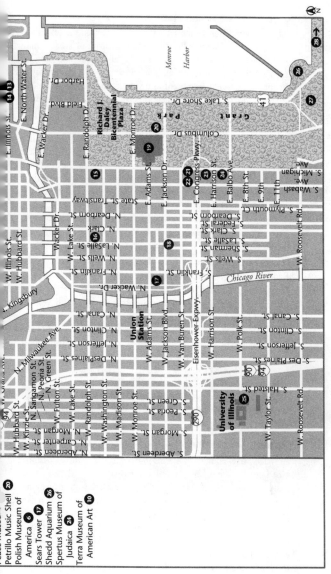

Petrillo Music Shell **20**
Polish Museum of America **6**
Sears Tower **17**
Shedd Aquarium **26**
Spertus Museum of Judaica **24**
Terra Museum of American Art **10**

5506

Admission (including daily tours at noon or 2pm): $3 adults, $2 seniors, free for children under 14 and students with ID.

Open: Tues noon–8pm, Wed–Sat 10am–5pm, Sun noon–5pm.
Bus: No. 3, 11, 125, 145, 146, 147, or 151. **Subway/El:** Take the Howard line to Grand or Chicago.

Chicago Board of Trade, 141 W. Jackson. ☎ **786-5600.**

The best live, improvisational acting in the city isn't necessarily at the theater. The Trading Pit at the Chicago Board of Trade, a massive citadel that stands at the foot of LaSalle Street, and the City Council chambers at City Hall (see below) can—on a given day—provide the best entertainment in town.

The Board of Trade Building is imposing in a bedrock sort of way, the no-nonsense gray countinghouse demeanor softened slightly by the whimsical statue of Ceres, goddess of grain, who dispenses her fecundity from her tower 609 feet above the ground. Inside, from a vantage point in the public galleries, you can watch the traders make their voluble deals, peaking in a shouting frenzy at the closing hour, after which these individual gamblers in pinstripes will count up their chips and learn if they've come out winners or losers for the day.

Admission: Free.

Open: Visitor center, Mon–Fri 8am–2pm. **Bus:** No. 1, 7, 60, 126, 151, or 156. **Subway/El:** Take the Ravenswood or Evanston line to Quincy or Van Buren.

City Council Chambers at City Hall, Washington, LaSalle, Randolph, and Clark Sts. ☎ **744-4000.**

Not far from the Board of Trade, power of a slightly different sort is being brokered during the public meetings of the equally volatile Chicago City Council, which meets in City Hall, a block-size complex. Faction fighting can be down and dirty when the right issue is being debated, and the political posturing can make for the best kind of theatrics. Call ahead to find out when the council is in session (☎ **744-3081**).

Admission: Free.

Open: When in session. **Bus:** No. 20, 56, 131, or 157. **Subway/El:** Take the Lake Street line to Clark or the O'Hare/Congress/Douglas line to Washington.

In Southern Grant Park

At Balbo Street and South Michigan Avenue, where the Blackstone Hotel stands on the corner, you could turn to the east and cross Grant Park, following the lakeshore route as you make the long trek to the Field Museum, the aquarium, and the planetarium. Or you can make your approach by continuing south on Michigan Avenue until you spot the wooden pedestrian bridge opposite 12th Street that crosses the tracks in the general vicinity of the Field Museum (the other establishments lie just beyond). The CTA no. 146 bus will take you to all three of these attractions. Call **836-7000** for stop locations and schedule.

Field Museum of Natural History, Roosevelt Rd. and Lake Shore Dr. ☎ **922-9410.**

For those who find the foundations of science—anthropology, botany, zoology, and geology—more intriguing than technology, the Field Museum of Natural History will be more compelling than the Museum of Science and Industry. Indeed, the Field Museum—

endowed by the redoubtable Chicago prince of dry goods, Marshall Field I—was initially mounted in the old Palace of Fine Arts following the World Columbian Exposition of 1893, the very same complex in Hyde Park that now houses the Museum of Science and Industry. The current home of the Field Museum, a tour de force of classicism in marble (designed by Daniel Burnham after the Erechtheum in Athens, but completed by others long after his death), was opened to the public in 1921. Spread over the museum's acres of floor space are the scores of permanent and temporary exhibitions—some interactive, but most requiring the enriching skills of observation, imagination, and reflection, notably those grand presentations in taxidermy and sculpture of the flora, fauna, and early peoples of the natural world.

One anthropological coup at the Field is a permanent exhibit entitled "Inside Ancient Egypt." In 1908 researchers excavated in Saqqara, Egypt, two of the original chambers from the tomb of Unis-ankh, son of the Fifth Dynasty ruler, Pharaoh Unis, and transported them to the museum in Chicago. This mastaba (tomb) of Unis-ankh now forms the core of a spellbinding exhibit that realistically depicts scenes from Egyptian funeral, religious, and other social practices.

Visitors can explore aspects of the day-to-day world of ancient Egypt, viewing 23 actual mummies and realistic burial scenes, a living marsh environment and canal works, the ancient royal barge, a religious shrine, and a reproduction of a typical marketplace of the period. Many of the exhibits allow hands-on interaction, and there are special activities for kids, like making parchment from living papyrus plants.

A permanent exhibit called "Traveling the Pacific" employs hundreds of artifacts from the museum's oceanic collection to re-create scenes of island life in the South Pacific. Highlighted in the exhibit are the art and rituals of Pacific cultures, including Hawaii, Tahiti, and Papua New Guinea, dramatized through display of objects of war, celebration, and ceremony.

The other perennial exhibits at the Field Museum include the valley of the dinosaurs, dazzling gemstones, a Pawnee earth lodge for storytelling on Native American life and lore, and those appealing dioramas that depict the ways and customs of ancient peoples.

A welcome change here—instead of the traditional cafeteria found in most museums, there's a McDonald's.

Admission: $5 adults; $3 children ages 3–17, students with ID, and seniors; free for children 2 and under, members, teachers, and armed forces personnel in uniform. Maximum family charge $16. Free admission on Wed.

IMPRESSIONS

This is a great uninteresting place.
—Matthew Arnold, Letter to Miss Arnold, January 23, 1884

Open: Daily 9am–5pm. **Closed:** Thanksgiving, Christmas, and New Year's days. **Bus:** No. 146.

Adler Planetarium, 1300 Lake Shore Dr. ☎ 322-0304, or 322-0300 for a recorded message.

A causeway across one end of Burnham Park Harbor links the mainland here to Northerly Island, which is occupied by two tenants, Miegs Field, the in-town landing strip for small, private aircraft; and the Adler Planetarium. The zodiacal 12-sided structure sits on a promontory at the end of ornamental Solidarity Drive, just up the road from the aquarium. The founder of this planetarium, Sears, Roebuck executive Max Adler, imported a Zeiss projector invented in Germany in 1923 to Chicago in 1930 because he wished to bring the sky closer to people, hoping the novelty of the artificial sky would redirect attention to the real experience of watching a night sky.

Today the Adler Planetarium offers a range of programs for both children and adults. Multimedia sky shows re-create the nighttime skies and current topics in space exploration. A closed-circuit monitor connected to the planetarium's Doane Observatory telescope allows visitors to view dramatic close-ups of the moon, the planets, and distant galaxies. In addition, there are exhibits of early scientific instruments, and a display on stars and galaxies called the "New Universe."

To find out what to look for in this month's sky, call the Nightwatch 24-Hour Hot Line (☎ 322-0334).

Admission: $4 adults, $2 children and seniors. Children's sky show (for children under 6) $2 per person.

Open: Sat–Thurs 9am–5pm, Fri 9am–9pm. Sky shows at numerous times throughout the day—call 322-0300 for current times. **Bus:** No. 146.

★ Shedd Aquarium, 1200 S. Lake Shore Dr. ☎ 939-2438.

Closest to the Field Museum is the Shedd Aquarium, a marble octagon, whose Doric exterior is decorated with a motif of marine symbols, and whose interior galleries are populated by thousands of denizens of river, lake, and sea. The aquarium's most popular entertainment is the twice-daily (at 11am and 2pm; additional show at 3pm on Saturday and Sunday) Coral Reef feeding of the sharks and other creatures of the reefs, from the hands of divers who swim them in a 90,000-gallon tank. It's also fun to watch the frolicking of the river otters in their naturalistic habitat, landscaped with plant life native to the Illinois prairie. But the true revelation comes from studying the collection of sea anemones, those odd flowerlike animals of the deep.

Already the world's largest indoor aquarium, the Shedd recently doubled its size with the opening of the Oceanarium, a marine mammal pavilion that re-creates a Pacific Northwest coastal environment. As you follow a winding nature trail, you encounter whales, dolphins, sea otters, and harbor seals. A colony of penguins in a separate exhibit area inhabits a naturalistic environment meant to resemble the Mariana Islands in the southern sea off Argentina. You observe all

South Michigan Ave./Grant Park

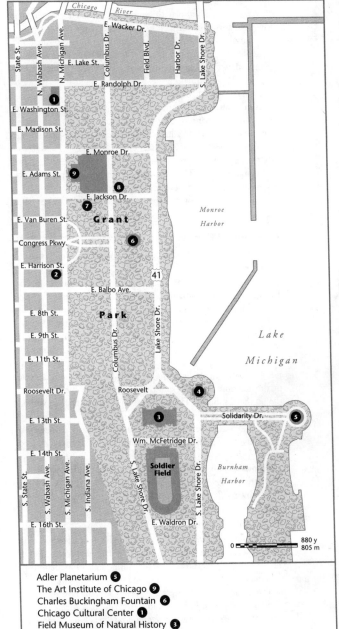

Adler Planetarium **5**
The Art Institute of Chicago **9**
Charles Buckingham Fountain **6**
Chicago Cultural Center **1**
Field Museum of Natural History **3**
John G. Shedd Aquarium **4**
Petrillo Music Shell **8**
The Seated Lincoln **7**
Spertus Museum of Judaica **2**

these sea mammals at play through large underwater viewing windows. On a fixed performance schedule in a large pool surrounded by an amphitheater, the whales and dolphins are put through their paces of leaps and dives by a crew of friendly trainers. If you want a good sit-down meal in a restaurant with a spectacular view overlooking Lake Michigan, check out Sounding's, right there inside the aquarium.

Admission: Both Aquarium and Oceanarium, $8 adults, $6 children 3–11 and seniors, free for children under 3. Oceanarium admission on Thurs, $4 adults, $3 children 3–11 and seniors. Original aquarium galleries only, $4 adults, $3 children 3–11 and seniors; free to everyone on Thurs. Aquarium tickets available on a limited, first-come, first-served basis, so it's recommended you purchase tickets in advance at any Ticketmaster outlet.

Open: Daily 9am–6pm; last entry into Oceanarium 5:15 pm. **Bus:** No. 146.

North of the Loop

John Hancock Observatory, on the 94th floor of the John Hancock Center, 875 N. Michigan. ☎ **751-3681.**

The John Hancock Observatory, locally known as "Big John," delivers an excellent panorama of the city, and an intimate view over nearby Lake Michigan and the various shoreline residential areas. On a clear day you can see portions of the three states surrounding this corner of Illinois (Michigan, Indiana, and Wisconsin), for a radius of 80 miles. The view up the North Side is particularly dramatic, stretching from the nearby Oak and North Street Beaches, along the green strip of Lincoln Park, the line of high-rises that you can trace up the shoreline until they suddenly halt just below the boundary of the northern suburbs. The lake itself seems like a vast sea without any boundaries at all.

Big John has three high-speed elevators that carry passengers to the observatory in 40 seconds. For wheelchair assistance, call prior to your visit.

Admission: $3.65 adults, $2.35 seniors and children ages 5–17.

Open: Daily 9am–midnight. **Bus:** No. 125, 145, 146, 147, or 151. **Subway/El:** Take the Howard line to Chicago Ave.

★ **Chicago Historical Society,** Clark St. (at North Ave.). ☎ 642-4600.

At the southwestern tip of Lincoln Park stands one of Chicago's most interesting exhibition halls. Don't let the phrase *historical society* put you off—this scholars' tower isn't only for eggheads and highbrows.

In the society's new permanent second-floor exhibition, called "We the People," among the objects that are my personal favorites are an original copy of the Ephrata Cloister Hymnal, a memento of a little-known early communal religious group in colonial Pennsylvania; and the Boweles' New Pocket Map (1784), which depicts Mount Desert Island and the Penobscot Bay along the coast of Maine in reverse order. Various other articles and documents reveal how the nation's mercantile interests prolonged the practice of importing slaves from Africa. Also rare—as both a document and the tale it refers to—was the copy of Herman Mann's 1866 biography of Deborah Sampson, the "female soldier in the war of Revolution." I had a hard time leaving because each time I started to go, my eye would catch something, like the touching painting of Washington's farewell to his staff at New York's Fraunces Tavern, which shows many of the officers openly and unashamedly weeping as they take leave of their commander-in-chief.

Probably the most exciting, emotionally charged exhibit on the Civil War you will ever see, **A House Divided** opened at the Historical Society in February 1990, and is scheduled to close in the year 2000. The exhibition is divided into eight sections and draws upon the society's antebellum Lincoln and Civil War holdings. Through a display of more than 600 artifacts, it examines the major political and social forces of mid-19th-century America, with a strong emphasis on Abraham Lincoln as the human perspective against which the monumental events of that time are explored. Some of the major artifacts include the "Railsplitter" painting of Lincoln, the Emancipation Proclamation table, the Appomattox table, Lincoln's deathbed, John Brown's Bible, and a diorama of the Lincoln-Douglas debates. Another exhibit of great appeal at the society is "The Chicago Street, 1860–2000," a replica of State Street including both the past and the future.

Adding to the museum's attractiveness is the recently opened restaurant, the **Big Shoulders Café,** on the ground floor past the gift shop, entered through a terra-cotta arch. Its facade is adorned with animals and historical figures in relief, and was removed intact from the old Stockyard Bank and reassembled here. The food is light, delicious and imaginative. A digression here is justified even if you don't dine, simply to see this magnificent archway.

Admission: $3 adults, $2 seniors and students, $1 children ages 6–17. Free admission on Mon.

Open: Mon–Sat 9:30am–4:30pm, Sun noon–5pm. **Bus:** Nos. 11, 22, 36, 72, 151, and 156 all stop nearby.

⭐ **Lincoln Park Zoo,** on the southern border of Lincoln Park. ☎ 935-6700.

The Lincoln Park Zoo is spread over 35 acres and is open 365 days a year. The animals occupy separate habitats according to their kind, and in most cases the viewing possibilities are maximized. The zoo is humanely and imaginatively designed. The seal tank, for example, has a lower passage with a wall of glass, so that these sleek arctic mammals can be seen swimming underwater as well as sunning and cavorting on the land portion of their den. The families of great apes in the ape house sometimes seem to be studying the humans as intently as we do them.

The best time to visit the zoo, of course, is in the summer, for that is when the park itself is at its most animated, overflowing with people, with thousands of local residents taking a stroll through the zoo as part of their daily constitutional. The zoo has a population of more than 2,000 animals, birds, and reptiles, with just the names of the large mammals enough to excite interest: gorillas, rhinos, wolves, bears, camels, bison, gazelles, big cats, zebras, orangutans, elephants, and hippos. For the adjoining children's zoo, see "Cool for Kids" later in this chapter.

Admission: Free.

Open: Daily 8am–5:15pm. Zoo buildings 9am–5pm. **Bus:** No. 145, 146, 147, 151, or 156.

In Hyde Park

Birthplace of atomic fission, home to the University of Chicago and to the Midwest's most popular tourist attraction, the Museum of Science and Industry, Hyde Park is also one of Chicago's most prosperous, attractive, sophisticated—and integrated—neighborhoods. Whatever you do, set aside at least one full day to explore this southeast corner of Chicago.

HISTORY   When Hyde Park was settled in 1850, it became Chicago's first suburb. A hundred years later, in the 1950s, Hyde Park added another first to its impressive résumé, one that the current neighborhood is not particularly proud of—it was selected as the prototype for the nation's first urban-renewal plan. At the time a certain amount of old commercial and housing stock was demolished rather than rehabilitated—just those kinds of buildings that would be much prized today—and replaced by projects and small shopping malls that actually make some corners of Hyde Park look more suburban, in the modern sense, than they really are. Beneath the grandstand of Stagg Field, where the legendary University of Chicago football team once played, Enrico Fermi's scientific team was allowed to perform its research, unleashing the terrible power of the split atom.

For the rest, Hyde Park seems to shine like the evening star. In racially balkanized Chicago, Hyde Park leads the way toward an alternative vision. The 1980 census numbered 17,000 whites and 11,000 blacks in the neighborhood's population, a racial balance that nevertheless once earned Hyde Parkers a witty barb from the sharp tongues of Mike Nichols and Elaine May: "Hyde Parkers: white and black, arm in arm, united against the poor." Hyde Park is decidedly middle class, with pockets of grand affluence in Kenwood that reflect the days when merchant princes and corporate magnates moved here with their families following the decline of Prairie Avenue as the city's Mansion Row around 1900. Among those "old" Chicago

IMPRESSIONS

SATAN (impatiently) to NEW-COMER: *The trouble with you Chicago people is, that you think you are the best people down here; whereas you are merely the most numerous.*
—Mark Twain, "Pudd'nhead Wilson's New Calendar," in *More Tramps Abroad,* 1897

families who once occupied the estates in Kenwood were meat packer Gustavus Swift; lumber merchant Martin Ryerson; Sears, Roebuck executive Julius Rosenwald (who endowed the Museum of Science and Industry); John Shedd (the president of Marshall Field who gave the city the aquarium that bears his name); and William Goodman (who sponsored the Art Institute and the theater to which his name is affixed). Among Hyde Park-Kenwood's well-known black residents in recent years were the late Elijah Muhammad and Muhammad Ali, along with numerous other Nation of Islam families who continue to worship in a mosque, formerly a Greek Orthodox cathedral, that is one of the neighborhood's architectural landmarks. Surrounding this unusual enclave, however, are many blocks of poverty and slum housing. For all its nobility, Hyde Park's achievement in integration merely emphasizes the obvious, that behind the bugaboo of racial prejudice stalks the more unyielding specter of poverty.

Hyde Park has gained a reputation as an activist community in the course of a long struggle for self-preservation. Rather than flee before the expansion of the "Black Belt" that began the radical transformation of Chicago's South Side from World War I onward, most whites here—aided by the strong institutional power and presence of the university—chose integration as the only realistic strategy to preserve their neighborhood. A certain vitality springs from acts of coping with the world as you find it, and it is this element that distinguishes Hyde Park from other middle-class neighborhoods in Chicago. Hyde Park, in a word, is self-assured and cosmopolitan.

The University of Chicago is widely hailed as one of the more intellectually exciting institutions of higher learning in the country. And certainly on the level of research scholarship the U of C, which has been home to some 58 Nobel laureates, takes a backseat to no one. The year the university opened its doors, 1892, was a big one for Hyde Park, but 1893 was even bigger. In that year, Chicago, chosen over other cities in a competitive international field, hosted the World Columbian Exposition, commemorating the 400th anniversary of Columbus's discovery of America.

To create a fairground, the landscape architect Frederick Law Olmsted was enlisted to fill in the marshlands along Hyde Park's lakefront and link what was to become Jackson Park to existing Washington Park on the neighborhood's western boundary with a narrow concourse called the Midway Plaisance. On the resulting 650 acres, at the cost of $30 million, 12 exhibit palaces, 57 buildings devoted to U.S. states and foreign governments, and dozens of smaller structures were constructed under the supervision of architect Daniel Burnham. Most of the building followed Burnham's preference for the Classical Revival style and exterior surfaces finished in white stucco. With the innovation of outdoor electric lighting, the sparkling result was the "White City" that attracted 27 million visitors in a single season, running from May 1 to October 31, 1893. The exposition sponsors, in that brief time, had remarkably recovered their investment, but within a few short years of its closing, most of the fair's buildings were destroyed by vandalism and fire. Only the Palace of Fine Arts, occupying the eastern tip of the midway, survives to this day, and now houses the Museum of Science and Industry.

GETTING THERE   From the Loop, the ride to Hyde Park on the **no. 6 Jeffrey Express bus** takes about 30 minutes. The bus originates on Wacker Drive, travels south along State Street, and ultimately follows Lake Shore Drive to Hyde Park. Weekdays the bus runs from around 5am to 10:30pm, and on weekends and holidays from around 7am to 8pm. The southbound bus adds a surcharge of 30¢ to the normal fare of $1.50. The **no. 1 local bus** originates at Union Station on Adams and Canal Streets.

The **Metra/Electric train** follows the old Illinois Central line—and is still referred to as the IC—arriving in Hyde Park in about 15 minutes from downtown. Trains run every hour Monday through Saturday from 5:15am to 12:50am, and at two-hour intervals on Sunday and holidays from 12:50am to 10:30pm. IC stations in the loop are at Michigan and Randolph and at Van Buren Street, where printed schedules are available. The fare is approximately $1.90 each way.

For CTA bus and Metra train information, call **836-7000.**

For **taxis,** dial TAXI-CAB (**829-4222**) for Yellow or Checker cabs. The one-way fare is around $12.

A SUGGESTED ITINERARY   A *long* one-day itinerary for Hyde Park should include the following: a selected tour of the U of C campus, a visit to several museums and cultural institutions, a tour of the Kenwood mansions (preferably by car), a walk through the area's commercial center, and a stroll around the lakeshore Promontory Point.

OFF-CAMPUS

★ **Museum of Science and Industry,** 57th St. and Lake Shore Dr. ☎ **684-1414,** or TDD 684-DEAF.

Hyde Park is on the itinerary of virtually every tourist who comes to Chicago. But it isn't the neighborhood that draws the tourists (most don't even realize the extent of Hyde Park's other charms); it's the Museum of Science and Industry, the granddaddy of every interactive museum, balm to all button-pushers, with something for children of all ages.

In statistical terms alone the museum's collection is awesome: some 2,000 exhibits spread over 14 acres in 75 exhibition halls. The current headliner attraction at the museum is the Henry Crown Space Center, where the story of space exploration, still in its infancy, is documented in copious detail, highlighted by a simulated space shuttle experience through sight and sound at the center's Omnimax Theater. Old hat now, but still my personal favorite, is the descent into a full-scale replica of a southern Illinois coal mine (for which there is a charge of $1). But whatever your particular techno-fetish—from submarines to space capsules, special effects to the mysteries of the human organism—you will find the object of your curiosity somewhere in this one-size-fits-all museum. The Omnimax Theater offers Friday and Saturday evening showings at 7 and 8pm.

Admission: Museum only, $5 adults, $4 seniors, $2 children ages 5–12, free for children under 5. Free on Thurs. Museum and Omnimax Theater, $9 adults, $7 seniors, $5 children; children under 5 admitted free if seated on an adult's lap. Omnimax Theater only, Thurs and evening shows $5.50 adults, $4.50 seniors, $3.50 children. Free parking.

Open: Summer daily 9:30am–5:30pm; fall–spring Mon–Fri 9:30am–4pm, Sat–Sun and holidays 9:30am–5:30pm. **Bus:** No. 151 or 156.

DuSable Museum of African American History, 740 E. 56th Place. ☎ **947-0600.**

The DuSable Museum is one of several repositories created in recent years of the history, art, and artifacts pertaining to the African-American experience and culture. Sadly, as interesting as many of the exhibits are, the bulk of the collection dates only from the WPA period in the late thirties and the black arts movement of the sixties, though there are some exhibits, albeit sketchy, tracing the earlier stages of the African-American experience in this country.

The museum, located on the eastern edge of Washington Park, also has a gift shop, a research library, and an extensive program of community-related events, including an annual carnival celebration.

Admission: $3 adults, $1 children ages 6–13, $2 students and seniors. Free on Thurs.

Open: Mon–Wed and Fri 10am–5pm, Thurs 10am–6pm, Sat 10am–5pm, Sun 10am–5pm. **Bus:** No. 4. **Subway/El:** Take the Howard line to Jackson Park.

THE UNIVERSITY OF CHICAGO

The University of Chicago offers visitors several campus tours, and an Activities Line (☎ **702-9559** for a recorded message) that lists current campus events. **Campus tours** are organized by the university's Office of Special Events (☎ **702-8374**). Tours begin at 10am on Monday to Saturday from Ida Noyes Hall, 1212 E. 59th St. Free campus maps and copies of the "Chronicle," a calendar of events put out by the university's information service, may be picked up at several locations on campus, among them Robie House, 5757 S. Woodlawn, and the Graduate Admissions Office in the Administration Building.

Just walking around the University of Chicago campus is bound to fill you with that old college feeling, as you wander over the paths from one inner quad to another, browsing among the buildings. Some stops to consider are the Henry Moore statue, *Nuclear Energy*, on South Ellis Avenue between 56th and 57th Streets next to the Roentgen Library, which marks the site of the old Stagg Field, where on December 2, 1942, the world's first sustained nuclear reaction was achieved. The **Seminary Co-op Bookstore,** 5757 S. University Ave. (☎ **752-4381**), has just about everything on the shelves you might

The Museum of Science and Industry

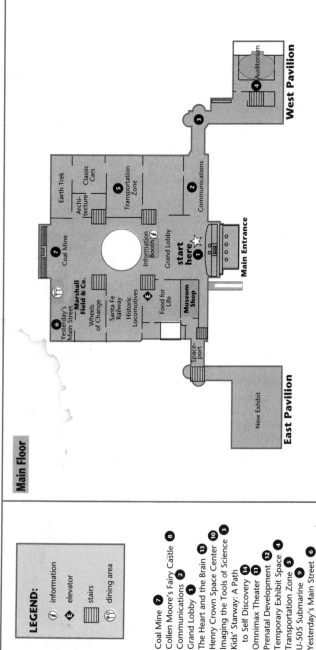

Main Floor

West Pavilion

Auditorium ④

③

Earth Trek

Classic Cars

Architecture

Transportation Zone ⑤

Coal Mine ⑦

Communications ②

Information Booth ⓘ

Grand Lobby

★ start here ①

Main Entrance

Marshall Field & Co.

Wheels of Change

Santa Fe Railway

Historic Locomotives

Food for Life

Yesterday's Main Street ⑥

Museum Shop

Space-port

New Exhibit

East Pavilion

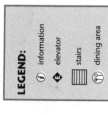

LEGEND:

ⓘ information
🔼 elevator
▥ stairs
🍴 dining area

Coal Mine ⑦
Collen Moore's Fairy Castle ⑧
Communications ②
Grand Lobby ①
The Heart and the Brain ⑬
Henry Crown Space Center ⑩
Imaging the Tools of Science ③
Kids' Starway: A Path to Self Discovery ⑭
Omnimax Theater ⑪
Prenatal Development ⑫
Temporary Exhibit Space ④
Transportation Zone ⑤
U-505 Submarine ⑨
Yesterday's Main Street ⑥

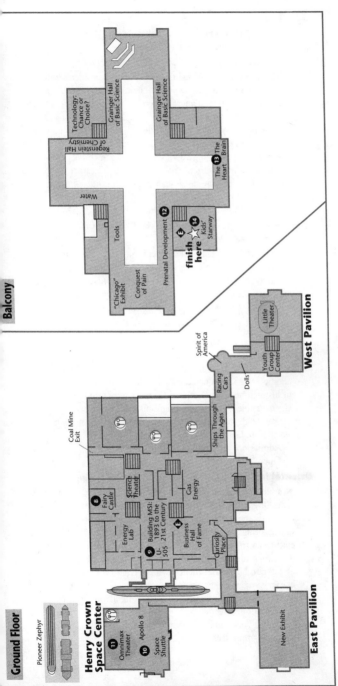

Ground Floor

Pioneer Zephyr

Henry Crown Space Center

Omnimax Theater

Apollo 8
10 Space Shuttle

11

Coal Mine Exit

Energy Lab

Fairy Castle **8**

Science Theater

Building MSI: 1893 to the 21st Century

U-505 **9**

Gas Energy

Business Hall of Fame

Curiosity Place

Ships Through the Ages

Spirit of America

Racing Cars

Dolls

West Pavilion

Little Theater

Youth Group Center

East Pavilion

New Exhibit

Balcony

"Chicago" Exhibit

Conquest of Pain

Tools

Water

Technology: Chance or Choice?

Regenstein Hall of Chemistry

Grainger Hall of Basic Science

Grainger Hall of Basic Science

Prenatal Development **12**

finish here

Kids' Starway **14**

The Heart **13** The Brain

9057

want, including the full collection of Penguin paperbacks. It's open Monday through Friday from 8:30am to 9pm, Saturday from 10am to 6pm, and Sunday from noon to 6pm.

Robie House, 5757 S. Woodlawn Ave. ☎ **702-2175.**

One of Frank Lloyd Wright's finest works is considered among the five masterpieces of 20th-century American architecture. A tour takes you to the first-floor living/dining room only (the other rooms serve the university as administrative offices). The open layout and craftsmanship are typical of a Wright design. Robie House, however, is by no means the most satisfying of Wright's houses in my opinion, its institutional-looking exterior having lost something of the delight of discovery in new forms that characterizes his earlier work, much of which can be viewed—at least from the outside—in Oak Park.

Admission: Free.

Open: Daily tours at noon. **Bus:** No. 55.

Rockefeller Memorial Chapel, 5850 S. Woodlawn Ave. ☎ **702-7000.**

The Rockefeller Memorial Chapel is on the campus grounds, just across from Robie House. Did someone say chapel? This is false modesty, even for a Rockefeller. When the university first opened its doors, the students sang the following ditty:

> *John D. Rockefeller, wonderful man is he*
> *Gives all his spare change to the U of C.*

John D. was a generous patron, indeed. He founded the university (in cooperation with the American Baptist Society), built the magnificent mini-cathedral that now bears his name, and shelled out an additional $35 million in donations to the institution over the course of his lifetime. The Memorial Chapel's outstanding feature is the circular stained-glass window high above the main altar that captures the sun's radiance with such intensity as to give new meaning to the words from Genesis, "Let there be light."

Admission: Free.

Open: Daily 9am–4pm. **Bus:** No. 55.

Oriental Institute, 1155 E. 58th St. ☎ **702-9520** for special tours.

Near the midpoint of the campus, just north of the Memorial Chapel, is the Oriental Institute, housing one of the world's major collections of Near Eastern art, dating from 9000 B.C. to the 10th century A.D., underscoring the maxim that archeologists are to grave robbers what epicures are to mere gluttons. These ancient objects are extraordinarily beautiful to the eye, subtle in form, texture, and hue.

The gift shop at the Oriental Institute, called the Suq, is renowned in its own right as a shopper's treasure trove. Deck yourself with the jewelry of the Fertile Crescent . . . and walk like an Egyptian.

Admission: Free.

Open: Tues and Thurs–Sat 10am–4pm, Wed 10am–8:30pm, Sun noon–4pm. **Bus:** No. 55.

David and Alfred Smart Museum of Art, 5550 S. Greenwood Ave. (at E. 56th St.). ☎ 702-0200.

The David and Alfred Smart Museum of Art is named for two of the founders of *Esquire* magazine, whose family foundation created the University of Chicago's fine arts museum that bears their name, housing a permanent collection of more than 5,000 works ranging from classical antiquity to the contemporary. The Smart also hosts an intriguing variety of temporary exhibitions with names like "Selected Work from the Prinzhorn Collection of the Art of the Mentally Ill" and "The Earthly Chimera and the Femme Fatale: Fear of Woman in Late Nineteenth Century Art."

Admission: Free, but donations welcome.

Open: Tues–Fri noon–4pm, Sat–Sun noon–6pm. **Closed:** Holidays. **Bus:** No. 55.

OUTDOOR ATTRACTIONS

Hyde Park is not only a haven for book lovers and culture aficionados—the community also has its open-air attractions. One unexpected corner of tranquility is the **Bergen Garden,** a one-acre formal garden three stories high built on the roof of the parking garage at an exclusive condominium called Regents Park, 5050 S. Lake Shore Dr. (☎ 288-5050). Self-guided public tours of the garden are permitted, and what you will see will amaze you: lagoons (with eight inches of water, but painted black to give the appearance of depth), live ducks, several fountains, a maze of pathways among scores of trees and 30,000 plants, and a small waterfall—a tour de force of urban landscape gardening that transformed a bleak concrete eyesore into a delightful sanctuary.

A number of additional worthy outdoor environments are located near Lake Michigan, including Lake Shore Drive itself, where many stately apartment houses follow the contour of the shoreline. A very suitable locale for a quiet stroll is Promontory Point, at 55th Street and Lake Michigan, a bulb of land that juts into the lake and offers a good view of Chicago to the north, and the seasonally active 57th Street beach to the south.

Farther south, just below the Museum of Science and Industry, is Wooded Island in **Jackson Park,** the site of the Japanese Pavilion during the Columbian Exposition, and today a lovely garden of meandering paths. The Perennial Garden in Jackson Park is located at 59th Street and Stony Island Avenue, where more than 180 varieties of flowering plants display a palate of colors that changes with the seasons.

2   More Attractions

A Loop Sculpture Tour

With the help of a very comprehensive pamphlet, **"The Loop Sculpture Guide,"** you can guide yourself through Grant Park and much of the Loop to view some 65 examples of Chicago's monumental public art. The best-known of these works are by 20th-century artists and include such familiar names as Picasso, Chagall, Miró, Calder, Moore, and Oldenburg. The guide also highlights the more traditional park monuments of such 19th-century sculptors as Augustus Saint-Gaudens and Lorado Taft. Thirty major works are illustrated by photographs and provided with detailed descriptions in the guide and are further identified on a foldout map of the Loop.

"The Loop Sculpture Guide" is available by mail order for $1.50. Send a check to the **Chicago Department of Cultural Affairs,** 78 E. Washington St., Chicago, IL 60602 (☎ **FINE-ART** or **346-3278**), which also sponsors some 800 free programs and exhibits annually. Call them for a listing of the art events that are current during your stay in Chicago.

Along South Michigan Avenue

Fashion may have moved north to the Magnificent Mile, but Chicago's grandest stretch of boulevard is still south of the river. From the Michigan Avenue Bridge to the Field Museum, South Michigan Avenue runs parallel to Grant Park on one side and the Loop on the other. A stroll along this boulevard in any season offers the visitor many visual and cultural treats. The attractions are listed from north to south.

Chicago Cultural Center, 78 E. Washington St. ☎ **427-7602** (office) or **939-3880** (auditorium).

The Cultural Center is an exhibit hall showcasing a wide variety of art. The center also presents a wide program of performances, some of them for children, in the form of film, puppet shows, movement, storytelling, and juggling.

Promoted as the "People's Palace," what was formerly the main branch of the Chicago Public Library has several features that lure visitors. The building itself dates from 1897, and can also be appreciated from without as a monumental object of Renaissance proportions. Most of the first floor of the Cultural Center on this side of the building houses the Museum of Broadcast Communications, which includes the Radio Hall of Fame and the Kraft TeleCenter. Access to the museum is free of charge. The Chicago Office of Tourism now has its offices here as well, and there is an information booth on the premises.

The ground floor on the Randolph Street side of the Cultural Center provides space for a large gallery/cafe where art from Chicago's neighborhoods is featured on a regular and rotating basis. The Chicago Cultural Center Gallery/Cafe is the perfect spot to hang out over a cup of gourmet coffee and a light snack. Many small tables with chairs are spread over a large area surrounded by walls of art.

Admission: Free.

Open: Mon–Thurs 9am–7pm, Fri 9am–6pm, Sat 9am–5pm. **Closed:** Most major holidays. **Bus:** 3, 4, 60, 145, 147, or 151. **Subway/El:** Take the Ravenswood or Lake/Dan Ryan line to Madison.

Fine Arts Building, 410 S. Michigan Ave. ☎ **427-7602.**

Built as a showroom for Studebaker carriages in 1885, the landmark Fine Arts Building was converted at the turn of the century into a concert hall whose upper stories sheltered a number of well-known publications (*Saturday Evening Post, Dial*) and provided offices for such luminaries as Frank Lloyd Wright, sculptor Lorado Taft, and L. Frank Baum, author of *The Wizard of Oz.* Harriet Monroe published her magazine, *Poetry,* here and first introduced American readers to Carl Sandburg, T. S. Eliot, and Ezra Pound. Movie buffs should take note that the two original ground-floor theaters have been converted into an art cinema with four separate screening rooms. Located throughout the building are a number of interesting musical instrument shops. Take a quick walk at least through the lovely marble-and-wood lobby, which suggests something monastic and cloisterlike, or visit the top floor (10th) to see the spectacular murals.

Admission: Free.

Open: Daily 8am–6pm. **Bus:** No. 3, 4, 60, 145, 147, or 151.

Subway/El: Take the Ravenswood or Lake/Dan Ryan line to Madison.

Auditorium Building and Theater, 50 E. Congress Pkwy. ☎ **922-4046.**

On the corner of Congress Parkway and Michigan Avenue is a national landmark that was designed and built in 1889 by Louis Sullivan and Dankmar Adler, the Auditorium Building and Theater. Considered Sullivan's masterpiece, the theater's interior is a glittering display of mirrors and stained glass and is equally renowned for its excellent acoustics and sightlines, making good seats of all 4,000 within its confines. The Auditorium Building, formerly a hotel, was the first building to be wired for electric light in Chicago, and the theater was the first in the country to install air conditioning. In the days when the Auditorium was the first theater of Chicago, the hydraulically operated stage could be lowered from view, creating a ballroom capable of accommodating 8,000 guests.

For ticket reservations or box office information, call **922-2110.**

Admission: Tours free.

Open: Tours offered Mon–Tues and occasionally Wed–Thurs. Call for details. **Bus:** No. 145, 147, or 151.

Museum of Contemporary Photography, 600 S. Michigan Ave. ☎ **663-5554.**

The Museum of Contemporary Photography is located in a wing of Columbia College, near the corner of Harrison Street. The museum exhibits, collects, and promotes contemporary photography. Related lectures and special programs are scheduled during the year.

Admission: Free.

Open: Mon–Fri 10am–5pm, Sat noon–5pm. Shorter hours in summer. **Bus:** No. 6 or 146. **Subway/El:** Take the Howard line to Harrison.

Spertus Museum of Judaica, 618 S. Michigan Ave. ☎ **922-9012.**
The Spertus Museum of Judaica houses intricately crafted and historic Jewish ceremonial objects, textiles, coins, paintings, and sculpture, tracing 3,500 years of Jewish heritage.

Admission: $3.50 adults, $2 children.

Open: Sun–Wed 10am–5pm, Thurs 10am–8pm, Fri 10am–3pm. **Bus:** No. 145, 147, or 151. **Subway/El:** Take the Howard line to Jackson.

On the Water

NORTH PIER

 Chicago's newest, and among its most popular year-round leisure playgrounds, is **North Pier,** 435 E. Illinois St. (☎ **836-4300**), a two-block-long complex fronting the Chicago River's Ogden Slip, and housing nightspots, museums, restaurants, and nearly four dozen specialty shops, boutiques, and galleries. Having outgrown its mercantile role as Chicago's largest warehouse and distribution center, North Pier has been gradually rehabilitated over the past few years as a one-of-a-kind entertainment center. For a selected list of shops, see Chapter 9.

North Pier shopping hours are Monday through Saturday from 11am to 9pm, and Sunday from noon to 8pm. Parking is available in lots adjacent to the complex for $4 for four hours with a validation ticket obtained with a minimum purchase. Six Chicago Transit Authority buses go directly to North Pier, nos. 29, 56, 65, 66, 120, and 121. Seasonal boat-docking facilities are also available; for information call **836-4252.**

NAVY PIER

If everything goes according to plan, the $150 million redevelopment of Navy Pier, 600 E. Grand Ave. (☎ **791-6568**) will have been completed in the spring of 1995. On its 50 acres of pier and lakefront property, you will encounter one of the premier entertainment environments in the world, a veritable Tivoli by the lake. Featured in this constellation of attractions is the Sky Line Stage, a state-of-the-art performance venue for world-class productions. The Family Pavilion will provide a new home for the Chicago Children's Museum, complete with IMAX theater. Permanent rides like a 15-story ferris wheel and a carousel will enhance the Pier's festive, carnival atmosphere. There will be various parks and promenades throughout, including an indoor botanical garden. A reflecting pool becomes an ice skating rink by winter, while in the summertime, dinner and cruise boats will embark directly from the Pier's spacious dockside marina. To round out this impressive entertainment infrastructure will be a host of restaurants, shops and outdoors markets, exhibitions spaces, and a beer garden.

North of the Loop

North of the Chicago River are a number of attractions that the visitor should not overlook. These include several museums and

The Loop Sculpture Tour

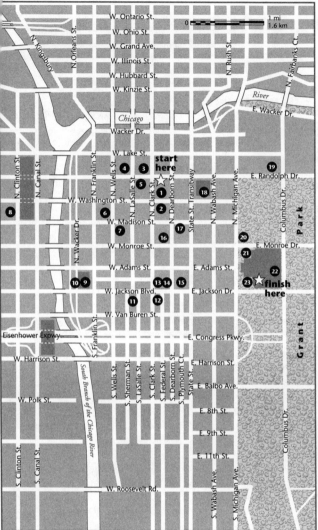

buildings, the city's most important park, a zoo, and one of the world's most impressive research libraries. What we might refer to as "official sightseeing" on the North Side is confined to two areas: the Magnificent Mile (North Michigan Avenue) and its surrounding blocks, and the Near North Side.

THE MAGNIFICENT MILE

I first read of Chicago's famous **Bughouse Square** in the *Studs Lonigan* trilogy by James T. Farrell, that "outdoor forum of garrulous hobohemia" on Walton Street, between Dearborn and Clark, where an oddball collection of soapbox orators expounding on anything from free love to a stateless society used to harangue each other and the crowds of derisive, delighted onlookers throughout the 1920s. Officially called **Washington Square,** it was one of Chicago's first parks, and the main attractions here today are some fine old mansions and renovated town houses, and the glorious Newberry Library, which, incidentally, sponsors a revival of the Bughouse Square debates on a designated weekend each September, an event in which the public is heartily encouraged to participate.

Here's Chicago, in the Water Tower Pumping Station, 163 E. Pearson (at the corner of N. Michigan Ave.). ☎ **467-7114.**

Frommer's Favorite Chicago Experiences

Going to a Cubs Day Game   Wrigley Field on Chicago's Mid-North Side was the last baseball park in the country to install lights for night games. The Cubs still play an extensive daylight schedule, however, and a game at historic Wrigley by sunlight is the way the game should be played and seen.

Spending the Weekend at a Hotel   Indulge yourself in the pleasures of a fine hotel some weekend in Chicago, when rates are half what they are during the workweek.

Cruising the Chicago River   Inner-city riverways are possessed of some intrinsic mystique; contact the Chicago Architecture Foundation or the Friends of the Chicago River (see "Organized Tours"), and cruise the river on a fascinating, informative guided tour.

Walking the Neighborhoods   The "real" Chicago experience is embodied in the many neighborhoods that make up the city and provide its multicultural diversity. Explore the neighborhoods as much as possible, and you won't regret it.

Eating Out   Any urban center worthy of the name "city" is inevitably a haven for the talents of great cooks, and its residents, who dine out frequently, will set high standards. Chicago is definitely that kind of city.

For a quick and painless orientation to the city, the visitor's first stop in this area ought to be *Here's Chicago,* a 45-minute sound-and-sight show. Both the Pumping Station and the Water Tower across the street—which one wag likened to a sandcastle at the bottom of a goldfish bowl, and which in 1892 Oscar Wilde dubbed a "monstrosity"—were among the only buildings in the path of the Great Fire of 1871 that survived. Despite his almost enviable, childlike sense of design, the architect must have been doing something right, for these two limestone monuments were the only ones that withstood the fiery holocaust when all the other buildings melted around them.

The show begins with a brief tour of the Pumping Station's machinery—which Wilde, anticipating the high-tech fashion craze by nearly a century, is said to have loved. Next, patrons are treated to a few minor exhibits, one on the Chicago Fire, another a tableau of life-size figures representing the denouement of the St. Valentine's Day massacre—the mannequin corpses of the gangsters are laid out in a neat line, including the gent who truly deserves the sobriquet "die-hard" for his parting words (when asked who shot him, he replied through clenched teeth, "Nobody shot me!"). The remainder—and the best part of the show—is visual. First comes a computerized slide show showing the varied scenes and human faces of Chicago, and finally a 70mm film entitled *City of Dreams,* which takes you on a simulated helicopter ride over the city, particularly exciting as the chopper tunnels through downtown by way of the river.

In the Pumping Station lobby you'll find a gift shop, a few fast-food stands, and of particular importance to visitors who are wandering through unknown streets, a Chicago Office of Tourism information desk, clean restrooms, and a bank of pay phones.

Admission: Show tickets $5.75 adults; $4.50 seniors, students, the handicapped, and children under 12; $12 family (including two adults with three or more children).

Open: Daily 9:30am–6pm. Shows presented every 30 minutes until 4pm Mon–Thurs, until 5pm Sat–Sun. **Bus:** No. 125, 145, 146, 147, or 151. **Subway/El:** Take the Howard line to Chicago Ave.

Newberry Library, 60 W. Walton. ☎ 943-9090.

The Newberry Library is a bibliophile's and researcher's dream. Established in 1887 at the bequest of the Chicago merchant and financier Walter Loomis Newberry, the library today contains many rare books and manuscripts, as well as a vast depository of published resources for those who are seriously delving into American and European history and literature, and many other aspects of Western civilization. The collections, many items of which are on display, include more than five million manuscripts and 75,000 maps, housed in a comely five-story granite building, designed in the Spanish-Romanesque style by Henry Ives Cobb, and built for the library in 1893.

Tours: Free 45-minute tours Thurs at 3pm and Sat at 10:30am.
Open: Tues–Thurs 10am–6pm, Fri–Sat 9am–5pm. **Bus:** No. 125, 145, 146, 147, or 151. **Subway/El:** Take the Howard line to Chicago Ave.

Museum of Contemporary Art, 237 E. Ontario. ☎ **280-2660,** or **280-5161** for a recorded announcement.

The MCA exhibits work that emphasizes experimentation in a variety of media—painting, sculpture, photography, video, dance, music, and performance. While the exhibits change frequently, the MCA also has a permanent collection of more than 3,300 pieces, highlighting the work of Chicago artists but gathered from all over the nation and the world as well.

In addition to a range of special activities and educational programming, including special films, tours, and lecture series, the MCA features a store with one-of-a-kind gift items, and the Site Café, made environmentally interesting by an exposed brick wall on which an artist has etched the evolution of an imaginary civilization.

Note: The museum is scheduled to move to its new home at Mies von der Rohe and Chicago Avenue (across from Water Tower Place) sometime in 1995.

Admission: $4 adults; $2 children ages 10–16, students, and seniors; free for children under 10. Free admission on Tues.

Open: Tues–Sat 10am–5pm, Sun noon–5pm. Cafe and store, Tues–Sat 11am–4:45pm. **Bus:** No. 157. **Subway/El:** Take the Howard line to Grand.

LINCOLN SQUARE

An organizational headquarters, **Dankhaus,** 4740 N. Western (☎ **561-9181**), is the local branch of the German-American National Congress, which serves as a meeting hall and as newsroom for the German-language paper *Amerika-Woche.*

More Museums

Chicago has a wealth of smaller museums devoted to a wide range of subjects. Many preserve in their collections the unique stories and heritage of a particular immigrant experience that has become inseparable from the history of the city as a whole.

American Police Center And Museum, 1705–1725 S. State St. ☎ **431-0005.**

A museum displaying police equipment and memorabilia, this must be where Nelson Algren brought Simone de Beauvoir to show her the electric chair, an event Algren refers to in an interview for the *Paris Review.* Tours are by reservation only and require a minimum of 20 people. However, the exhibits are self-explanatory and the museum brochure helps.

Admission: Suggested donation, $2 adults, $1 children.

Open: Mon–Fri 8:30am–4:30pm. **Bus:** No. 29, 44, 62, 99, or 164.

Balzekas Museum of Lithuanian Culture, 6500 S. Pulaski Rd. ☎ 582-6500.

The Balzekas Museum of Lithuanian Culture gives insight into the history and ancient culture of the tiny Baltic state that was absorbed into the former Soviet Union and whose people achieved complete independence in August 1991. The collection contains a range of objects from books to artworks, arms and armor, maps, and decorative ornaments.

Admission: $4 adults, $3 students and seniors, $1 children.

Open: Sat–Thurs 10am–4pm, Fri 10am–8pm. **Bus:** No. 53A.

Martin D'Arcy Gallery of Art, Loyola University, 6525 N. Sheridan Rd. ☎ 508-2679.

A treasure trove of medieval and Renaissance art, the Martin D'Arcy Gallery of Art covers the years A.D. 1100 to 1700. All the rich symbolism of Catholicism through the baroque era is embodied in such works as a gem-encrusted sculpture in silver and ebony of Christ's scourging, a head of John the Baptist on a silver platter, golden chalices, rosary beads carved with biblical scenes, and many other highly ornamented ritual objects.

Admission: Free.

Open: Mon, Wed, and Fri noon–4pm; Tues and Thurs noon–4pm and 6–9pm; Sun 1–4pm. **Bus:** No. 151. **Subway/El:** Take the Howard line to Loyola.

Hull House Museum, 800 S. Halsted. ☎ 413-5353.

Three years after the Haymarket Riot, a young woman named Jane Addams bought an old mansion on Halsted Street that had been built in 1856 as a "country home," but was now surrounded by the shanties of the immigrant poor. Here Addams and her co-worker, Ellen Gates Starr, launched the American settlement house movement with the establishment of Hull House, an institution that endured in Chicago until 1963. In that year all but two of the settlement's 13 buildings, along with the entire residential neighborhood in its immediate vicinity, were demolished to make room for a new university campus. The story of the opposition to this project is eloquently told in the words of the participants themselves, who appear among the scores of others interviewed by Studs Terkel for his book *Division Street America*.

Of the original settlement, what remains today is the Hull House Museum, the mansion itself, and the residents' dining hall, snuggled among the ultramodern, poured-concrete buildings of the University of Illinois Chicago campus. Inside are the original furnishings, Jane Addams's office, and numerous settlement maps and photographs. Rotating exhibits re-create the history of the settlement and the work of its residents. Addams had greatly admired the work of Jacob Riis, whose pictures—though they concentrate on the slum dwellers and conditions of New York City—were visually descriptive of the streets in her midst when Addams moved in 100 years ago. In time, however, those streets—due in part to the work of the settlement—evolved into stable inner-city environments worth fighting over, which happened when the city finally decided to demolish them in favor of a new college campus.

Admission: Free.

Open: Mon–Fri 10am–4pm, plus Sun in summer noon–5pm.

Bus: No. 8. **Subway/El:** Take the O'Hare/Congress/Douglas line to Halsted/University of Illinois.

International Museum of Surgical Sciences, 1524 N. Lake Shore Dr. ☎ 642-3555.

Housed in a 1917 Gold Coast mansion, the museum has a collection of surgical instruments, paintings, and sculpture depicting the history of surgery. A turn-of-the-century apothecary shop and dentist's office are re-created in a historic street exhibit. There's handicap access, but there are a few steps near the entrance.

Admission: Free, but donations requested. Children under 11 not admitted.

Open: Thurs–Sat 10am–4pm, Sun 11am–5pm. **Bus:** No. 147.

Mexican Fine Arts Center Museum, 1852 W. 19th St. ☎ 738-1503.

The Mexican Fine Arts Center Museum features the work of Mexican and Mexican-American artists.

Admission: Free.

Open: Tues–Sun 10am–5pm. **Bus:** No. 9. **Subway/El:** Take the O'Hare/Douglas line to 18th St. or Hoyne.

Museum of Broadcast Communication, 78 E. Washington St. ☎ 629-6000.

Recently relocated to the Chicago Cultural Center, this is the place to listen to or watch the classic programs from the past of radio and television.

Admission: Free.

Open: Mon–Sat 10am–4:30pm, Sun noon–5pm. **Bus:** No. 3, 4, 60, 145, 147, or 151. **Subway/El:** Take the Ravenswood or Lake/Dan Ryan line to Madison.

The Peace Museum, 350 W. Ontario. ☎ 440-1860.

Exhibits, performances, and other programs serve as vehicles for the ideas and messages of the World Peace Movement.

Admission: $2 adults, 50¢ seniors and children.

Open: Tues–Wed, Fri, and Sun noon–5pm; Thurs noon–8pm.

Bus: No. 37 or 41. **Subway/El:** Take the Howard line to Bryn Mawr.

Polish Museum of America, 984 N. Milwaukee. ☎ 384-3352.

Located in the heart of the first Polish neighborhood in Chicago, this is one of the most important collections of Polish art and historical materials outside Poland. And it is also the largest museum in the country devoted exclusively to an ethnic group. The museum's central rotunda is decorated with huge murals that depict Polish accomplishments in science, art, and culture. PMA's programs include rotating exhibitions, films, and lectures.

Admission: Suggested donation $2 adults, $1 children.

Open: Daily 11am–4pm.

Swedish American Museum, 5211 N. Clark. ☎ **728-8111.**

A storefront exhibit chronicles the Swedish immigrant contribution to American life and is also a gift shop for typical items of Scandinavian manufacture. I once saw an exhibit on Alfred Nobel, inventor of dynamite and founder of the Nobel Prizes.

Admission: Free.

Open: Tues–Fri 11am–4pm, Sat–Sun 11am–3pm. **Bus:** No. 22. **Subway/El:** Take the Howard line to Bryn Mawr.

Ukrainian National Museum, 2453 W. Chicago Ave. ☎ **276-6565.**

The Ukrainian National Museum possesses an unmistakably old-world atmosphere; few cultures have seemed to change as little over the ages as that of the Ukrainians. Throughout the two upper stories of this converted brownstone, you will find decorative Easter eggs, fine embroidery, wood carvings, artwork, crafts, and folk costumes, all of which reflect an incredible continuity in technique over the years.

Admission: Donations requested.

Open: Mon–Wed by appointment, Thurs–Sun 11am–4:30pm. **Bus:** No. 49 or 66.

Morton B. Weiss Museum of Judaica, K. A. M. Isaiah Israel Congregation, 1000 E. Hyde Park Blvd. ☎ **924-1234.**

Among other fascinating artifacts of Jewish culture, you'll see some of the findings unearthed at digs in the Holy Land by amateur archeologist Gen. Moshe Dayan. Also of note are the illuminated (illustrated) marriage contracts on parchment from the Middle Ages and the Byzantine-style temple itself, built in 1924.

Admission: Free.

Open: Call for an appointment, or visit following weekly services. **Transportation:** Take the Metra train to Hyde Park; then take a cab.

Chicago's Parks

GRANT PARK

Grant Park is really a patchwork of giant lawns etched by major roadways and a network of railroad tracks, over which are spread a variety of public recreational and cultural facilities. The immense **Buckingham Fountain,** accessible along Congress Drive, is the baroque centerpiece of the park, patterned after—but twice the size of—the Latona Fountain at Versailles, with adjoining esplanades beautified by rose gardens in season. Throughout the late spring and summer, the fountain spurts columns of water up to 100 feet in the air, illuminated after dark by a whirl of colored lights.

Popular outdoor concerts are staged at the **Petrillo Music Shell,** at Jackson and Columbus Drives, over a 10-week summer period every Wednesday, Friday, Saturday, and Sunday evening. Other favorite annual events are the free outdoor jazz festival (around Labor Day), and the blues festival (in June). For program information, call **294-2920.**

Recently completed at the north end of the park is a covered, outdoor **sports plaza** with 12 lighted tennis courts, a rink for ice skating in the winter and roller skating in the summer, a cross-country ski trail that operates during January and February, and a field house.

Scattered about the park are a number of sculptures and monuments, including the Native American on horseback (at Congress Drive and Michigan Avenue), which has become the park's trademark, as well as likenesses of Copernicus, Columbus, and Lincoln, the latter by the American genius Augustus Saint-Gaudens, located on Congress Drive between Michigan Avenue and Columbus Drive. At the south end of the park, deceptively distant from the Art Institute, are the Field Museum of Natural History, the Adler Planetarium, and the Shedd Aquarium (see Section 1, "The Top Attractions," earlier in this chapter).

To get to the park, take bus no. 3, 4, 6, 60, or 146. If you want to take the subway or the el, get off at any stop in the Loop along State or Wabash.

LINCOLN PARK

Lincoln Park is the city's largest, and certainly one of the longest parks around. Straight and narrow, Lincoln Park begins at North Avenue and follows the shoreline of Lake Michigan northward as far as Ardmore Avenue (not far from the "new" Chinatown, and Andersonville). Within its elongated 1,200 acres are a first-class zoo, a half-dozen bathing beaches, a botanical conservatory, two excellent museums, a golf course, and the usual meadows, formal gardens, sporting fields, and tennis courts typical of inner-city parks everywhere. To get to the park, take bus no. 145, 146, 147, 151, or 156.

A group calling itself **Friends of Lincoln Park,** 900 W. Fullerton (☎ 472-7275), has initiated an "adopt-a-monument" program, asking corporate sponsors to underwrite the cleanup and repair costs for a very fine selection of public statues honoring a group of great men: LaSalle, Schiller, Benjamin Franklin, U. S. Grant, Shakespeare, Hans Christian Andersen, Goethe, and, of course, Lincoln. The statue of Lincoln in the park that bears his name is one of two in Chicago by Augustus Saint-Gaudens (the other statue is in Grant Park). Saint-Gaudens also did the Bates Fountain near the conservatory. In the area near the conservatory is the bust of a contemporary figure that the Friends do not cite in their appeal, that of Sir Georg Solti, laureate music director of the Chicago Symphony, one of those rare cases where a man is so memorialized before his death.

Lincoln Park Conservatory, Fullerton Dr. (at Stockton Dr.).
☎ 294-4770.

Inside are four great halls filled with thousands of plants, the closest thing (other than several smaller conservatories scattered in a few neighborhood parks) that Chicago has to a botanical garden within the city limits. The Palm House features giant palms and rubber trees, the Fernery nurtures the plants that grow close to the forest floor, and the Tropical House is a symphony of shiny greenery. A fourth environment is aptly named the Show House, for here the seasonal flower shows are held.

Admission: Free.

Open: Daily 9am–5pm (10am–6pm during flower shows). **Bus** No. 151 or 156.

Chicago Academy of Sciences Museum, 2001 N. Clark St. ☎ 871-2668.

The other nature-oriented institution in the park is the Chicago Academy of Sciences Museum, the oldest science museum in the Midwest. The museum is relatively small, but packs a lot in, and is particularly good at showing dioramas on the variety of ecosystems surrounding Chicago. The Children's Gallery, open daily from 10am to 3pm, features puzzles, games, live animals, fossils, artifacts, and more for kids to explore.

Admission: $2 adults, $1 seniors and children. Free on Mon.

Open: Daily 10am–5pm. **Bus:** No. 151 or 156.

Café Brauer, 2000 N. Cannon Dr. ☎ 935-6700.

A onetime Chicago institution near the zoo, Café Brauer has reopened its doors to the public following a massive restoration costing more than $4 million. Operating a cafe and ice-cream parlor on the ground floor, and a banquet area called the Great Hall on the second floor, the Brauer's return restores some of the atmosphere of ease and elegance characteristic of the park around the turn of the century, when this landmark building was erected.

Open: Daily 10am–5pm. **Bus:** No. 151 or 156.

3 Cool for Kids

There are plenty of places to take the kids in Chicago—places, in fact, that make every effort to gear their exhibits to the interests and tactile needs of children. All the city's museums are leaders in this "please touch me" school of interactive exhibitions, exhibits with buttons and lights and levers and sound and bright colors. Most of the museums and institutions listed below have already been described in greater detail elsewhere in this chapter. They are repeated here primarily as a convenience for parents visiting Chicago in the company of children and to provide a ready reference of activities in those places that are particularly hospitable to inquisitive children.

The **Museum of Science and Industry,** 57th Street and Lake Shore Drive (☎ 684-1414), has nothing but high-tech, push-button exhibits for children, and kids are particularly awed by the large-screen Omnimax Theater. (See Section 1 of this chapter for a more detailed listing.)

The **Chicago Academy of Sciences Museum,** 2001 N. Clark St. (☎ 871-2668), has a special Children's Gallery. (See Section 2 of this chapter for details.)

The **Chicago Historical Society,** at Clark Street and North Avenue (☎ 642-4600), has many displays, especially in the "Chicago

Street" exhibit, such as an old locomotive, a real taxicab, pushcarts, and so on, that are inherently interesting to children. (See Section 1 of this chapter for details.)

The **Field Museum of Natural History,** Roosevelt Road and Lake Shore Drive (☎ 922-9410), has a "place for wonder" with many curiosities that children can touch. (See Section 1 of this chapter for details.)

The **Adler Planetarium,** 1300 Lake Shore Dr. (☎ 322-0300), offers special "sky shows" for children on Saturday mornings. (See Section 1 of this chapter for details.)

The **Shedd Aquarium,** 1200 S. Lake Shore Dr. (☎ 939-2426), shows divers hand-feeding sharks while swimming in the same tank and explaining everything via an underwater intercom. (See Section 1 of this chapter for details.)

The **Chicago Cultural Center,** 78 E. Washington St. (☎ 269-2820, or 744-6630 for a listing of current events), offers films for children every Saturday, and a special program of activities in the summertime. (See Section 2 of this chapter for details.)

The **Art Institute of Chicago,** Michigan Avenue at Adams Street (☎ 443-3600), has designated five galleries as a "junior museum" where children can engage in art projects of their own. (See Section 1 of this chapter for details.)

The **DuSable Museum of African American History,** 740 E. 56th Place, in Hyde Park (☎ 947-0600), also has a summer program offering cultural and educational activities for children. (See Section 1 of this chapter for details.)

More Attractions

Chicago Children's Museum, North Pier, 465 E. Illinois St. ☎ 527-1000.

The Chicago Children's Museum is especially good for preschoolers and children in the early grades. Several permanent exhibits allow kids a maximum of hands-on fun. "Amazing Chicago," for example, is a mini-version of Chicago represented by playhouse-size constructions of several well-known Chicago buildings where the kids can go in and play. In the miniature "Art Institute" they can draw and hang up their own art, or in the "Sears Tower" they learn about architecture and play with decorating materials. "Touchy Business" is a tactile tunnel for kids ages three to seven, where the labyrinth leads through a Lighted Forest to the pretend house of the Three Bears, with lots of stuff to touch and learn about along the way. There are also collections of masks and clothes for fantasy and dress-up, and craft projects that allow kids to make puppets or jewelry that they can take home with them.

Note: The museum will be moving to its new home at Navy Pier sometime during 1995.

Admission: $3.50 nonmember adults, $2.50 nonmember children and seniors; membership fee $35 a year per family.

Open: Tues–Fri 12:30–4:30pm, Sat–Sun 10am–4:30pm. **Bus:** No. 29, 56, or 65.

Lincoln Park Children's Zoo and Nursery, adjacent to the Lincoln Park Zoo. ☎ **294-7847.**

The Children's Zoo is a delight for children and adults alike. Any species of animal young might be on hand, from tiger cubs to baby chimps, and there are even a few critters like rabbits or gerbils that can be petted or held. An exhibit called the "animal garden" gives you a close-up look at prairie dogs and raccoons.

The Farm-in-the-Zoo is another major and totally separate Lincoln Park Zoo environment, in this case a working reproduction of a midwestern farm, complete with barnyard, chicken coops, and stalls filled with livestock, including cows, sheep, and pigs.

Admission: Free.

Open: Daily 9am–5pm. **Bus:** No. 151 or 156.

4   Organized Tours

If you want someone else to organize your sightseeing, by bus or by boat, Chicago has a number of experienced companies that provide just about any kind of itinerary you can imagine.

Land Tours

For a narrated city tour by bus, contact **American Sightseeing,** 530 S. Michigan Ave. (☎ **427-3100**), which offers a varied selection of two- to five-hour tours covering daytime sights and nightlife.

Double Decker Bus Rides, narrated one-hour tours of the Loop, downtown, and the lakefront, are offered daily from 9:30am to 5pm by Chicago Motor Coach (☎ **922-8919**). Board the buses at the Sears Tower, the Water Tower, or Mercury Boat, and buy your ticket from the driver, who will then give you a brochure describing the day's stops. You can get off at any number of attractions along the way and reboard throughout the day. The cost is $7 for adults, $5 for children.

The **Untouchable Tours,** or so-called Gangster Tours, P.O. Box 43185, Chicago, IL 60643 (☎ **881-1195**), is the only bus tour in Chicago of all the old hoodlum hangouts from the Prohibition era. See the old hotel where Capone had his command center, the site of O'Bannion's flower shop, and the site of the St. Valentine's Day massacre, plus much more; $20 per person. Tours run Monday to Thursday at 10am; Friday at 10am, 1pm, and 7:30pm; Saturday at 10am and 5pm; and Sunday at 11am and 2pm.

And of course, don't forget the **Chicago Architecture Foundation,** 224 S. Michigan Ave. (☎ **922-3432**), with its guided programs by foot, bike, and bus to more than 50 different architectural sites and environments in and around Chicago. Hyde Park is included in its "Chicago Highlights Bus Tour." The foundation also offers walking tours of Hyde Park and neighboring Kenwood during alternating months from May through October. Both locales are listed on the National Register of Historic Places: Hyde Park features the work of many notable architects, particularly Wright and van der Rohe, while Kenwood is noted for the highest concentration of mansions in Chicago.

In addition to Robie House, several of Wright's earlier works, still privately owned, decorate the streets of Hyde Park, such as the Heller House, 5132 S. Woodlawn (1897); the Blossom House, 1332 E. 49th St. (1882); and the McArthur House, 4852 S. Kenwood Ave. (1892).

A BUGGY RIDE

Coach Horse Livery Ltd., Pearson Street and Michigan Avenue (☎ 266-7878), maintains a fleet of old-fashioned horse carriages stationed around Water Tower Square. Each driver has his or her own variation on the basic Magnificent Mile itinerary, and the charge is $30 for each half hour.

A River Runs Through It —————————————

With apologies to the late Norman Maclean for appropriating the title of his wonderful collection of fiction, *A River Runs Through It,* the words here refer to the river in Chicago, not to the one in the writer's native Montana. Chicago not only owes its name, but very likely its existence, to its river. Native Americans referred to the land around the river with a word in their language that to the ears of the early Europeans sounded like "chicago," meaning "powerful," presumably owing to the strong odors of either the swampy decay or the plant life pervasive along the riverbank. And Chicago was destined to grow into the nation's great midcontinental hub of transportation and transshipment precisely because the Chicago River provided a crucial link in the inland water route between the Great Lakes and the Mississippi, thus facilitating travel and trade between the eastern settlements and the frontier.

Today the **Chicago River** remains one of the most visible yet enigmatic of Chicago's major physical features. The river branches into so many neighborhoods that its presence is always popping up when you least expect it. The effect is similar to that famous Revolutionary-era flag of the segmented snake; you only see the river in isolated snatches, each of which usually includes one of the city's 50 some-odd bridges. At any given time while downtown, you might witness all the bridges that span the main and south branches—connecting the Loop to both the West Side and the Near North Side—flap up and then down like the syncopated human wave of spectators at a ball game, as the drawbridges are raised to allow for the passage of some ship or barge, and then lowered. When this happens, all traffic in downtown Chicago grinds to a halt, but only for a moment, because the choreography involving drawbridges and traffic in Chicago is well practiced and smoothly performed.

The Chicago River has long outlived the critical commercial function it once performed for the city that developed along its banks. Most of the remaining millworks that still occupy these banks have long ceased to depend on the river alone for the transport of their materials, raw and finished. The river's main function today is to serve as a fluvial conduit for sewage which, owing to an engineering feat that reversed its flow inland in 1900, no longer pollutes the waters of Lake Michigan. But recently the river has begun to develop another role for itself, as a leisure resource providing a variety of short cruises, many of which combine music, food, and local history.

RIVER TOURS

The **Chicago Architecture Foundation** (☎ **922-3432**) organizes river trips that leave from the south side of the Chicago River, at Michigan Avenue and Lower Wacker Drive, and cruise for an hour and a half at midday along both the north and south branches, accompanied by a lecturer. I learned that Jefferson Davis was among the army engineers to survey the Chicago River in 1825, and other such historical facts, but mostly our guide pointed out the principal architectural sights. These are the very same buildings you see from the land perspective by walking along Wacker Drive, or along the river's north-bank esplanade.

For the first stretch of the cruise on the main branch, most of the buildings are contemporary, since this is a site of vigorous development in Chicago within recent years. Noteworthy is the new **NBC Building,** constructed in wedding-cake style to reflect the city's old zoning codes that allow light to come to the street. The result is to make the building look stylishly old-fashioned. Next you'll float past the "gateway" buildings, and then more modern structures, including Mies van der Rohe's **IBM Building.** Mies van der Rohe once opined, when holding forth on his philosophy of architecture, that "God is in the details," yet in practice his clunky, repetitive building-block style seems devoid of any compelling detail to please the eye. Also in this section, which is just beyond the Michigan Avenue Bridge, are Bertrand Goldberg's whimsical **Marina Towers,** tall cylindrical tubes that look like multistoried bird feeders.

Just before the boat approaches the fork in the river and heads up the north branch, it sails by the enormous **Merchandise Mart,** center of the midwestern wholesale trade in interior decorating, furniture, and apparel. The building seems to bend with the river, and sitting atop a line of pillars that face the water are the larger-than-life busts of giants of American merchandising, including Marshall Field, Edward Filene, George Huntington Hartford (A&P), Julius Rosenwald (Sears), John R. Wanamaker, and Aaron Montgomery Ward. On the opposite shore, however, **333 West Wacker** is an ultramodern shell of steel and glass with a curved and mirrored surface. Looking at the building while you cruise by is like watching a gigantic Technicolor film of the river in motion. Its shore lined with plants, warehouses, and storage yards, the north branch retains its commercial aspect, and justifies the claim that this is still "a working

IMPRESSIONS

Nothing missed by these Chicago papers. If world came to an end tomorrow Tribune *would come out day after with illustrations and an interview with God Almighty.*
—John Foster Fraser, *Round The World on a Wheel,* 1899

river." The river forks again and you enter the east branch, where the boat turns around opposite Ogden or **Goose Island,** so named for the early Irish and German shanty dwellers who kept noisy flocks of these birds here when Chicago was still a frontier town.

The tour of the south branch goes no farther than the end of the Loop, but it, too, is dramatic, and as decidedly urbane as the scene along the north branch is industrial. Here your river view includes several interesting angles on Helmut Jahn's contemporary **North Western Atrium Building,** and the old **Civic Opera House,** where the very popular season runs from September to February.

The architecture foundation boat tour costs $15 and operates from early May through October.

Mercury Chicago Skyline Cruises at Michigan Avenue and Wacker Drive (☎ **332-1353**), also offers frequent water tours, usually combining a cruise on both the river and the lake. Tickets range from $3.50 to $4.50 for children under 12, and $7 to $9 for adults, depending on the length of the cruise.

FRIENDS OF THE CHICAGO RIVER

The Friends of the Chicago River, 407 S. Dearborn St. (☎ **939-0490**), is a nonprofit organization devoted to the preservation and public utilization of the city's riverfront. Each summer the organization sponsors walking tours, canoe trips, festivals, and cruises. The organization also publishes and sells five excellent maps—"Chicago River Trails"—for self-guided walking tours along the north and south branches and the downtown section of the river.

The Friends of the Chicago River offers docent-guided walks along eight sections of the river, scheduled on many Saturdays and Sundays from May through October. Bicycle tours are also offered. All tours meet at 10am or 2pm at varying locations depending on the tour in question, are approximately two hours long, and cost $5 per person. Typical of the excursions is a walk around the perimeter of Goose Island, Chicago's only island.

Boat Tours on Lake Michigan ─────────────────

Tired of just looking at the water from the dozens of vantage points that touring around Chicago provides? Reverse your perspective. Take a sightseeing cruise and look at that incredible skyline from an offshore vantage point. Offering one- and two-hour water tours between late April and early October that take in a stretch of the Chicago River, as well as the area of the lake off the downtown district, are the **Mercury Chicago Skyline Cruises** (☎ **332-1353**) and the **Wendella Streamliner** (☎ **337-1446**), both located under the Michigan Avenue Bridge, at Michigan and Wacker Drive. Scheduling for these cruises depends on both the season and the weather, so call ahead for the current hours. Prices range from $7 to $11 for adults, and $3.50 to $5.50 for children under 12, depending on the duration of the cruise. One of the most dramatic events during the boat tours is passing through the locks that separate river from lake.

For the kids, the Mercury Line also offers a **Wacky Pirate Cruise,** an hour of singing and surprises, departing from their dock at 10am every Thursday, Friday, Saturday, and Sunday from mid-June to early September. The cost is $7.50 for adults, $5 for kids. Reservations required.

Shoreline Marine Sightseeing (☎ 222-9328) schedules one-hour lake cruises from three different dock locations: the Shedd Aquarium, the Adler Planetarium, and Buckingham Fountain. Cruises operate between Memorial Day and Labor Day, and tickets cost $6 for adults and $3.50 for children under 10.

Chicago from the Lake Ltd., 455 E. Illinois (☎ 527-2002), home ports in the Ogden Slip adjacent to North Pier (not Navy Pier) at the end of East Illinois Street. Architectural River Tours and Lake and River Historical Tours are offered from May through September. Tickets are $16 for adult, $14 for seniors $11 for children ages 9–18, free for children under 9.

The *Spirit of Chicago* (☎ 836-7899) has evening dinner cruises that depart daily from Navy Pier at 7pm, offering dancing to a live band and a floor show, returning to port at 10pm. The price is $59.95 on Sunday and weekdays, and $74.35 on Friday and Saturday, plus service. The company also offers other programs, such as weekday luncheon trips at $31.80, moonlight cocktail cruises on Friday and Saturday for $37.80, and a Sunday brunch sailing for $37.80.

National Heritage Corridor

Another Mercury Line offering is a cruise along the river route that links Chicago with the Mississippi River, taking in everything from the cityscape to the prairielands. Spring and fall dates are to be announced; call for details (☎ 332-1353). Price is $39.50 per person, including coffee and breakfast pastries.

Offbeat Tours

THE HARP FACTORY See how the world's most beautiful musical instrument is built—in the harp factory. **Lyon-Healy,** with a store downtown in the Loop at Wabash and Jackson, manufactured the first harp in America in 1889. The harp factory itself is located at 168 N. Ogden (☎ 786-1881), and offers tours "on a limited basis, by appointment only."

GOIN' TO GRACELAND If you really want to stretch your legs, walk all the way north along Clark Street as far as Andersonville, another of Chicago's fascinating neighborhoods with an ethnic past, in this case Swedish. The land between Irving Park Road and Montrose Avenue, running for approximately a mile along Clark, is occupied exclusively by cemeteries—primarily Graceland. Here the tombs and monuments of many Chicago notables may be viewed on walking tours organized by the Chicago Architecture Foundation. When Graceland was laid out in 1860, public parks as such did not exist. The elaborate burial grounds that were constructed in many large American cities around this same time were meant both to relieve the congestion of the municipal cemeteries closer to town, and to provide pastoral recreational settings for the Sunday outings of the living as well. Indeed, cemeteries like Graceland (and Green-Wood in Brooklyn) were the precursors of the great municipal green spaces like Lincoln Park in Chicago and Central Park in New York. Much of the land currently occupied by Lincoln Park, in fact, had been in use as a public cemetery since Chicago's earliest times. Many who once rested there were reinterred in Graceland when the plans for building Lincoln Park went forward.

The Chicago Architecture Foundation (☎ 922-3432) offers **walking tours of Graceland** on selected Sundays during August, September, and October. They cost $5 per person, and they last about two hours. Among the points of interest you will discover as you meander the pathways over these 119 beautifully landscaped acres are the Carrie Getty and Martin Ryerson tombs, famous architectural monuments designed by Louis Sullivan. Sullivan himself rests here in the company of several of his most distinguished colleagues: Daniel Burnham, Ludwig Mies van der Rohe, and Howard Van Doren Shaw, an establishment architect whose summer home in Lake Forest, called Ragdale, now operates as a writers' and artists' colony. Some of Chicago's giants of industry and commerce are also buried at Graceland, including Potter Palmer, Marshall Field, and George Pullman. An ambiguous reference in the *WPA Guide to Illinois* (New York: Pantheon Books, 1983), reprinted without revisions, records that Graceland also contains the grave of Chicago's first white civilian settler, John Kinzie. The racial adjective is a reminder that Chicago's real first settler was a black man named DuSable.

5 Sports & Recreation

Baseball is imprinted in the national consciousness as part and parcel of Chicago—from the Black Sox scandal at Comiskey Park to the pennant-chasing of the Cubs and the White Sox. There are also many other options in the world of sports in this city. Here are the basics for the major ones.

Spectator Sports

AUTO RACING   Go to **Raceway Park,** 130th Street and Ashland Avenue (☎ 385-4035), or the **Santa Fe Speedway,** 9100 S. Wolf Rd. (☎ 839-1050).

BASEBALL   Sure they have lights at **Wrigley Field** now. So what? For some of us, baseball will always be a daylight game, played on grass. The emphasis here is on *game.* You go to watch the boys who play it best. And when the experience is packaged in as much tradition as the Cubs have, so much the better. Some of the old-time elements retained at Wrigley are the hand-manipulated scoreboard, the ivy-covered walls around the outfield, and the flag that flies over the stadium announcing with a "W" or an "L" the outcomes of the day's contest. Quiet ecstasy in the form of a day game at Wrigley can still be purchased for about $20 a head, if you add a beer or two and a hot dog to the price of your ticket.

The spirit and pure pleasure associated with baseball still thrive in this North Chicago neighborhood called Wrigleyville, and are best expressed in the words of Ernie Banks, the Cubs' legendary second baseman from the fifties, an era when the team seldom climbed more than a rung or two above the cellar in the standings. "It's a beautiful day, so let's play two," said the immortal Ernie, or words to that effect. Today a star ballplayer would probably say, "It's a beautiful day, so talk to my agent." Wrigleyville was—and remains in essence—a working-class neighborhood where the only criterion for residency seems to be that you have to be a Cubs fan. Race, color—forget about it.

Wrigley Field, 1060 W. Addison St. (☎ 404-2827), is easy to reach. Take the B train on the north-south line to the Addison stop, and you're there. The entire area around the stadium is surrounded by souvenir shops, sports bars, and restaurants. One sandwich shop, the **Friendly Confines,** is actually located within the stadium itself, just off the sidewalk. **Sluggers,** a sports bar with real batting cages, is right around the corner from Wrigley at 3540 N. Clark St. (☎ 248-0055).

The **Chicago White Sox** are at Comiskey Park, 333 W. 35th St. (☎ 924-1000); to get there by subway/el, take the Lake/Dan Ryan line to Sox/35th St. As baseball legend has it, some young fan confronted Shoeless Joe Jackson with the words "Joe, say it ain't so!" hoping his idol would deny his role in the conspiracy that has come down to us as the Black Sox scandal—the alleged sellout of eight White Sox players to the bookmakers and the throwing of the 1919 World Series. That drama, emblematic of the end of the age of innocence for America after World War I, is very much a part of Bridgeport's story as well, since Comiskey Park is located a few blocks east, nestled in the shadow of the Dan Ryan Expressway. For a while recently it looked as if the White Sox would finally be leaving Chicago for a more genteel setting, but the Illinois state legislature voted money for a new stadium across from the original "baseball palace of the world," which stood there since opening on July 1, 1910. The new third base stands on the spot once occupied by a well-known baseball bar called McCuddy's saloon.

Game times and schedules for each month are available by writing to the **Chicago Office of Tourism,** 78 E. Washington Chicago, IL 60602.

BASKETBALL   The **Chicago Bulls,** NBA Champs in 1991, 1992, and 1993, play at the Chicago Stadium, 1800 W. Madison St. (☎ 943-5800). The **De Paul Blue Demons,** the local college team, play at Rosemont Horizon, 6920 N. Mannheim Rd. (☎ 341-8010).

BEACH VOLLEYBALL   Call the **Association of Mid-west Volleyball Professionals,** 1848 N. Mohawk St. (☎ 266-8580), for dates, times, and locations.

CLINCHER   In the summertime you are likely to pass a park where two teams are engaged in playing something that looks a lot like softball, but with an oversize, 16-inch ball, and generally without gloves. This is "clincher," and it's only played in Chicago (or in a few other places by former Chicagoans). Championship clincher, incidentally, is big business in Chicago, with players making a fair bundle in exchange for their services. Look for the tournaments at Mount Prospect Park, near O'Hare International Airport. Or catch a more informal game in Oz Park, in the Lincoln Park West neighborhood.

FOOTBALL   The **Chicago Bears** play at Soldier Field, 425 E. McFetridge Dr. (☎ **663-5408**). The **Northwestern Wildcats** play college ball at Dyche Stadium, 1501 Central Ave., in nearby Evanston (☎ **708/491-7070**).

HOCKEY   The **Chicago Blackhawks** play at Chicago Stadium, 1800 W. Madison St. (☎ **733-5300**).

HORSE RACING   There's Thoroughbred racing at **Arlington International Race Course,** Euclid Avenue and Wilke Road, Arlington Heights (☎ **708/255-4300**), and at **Hawthorne Race Track,** 3501 S. Laramie, in Cicero (☎ **708/780-3700**); thoroughbred and harness racing at **Balmoral Race Track,** Illinois 1 and Elms Court Lane, in Crete (☎ **312/568-5700**); and harness racing at **Maywood Park Race Track,** 8600 W. North and Fifth Avenues, in Maywood (☎ **708/343-4800**).

TENNIS   Chicago has a number of international tennis tournaments throughout the year, including the Virginia Slims Women's Pro Tournament. Call the **Chicago District Tennis Association** (☎ **834-3727**) for information.

Recreation

BEACHES   There are a number of public beaches in Lincoln Park. The North Avenue Beach House is close to downtown and the zoo. Montrose, Foster, and Hollywood beaches attract families, while yuppies flock to Fullerton, and gays congregate at the strand off Belmont Avenue. Oak Street Beach, along the Gold Coast, is crowded and lively on the weekends.

BOWLING   The bowling alley located closest to the major hotels is **Spenser's Marina City Bowl,** 300 N. State St. (☎ **527-0747**).

GOLF   There are a number of public golf courses within the Park District jurisdiction. For information on hours, greens fees, and price per bucket of balls for driving ranges, call the **Park District** (☎ **245-0909**).

MARATHONS & JOGGING   Chicago, with its many parks and lakeshore avenues, is inviting to the casual jogger as well as to the hardy marathoner.

For information about competitive marathons, call the **Chicago Area Runners Association** (☎ **666-9836**) and the **Chicago Marathon** (☎ **527-1105**). There are also exercise stations with outdoor apparatus and athletic fields available to the public. For other information call the Park District (☎ **294-2200**).

TENNIS For the hundreds of tennis courts where you can personally lob the ball, call the **Park District** (☎ **294-2200**).

8

Strolling Around Chicago

"IT ISN'T HARD TO LOVE A TOWN FOR ITS GREATER AND ITS LESSER TOWERS, its pleasant parks, or its flashing ballet. Or for its broad boulevards.... But you can never truly love it till you can love its alleys too," wrote Chicago's own Nelson Algren in *Chicago: City on the Make.* Maybe you have to have a poet's heart and an appetite for wandering close to the edges of things to be able to love a city's alleys as well as the images it reserves for its postcards. But Nelson Algren's words challenge the visitor to look beyond the skyline and the glitter of Chicago to its many "old world villages crowding hard one upon the other."

In plain English and cold arithmetic these amount to some 77 neighborhoods within the city limits, each in itself every bit as entertaining and educational as going to a museum, an exhibit, or an event. More offbeat adventures often deliver far greater rewards. The three tours listed here provide an introductory profile of Chicago; the remainder of the chapter describes more outlying city neighborhoods in narrative detail.

Walking Tour 1
The Loop

Start   Sears Tower, 233 S. Wacker Dr.

Finish   Dearborn Station, 47 W. Polk St.

Time   Two hours, not counting food stops.

Best Times   Daytime. On weekdays, during business hours, you witness the city's business district in full swing. On weekends, the Loop is very quiet, an ideal time for a long walk; but keep in mind that some restaurants and attractions will not be open.

Worst Times   Nighttime. The Loop, except for its seedier fringes, is virtually abandoned after dark, and probably not a very safe place to be wandering about on the empty sidewalks. This rule of thumb does not apply to the strip of South Michigan Avenue, which forms a segment of this tour, along which many large, convention-style hotels are located, and where therefore street movement continues until well after dark. And, of course, there are many nighttime cultural activities—theater, opera, classical and popular music concerts—that draw the public to the Loop area after dark. But coming to these does not involve a lot of walking through the Loop's innermost streets.

We begin this tour at the:

1. **Sears Tower,** the world's largest skyscraper, where the sky deck is open daily from 9am to midnight. From the 103rd floor, you can get a pretty good orientation of where you'll be walking during the remainder of your tour.

To make sure you have enough energy for the long walk, you could head a few blocks to the west, across the Chicago River near Union Station, to a:

Refueling Stop

    Lou Mitchell's, 625 W. Jackson (☎ **939-3111**), is one of the great breakfast spots in Chicago, open Monday to Saturday from 5:30am. You can arrive close to the restaurant by the no. 151 or 157 public bus, both of which run down North Michigan Ave.

    From the Sears Tower, begin walking north along:

2. **Wacker Drive,** which follows the contour of the Chicago River and borders two legs of this tour. Strolling Wacker Drive gives you a chance to observe the architectural gems that line the riverside, and to see many of the bridges that cross it at strategic points. The first building of note is:

3. **U.S. Gypsum,** 101 S. Wacker, which rises at a 45° angle from the sidewalk and is said to resemble a gypsum crystal.
    Continuing north along Wacker, you will next come to:

4. **The Chicago Mercantile Exchange,** 31 S. Wacker. The "Merc" has been the great commodities exchange of the heartland since 1919. Visitors are welcome during trading hours.
    Wacker Drive now curves to the east. At LaSalle Street, enter to the right and walk two blocks to Randolph Street. Occupying this entire block is:

5. **The State of Illinois Building,** built in 1985 after a design by Helmut Jahn, a tour de force of glass and steel, and very controversial among Chicagoans. The monumental sculpture near the entrance is by Dubuffet.
    Return to Wacker Drive, and continue east. As you approach Wabash Avenue, note the:

6. **Heald Square Monument,** Lorado Taft's final work, completed in 1941, portraying an odd pair of heroes from the American Revolution, Haym Salomon and Robert Morris, with George Washington between them.
    The next block brings you to the:

7. **Michigan Avenue Bridge,** on the other side of which the Magnificent Mile—Chicago's strip of elegant hotels and shops—begins. As you approach the bridge, you may see signs for river tour boats and the double-decker tour bus that makes a circuit of this area.
    We will turn to the right on Michigan Avenue, and note—on the left—the:

8. **Stone Container Building,** 360 N. Michigan, an architectural landmark in Chicago since 1923. Notice the domed roof supported by columns, and the building's trapezoidal shape.
    Continue south along Michigan Avenue until Washington Street; half a block west is the:

9. **Chicago Cultural Center,** 78 E. Washington, with many programs of interest to the public, and the new home of the Museum of Broadcasting.

Walking Tour—The Loop

- 1 Sears Tower
- 2 Wacker Drive
- 3 U.S. Gypsum
- 4 The Chicago Mercantile Exchange
- 5 The State of Illinois Building
- 6 Heald Square Monument
- 7 Michigan Avenue Bridge
- 8 Stone Container Building
- 9 Chicago Cultural Center
- 10 Art Institute of Chicago
- 11 State Street Pedestrian Mall
- 12 Orchestra Hall
- 13 ArchiCenter
- 14 Fine Arts Building
- 15 The Rookery Building
- 16 Monadnock Building
- 17 The Fisher Building
- 18 The Old Colony Building
- 19 The Manhattan Building
- 20 Auditorium Building and Theater
- 21 Printer's Row
- 22 Dearborn Station

Three more blocks to the south along Michigan Avenue to Adams Street will bring you to the:

10. **Art Institute of Chicago,** the city's most prestigious museum, nestled within the confines of Grant Park, which accompanies this walk the entire length south along Michigan Avenue.

Turn right on Adams and cross State Street until you see the sign for Berghoff's.

Refueling Stop

Berghoff's, 17 W. Adams (☎ **427-3170**), has been a favorite Chicago watering hole and restaurant from nearly the turn of the century. Have a light pick-me-up here at the bar. A glass of Maibock beer, and a bratwurst, will cost about $6.

On the way back to Michigan Avenue, make a digression along the:

11. **State Street Pedestrian Mall.** One of the most famous department stores along this strip is Carson Pirie Scott, 1 S. State, a Chicago architectural gem designed by Louis Sullivan. Return to Michigan Avenue and continue south to:

12. **Orchestra Hall,** 220 S. Michigan, home of the Chicago Symphony, and one of the avenue's grandest buildings dating from 1905. One door down from here you can drop in on the:

13. **ArchiCenter,** 224 S. Michigan, gift shop and tour center of the Chicago Architecture Foundation (call **922-TOUR** for a recorded message of available tours). Here you can arrange for a more intensive tour of the downtown architectural highlights.

Two blocks farther south is one of Chicago's most beautiful and romantic buildings, the:

14. **Fine Arts Building,** 410 S. Michigan (for more details, see Chapter 7).

A digression here to the interior streets will pick up one of the outstanding architectural sights in Loop. Walk west along Jackson to LaSalle and turn right. You'll come to:

15. **The Rookery Building,** 209 S. LaSalle, a Root and Burnham building, the lobby of which was designed by Frank Lloyd Wright. Return east along Jackson to see the:

16. **Monadnock Building,** 53 W. Jackson, the north half of which was designed in 1891 by Burnham and Root, the south half by Holabird and Roche. It's the tallest masonry building in Chicago. Continue south along Dearborn Street and note some other standout relics of Chicago's revival after the great fire of 1871:

17. **The Fisher Building,** 343 S. Dearborn.

18. **The Old Colony Building,** 407 S. Dearborn.

19. **The Manhattan Building,** 431 S. Dearborn.

Turn left onto Congress Parkway to see the:

20. **Auditorium Building and Theater,** 50 E. Congress. Dankmar Adler and Louis Sullivan designed this masterpiece and supervised its construction in 1889. Much of the building now houses Roosevelt University, but the

theater is still in use, and it is considered to be one of the most acoustically perfect performing spaces in the world.

An ideal place for lunch or dinner is the next:

Refueling Stop

Prairie, 500 S. Dearborn (☎ **663-1143**), offers a menu of gourmet dishes from heartland recipes and ingredients.

Continue south along:

21. **Printer's Row,** as this stretch of old Dearborn Street is known, where the oldest concentration of the city's post-fire buildings is found. Today this neighborhood has undergone a revival, and it's fast becoming one of the city's most fashionable districts. Many interesting shops and restaurants line the row.

The street dead-ends at our tour's final stop:

22. **Dearborn Station,** the oldest surviving train station in Chicago, but now converted into a mall of shops and restaurants. From here, the three great museums at the lower end of Grant Park, the Field, the Shedd Aquarium, and the Adler Planetarium, are only a short cab ride away; the same is true for Chinatown, the Prairie Avenue Historical District, and McCormick Place Convention Center.

Walking Tour 2
Lincoln Park

Start   Chicago Historical Society, Clark Street and North Avenue.
Finish   Ben and Jerry's, 338 W. Armitage.
Time   Two to three hours or more, depending on how long you linger in Lincoln Park and at the various museums, whether or not you elect the digression to the Clybourn Corridor, and how long you stop to refuel. You might elect to make this tour by bike, but remember to bring along a good lock.
Best Times   Anytime after 11am, when most of the stores, restaurants, and attractions are open, until dark. The weekends are preferable, since that's when the streets are liveliest.
Worst Times   After dark. This is a nightlife and entertainment area after dark, but that's not the time of day to take a walking tour.

This tour will take you through a series of neighborhoods on the Near North Side, but primarily through the area called Lincoln Park and DePaul, highly gentrified in recent years, and loaded with interesting attractions, shops, restaurants, and nightspots. Some of the highlights are the Chicago Historical Society (where the tour begins), Lincoln Park—with its zoo, beach, and conservatory—and the North Halsted Street shopping and restaurant strip.

Begin at:

1. **The Chicago Historical Society,** North Avenue and Clark
Street (☎ **642-4600**). For more detail on the exciting
exhibits housed in the historical society, see Chapter 7.
Public transportation runs close to this location. By
subway, you would have to walk north from Division
Street, but the no. 151 bus running through the Loop and
along North Michigan Avenue will bring you closer, to
North Avenue and the Inner Drive.

Refueling Stop

The **Big Shoulders Café,** on the ground floor of the
Chicago Historical Society, is an excellent choice for a light
lunch and that extra cup of coffee to get you started on
your tour.

After leaving the historical society, cross LaSalle Street
on the edge of Lincoln Park, and continue north along
Clark. At the Lincoln Avenue intersection, look to the right
for the:

2. **Farm in the Zoo,** the children's zoo in Lincoln Park. Here
you could enter the park to visit the farm, the zoo, North
Beach, and the historic Café Brauer.

Continue straight on Lincoln Park West, the street
running along the edge of the park, and you will come to
the:

3. **Chicago Academy of Sciences,** an interesting museum
with many exhibits relating to the local environment and
lots of programs for kids.

From here, continue north on Lincoln Park West. On
the corner of Dickens, is another:

Refueling Stop

R. J. Grunts, 2056 Lincoln Park West (☎ **929-5363**),
offers excellent burgers, chili, and a salad bar brimming
over with a wide variety of fresh items.

Continue north on Lincoln Park West until Belden,
where another choice awaits you. Just inside the park is an
interesting:

4. **statue of William Shakespeare.** And just beyond the
monument, signs mark another entrance to the zoo, and
the:

5. **Lincoln Park Conservatory,** with its permanent botanical
displays and periodic floral shows.

Across from the park, the Belden Stratford Building,
formerly a grand hotel, houses two very fine restaurants,
Ambria and Le Grand Café. We will turn left here on
Belden and walk west to the corner of Clark Street, where
you will note the huge branch of:

Walking Tour—Lincoln Park

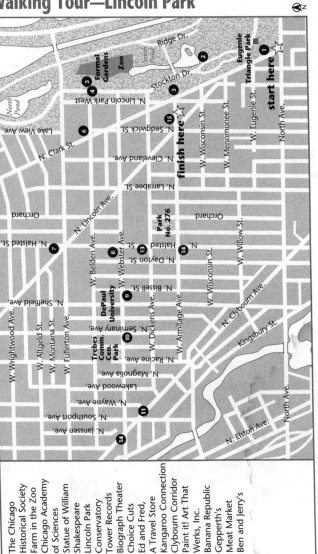

1. The Chicago Historical Society
2. Farm in the Zoo
3. Chicago Academy of Sciences
4. Statue of William Shakespeare
5. Lincoln Park Conservatory
6. Tower Records
7. Biograph Theater
8. Choice Cuts
9. Ed and Fred, A Travel Store
10. Kangaroo Connection
11. Clybourn Corridor
12. Paint it! Art That Werks, Inc.
13. Banana Republic
14. Gepperth's Meat Market
15. Ben and Jerry's

6. **Tower Records,** corner of Clark and Belden, mezzanine
   (☎ 477-5994), stocking all the latest videos, tapes, and
   CDs.

   Cross Clark and continue west on Belden for the
   residential view along this attractive, tree-shaded block.
   Where Belden, Lincoln, and Orchard intersect, turn right

past the John Barleycorn Memorial Pub, and continue north along Lincoln Avenue. This is a somewhat drab stretch of road that ends when you reach Halsted, which crosses Fullerton, as will you. Halsted here offers many appealing choices of restaurants, bars, and stores, and one very historic site, the:

7. Biograph Theater, 2433 N. Lincoln (☎ 348-4123), which is still a functioning movie house, but best known as where the fledgling FBI put a violent end to John L. Dillinger's wicked career of murder and crime.

From here, double back and recross Fullerton, continuing south along Halsted. After a relatively long, nondescript stretch as you approach Webster Street, you will see on your left one of the best restaurants in Chicago, Carlucci's (see Chapter 6).

From this point, you can continue down Halsted and pick up this tour at no. 14 below, or you can turn right on Webster for a long digression to Clybourn Avenue. If you choose the detour, it may be time for another quick:

Refueling Stop

As if by special request, a branch of one of the best java houses in town, **Starbucks,** is right on the corner of Webster and Halsted. Treat yourself to a rich espresso, or a creamy cappuccino before continuing west on Webster, where immediately in from the corner you will see a lovely neighborhood flower shop, called:

8. Choice Cuts. As you wander down Webster, you will pass the north boundary of the De Paul University campus on the right. There are a number of other interesting shops along this street, such as:

9. Ed and Fred, A Travel Store, 1007 W. Webster (☎ 477-6220), near the corner of Sheffield, outfitters of travel gadgets and books.

Farther along, also on the south side of the street, is the:

10. Kangaroo Connection, 1113 W. Webster (☎ 248-5499), dry goods and fashions from down under; also bottled water for the thirsty urban trekker at $1 a bottle, chilled.

At Magnolia Street, which crosses Webster, more or less in the vicinity of Charlie's Ale House, a banner suspended from a telephone pole announces that you have left the neighborhood of DePaul and entered that of Sheffield. In a few short blocks, you will have arrived at the:

11. Clybourn Corridor. Clybourn Avenue is one of the shorter of the diagonal streets that punctuate the Chicago grid. Along this "corridor," formerly a warehouse and light industrial district, a growing number of fashionable shops and restaurants have opened in recent years. Right on the corner of Webster and Clybourn is a one-of-a-kind enterprise, a shop called:

12. Paint It! Art That Werks, Inc., 1422 W. Webster (☎ **880-6400**), a showroom and studio for marbleizing and other modern decorative painting techniques. Next door is a potential:

Refueling Stop

Batteries Not Included, 2201 N. Clybourn (☎ **472-9920**). This is a storefront restaurant featuring an intriguing menu of French-Caribbean dishes.

Walking south from here, you may explore the Clybourn Corridor and rejoin the tour near the end on Armitage. This is a more reasonable option for those with bikes than for those on foot, since sections of the neighborhood you must pass through are not the safest, though they're not likely to be a problem during the daytime.

From here, we pick up the tour back on Webster and Halsted, heading south to explore the many shops, including an outlet of:

13. Banana Republic, 2104 N. Halsted St. (see Chapter 9 for details).

One stop not to be missed for lunch or dinner, either now or when personal scheduling permits, is Café Ba-Ba-Reeba!

Refueling Stop

Café Ba-Ba-Reeba!, 2024 N. Halsted (☎ **935-5000**), a Chicago version of a Spanish tapas bar. Tapas are appetizer-size portions featuring inventive combinations of foods, both hot and cold. Bet you can't eat just one.

Some of the other great restaurants to consider along North Halsted, depending on your appetite and mood, are **Café Bernard** for French food bistro-style, **Grants** tavern for burgers and platters, **Edwardo's** for pizza, **Nookies, Too** for breakfast anytime (open 24 hours over the weekend), and **P. S. Bangkok** for Thai food. (Each of these restaurants is detailed in Chapter 6).

As you descend North Halsted Street, you will come to Armitage. We will eventually turn left, or east, here, but many other interesting shops are to be found as Halsted continues south, including:

14. Gepperth's Meat Market, 1970 N. Halsted (☎ **549-3883**), a specialty food market I mention for anyone considering a picnic in nearby Lincoln Park.

One of the most highly praised and elegant restaurants in Chicago, Charlie Trotter's (see Chapter 6), open for dinner only, is located on Armitage just west of Halsted Street. You might want to file away the location for later.

As we approach Lincoln Avenue, not far from where we began, our walking tour draws to an end. You'll pass Geja's, another restaurant recommended in Chapter 6. But we will end on a simple, sweet note at:

15. **Ben and Jerry's,** 338 W. Armitage, for a well-deserved ice-cream cone.

Walking Tour 3
Hyde Park

Start   53rd Street station of the Metra Railroad.

Finish   Museum of Science and Industry, 57th Street and Jackson Park.

Time   3 hours, depending on stops and digressions.

Best Times   Any day of the week before dusk. Check with the Hyde Park–Kenwood Development Corporation (☎ **667-3932**) about special programs that may be taking place in the neighborhood during the time of your visit, and schedule your tour accordingly.

Worst Times   After dark. This walking tour must be taken during daylight hours, since the experience is largely visual.

Hyde Park is described in detail under the "Top Attractions" in Chapter 7. Assuming you are staying in or near downtown Chicago, you may get to Hyde Park in a half hour or less on one of several modes of public transportation or by cab.

This tour begins at the:

1. **53rd Street station** of the Metra train. The Metra train has two stops on South Michigan Avenue. Make sure you board the South Chicago train, otherwise you may have to ride to the 57th Street station, still in Hyde Park, but several long blocks from where the tour begins.

If you're going to make a day of it in Hyde Park, you might as well start off with a traditional breakfast:

Refueling Stops

Valois, 1518 E. 53rd St. (☎ **667-0647**). "See Your Food" is the slogan that greets you on the sign outside Valois, a small cafeteria-style restaurant and hangout for the whole Hyde Park community for several generations. Short-order meals are the specialty here. An alternative for a refueling stop at this point is near the tour's first stop, a **Starbucks** coffee shop on the corner of Harper and 53rd.

After leaving the train station, or Valois, as the case may be, start heading west on 53rd Street until you come to:

2. **Harper Court,** a complex of interesting shops and restaurants. For a sampling of the shops, see Chapter 9.

From Harper Court, continue west on 53rd Street until you reach Dorchester Avenue, where, on the southeast corner, directly beyond a vacant lot, you will see:

3. **the oldest house in Hyde Park,** circa 1840. Actually it is the rear section of a more recent structure, with a steep roof and something of the shed or outbuilding about it.

Double back along 53rd Street to Blackstone Avenue, and proceed west. At the end of the first block are a row of unadorned

4. **cottages,** built for workers and their families at the time of the Columbian Exposition in 1893.

Continue south on Blackstone Avenue until 55th Street. The massive block of buildings in front of you is the:

5. **University of Chicago Towers,** designed by I. M. Pei in the fifties, when this entire street, along with other sections of the neighborhood, fell prey to the ideology of urban renewal. This stretch of street today is known locally as "monoxide island," because traffic heading east or west must first circumvent the Towers, which block the way.

Directly west of the Towers is a small:

6. **swimming pool,** encircled by tall conifers and a wrought-iron fence, belonging to the university, but open to the public.

At the next block, across 55th Street on the corner of Kimbark Avenue, notice:

7. **St. Thomas Apostle school and church.** The lacy terra-cotta trim at the church entrance was designed in 1922 by an apprentice of Frank Lloyd Wright.

Turn left, or south, on Kimbark and enter the:

8. **Golden rectangle,** an area bordering the U of C campus where the neighborhood's priciest real estate is located. On the west corners, on both sides of 56th Street is a complex of homes called:

9. **Professor's Row,** dating from 1904 to 1907, some of the most desirable residences in Hyde Park. Migratory parrots, which have somehow drifted here from the South American rain forests, have nested within the confines of Professor's Row, causing a heated controversy in recent years between local "Friends of the Birds" and Illinois farmers who claim the presence of the parrots is a danger to crops.

Now walk one block west to Woodlawn Avenue and see:

10. **no. 5537 Woodlawn,** the former home of Enrico Fermi, the physicist responsible for the first sustained nuclear chain reaction.

Now reverse direction on Woodlawn, and head south. Turn right on 57th Street and enter the:

11. **University of Chicago campus.** You have two options here. Either continue on this self-guided tour, or depending on the time of day, take the official university tour, which departs from Ida Noyes Hall, 1212 E. 59th St., on Monday to Saturday at 10am. The main attractions for those continuing on the self-guided tour are listed below in a logical order. Given the campus layout, you'll probably have to ask directions. Near where you entered the campus is:

12. **The Reynold's Club building,** housing the student union and the University Theater. The old U of C stadium, Stagg Field, was here, where the Regenstein Library now stands. Go through:

13. **Cobb Gate** to the Main Quad, where you will find the:

14. **Visitors Center,** the university's original science building, including Botany Pond, designed by the two sons of Frederick Law Olmsted. On the opposite side of the quad is:

15. **The Renaissance Society,** on the fourth floor of Cobb Hall, which introduced such artists as Klee, Miró, and Matisse to the Midwest, and continues to exhibit vanguard artists. Between Classics and Harper Quads, you must visit the:

16. **Bond Chapel,** a strikingly ornate masterpiece of stained glass and carved wood. Walk to 59th Street, where the:

17. **Midway Plaisance** divides the main campus from a number of satellite buildings, many of which were designed by well-known modernist architects like Eliel Saarinen, Edward Durell Stone, and Ludwig Mies van der Rohe.

    Walk to Ellis and 58th Street, where you'll find the:

18. **University Bookstore,** a good place to shop for U of C souvenirs, like T-shirts.

    Also on Ellis, between 57th and 56th Streets is the famous bronze sculpture:

19. *Nuclear Energy* by Henry Moore. A short cab ride (you could also walk) from 57th and Ellis will bring you to the:

20. **DuSable Museum of African American History,** 740 E. 56th Place. Continuing by foot along Ellis, it is a short walk to the:

21. **Court Theatre,** an Equity house of some 250 seats; and just behind the theater, the:

22. **Smart Museum of Art,** 5550 S. Greenwood Ave. (at E. 56th Street), where the university's impressive collection of nearly 7,000 works is housed.

    From here another lengthy digression is possible. Those wishing to walk through the elegant Kenwood neighborhood might continue toward the north here about 5 blocks, preferably along Woodlawn. Or you may make a prior contact with the Hyde Park–Kenwood Development Corporation (☎ **667-3932**) for information on organized

Walking Tour—Hyde Park

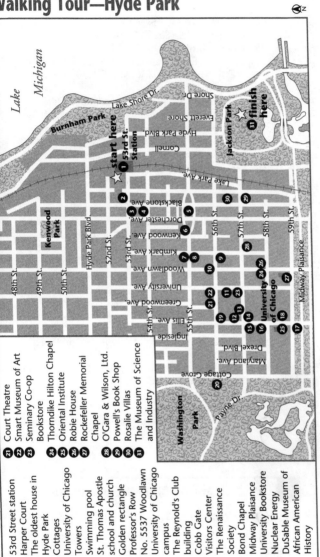

Map legend:

1. 53rd Street station
2. Harper Court
3. The oldest house in Hyde Park
4. Cottages
5. University of Chicago Towers
6. Swimming pool
7. St. Thomas Apostle school and church
8. Golden rectangle
9. Professor's Row
10. No. 5537 Woodlawn
11. University of Chicago campus
12. The Reynold's Club building
13. Cobb Gate
14. Visitors Center
15. The Renaissance Society
16. Bond Chapel
17. Midway Plaisance
18. University Bookstore
19. Nuclear Energy
20. DuSable Museum of African American History
21. Court Theatre
22. Smart Museum of Art
23. Seminary Co-op Bookstore
24. Thorndike Hilton Chapel
25. Oriental Institute
26. Robie House
27. Rockefeller Memorial Chapel
28. O'Gara & Wilson, Ltd.
29. Powell's Book Shop
30. Rosalie Villas
31. The Museum of Science and Industry

or self-guided tours of Kenwood. Now return along University Avenue to 57th Street, where you can drop in at the:

23. **Seminary Co-op Bookstore,** 5757 S. University Ave., making sure to also take a peek into the lovely and diminutive:

24. **Thorndike Hilton Chapel,** in the same building. Across the street, at 58th Street, visit the unique:

25. **Oriental Institute,** 1155 E. 58th St., an extraordinary collection of ancient art and artifacts dating from 9000 B.C. At 58th Street and Woodlawn Avenue is one of the highlights of this tour:

26. **Robie House,** 5757 S. Woodlawn Ave., the ultimate expression of Frank Lloyd Wright's Prairie School style. Robie House can be toured every day at noon, free of charge.

    Our final stop on the U of C campus is the:

27. **Rockefeller Memorial Chapel,** at 59th and Woodlawn, a tour de force of modern Gothic architecture, housing the world's second-largest carillon. Carillon concerts may be heard Sunday at 11:30am and Monday to Friday at 6pm.

    We will now begin to head east again. Either walk down 57th Street, taking note of two interesting book-stores, first:

28. **O'Gara & Wilson, Ltd.,** 1311 E. 57th St. (☎ **363-0993**), Chicago's oldest book dealer just south of Kimbark, and then farther down the street:

29. **Powell's Book Shop,** 1501 E. 57th St. (☎ **955-7780**), crammed with used titles in every subject from the classics to the social sciences.

    Or, follow 59th Street and recross to 57th along Harper, and see the:

30. **Rosalie Villas,** where the cottages once formed a miniature planned community constructed in the 1880s.

    From here, continue into Jackson Park until you reach our final stop on this tour:

31. **The Museum of Science and Industry,** 57th Street and Lake Shore Drive, one of the most popular tourist attractions in Chicago.

4 Strolling Around Other Neighborhoods

Exploring the Gold Coast

In Chicago the "Gold Coast" refers not only to the short strip of privileged shorefront on the Near North Side along Lake Michigan, between Division Street and North Avenue (right below Lincoln Park), but also to the interior blocks off the lake as far as Old Town.

SUNRISE ON THE DRIVE

A very pleasant activity for an early riser staying the weekend at a hotel in or near the Gold Coast is a Sunday-morning constitutional stroll along the Oak Street Beach or on Lake Shore Drive itself between the end of the Magnificent Mile and the beginning of Lincoln Park. If you want to be a real fanatic about it, you could even see the sun as it rises magnificently over the inland sea that is Lake Michigan.

A bit later in the morning, you may find that walking along the stone path that borders the street side of the beach, while not exactly precarious, will keep you on your toes. In truth, the experience can be somewhat uncomfortable for pedestrians, as packs of racing bike enthusiasts swish by. Here's a palpable example of Algren's "City on the Make" syndrome, "where three and a half million bipeds swarm with a single cry, 'One side or a leg off, I'm getting mine.'" The slow lane is on the sand, for anyone old-fashioned enough to want to enjoy the breeze and the sea/city view in a less agitated frame of mind. Joggers, on the other hand, have a lakeshore route that will take them up the Gold Coast and deep into nearby Lincoln Park. Among the sights you will pass as you jog along this 10-mile course are the Chess Pavilion, the zoo, the conservatory, an exercise station with outdoor apparatus, various harbors, beaches, tennis courts, and athletic fields.

HISTORIC GOLD COAST ARCHITECTURE

This particular stretch of Lake Shore Drive, as well as those streets in the immediate vicinity, first received the appellation "Gold Coast" because many of Chicago's wealthiest families built their mansions here in the years following the Chicago fire, which had virtually destroyed all of the Near North Side, once a prosperous neighborhood of artisans and craftspeople, primarily German immigrants. State Street merchant Potter Palmer began the trend in 1882 with his million-dollar castle at what is now 1359 N. Lake Shore Dr. Other worthies followed Potter's example, but with the exception of several survivors like those now housing the International College of Surgeons (no. 1516) and the Polish Consulate General (no. 1530), most of these shoreside estates have long been replaced by elegant apartment buildings.

A winding, self-guided architectural tour through the interior streets of the Gold Coast is a must for the eclectic variety of building styles that flowered in Chicago after the Great Fire of 1871. On these streets, the preservation of Chicago's oldest mansions and fine town houses has fared better than on the drive itself, though the architectural relics here are likewise sheltered beneath the shadows of the neighborhood's many high-rise towers.

A block from the water is **Astor Street,** a designated national landmark along its entire length between Division Street and North Avenue, with many fine houses preserved from the era of "Old Chicago." Some of the standouts to look for are the houses at nos. 1316 to 1322, which show a Romanesque influence in the manner of the Boston architect H. H. Richardson's chosen style. (The only actual sample of Richardson's work in Chicago, however, is on the South Side, the Glessner House in the Prairie Historical District, which today serves as headquarters for the Chicago Architecture Foundation; it's discussed later in this chapter.) **Charnley House,** on the other hand, at 1365 N. Astor St., at the corner of Schiller Street, is distinctly Chicago, built in 1892 by Adler and Sullivan during the period when Frank Lloyd Wright (who presumably had a hand in the design) worked for the firm. On a side street off Astor, at 20 E. Burton, is the **Patterson-McCormick Mansion.** The original building, an Italianate palazzo, was designed by Stanford White as a wedding present for the daughter of the *Chicago Tribune*'s publisher, and later expanded in 1927 by David Adler for Cyrus McCormick II. Today the complex has been broken up into condos. At 1406 N. Astor St. is the **Ryerson House,** also by David Adler, whose design in this case was inspired by the hotels of Paris constructed during the Second Empire. Another sturdy example of the Romanesque style is the **May House,** at 1443 N. Astor, built in 1891, while the **Russel House,** at no. 1449, constructed 40 years later by Holabird and Root, is distinctly art deco, and the Tudor house at no. 1451 was designed by architect Howard Van Doren Shaw.

On the corner of North Boulevard, between Astor and North State Parkway, is Chicago's Catholic **Archbishop's Residence,** 1555 N. State Pkwy. The red-brick mansion with many chimneys, in the Queen Anne style, was one of the first houses built in the district in the 1880s on land that had previously been a cemetery. At **1550 N. State** is a building where each of the 10 floors originally housed a single apartment of 9,000 square feet, designed by Benjamin Marshall, the architect for the Blackstone and Drake hotels. At 4 W. Burton St. is the **Madlener House** (ca. 1900) by the firm of Richard E. Schmidt, one of the city's earliest examples of the horizontal architecture that would come to characterize the Prairie School and the work of Frank Lloyd Wright. Today the building is home to the Graham Foundation for Advanced Studies in Fine Arts. The **George S. Isham House** at 1340 N. State St., built in 1889, has been better known in recent years as Hugh Hefner's Playboy Mansion, and is now a women's dormitory for the School of the Art Institute. Half a block farther south, at 1301 N. State, at the corner of Goethe, is the **Omni Ambassador East Hotel** and its famous Pump Room restaurant. Finally, near Division Street there's the **Frank Fisher Apartments,** 1207 N. State, a small white-brick building with a curved, glass-block facade in the art moderne tradition, that is built around an appealing inner courtyard.

Continuing up North Dearborn Street there are also several notable examples of early Chicago architecture, beginning with the landmark **Three Arts Club,** at 1300 N. Dearborn, built in 1912 by Holabird and Root, and still functioning as a residence for women students who are enrolled in music classes and courses in the arts. **St. Chrysostom's Episcopal Church,** at 1424 N. Dearborn, often enlivens the neighborhood with its 43-bell carillon. Above North Boulevard begins Lincoln Park (see Chapter 7 and the walking tour earlier in this chapter), and to the left from Dearborn Street the neo-colonial brick structure of the **Chicago Historical Society** standing alone in a large meadow (see Chapter 7). Three additional architectural sites close to the south end of the park, along Lincoln Park West, should not be overlooked. They are **Tonk House,** 1817 N. Lincoln

Park West, noteworthy for its carved wooden doors; the **Louis Sullivan Town Houses,** nos. 1826 to 1834, built in 1885 and still in very good repair; and no. 1838, the boyhood **home of Charles Wacker,** built in 1874, whose idea it was to create a double-decker street along the edge of the Chicago River, today called Wacker Drive in his honor.

THE DIVISION STREET AREA

Two blocks south from the Claridge Hotel, Dearborn Street intersects with Division Street. Division Street is also the name Studs Terkel used as the title for his best-selling chronicle about the lives of mostly ordinary Chicago folk. The name, he says, is meant to stand not for a real street, but for a kind of geographic archetype of the American reality. It is not far-fetched to imagine that it was on this Division Street that Terkel, who as a boy lived in the former boardinghouse district around nearby LaSalle Street, first heard that gaggle of unheralded voices of Chicago's working stiffs that he transmits so faithfully to his readers. Some of Chicago's rougher edges still cling to this street, but the area is increasingly succumbing to the forces of gentrification that surround it.

Division Street, on the other hand, has a slew of singles bars (see Chapter 10 for specific bar information). There's also a good hot-dog stand on Division about mid-block on the north side of the street between State and Dearborn.

To the north of Division, State *Parkway* is strictly Gold Coast, but to the south it's State *Street* once again, and all commercial— not in the downtown sense of department stores, as in "State Street, that Great Street," but lined with storefronts, like the neighborhood dry cleaner and the mom-and-pop newsstand-*cum*-smoke shop. **Rush Street** doesn't actually extend all the way to Division, but ends a block to the south, where it stems diagonally into *State* at the corner of Bellevue. Le Meridien Chicago, a popular cafe, is on this corner (see Chapter 6).

Not to be overlooked while in the vicinity is the opportunity for some serious high-fashion window shopping along **Oak Street,** where most of the buildings have been restored and remodeled in recent years to accommodate a host of designer-apparel boutiques (see Chapter 9). One holdover from Oak Street's seedier past is the Esquire Theater, recently rehabbed to house six screening rooms and a few more retail shops.

Old Town

West of LaSalle Street stretches a strip of old Chicago bohemia called Old Town, separating the Gold Coast from Cabrini Green, one of the city's most notorious public housing projects, west of Sedgwick Street. LaSalle itself, before the street was widened in the 1930s to accommodate Loop-bound car commuters, was an elegant quarter of private residences considered the western boundary of the Gold Coast. For years thereafter, many a foreshortened structure along LaSalle, whose facade was lopped off to accommodate the broadened avenue, functioned as a rooming house or a hotel for transients. Today LaSalle Drive, as it has been renamed, is undergoing a revival toward upscale housing once again, in response to the pressures of development pressing ever-westward on the North Side. One old building, the **LaSalle Towers,** on the northeast corner of Division and LaSalle, seems itself a wry commentary on the latest transformation of the "Drive." The artist Richard Hass has painted the exterior walls of this circa-1920s apartment hotel with a series of trompe l'oeil murals as an homage to Chicago's architectural heritage. On the front of the building Hass has re-created an image of Louis Sullivan's archway entrance to the Transportation Building that the famous architect designed for the Columbian Exposition of 1893.

Old Town's main drag is a block west of LaSalle on **Wells Street,** covering a stretch three-quarters of a mile long between Division Street and Lincoln Avenue, the diagonal extension of Wells that continues on a northwesterly route beyond the city limits into suburban Skokie. Old Town, like much of the Near North Side of Chicago, was once a German neighborhood. But around the beginning of the Great Depression in the early thirties the area around Wells had begun to fray, becoming in the process both attractive and accessible to a new generation of artists and writers who were trying to eke out a living on the government's Works Progress Administration. Under these circumstances, Old Town became the center of Chicago's bohemian life, a status it maintained through the hippie era of the sixties and until the recent onslaught of gentrification that has swept through the area in the eighties. Today Wells Street is lined with specialty shops and boutiques, bars and restaurants, and several popular cabarets and nightspots. Each year in mid-June, Wells Street is transformed into an outdoor gallery for its annual Art Fair.

The residential part of the neighborhood, referred to as the **Old Town Triangle,** begins roughly above North Avenue, only two blocks west of Lincoln Park at this point. A walk through these quiet streets is rewarded by a vision of Old Town the way it was around the turn of the century and before. Many of the wood-frame houses built after the Chicago Fire are still standing and coexist with residential creations of more recent vintage, notably the 10 luxury town houses on Sedgwick Street between Wisconsin and Menomonee, designed by nine of Chicago's top contemporary architectural firms. On the corner of nearby Eugenie and Cleveland Streets is an enormous Bavarian baroque church, **St. Michael's,** rebuilt from its standing walls after the fire, and for most of the second half of the 19th century the parish center of Chicago's largest German Catholic community.

The Near West Side

Late Sunday evening on October 8, 1871, a fire broke out somewhere near the home belonging to a family named O'Leary. Legend has it that the fire began in the O'Learys' barn, a freak accident caused when a cow upended an oil-filled lantern. The fire raged mostly to the east and north, jumping the Chicago River in both directions, leveling all of downtown Chicago and most of the Near North Side as far as the city line along Fullerton Avenue. Two days later as the city lay in smoldering ash, the O'Leary home stood unscathed, marking the western limit of the fire that, owing to the direction of the wind and to otherwise inexplicable good fortune, left much of the Near West Side intact. A monument shaped like a pillar of fire stands today in the courtyard of the Chicago Fire Academy at Jefferson and DeKoven Streets, where the O'Learys lived and the fire was believed to have started.

From the 1850s onward, the Near West Side was a study in social contrasts, the town houses of wealthy merchants standing near the most wretched hovels of the immigrant families: at first the Irish, Germans, and Bohemians; later the Jews, Greeks, and Italians; and still later, Mexicans and southern African Americans. Urban-renewal schemes over the years and the construction of the **University of Illinois Chicago campus** have forever transformed the once residential character of the neighborhood, but a number of important landmarks and vest-pocket neighborhoods have been preserved from the wrecker's ball, more by accident than design. There is, for example, Chicago's oldest church, **St. Patrick's,** at Des Plaines and Adams, dwarfed today by the Presidential Towers, a luxury apartment complex. Within the **Jackson Boulevard Historic District,** the 1500 block of Jackson (between Ashland and Laflin), some 31 Victorian-era middle-class homes were intentionally spared and restored to their spit-and-polish appearances through the sweat equity of some urban homesteaders in the early seventies.

There is nothing in particular today to remind you of the significance of the area around Des Plaines and Randolph Streets. The city's open-air market was once located here in a place called **Haymarket Square,** scene in 1886 of a political riot that in turn led to one of the great miscarriages of American justice. Workers staged a protest at the square on May 4 to denounce the killing of a fellow worker by the police at the nearby McCormick Reaper Works the day before. Mayor Carter Harrison personally surveyed the rally and concluded that there was no cause for alarm. Acting on his own authority, however, the commander of a reserve police force ordered the workers to disperse soon after the mayor left for home. Suddenly, in the moments preceding the dispersal, a bomb exploded and a policeman lay dead. The remaining police attacked the assemblage, leading to the deaths of six additional policemen and four civilians, not to mention scores of injured among both groups. Six of the eight labor and political leaders subsequently indicted and tried for conspiracy in the death of the murdered policeman were not even present at the rally. Of these, four were hanged, one took his own life in prison, and the remaining three were pardoned by Illinois Gov. John Peter Altgeld in 1893. Altgeld's gesture of personal honor was also an act of political suicide; the governor was himself pilloried in the press and thereafter shunned as a virtual renegade. But his heroic action came to be immortalized in Vachel Lindsay's widely known poem, "Sleep Softly, Eagle Forgotten." The bomb thrower himself was never found. (Some years ago I read a wire story in the *New York Daily News* reporting on the outcome of a scholarly investigation whose authors had uncovered a plausible suspect, a deranged German immigrant who, they claim, acted completely alone.) A monument called the "Haymarket Statue" once stood in this square to commemorate the seven policemen who fell that day. But the monument was "repeatedly blown up in the 1960s" and so it now stands in the atrium of the Police Training Academy, 1300 W. Jackson Blvd.

The Prairie Avenue Historical District

The two public attractions of the Prairie Historical District are the Glessner House, where the Architecture Foundation has its headquarters, and the Clarke House, Chicago's oldest surviving structure. From downtown, on South Michigan Avenue, the no. 18 bus will take you there. Get off at 18th Street and walk the two blocks east to Prairie. As far back as the Civil War, this geographic swath of the Near South Side had been a desirable residential choice for the wealthy, with its proximity to downtown. On Prairie Avenue alone were the houses of such giants of industry and commerce as George Pullman, George Armour, Marshall Field, Joseph Sears, Charles P. Kellogg, William Kimball, and John Jacob Glessner, of which only the homes of Glessner and Kimball, a piano manufacturer, survive to this day. Since the Near South Side was not destroyed by the Great Fire, the popularity of the area as the site for the mansions and town houses of city's "best families" increased proportionally after 1871.

The area's desirability lasted for less than two decades beyond this, declining steadily with the encroachment on the periphery of the neighborhood by "houses of vice" that had been pushed south by the commercial development of downtown State Street. The final blow was the arrival of the railroad. Tracks were laid nearby and warehouses sprang up where most local residents had assumed fine houses would someday stand. Some citizens who were farsighted in their day fought the plan to construct tracks so close to the lakefront, but they were defeated. Today the rail lines that once traveled these tracks are mostly idle. But the scar of land occupied by the tracks— running on the surface all the way to Grant Park, just opposite the Loop—remains an incongruous strip of ugliness cutting into the heart of a city that rightly prizes the beauty of its center.

Practically speaking, this same system of tracks occupies a forlorn no-man's-land that separates a long stretch of residential Chicago from the beautiful parklands that line the lakefront. Here in the Prairie Historical District, for example, Burnham Park can be reached only by crossing a long footbridge over the tracks. Only 23rd Street, several blocks to the south, crosses the tracks en route to the McCormick Place Convention Center, which sits on land within the park. (For the downtown pedestrian, the tracks also stand as an obstacle to negotiate between the Loop and several of Chicago's most important cultural institutions—the Field Museum, the Shedd Aquarium, and the Adler Planetarium.)

Like a shadow of the past, **Glessner House** (1886), at 1800 S. Prairie, stands practically alone on a block once lined with old mansions, and guards a corner of historic Prairie Avenue at the intersection of 18th Street. The carriage house of the dramatic Romanesque stone building houses the architecture foundation's information desk, as well as a small gift shop with a wide selection of books pertaining to Chicago architecture, and some wonderful prints and postcards. In the main house, most of the common spaces and bedrooms are open to the public on an escorted tour, while the foundation's administrative offices are happily sequestered under the eaves in the upstairs quarters that in former times were the domain of the servants. Glessner House was designed by the Boston architect H. H. Richardson—Louisiana-born, Paris-educated, and a great-grandson of Joseph Priestley, the famous English clergyman and chemist. Richardson's Romanesque designs were widely imitated in commercial and residential buildings of that day, until their vogue lapsed in favor of the simpler lines—vertical with skyscrapers, horizontal with dwellings—that reflected the rise of steel and the emergence of the "Chicago School" of architecture. Richardson's work, unlike that of his many imitators, was infused with intellectual and artistic notions that had emerged among thinkers and artists in Victorian England. He built Glessner House after a stone abbey he'd seen in the English country town of Abingdon, and designed the warm interior in the spirit of the Arts and Crafts Movement that spurned the products of mass production in favor of those crafted by hand.

Ironically, men like Glessner—then vice-president of International Harvester—defended in their personal life the values and comforts they associated with genteel rural living against the leveling of tastes and decline in quality that their own industrial innovations had ensured. Everywhere in America in those days people were reawakening to the beauties of nature and of a wilderness that was shrinking rapidly before the ever-widening circumference of progress. The rusticators believed—and the Glessner family was no different—that only in the country could you let your hair down and escape the creeping hardness of the modern city. Town houses in the city were also necessary—even desirable for work and society. But life here—except for those within one's charmed circle—turned inward, away from the harsh urban surroundings, and Richardson's fortresslike designs only expressed more forthrightly than most domestic architecture of the day this widely perceived contrast between the tranquility within and the barbarism without.

Even today the uninhabited rooms of the Glessner House radiate with a warmth that reflects not prosperity alone but a sensibility that can only be described as secure and "homelike." The 35-room house was filled with wallpaper and fabric designed by William Morris, and contains many of the family's original furnishings designed by Frances Bacon and by the Glessner family friend, Isaac Scott, who also personally hand-carved many of the picture frames that decorate the walls. This appreciation and practice of manual crafts, like woodworking, was typical of those, like Scott, who were influenced by the Arts and Crafts Movement. (Many Chicago architects in those days—Wright included—could work as well with their hands as with their minds.)

The Glessner House is the only surviving memorial to the fertile and complex imagination of H. H. Richardson that remains in Chicago—the others were demolished for one reason or another—and a visit here is worthwhile. But that's more than I can say about **Clarke House,** at 16th Street and South Michigan Avenue. The restoration of the city's oldest home and building (1836) is as discordant as the Glessner House is harmonious and internally consistent. Much effort was made to preserve Clarke House, which had fallen into ruin in the service of many tenants, domestic and institutional, over the years. This restoration project is documented by an interesting display in Clarke House of black-and-white photographs, where—however decayed—at least the old homestead looked like what it was, the wreck of a timber-frame house about to go horizontal. Now it looks like an idealization of something that never existed. Rooms are done up in different periods to accommodate imaginary former residents. Most of the materials and finishing techniques used in the restoration make Clarke House seem much too contemporary, not frontier colonial. It's not only the look; it's the texture of the place. The boards aren't old or worn, the banister looks like it's fresh from the lumberyard, the wallpaper sparkles, and the paint job would be acceptable as a model for the latest in decorator interiors by *House Beautiful.* If the original Clarke family could see their frontier home today—built when most of their neighbors still inhabited log cabins—they'd probably die of shame at its pretentiousness. The most authentic thing about Clarke House is outside on the well-cropped grounds. But that's not a lawn you're walking on—it's prairie grass, Chicago au naturel.

The combined tour of these two houses costs $8 ($5 for just one house) and is led by one of the architecture foundation's 250 volunteer docents, or guides, who receive formal training in their areas, but whose real knowledge of their subject often stems from individual research and study.

Pilsen

Most of Pilsen still remains an immigrant neighborhood, a narrow, rectangular box of streets stretching as far west as Damen Street, and shaped north and south by the old railyards and the remaining industrial infrastructure of the 19th century. The area is named for the second-largest city in what was then Bohemia—a country best remembered in history as the *causa belli* of Europe's Thirty Years' War. English is still the second language of Pilsen, but the first is no longer Czech—it's Mexican Spanish. The Bohemians left their mark on the physical appearance of the neighborhood, however, with the colorful brick- and stonework that decorates the facades on many houses.

Every September, before summer officially draws to a close, many artists and artisans of Pilsen throw open their studio doors and invite the public to view the work they've produced over the preceding year. The epicenter of the Pilsen art scene is located in the eastern corner of the neighborhood at Halsted and 18th Streets. The majority of the studios occupy spaces in what are some of the oldest and most charming houses and commercial buildings that remain in Chicago within a single, unified residential zone. Behind the block-long row of buildings along the 1800 block of North Halsted (between 18th and 19th Streets), a large interior area lies hidden from public view and serves as a courtyard for the residents whose studios and homes surround it. The courtyard is filled with artists and their patrons sipping white wine from plastic glasses on summer days.

Even if your stay in Chicago does not coincide with the Pilsen Artists' Open House, you can spend a profitable afternoon and evening in this neighborhood. *Explore* is the key word here, so it is wise to arrive with several daylight hours still before you. I would suggest catching the Halsted Street bus, if you are coming from the general vicinity of the Loop. Just walk west to Greek Town, crossing the south branch of the Chicago River until you get to Halsted Street, heading south from there until reaching 18th Street.

First wander among the side streets that encircle the intersection of Halsted and 18th, delightful, simple residential settings. Heading in a westerly direction, and zigzagging the streets between 18th and Cermak, see how many of the murals you can find among the 30 or more that have been painted on the exterior walls of buildings by artists and their friends in the community, many of whom draw heavily from pre-Columbian myths and customs for their imagery, and combine them with a vision of social realism in the manner of Diego Rivera and other great muralists of Central America.

One of Chicago's most controversial experimental theaters, the Blue Rider, is in Pilsen (see Chapter 10). See Chapter 6 for some restaurant ideas in this area.

Chinatown

Chicago's original Chinatown centered around Clark and Van Buren Streets, but later settled around Cermak Road and Wentworth Avenue. Today's Chinatown, like New York's, abuts its "Little Italy," and the restaurants and shops in the area on the periphery—26th Street from Halsted to Canal Street—reflect this mixture. See Chapter 6 for restaurants in Chinatown.

9

Shopping A to Z

Sʜᴏᴘᴘɪɴɢ ɪs Cʜɪᴄᴀɢᴏ's ᴍɪᴅᴅʟᴇ ɴᴀᴍᴇ. Tʜᴇ ᴀʀᴛ ᴏꜰ ᴍᴇʀᴄʜᴀɴᴅɪsɪɴɢ—big-time merchandising—was practically invented here. There was a time in this nation when every privy and outhouse along the frontier contained a catalog from Sears, Roebuck or Montgomery Ward—both of which grew up in Chicago. All the wondrous items that Americans discovered in the pages of those dream books (including houses sold section by section), and coveted to bring pleasures and convenience to their lives, were shipped from Chicago warehouses. The merchant princes of Chicago built the greatest merchandising empire the world had ever seen. At the height of its power, this empire depended on its monopoly—first over the inland sea trade, and later over the rail trade. If you produced something in the East, and wanted to develop a western market, you sent your goods through Chicago; the grain and livestock of the prairie and the range flowed in the opposite direction, but also through Chicago.

For many generations, "ambitious young men" consciously left their hometowns, bound for Chicago with the single intent of making their fortunes by becoming masters in the trade of the middleman. They shared with gangsters, hustlers, corrupt public officials, and shady entrepreneurs the idea that the only reasonable end in life was to make the barrels of money for which wide-open Chicago provided so many opportunities. The difference, of course, is that they would work extremely hard for their success, and for the most part within the system, and only a few would arrive anywhere near the pinnacle. But so prevalent was the drive to "make money" among a segment of the citizens in Chicago that, in 1877, the president of the Historical Society was to warn the city fathers that, "We have boasted long enough of our grain elevators, our railroads, our trade.... Let us now have libraries, galleries of art, scientific museums, noble architecture, and public parks.... Otherwise there is the danger that Chicago will become a place where ambitious young men will come to make money...and then go elsewhere to enjoy it."

It is now apparent that the powers-that-be heeded that practical scholar's advice. In the meantime, Chicago's privileged position as a center for the transshipment of goods was gradually superseded by the installation of a national highway system, and by trucks that covered distances between points more efficiently and directly than rivers or railroads. The great merchandising combines—like Sears and Montgomery Ward—have either substantially dissolved or become completely decentralized since the reorganization of the national economy that followed the Great Depression. Today every major shopping mall in the country has its own Sears; the catalog trade, too, has been fragmented into thousands of specialty businesses, from L. L. Bean to Burpee Seeds. The power of merchandising and transportation in Chicago has long been transformed into the power of finance and corporate management. But the general air of prosperity, and the urge to consume and live well, has not diminished an iota in Chicago. Seen in one light, Chicago can be characterized as an endless, movable shopping center, stretching from one end of town to the other. In addition to its two principal malls—the Magnificent Mile and State Street—each neighborhood radiating from the center is speckled more or less densely with every manner of enterprise. This section will concentrate exclusively on the great department stores and on the trendy downtown shopping scene.

SHOPPING HOURS   As a general rule, shop hours are Monday through Saturday from 10am to 6pm and on Sunday from noon to 5pm. Department stores generally keep later hours, remaining open until 8pm Monday through Saturday, and until 6pm on Sunday. Many shops located within the vertical malls, such as Water Tower Place and Avenue Atrium, are open most nights until midnight.

The vast majority of stores in the Loop are open for daytime shopping only, generally between the hours of 9 or 10am until no later than 6pm Monday through Saturday. (The big department stores do have some selected evening hours; see below.) On Sunday, the Loop—except for a few restaurants, movie theaters, and cultural attractions—is shut down tight.

1   The Magnificent Mile

North Michigan Avenue between the Chicago River and Oak Street—roughly a mile in length, whence the glitzy nickname—is everything that New York's Fifth Avenue aspires to be, and then some. People in Chicago really dress to kill, and nowhere is this propensity more obvious than among the fashion-plate crowd that cruises North Michigan Avenue on both workdays and weekends. If you want a living fashion show, just head for this avenue and watch the fashion spectacle on parade. And just where do these well-cut threads come from? Why, from any number of stores and shops that occupy the buildings of this high-rent strip for the privilege of serving the consumer public, especially the hip and the well-heeled.

Michigan Avenue

Let's stop at a select few of the best-known shops along North Michigan Avenue and on nearby side streets. Unlike the following sections, which are organized alphabetically, here we'll take each shop as it comes, beginning at the river and heading northward.

Great Lakes Hot Tubs, Inc., 15 W. Hubbard. ☎ **527-1311.**

Not for everyone, but a curiosity nonetheless, is Great Lakes Hot Tubs where you can actually relax in a working hot tub in one of the store's separate rooms, by reservation, if you think you might want to buy one but wish to try it out first.

Jazz Record Mart, 11 W. Grand. ☎ **222-1467.**

You can uncover some super finds in recycled jazz records (also big band, bebop, Latin, and so on) at the Jazz Record Mart, where a full jazz and blues line of new records is also sold.

Avenue Five-Forty, 540 N. Michigan Ave. ☎ **321-9540.**

This is a unique boutique for artsy clothing and accessories.

Timberland Company, 545 N. Michigan Ave. ☎ **494-0176.**
Outfitters for the great outdoors.

★ **Hammacher Schlemmer,** 618 N. Michigan Ave.
☎ **664-9292.**
Be sure to stop at this favorite gadget shop—the ultimate choice when looking to buy a gift for "the person who has everything."

ACA Joe, 622 N. Michigan Ave. ☎ **337-0280.**
Banana Republic look-alike sportswear in rough cotton and khaki is the order of the day at ACA Joe.

Burberry's Limited, 633 N. Michigan Ave. ☎ **787-2500.**
When you want to come in from the cold or go out in the rain, drape yourself in a traditional trench coat from Burberry's Limited where the style hasn't changed appreciably since creator Thomas Burberry furnished "impermeables" for the British quartermaster during World War I. Today's Burberry's can also furnish your wardrobe with sports coats and other sportswear, plus Shetland and cashmere sweaters for men and women.

★ **Hoffritz,** 634 N. Michigan Ave. ☎ **664-4473.**
Hoffritz always displays a wealth of attractive cutlery in its store window. The store is noted for its wide selection of Swiss army knives.

B. Dalton Bookseller, 645 N. Michigan Ave. ☎ **944-3702.**
This mass-market/best-seller specialist has shelf after shelf of the latest fiction, nonfiction, how-to, and computer titles. Computer software and video systems have also been added to the store's inventory. Look for the special table of remaindered books for some good reads at a big discount. Those who purchase a Book-saver membership save 10% on all purchases.

★ **Crate & Barrel,** 646 N. Michigan Ave. ☎ **787-5900.**
The window displays in Crate & Barrel are little stage sets of interior environments: a butcher-block counter with all the accessories, an inviting and fully set dining room table, and that sort of thing. What better way to demonstrate the intimate appeal of functional, ordinary objects of daily life: kitchen gadgets, cookware, plates and glasses, and space-saving wire storage shelves and bins.

Sony Gallery Of Consumer Electronics, 663 N. Michigan Ave.
☎ **943-3334.**
A hands-on showcase of Sony's consumer electronic products, including a video "shooting gallery" for live camcorder demos, and an area for portables to check out boomboxes, tape and disc players, telephones, etc.

Nike Town, 669 N. Michigan Ave. ☎ **642-6363.**
Nike Town is built like a theater, housing shoes and fitness products for 20 different sports over several stories and in a variety of environments, like the "museum" with its memorabilia (including an autographed pair of sneakers Michael Jordan used while a member of the Olympic Dream Team).

Stuart Brent Books, 670 N. Michigan Ave. ☎ 337-6357.

Serious readers and book collectors will adore Stuart Brent Books, named for the owner who has patterned his inviting shop after those booksellers in Oxford, or off the Strand in London. Follow the carpeted stairway to the lower level where you will find one of the best selections of children's books in the city.

Tiffany & Company, 715 N. Michigan Ave. ☎ 944-7500.

Fortunately Tiffany & Company always has something on hand around the cash registers that is moderately affordable for all the folk who want to give or receive a glittery gift with the shop's famous name stamped on it; otherwise, at this jeweler the sky's the limit.

Manifesto, 200 W. Superior. ☎ 664-0733.

This is a serendipitous furniture store selling first-class reproductions of architect-designed furniture by such superstars as Frank Lloyd Wright and Mies van der Rohe.

Joan & David, 717 N. Michigan Ave. ☎ 482-8585.

Stylish shoes of fine leather for men and women.

The Elizabeth Arden Red Door Salon, 717 N. Michigan Ave.
☎ 988-9191.

Chicago's innovative daytime spa, with 8,000 square feet of beauty care services in an atmosphere of elegance.

Neiman-Marcus, 737 N. Michigan Ave. ☎ 642-5900.

At Neiman-Marcus, merchandising has been elevated to an art form. The store's buyers seem to function as curators of rare objects, and the attractive staff might be as comfortable modeling the wares as selling them. You can just as easily visit the store as a form of fantasy entertainment as much as to shop here; for anyone who wins the $20-million lottery and wants to know how the other half spends their money, this store should be your first stop after you cash in your winnings. Visually and architecturally, the store is a stunner. The four-story lobby has a 75-foot wood sculpture as a centerpiece, and is otherwise plush with marble and brass trimmings. The central elevator will convey you to a wide variety of ritzy displays and boutiquelike environments, selling everything from high-fashion designer togs to the best caviar to furs stitched from the most-prized pelts available throughout the animal kingdom. If your mouth begins to water, you can't eat the merchandise, but there are two in-house restaurants that will satisfy most appetites: the relaxed Fresh Market, and the more formal Zodiac.

Walgreen's Drugs, Michigan and Chicago Aves. ☎ 664-8686.

This pharmacy is open 24 hours a day.

★ **Write Impressions**, 42 E. Chicago Ave. ☎ 943-3306.

This is one of those magical stationery stores that stocks all the desktop materials you may need, from the mundane to the whimsical.

Plaza Escada, 840 N. Michigan Ave. ☎ 915-0500.

The most comprehensive collection of Escada apparel and accessories in the country is housed in this elegant free-standing four-story

The Magnificent Mile

0 ⟨scale bar⟩ 218 y / 239 m

N

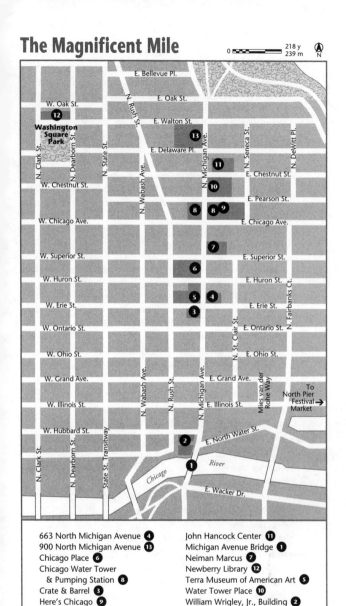

663 North Michigan Avenue ④
900 North Michigan Avenue ⑬
Chicago Place ⑥
Chicago Water Tower
  & Pumping Station ⑧
Crate & Barrel ③
Here's Chicago ⑨
John Hancock Center ⑪
Michigan Avenue Bridge ①
Neiman Marcus ⑦
Newberry Library ⑫
Terra Museum of American Art ⑤
Water Tower Place ⑩
William Wrigley, Jr., Building ②

building. The fourth-floor cafe offers a small but excellent lunch and dessert menu with a terrific view over Michigan Avenue.

Williams-Sonoma, 17 E. Chestnut. ☎ **642-1593.**

Just like its San Francisco original. Here you can get all the latest snazzy and utilitarian high-tech kitchen gadgetry that is on the market today.

Water Tower Place

We now approach one of Chicago's great vertical palaces of retail, Water Tower Place, a block-size building occupying the east side of North Michigan Avenue, between East Pearson and East Chestnut Streets, where some 130 separate stores are dispersed, atrium style, over the bottom eight floors of the 74-story building. Roughly half of all the retail trade transacted along the Magnificent Mile takes place within these premises—though with the opening of a rival mall a bit farther up the block (with Bloomingdale's among its tenants), Water Tower Place is in for a real old-fashioned retail shoot-out over the next few years, and the outcome is still very much in question. Operating in its favor is the added fact that Water Tower Place also provides quarters for the 22-story, 431-room Ritz-Carlton Hotel, very convenient digs for the carriage trade from out of town.

Some of the shops at Water Tower Place fall roughly into the following categories: apparel (men's and women's, some two-score shops in all), beauty services, cards and flowers, specialty foods, home furnishings, jewelry, leather goods, paintings and graphics, shoes, sporting goods, tobacconists, toys and games, and of course, dining in one of a dozen different cafes and restaurants. For entertainment, seven separate cinemas are also scattered throughout the premises.

Accent Chicago, Inc. Water Tower Place. ☎ 944-1354.

Great Chicago souvenirs from wrapping paper to photos, and other tasteful gifts.

F. A. O. Schwarz, Water Tower Place. ☎ 587-5000.

The New York toy maven. Watch other adults demo many innovative playthings. You won't stand on the sidelines for long.

Kroch's & Brentano's, Water Tower Place. ☎ 943-2452.

This branch of the big book chain is a choice option, by the way, for remaindered copies (discounted books that may not be selling well, but are still just what you're looking for).

Lord & Taylor, Water Tower Place. ☎ 787-7400.

Lord & Taylor, the other large department store in Water Tower Place (see Marshall Field's, below), provides for the day-to-day fashion and household needs of the city's working gals and guys.

Marshall Field & Company, Water Tower Place. ☎ 781-1234.

The flagship enterprise at Water Tower Place is an elegant branch of Chicago's hometown department store, Marshall Field's, which occupies some portion of all those eight stories—all accessible by escalator—that the building devotes to its retail trade. I won't go into detail here about Marshall Field's because we will also visit the chain's original Loop location (described below).

Rizzoli International Bookstore and Gallery, Water Tower Place. ☎ 642-3500.

This bookstore specializes in well-crafted coffee-table books.

Chicago Place

Inaugurated in 1991 at 700 N. Michigan Ave., this is Chicago's newest entry in the lists of vertical shopping malls. About 80 distinct retailers have joined Saks Fifth Avenue in the vast eight-story shopping environment. The eight-floor atrium cafe, a cluster of tables under a skylight complete with fountain and potted greenery, is surrounded by some interesting fast-food counters.

Hello Chicago, 700 N. Michigan Ave. ☎ **787-0338.**

This is a well-located souvenir shop for Chicago-related paraphernalia, like Bulls T-shirts and other Michael Jordan merchandise.

Petite Sophisticate, 700 N. Michigan Ave. ☎ **787-4923.**

This store specializes in women's clothes in sizes 2 to 12, while knit items are stocked from petite to large.

Politix, 700 N. Michigan Ave. ☎ **440-9222.**

Politix was described to me as Armaniesque men's fashions, in similar materials and patterns, straight from Milan, but at much lower prices.

Saks Fifth Avenue, 700 N. Michigan Ave. ☎ **944-6500.**

This department store seems to offer something for everybody. There are men's and women's departments, children's clothes, jewelry and makeup counters galore, and a good range of prices not available in some of the more evening wear–oriented giants up the block—plus there's always something attractive on sale for the bargain-conscious. Saks offers one-on-one personal-shopping consultants, interpreters, and shipping services. The store can also boast a very reputable beauty salon. It's open Sunday, too, from noon to 5pm.

900 North Michigan Avenue

Here you'll find the first-ever branch of the very exclusive **Henri Bendel's** (☎ **620-0140**) that has ventured off Fifth Avenue in New York City, as well as 85 additional shops and restaurants.

Art Institute Museum Store, 900 N. Michigan Ave. ☎ **482-8275.**

The Art Institute has opened several gift shops throughout the city, including this one. It has the same selection of prints, books, and postcards that you will find at the actual museum, plus attractive and unusual craft items.

★ **Bloomingdale's,** 900 N. Michigan Ave. ☎ **440-4460.**

You'd have thought the Cubs had won the pennant for all the press and hoopla that surrounded the September 1988 opening of Bloomie's in the somewhat-daunting vertical mall called Avenue Atrium. Bloomie's is the hippest of the hip, with a lock on Ralph Lauren to boot.

Chicago Trunk & Luggage, 900 N. Michigan Ave. ☎ **787-1987.**

Here you'll find a great selection of transportables to fit any traveler's needs.

Episode, 900 N. Michigan Ave. ☎ **266-9760.**

Episode has three stores in Chicago, including this one, and caters to working women who like clothes made from natural fibers, primarily cotton and silk.

Fogal Legware, 900 N. Michigan Ave. ☎ **944-7866.**

This shop carries everything for the legs, including stockings, panty hose, and socks for men.

Glasses Ltd. 900 N. Michigan Ave. ☎ **751-0330.**

This is one of several Chicago branches of this top-quality eyeglass boutique, with full service.

H20 Plus, 900 N. Michigan Ave. ☎ **440-0171.**

H20 Plus features bath and shower products, plus ointments and lotions for hair and skin care.

Upper Michigan Avenue ─────────────────

In the final block along the Magnificent Mile before the avenue makes its transition into Lake Shore Drive (near attractive Oak Street Beach) and marches on up the Gold Coast, there are two other important clusters of retail shops. One of these is a building crammed with good shops, known as **1 Magnificent Mile,** where you will find the pricey **Spiaggia** (☎ **280-2750**), one of the best Italian restaurants in the city.

Bally Of Switzerland, 919 N. Michigan Ave. ☎ **787-8110.**

This is the place to come for high-toned leather goods, including shoes, attaché cases, handbags, and accessories.

Polo Ralph Lauren, 1 Magnificent Mile. ☎ **280-1655.**

This is a branch of the famous designer's store, his beachhead before the arrival of Bloomie's.

2 Other Shopping Areas

Oak Street ─────────────────────────────

Just past the Drake hotel on Walton Street, which marks the northern boundary of the Magnificent Mile, and to the west, is Oak Street. Along this single block, from Michigan Avenue to Rush Street, a major rehabilitation has taken place in recent years, transforming what was once a marginal, even seedy, commercial block into the highest-priced boutique row in Chicago. Here's a sampling of the shops to be found on this posh strip.

Alaska Shop, 104 E. Oak St. ☎ **943-3393.**

Somewhat offbeat, given its company, is the Alaska Shop, a showcase for Eskimo arts and crafts. The shop offers a unique variety of soapstone sculptures, ivory carvings, and stone-cut prints by Canadian and Alaskan artists. It's the largest and most comprehensive collection of Eskimo art in the world.

Gianni Versace, 101 E. Oak St. ☎ **337-1111.**

This boutique offers finely tailored clothes for both sexes.

Giorgio Armani, 113 E. Oak St. ☎ **427-6264.**

The severe and striking fashions of Giorgio Armani can be found only at this boutique.

Jil Sander, Chicago, 48 E. Oak St. ☎ **335-0006.**

The German-based designer of women's high fashion, ready-to-wear, accessories, cosmetics, and fragrances, in the only free-standing Jil Sander store in the world.

Marilyn Miglin, 112 E. Oak St. ☎ **943-1120.**

Marilyn Miglin is a very "in" makeup and skin-care salon.

Ultimo, 114 E. Oak St. ☎ **787-0906.**

Ultimo has snob appeal in the men's and women's apparel market.

Maple Street

Maple Street is just west of State Street, and two blocks south of Division Street in the center of the old Gold Coast residential district. The Newberry Library is the principle attraction in the neighborhood, along with a cluster of fine old mansions lining a little park called Washington Square. But the setting on Maple Street is equally serene, the perfect place for an afternoon massage.

★ **Urban Oasis**, 12 W. Maple St. ☎ **587-3500.**

Soothe your ruffled feathers with a professional massage in an atmosphere that is subdued and Zen-like. Variable lighting and piped-in music encourage one to "come in and leave the city behind," says owner Peter Rubniz, whose emphasis for massage is on health, not sensual escapism. The ritual begins with a steam or rain shower in a private changing room, followed by the spa treatment you elect—various forms of massage, mud or herbal body wrap, aromatherapy, and so forth. Fruit, juices, or herbal teas are offered on completion. The fee for a one-hour treatment is $60; $35 for 30 minutes. Open every day but Monday; call for exact scheduling.

River North

The rapid development of Chicago's new art-gallery district—designated River North—has also attracted many shops to the area west of the Magnificent Mile. Most of the action seems to be along Wells Street, from Kinzie Street to Chicago Avenue.

Elements, 738 N. Wells St. ☎ **642-6574.**

Elements is a showroom for artist-made crafts and jewelry.

Table Of Contents, 448 N. Wells St. ☎ **644-9004.**

In the shadow of the Merchandise Mart, Table of Contents is your shop for both everyday and fancy table settings and service.

Tuscany Studios, 601 N. Wells St. ☎ **664-7680.**

Tuscany is a fun place, though it's unlikely that the average visitor to Chicago will take home any of the garden statuary or birdbaths.

North Pier

North Pier, located at 435 E. Illinois St., is more than a shopping mall. Think of it as a shopping-entertainment center. A select listing of North Pier's many unusual shops will show you why.

Battletech Center, North Pier. ☎ **836-5977.**

This is the ultimate video arcade. Using the same kind of simulator technology as NASA, you engage in a 24-minute, action-packed, life-like, high-tech battle. The cost is $6 to $8, depending on the day. Open daily from 11am until as late as 1am on Saturday.

City of Chicago Store, North Pier. ☎ **332-0055.**

It's a wonder that no one has thought of it sooner. A store that recycles "real" street signs, manhole covers, parking meters, old-fashioned ballot boxes, even voting machines—all retired from active city service—and sells them to the public. It's all here at the City of Chicago Store, created under the cosponsorship of the Chicago Office of Tourism and the city's Department of Cultural Affairs, with proceeds to benefit cultural and promotional programs. But that's not all you'll find here. The store also stocks a full inventory of T-shirts from every museum in Chicago, plus craft items, jewelry, calendars, and much, much more.

Ditto-2, North Pier. ☎ **836-4224.**

This shop turns your one-dimensional photograph into a two-dimensional cutout sculpture, fixed to a stand-up acrylic backing. Open Monday to Saturday from 10am to 10pm (to 6pm on Sunday).

⭐ **The Kite Harbor**, North Pier. ☎ **321-5483.**

The store's slogan is "kites aren't just for kids anymore." No doubt some of these enormous, colorful flying objects would require a whole team of adults to launch and control them. Open Monday to Thursday 10am to 8pm, Friday and Saturday 10am to 10pm, and Sunday noon to 8pm.

Light Wave Galleries, North Pier. ☎ **321-1123.**

This gallery specializes in holographic art created with lasers. Portraits and custom holograms are available. Open Monday to Thursday 10am to 9pm, Friday and Saturday 10am to 10pm, and Sunday noon to 6pm.

Turin Bikes, North Pier. ☎ **923-0100.**

Here you'll find a professional bike shop for rentals and repairs, as well as top-of-the-line mountain bikes and accessories for sale. Open Monday to Friday 11am to 8pm, Saturday 10am to 6pm, and Sunday noon to 5pm.

Clybourn Corridor

⭐ **Wear In Good Health, Clothes Plain And Simple**, 2202 N. Clybourn Ave. ☎ **929-0883.**

Two young artist-designers, Julie Jordan and Laura Ledford, have "bucked the system" by managing to create, manufacture, and retail exclusive women's fashions from their own shop. Writes Susie Evans in *Today's Chicago Women*, "The clothes are fun, with strong, simple lines. Some have bright patterns or colors. Others are intriguing because of intimate detail. They're sophisticated without being stuffy or staid. The styles rival those seen on New York and Paris runways, but are still wearable for regular people."

State Street

DEPARTMENT STORES

⭐ **Carson Pirie Scott & Company,** 1 S. State St.
☎ **744-2000.**
This store still basically appeals to working- and middle-class shoppers. But this venerable Chicago institution that was almost wiped out by the Chicago Fire has made a recent bid to capture the corporate, if not the carriage, trade. A number of upscale lines in designer clothes, casual and formal, plus a trendy housewares department, have been added to appeal to the moneyed crowd that works in the Loop. The store also has a team of interpreters who can communicate with practically anyone. Open Tuesday, Wednesday, Friday, and Saturday 9:45am to 5:45pm; Monday and Thursday 9:45am to 7:30pm.

⭐ **Marshall Field & Company,** 111 N. State St. ☎ **781-1000.**
Before the Magnificent Mile grew into Chicago's first boulevard of fashion, State Street, "That Great Street," was the center of retailing in Chicago for more than 100 years, ever since Potter Palmer's decision to develop the street and to establish his dry goods business there in 1852. Palmer's original emporium evolved over time into Marshall Field's.

Field's and Carson Pirie Scott became competitors, like Macy's and Gimbels in New York—though these two Chicago stores have always been a bit more fancy than their New York counterparts. Both buildings are city landmarks, with the Louis Sullivan–designed Carson Pirie Scott building the more celebrated of the two. But Marshall Field's, with its Tiffany-domed and skylit courts and galleries also creates a very dramatic environment.

Spread over 73 acres of floor space, with 450 departments, Marshall Field's provides as great a range in merchandising variety as shoppers will find anywhere. A perennial ground-floor favorite is the store's maze of candy counters, where the confectioners of the world get to flaunt their caloric specialties (Marshall Field's own contribution is a much-procured mint called the "Frango"). The Victorian Antique Jewelry Department is also a "must see" for out-of-towners. But the store is not merely a curiosity. The emphasis is on the variety of goods, practical and fanciful, and on service; store craftspeople are still on hand to fix antique clocks, repair jewelry, or restore an old painting. Other noteworthy departments on the premises are the antiquarian bookshop, the gallery of antique furniture, a boutique offering designer originals called the 28-Shop, and a bargain basement. To aid its foreign or non-English-speaking customers, there are also interpreters on hand who are conversant in more than 20 languages. Open Tuesday, Wednesday, Friday, and Saturday 9:45am to 5:45pm; Monday and Thursday 9:45am to 7pm.

THE STATE STREET MALL

By the early seventies the Loop was no longer a place that many Chicagoans wished to visit; in the euphemistic language of the popular tongue, "The neighborhood had changed." As was typical of inner-city environments throughout the country during those years, the Loop—especially the old entertainment and shopping quarters—had disintegrated badly. And the decay seemed to occur in direct proportion to the rise of the center of retail trade and fashion that had gradually flowered on the opposite bank of the river, along North Michigan Avenue. Many of the Loop's grand old department stores—Sears, Roebuck & Co., Montgomery Ward, Goldblatts, Wieboldt—closed their doors and shifted their inventories to more promising suburban outlets. Somehow, Marshall Field's and Carson Pirie Scott managed to hang on, for if they had fallen, surely State Street—as a major Chicago shopping zone—would have ceased to exist. But with a kind of tidal predictability, development began to flow back into the former commercial basin, and the ebb of decline has been—at least momentarily—reversed.

Between Wacker Drive and the Congress Expressway, State Street was closed to all traffic but CTA buses (and cabs between 7pm and 6am), a move designed to create a modified pedestrian mall. The experiment, apparently, has met with mixed success. State Street today seems to be hanging in the balance. You couldn't say that the old glamour has been recaptured, but the downward spiral has definitely been checked. The jury is still out as to whether State Street will recover any portion of its previous status in Chicago's world of retail. Time, it would seem, is in its favor, however. The rapid residential development of nearby Burnham Park throughout the old streets of the South Loop is bound to have a positive impact on State Street's recovery—though in what form, it is hard to predict. Many of the storefronts along State Street today are filled with shops offering nine-to-five necessities, or brand-name fast foods. There remain, however, numerous pockets of specialty and fancy retail stores throughout the district, like those occupying the arcade on the ground level of the Palmer House Hotel at the corner of Monroe Street.

Some of State Street's fast-food eateries are described in Chapter 6. State Street (and its surrounding blocks) also seems to be hospitable to shops catering to women whose figures do not fit the exacting mold of fashion or convention. Notable in this category is **Lane Bryant,** 9 N. Wabash Ave. (☎ **621-8700**). (*A reminder:* If the quick change from north to south confuses you here, keep in mind that in Chicago, point zero for the purposes of address numbering is the intersection of State and Madison.) A popular maternity shop is **Mother's Work,** 50 E. Washington, on the second floor (☎ 332-0022).

SHOPS JUST OFF STATE STREET

Scattered among the side streets of the Loop are a number of other shops, some well-known, others that I include here on the strength of their uniqueness.

★ **Brooks Brothers,** 209 S. LaSalle St. ☎ 263-0100.

Businessmen of a certain set would probably go naked were it not for the existence of Brooks Brothers, where the label on the suit or tie is as important as the cut and color of the cloth.

E. B. Collinton Ltd., 318 S. Dearborn. ☎ 431-1888.

This store, in the Monadnock Building, specializes in old-fashioned fountain pens, "once written off, now a status symbol," says one Chicago trade paper. It's the only "full-service" pen (and pencil) store in Chicago.

Favor Ruhl Co., 23 S. Wabash Ave. ☎ 782-5737.

Whether you are an artist or not, you are bound to find something to strike your fancy at Favor Ruhl, one of Chicago's most popular art-supply houses. Custom framing is also available.

Old Chicago Smoke Shop, 169 N. Clark St. ☎ 236-9771.

While you may not be able to smoke those tasty stogies on board your homecoming flight—or anywhere else but the proverbial smoke-filled room—you can still stock up on exotic cigars at this smoke shop. There are no L'Abanas, unfortunately, but you'll find good hand-rolled cheroots from Jamaica, the Philippines, and the Canary Islands.

Riddle-Mcintyre, Inc., 175 N. Franklin St. ☎ 782-3317.

Every man should walk around at one time or another in a custom-made shirt, the only product sold by Riddle-McIntyre—but you must order a minimum of three shirts at a clip.

Hyde Park

Commercial Hyde Park is centered around 53rd Street close to the lakefront, although there are many shops and restaurants along the other numbered streets as well.

Harper Court, on Harper Avenue between 52nd and 53rd Streets, was urban renewal's answer to the old colony of artists and writers that once added a bohemian dimension to Hyde Park. The 57th Street art colony once harbored such luminaries as Carl Sandburg, Theodore Dreiser, Sherwood Anderson, Vachel Lindsay, Edgar Lee Masters, and many more. The ramshackle wood houses they occupied were originally built during the Columbian Exposition as souvenir and popcorn stands. When these structures were demolished, Harper Court was built to offer space to the displaced artists. Today, only a single artist-in-residence remains, but the Harper Court Foundation is expanding its cultural programs now that the entity's mortgage has been retired.

Today Harper Court is mostly an arts-oriented mall of retail shops, with 20 stores and two restaurants. The old art colony is also remembered each year at the springtime **57th Street Art Fair** (☎ 667-0508), a weekend outdoor art show scheduled in early June.

HARPER COURT SAMPLER

Beads, Harper Court. ☎ **752-4660.**

Here you'll find enchanting beads from around the world.

Cafe Coffee, 5211 S. Harper. ☎ **288-4063.**

The casual Café Coffee gives you a choice of fresh-roasted coffee and the daily newspaper to read. This is a nice vantage point from which to enjoy one of the musical events featured at Harper Court in the summertime (open from 10am to 7pm Monday through Friday, from 9am on Saturday).

Dr. Wax Records, Harper Court. ☎ **493-8696.**

New and used LPs, tapes, and CDs, with a first-rate selection of jazz and classical music.

★ **Windows To Africa,** 5210 S. Harper. ☎ **955-7742.**

This eye-catching shop is full of masks, fabrics, wood carvings, baskets, drums, collectibles, and many other artifacts imported from contemporary Africa. A new line of contemporary urban wear has also been added. Look for the occasional fashion shows based on African designs and fabrics. A second store was recently opened at 706 N. Wabash Ave. (☎ 787-1708), three blocks west of Water Tower Place.

THE HYDE PARK BOOKSTORES

57th Street Books, 1301 E. 57th St. ☎ **684-1300.**

This is the largest used-book store in Chicago and is known especially for its children's books. They also have a small fireplace, used in the wintertime, and sell coffee, amenities of particular importance to the professional book browser.

★ **O'Gara & Wilson, Ltd.,** 1311 E. 57th St. ☎ **363-0993.**

O'Gara and Wilson, a rumpled storefront of a bookseller who might easily have migrated from a back street in London or Cardiff, has good used-book and old titles by the hopperful.

3   Shopping A to Z

As can be expected of any metropolitan city in the United States, Chicago has shops selling a plethora of merchandise—from the functional to the decorative, whimsical, and exotic. The following list is certainly not complete, but it will give you an idea of the range of items available.

Antiques

The greatest concentration of antiques shops can be found west of Sheffield Avenue on Belmont, or along intersecting Halsted Street. In addition to the stores detailed below, there's **Caledonian,** 209 W.

Illinois St. (☎ **923-0098**); **Chicago Antique Mall,** 3050 N. Lincoln Ave. (☎ **929-0200**), with more than 50 dealers under a single roof; **Formerly Yours,** 3443 N. Halsted St. (☎ **248-7766**); **Hamill and Barker,** 1719 Howard St. (☎ **475-1724**), the city's most venerable antiquarian book dealer; and **Jay Roberts Antique Warehouse,** 149 W. Kinzie St. (☎ **222-0167**).

Antique Palace, 3020 N. Lincoln Ave. ☎ **477-6700.**

The Antique Palace boasts the neighborhood's most voluminous display of old furnishings and artifacts spread over 55,000 square feet of floor space on two levels.

Penn-Dutchman Antiques, 4912 N. Western. ☎ **271-2208.**

There's really nothing particularly German about this place except the name, but collectors of odd bric-a-brac and similar curios, such as old photos, will find the pickings interesting.

★ **Victorian House Antiques,** 806 W. Belmont. ☎ **472-0400.**

A certain brand of hedonism is conducive to the acquisition of antiques. Those who count themselves of this denomination will find Victorian House an obligatory station stop. You don't even need to enter the shop to enjoy the show. The old manse is a bona fide Victorian-era sampler in every detail, from its ornate bay window and trim boards to the rickety wrought-iron fence and gate that make the place look like a set from "The Addams Family." Open Monday noon to 8pm, and Tuesday to Sunday noon to 5:30pm.

Art

Fly-By-Night Gallery, 714 N. Wells St. ☎ **664-8136.**

This gallery is a treasure house for art deco and art nouveau objets d'art.

Okee Chee's Wild Horse Gallery, 5337 N. Clark St. ☎ **271-5883.**

Illustrative of the Native American presence that has reappeared on the Far North Side of Chicago in recent years are a number of shops that showcase the work of Native American artists and craftspeople. Such is Okee Chee's Wild Horse Gallery, which in addition to artworks, offers numerous books on Native American culture, as well as pots, beadwork, and jewelry. Open Tuesday and Thursday to Friday noon to 7pm, and Saturday 10am to 6pm.

★ **Paint It! Art That Werks, Inc.,** 1422 Webster (at the corner of Clybourn). ☎ **880-6400.**

This shop is part showroom, part studio, specializing in objects that have been marbleized or otherwise decoratively painted. Most of the shop's work is done off-site in the form of murals, frescoes, and set pieces for commercial firms and restaurants. But samples of work produced in the attached studio—where weekly classes are given—are for sale. By the way, "Werks" is how they spell it. Open Saturday and Sunday noon to 5pm.

★ **The Palate & Chisel Academy of Fine Arts,** 1012 N. Dearborn Pkwy. ☎ **642-4400.**

The Palate & Chisel is a nonprofit cooperative of painters and sculptors, who, beginning in 1921, pooled their funds to purchase this ca. 1870s mansion, one of the first buildings erected after the Chicago Fire. Currently, 200 professional artists use the facilities to paint and sculpt, and to exhibit work in their own galleries and private studio areas. Weekend visits are best; call for hours.

State Street Collection, 609 N. State St. ☎ **951-1828.**

The State Street Collection has art deco kitchen collectibles.

⭐ **Steve Starr Studios,** 2654 N. Clark St. ☎ **525-6530.**

Steve Starr carries some of the city's finest art deco items. If it's after two in the afternoon, you might get to meet Mr. Starr himself. Mr. Starr's book, *Picture Perfect,* a striking collection of deco frames filled with glamorous movie star photos, was recently published by Rizzoli International and is available at the studio.

Tobai, 320 N. Dearborn Ave., in the Nikko Hotel. ☎ **661-0394.**

Contains an extensive collection of Japanese prints and also features classic Korean temple paintings, and contemporary Chinese artists.

To Life!, 224 S. Michigan Ave. ☎ **362-0255.**

A gallery of fine crafts in life forms and music themes; marionettes/puppets; music boxes; handmade jewelry; ceramic sculptures; wood puzzles, toys, and games. There's another branch at 333 N. Michigan Ave. (☎ **541-1951**).

Books

Chicago is book country and its stores compare favorably with the best of New York, both in variety and number. The nationwide chain stores make a strong showing, with Crown, Waldenbooks, and B. Dalton's especially well represented.

Aspidistra Bookshop, 2630 N. Clark St. ☎ **549-3129.**

Aspidistra Bookshop is one of the city's best used-book stores, stocking 20th-century literature.

⭐ **Barbara's Bookstore,** 1350 N. Wells St. ☎ **642-5044.**

Barbara's is a haven for small, independent press titles, as well as extensive selections of everything current. In addition, it has a well-stocked children's section, with sitting areas for the tots to peruse the books.

There are four branches in all, including 3130 N. Broadway (☎ **477-0411**), 1800 N. Clybourn (☎ **664-1113**), and one in Oak Park at 1100 Lake St. (☎ **708/848-9140**).

Bookseller's Row, 2445 N. Lincoln Ave. ☎ **348-1170.**

Bookseller's Row is bookstore with some 40,000 used and rare books.

The Children's Bookstore, 2465 N. Lincoln Ave. ☎ **248-2665.**

This is Chicago's largest children's bookstore, and it has storytelling hours several days a week. There's free parking in the rear of the store.

Chinese American Book Co., 55 E. Washington, Suite 1003.
☎ **782-6004.**

China Books has lots to read on the People's Republic, though the little red Mao books are in short supply.

Fiery Clock Face, 5311 N. Clark St. ☎ **728-4227.**

The Fiery Clock Face is a secondhand bookshop and collectibles store that displays its wares with flair. Their programs include storytelling, play readings with audience participation, and special readings for particular holidays.

Grand Tour, 3229 N. Clark St. ☎ **929-1836.**

This is the city's best source for foreign-language books and "probably the most complete travel store in the United States," claims manager Robert Katzman.

Illinois Labor History Society Bookstore, 28 E. Jackson Blvd.
☎ **663-4107.**

Here you will find rare and half-forgotten titles on labor history.

I Love A Mystery Bookstore, 55 E. Washington, Suite 250.
☎ **236-1338.**

Cloak-and-dagger buffs will adore this bookstore.

N. Fagin Books, 1039 W. Grand Ave. ☎ **829-5252.**

N. Fagin Books is home for the person who yearns for natural-science books—from dinosaurs to primitive art and anthropology and from botany to zoology.

Powell's Book Warehouse, 828 S. Wabash Ave., 4th floor.
☎ **341-0748.**

Used textbooks, dog-eared paperbacks, hardcover classics, and former best-sellers fill the shelves at Powell's.

Rand McNally Map Store, 23 E. Madison. ☎ **332-4628.**

If maps are your thing, don't miss the Rand McNally Map Store. The store also stocks, among its 15,000-item inventory, travel guides, videotapes, globes, and travel-related gift items from around the world.

Sandmeyer's Bookstore, 714 S. Dearborn. ☎ **922-2104.**

This historic Printer's Row shop invites browsing with its fine literature and children's books as well as with all of its travel literature.

Savvy Traveller, 50 E. Washington, 2nd floor. ☎ **263-2100.**

Smart travelers can buy their Frommer's Guides from Savvy's. "Our aim is to provide everything a traveler needs to plan and take a trip except tickets—a one-stop shop for travelers."

Seminary Co-op Bookstore, 5757 S. University Ave.
☎ **752-4381.**

This store, located near the University of Chicago campus, has just about everything on the shelves you might want. Their philosophy and theology sections are extensive. This is one of the premier academic bookstores in the country.

The Stars Our Destination, 2942 N. Clark St. ☎ **871-2722.**
The Stars Our Destination should satisfy all sci-fi fanatics. They carry everything in print in the science-fiction and fantasy genres, and they have a large used-book selection too.

Unabridged Books, 3251 N. Broadway. ☎ **883-9119.**
Unabridged has strong sections in travel, film, sci-fi, and gay and lesbian literature. Their "Chicago Writers Reading" Program on the last Tuesday of each month features the best and up-and-coming authors reading from their work, and work in progress, at 7:30pm. Free admission.

Women And Children First, 1967 N. Halsted St. ☎ **440-8824.**
Women and Children First holds the best selection in the city of titles for, by, and about women. Co-owner Linda Bubon holds a children's storybook hour each Wednesday at 10:30am.

Ceramics

Lill Street Gallery, 1021 W. Lill St. (in Lincoln Park). ☎ **477-6185.**
Located just 3 blocks north of Fullerton, at Sheffield, is the Midwest's largest ceramics center housing private and group studios, a gallery, a retail store, and six classrooms. Among the wares for sale is a large selection of high-quality, handcrafted artwork for home or office. Director Bruce Robbins says, "There is constantly something new to see or do at Lill Street, a show opening, a class going on, an artist working, or a new event being planned."

Clocks

Chicago Clock Co., 1502 N. Wells St. ☎ **751-1980.**
Check out the Chicago Clock Co., a very attractive building of poured concrete suggesting the inspiration of Frank Lloyd Wright. Clocks, clocks, and more clocks, over a thousand are on display. Other specialties are music boxes, and clock repair is done on the premises. Open Monday to Friday 11am to 7pm, Saturday 11am to 6pm, and Sunday noon to 5pm.

Fashions

The stores listed in this section are only a sampling of those not mentioned above in the main shopping districts.

CHILDREN'S

Besides such well-known chain stores as Benetton and Gap Kids, Chicago is well supplied with shops offering children's wear.

All Our Children, 2217 N. Halsted St. ☎ **327-1868.**
All Our Children is a small and friendly boutique carrying all sizes, from newborn to size 6X-7.

Gap Kids, 2108 N. Halsted St. ☎ **281-0354.**
Just what the name implies: American casual for the small-fry.

Lollipop, 2828 N. Clark St. ☎ **248-7311.**
For trendy designer children's wear, try Lollipop.

The Second Child, 954 W. Armitage Ave. ☎ **883-0880.**

The Second Child is a resale boutique that offers quality clothing for a fraction of the price. They also carry maternity clothes, furniture, equipment, and toys.

MEN'S

Arbetman-Goldberg, Inc., 350 N. Orleans St. ☎ **467-0377.**

Men's clothing and accessories from all over the continent.

Bigsby & Kruthers, Water Tower Place, 835 N. Michigan Ave. ☎ **944-6955.**

Number one in its field for years, with five locations in Chicago.

M. Myman & Son, 100 E. Walton St. ☎ **266-0060** or toll free **800/735-5009.**

"We suit the big guys," says the perky sales staff. In addition to this outlet off the Magnificent Mile, there are also five branch stores in the 'burbs.

WOMEN'S

Fitigues, 2130 N. Halsted. ☎ **404-9696.**

Fitigues features sports and denim wear for fashion-conscious women and girls.

Isis, 38 E. Oak St. ☎ **664-7076.**

At Isis, the fashions are an unusual mix of textures, patterns, and colors.

Sugar Magnolia, 110 E. Oak St. ☎ **944-0885.**

This store offers lively, easy-to-wear fashions and accessories for women and girls.

This Little Piggy, 835 N. Michigan Ave. ☎ **943-7449.**

This Little Piggy, in Water Tower Place, is the ultimate in shopping for socks—great designs with a sense of humor. The store also carries a selection of panty hose.

Victoria's Secret, 835 N. Michigan Ave. ☎ **440-1169.**

Victoria's Secret, in Water Tower Place, has more merchandise than what is offered in their mail-order catalogs.

UNISEX

Banana Republic, 2104 N. Halsted St. ☎ **549-5505.**

Togs for the expeditionary, the adventuresome trekker, and the amateur or professional photojournalist, among others. The ultimate in travel wear.

Eddie Bauer, 123 N. Wabash Ave. ☎ **263-6005.**

Once an outdoors outfitter, Eddie Bauer now carries reasonably priced clothing for the entire family.

The Gap, 2128 N. Halsted St. ☎ **528-6884.**

The great American store, for men and women of all ages.

Jennings, Inc., 1979 N. Halsted ☎ **587-7866.**

Jennings bills itself as an accessory "bar" for men and women, including belts, bags, jewels, and specialty items. The design and ambience of the shop are similar to that of a neighborhood pub. Complimentary cappuccino and espresso are served.

Kangaroo Connection, 1113 W. Webster. ☎ **248-5499.**

This shop carries fashions from down under, such as oilskins of the outback, slouch hats, T-shirts, Aussie "football" jerseys, and more.

Food

BAKERIES

Cheesecakes by J. R., 2841 W. Howard St. ☎ **465-6733.**

Cheesecakes by J. R. offers 20 varieties, all baked on the premises, and an exclusive line of specialty cakes.

Dinkel's Bakery, 3329 N. Lincoln Ave. ☎ **281-7300.**

Dinkel's specializes in authentic old-world German flavors. Decorated cakes are available for all occasions. Gourmet sandwiches and coffee are served daily.

Let Them Eat Cake, 60 E. Chicago Ave. ☎ **708/863-4200.**

The chain Let Them Eat Cake is a major Chicago supplier of fresh-fruit tarts and banana-walnut fudge cakes. Traditional and contemporary wedding cakes are also available.

The Swedish Bakery, 5348 N. Clark St. ☎ **561-8919.**

For nearly 60 years, this bakery has set the standard in European and Swedish-style baked goods, specializing in marzipan and fruit-glazed cakes.

MARKETS

When you're shopping in Chinatown, try the **Chinese Trading Company,** 2263 S. Wentworth (☎ **842-2820**), and **Sun Chong Lung,** 2220 S. Wentworth (☎ **225-6050**).

Burhops, 745 N. LaSalle St. ☎ **642-8600.**

Burhops at One Fish Plaza is one of the best seafood markets in the city.

Chicago Fish House, 1250 W. Division St. ☎ **227-7000.**

This is another excellent seafood market with fresh fish flown in daily from Alaska, Hawaii, Florida, the Great Lakes, the Gulf of Mexico, New Zealand . . . you see the point?

Gepperth's Meat Market, 1970 N. Halsted St. ☎ **549-3883.**

Gepperth's has one of the best reputations in town for carrying Chicago's prime export—meats. It also sells cheeses.

Kuhn's Delicatessen, 3053 N. Lincoln Ave. ☎ **525-9019.**

Kuhn's is probably the best German deli in town. Gift baskets and party trays are also available for all occasions.

L'Appetito, 30 E. Huron St. ☎ **787-9881.**

L'Appetito sells everything Italian and is a favorite of the lunch crowd for its 10-inch Italian subs.

Oriental Food Market, 2801 W. Howard St. ☎ **274-2826.**

Here you'll find cooking staples from the Philippines, Japan, Thailand, and China—as well as the freshest of vegetables. Call for a schedule of weekly cooking classes.

Furniture

Henry A. W. Mundt, 4143 N. Lincoln Ave. ☎ **935-5115.**

This store is worth a peek for the old-world artisanship of the furniture.

Galleries

Landmark, 5301 N. Clark St. ☎ **728-5301.**

The Landmark is a gallery of shops on three floors, all individually owned businesses with a broad range of products—lamps, weavings, quilts, paper supplies, toys, handcrafts, and women's clothes—and services, from cross-stitch classes to photo restoration.

Toys

★ **Saturday's Child**, 2146 N. Halsted St. ☎ **525-8697.**

The clever toys and standbys range from rubber snakes and frogs to sidewalk chalk, from kid's large-faced wristwatches to books.

A Travel Outfitter

★ **Ed And Fred: A Traveler's Store**, 1007 Webster (near corner of Sheffield). ☎ **477-6220.**

This store carries little and big things to smooth the traveler's journey, such as electric-current converters and transformers, water purifiers, maps, and flashlights, plus a full line of guides and travel literature.

Wine & Liquor

Sam's Wine & Liquors, 1000 W. North Ave. ☎ **664-4394.**

A reader writes, "This is the most extensively stocked wine and spirits merchant I've encountered; a gold mine for anyone interested in the finer appellation."

10

Chicago Nights

Aₛ IN MOST LARGE CITIES, CHICAGO'S NIGHTLIFE SPANS THE TRADITIONAL and the contemporary. Showcases for symphonic concerts, opera, ballet, and professional dance, as well as dramatic and musical theater, are primarily located on the periphery of the Loop, mostly along South Michigan Avenue. Pop concerts, on the other hand, are generally hosted in stadiums, sports arenas, or convention centers in more outlying areas. More laid-back is the city's club and cabaret scene, scattered throughout Chicago, and also concentrated in several distinct quarters that border downtown on the Near North Side, most prominently Rush Street, Old Town, Lincoln Park, and New Town. Chicago's vibrant and innovative off-Loop theaters are also dispersed throughout a wide range of neighborhoods. Many of the larger hotels provide on their premises some form of nighttime entertainment, minimally a cozy piano bar, but in a few cases, full-blown nightclub acts and plays. And, of course, every Chicago neighborhood seems to have its favorite hangouts and taverns, and always at least one local movie theater exhibiting first-run features or a repertory of film classics.

Local newspapers and magazines are generally the best sources of information for up-to-date entertainment listings. The "Weekend" and "What's Happening" sections of the two dailies, the *Chicago Tribune* and the *Chicago Sun-Times,* as well as the entertainment sections of the free weekly tabloid, *The Reader,* and the monthly *Chicago* magazine all fall in this category. Most hotels stock their rooms with a variety of promotional materials to orient guests as to current events and activities taking place throughout the city.

1   The Performing Arts

Major Performing Arts Companies

CLASSICAL MUSIC

The Chicago Symphony Orchestra, performing in Orchestra Hall, 220 S. Michigan. ☎ **435-8111.**

Orchestra Hall is the home of the acclaimed **Chicago Symphony Orchestra,** now entering its second century with new Music Director Daniel Barenboim and Music Director Laureate Sir Georg Solti.

A Chicago Symphony concert is possibly the hottest ticket in town; however, good seats often become available on concert day. Call the number above or stop at the box office for the latest information. Tickets cost from $14 to $50. Those who visit Chicago during the summer still have an opportunity to hear a performance by the orchestra at the Ravinia Festival (☎ **312/RAVINIA**), led by well-known guest conductors; see Chapter 11 for details.

The **Civic Orchestra of Chicago,** the training orchestra of the Chicago Symphony since 1919, is also highly regarded and presents free programs at Orchestra Hall.

Box-Office Hotlines

A number of hotlines provide specific information on the performing arts:

Classical Musical Alliance (☎ **987-9296**) for information on classical music concerts and the opera.

Concert Line (☎ **666-6667**) for rock, country, blues, and pop music concert information.

Dance Hotline (☎ **419-8383**) for information on the dance scene.

Hot Tix Hotline (☎ **977-1755**) offers a recorded message listing all performances for the evening on which you call, and on Friday the message lists the weekend theater schedule for the entire city.

Jazz Hotline (☎ **666-1881**) for jazz club and concert listings.

Chicago Chamber Musicians, performing at various locales, including the Museum of Science and Industry. ☎ **558-1404.**

The Chicago Chamber Musicians present chamber music concerts by groups from around the world. Their resident quartet, the Vermeer Quartet, gives a series of concerts at the Chicago Historical Society. Ticket prices vary with the concerts; often they're free. You can write to them for more information; their office is at 410 South Michigan Ave., Suite 911, Chicago, IL 60605.

Chicago Chamber Orchestra, performing at various locales. ☎ **922-5570.**

The Chicago Chamber Orchestra, under the direction of Dieter Kober, performs frequently at major museums and at the Chicago Public Library. The group's premier yearly concert, the Blair Memorial, takes place in May at the Cathedral of St. James, 61 E. Huron St.

Grant Park Symphony And Chorus, performing in Grant Park at the James C. Petrillo Music Shell. ☎ **294-2420.**

Free outdoor classical music concerts can be attended all summer from late June through August in Grant Park.

OPERA

Lyric Opera Of Chicago, performing in the Civic Opera House, at Madison St. and Wacker Dr. ☎ **332-2244.**

The Lyric's season runs from September through February and is a sold-out event. A major American opera company, it attracts noted singers from all over the world, and its general director is the innovative Ardis Krainik. The opera has an adjunct, the Lyric Opera Center for American Artists, that also gives performances.

DANCE

Chicago has a lively dance scene, with many local groups as well as visiting companies, such as the Kirov Ballet and Ballet Theatre. For complete information, contact the Dance Hotline.

Ballet Chicago, 222 S. Riverside Plaza. ☎ **993-7575.**

Ballet Chicago is notable on the Chicago dance scene. Under artistic director Daniel Duell, the company specializes in the ballets of Balanchine.

Hubbard Street Dance Company, 218 S. Wabash. ☎ **663-0853.**

Lou Conti is the artistic director of this major Chicago contemporary dance company.

Major Concert Halls & Auditoriums

Auditorium Theater, 50 E. Congress Pkwy. ☎ **922-4046.**

Designed in 1888 by Louis Sullivan and Dankmar Adler, the Auditorium Theater is today a national landmark. Most of the building is now occupied by Roosevelt University, but the theater—one of the premier concert halls of the century—was restored in 1967 and now hosts a season of fine dance and musical performances and plays attracting such names as Twyla Tharp, Itzhak Perlman, Luciano Pavarotti, Alvin Ailey, Pilobolus, the American Ballet Theatre, and the Moscow Ballet. For ticket reservations or box office information, call **922-2100.** Tours are available on request.

Civic Opera House, at Madison St. and Wacker Dr. ☎ **346-0270.**

The 3,600-seat art deco Civic Opera House, home of the Lyric Opera company, was built in 1929. It is the enduring monument of its founder, Samuel Insull, who was probably the most hated man in Chicago during the Great Depression. His speculative empire crumbled during the 1929 stock market crash, dragging down thousands of small investors in its wake, and he himself died penniless.

Theater

Chicago is the home of more than 120 theaters; on a given weekend, a visitor may have the opportunity to choose from as many as 70 different productions in a range of theaters capable of seating audiences numbering anywhere from 40 to 4,000.

To order tickets, call **Ticketron** (☎ **902-1888**), a centralized phone-reservation system allowing you to charge, with a major credit card, full-price tickets for productions at more than 50 Chicago theaters. For half-price tickets on the day of the show, drop by the **Hot Tix Ticket Center,** located in the Loop at 24 S. State St.; or call **831-2822** to order by phone, **977-1755** for information. Hot Tix also offers advance-sales tickets at full price. It's open on Monday from noon to 6pm, Tuesday through Friday from 10am to 6pm, and on Saturday from 10am to 5pm.

DOWNTOWN

Arie Crown Theater, McCormick Place, 23rd St. and Lake Shore Dr. ☎ **791-6000.**

Another showcase for Broadway-style traveling companies, performing mostly musicals, is the Arie Crown Theater. This gigantic house, despite casts that often feature big-name stars, has a reputation for tinny acoustics and poor sightlines from all but the first 15 rows of the almost 3,400 seats.

Chicago Theater, 175 N. State St. ☎ 443-1130.

From a later era, and the product of a vastly different fantasy, is the Chicago Theater, the baroque centerpiece of the Balaban and Katz movie-house chain. The interior of this 1921 extravaganza defines the outer limits of the term *ornate,* the decor inspired as it was by the grandeur of Europe from antiquity through the Renaissance. By the end of the Vietnam War, the Chicago Theater had deteriorated badly, and was about to fall victim to the wrecker's ball when developers' plans were uncharacteristically foiled by a group of hearty preservationists who restored the landmark and reopened it in 1986. The Chicago Theater is used as a performing arts center by local companies and hosts dance companies, touring concerts, Broadway shows, and private industrial shows. On many occasions, it fulfills a role similar to that of Radio City Music Hall in New York, as a venue for star-studded nostalgia performances by such perennial draws as Frank Sinatra.

Columbia College Theater/Music Center, at Columbia College, 62 E. 11th St. ☎ 663-9465.

Located along South Michigan Avenue, the Columbia College Theater/Music Center presents large-scale productions with big-name guest actors staged in comely art deco surroundings.

Goodman Theatre, 200 S. Columbus Dr. ☎ 443-3800.

The dean of legitimate theaters in Chicago is the Goodman, where both original productions and familiar standards are staged in a house seating 683. The Goodman also houses a 135-seat auditorium for experimental stagings, called the Studio Theater. The Goodman occupies a wing of the Art Institute complex in Grant Park. Gourmet buffet meals are served prix-fixe on the premises in the Rehearsal Room, open after 6pm Wednesday through Saturday.

Mayfair Theater, 626 S. Michigan. ☎ 786-9120.

At the Blackstone Hotel's Mayfair Theater, located along South Michigan Avenue, the popular audience participation spoof, *Shear Madness,* has been running for years, and is likely to continue for some time to come. Tickets cost $23 Sunday through Thursday, $28 on Friday and Saturday.

O'Malley Workshop Theater, at Roosevelt University, 420 S. Michigan. ☎ 341-3720.

The O'Malley Workshop Theater features performances by well-known Chicago stage personalities.

Shubert Theater, 22 W. Monroe. ☎ 977-1700.

Road shows that originated on Broadway are presented at the Shubert Theater.

OFF-LOOP

Chicago's most successful off-Loop theaters have produced a number of legendary comic actors, including comic-turned-director Mike Nichols and current box-office favorite Bill Murray. But the vital organ of Chicago's theater remains the little non-Equity house, doggedly sustained by a handful of volunteers and supporters, and that in most cases occupies a small storefront or rehearsal space on a remote block in one of the city's more obscure neighborhoods.

American Blues Theater, 3212 N. Broadway. ☎ **728-5844.**

The American Blues Theater is similar to the Bailiwick Repertory, though its focus is on themes inspired by the midwestern experience.

Apollo Theater Center, 2540 N. Lincoln Ave. ☎ **988-9000.**

The Apollo, which occupies a middling-size house of 350 seats, is a neighborhood showcase for successful musical revues that in most cases were developed elsewhere.

Bailiwick Repertory, 1225 W. Belmont. ☎ **327-5252.**

The Bailiwick Repertory is one of Chicago's young and exciting regional theaters, each year producing a main-stage series of classics (such as *The Count of Monte Cristo*), a Director's Festival of one-act plays, and the Pride Performance Series.

Blue Rider, 1822 S. Halsted. ☎ **733-4668.**

One of Chicago's most controversial experimental theaters, the Blue Rider, is located on the artistic fringe of Pilsen, essentially a Mexican immigrant neighborhood. The group was founded by Donna Blue Lachman—the color blue, as you can see, bears a certain thematic load for this quirky ensemble. Why blue? Donna once played the streets of San Francisco as a "loud mime" she called "Blue the Clown." But the deeper inspiration for the name, she says, comes from the title of the Kandinsky painting *The Blue Rider.*

Blue Rider produces only a single, original work each year, with a running time of three to four months. The remainder of the time is devoted to writing and polishing upcoming productions.

Body Politic Theater, 2261 N. Lincoln. ☎ **348-7901.**

The Body Politic Theater offers subscribers a season of varied selections.

Briar Street Theater, 3133 N. Halsted. ☎ **348-4000.**

The Briar Street Theater seats approximately 400 and has premiered the work of Chicago native David Mamet, featuring as well the work of such other well-known playwrights as Tom Stoppard.

Steppenwolf Theater, 1650 N. Halsted. ☎ **335-1650.**

One of the great Chicago success stories of recent years is the brilliant repertory company Steppenwolf Theater. Steppenwolf has garnered many awards, including five Tonys—one for regional theater excellence. Steppenwolf's breakthrough, following the usual years of artistic struggle, now provides inspiration for other small theater companies that dream of following in its footsteps. Many of those kindred workshops and theaters can similarly be found on the city's Near North Side.

Victory Gardens Theater, 2257 N. Lincoln. ☎ **871-3000.**

Victory Gardens is a nonprofit group devoted to the development of the playwright. There are free weekly readings of new works.

2 The Club & Music Scene

Comedy Clubs

In the mid-seventies, "Saturday Night Live" once again brought Chicago's unique brand of comedy to national attention. But in those years John Belushi and Bill Murray were just the latest brood to hatch from the number one incubator of the Chicago-style humor, Second City, not to mention the added nurturing the comics gained from an odd assortment of other zany habitats throughout the city. From Nichols and May, Robin Williams, and Robert Klein to Joan Rivers, John Candy, and David Steinberg, two generations of American comics have won their spurs on the boards of Chicago before making their fortunes as recording artists, film stars, and talk-show celebrities.

Funny Firm, 318 W. Grand. ☎ **321-9500.**

The Funny Firm has the most spacious and comfortable comedy showroom in Chicago and features national headliners from the Tonight Show, Letterman, HBO, and Showtime.

Admission: Thurs–Sun $7–$10, Fri–Sat $12–$15.

Improvisation Institute, 2319 W. Belmont. ☎ **929-2323.**

The Improv Institute Players perform totally improvised comedy shows in a casual but intensely audience-interactive atmosphere. The company also hosts Fun Nite, an open stage for aspiring improvisers.

Admission: Wed (Fun Nite) $5, Thurs–Sat $10.

Second City, 1616 N. Wells. ☎ **337-3992.**

After decades of continuous service, Second City remains the top comedy club in Chicago. After the show, you can stick around for the "schtick," to handicap the stars of the future as they grind through their improvisational routines; no ticket is necessary if you skip the show.

Admission: Mon $5, Tues–Thurs and Sun $10, Fri $12, Sat $16.

Zanies, 1548 N. Wells. ☎ **337-4027.**

Another Old Town stalwart is Zanies, which often draws its headliners straight off "The Late Show with David Letterman" and "The Tonight Show." Satirical skits, improvisations, and stand-up comedy routines are the usual fare, played to packed, appreciative houses.

Admission: $12, plus two-drink minimum.

Jazz

Andy's, 11 E. Hubbard. ☎ 642-6805.

Andy's, a full restaurant and bar, is popular with both the hard-core and the neophyte jazz enthusiast. There are sets Monday through Friday from noon to 2:30pm and 5 to 8:30pm, Saturday at 9pm, and Sunday from 6 to 11pm, when you can hear Dr. Bop and the Headliners Rock and Roll Revival.

Admission: Before 5pm, free; after 5pm, Mon–Fri and Sun $3–$5, Sat $5–$7.

Gold Star Sardine Bar, 666 N. Lake Shore Dr. ☎ 664-4215.

The Gold Star Sardine Bar, toward the lake, is true to its name. It is lilliputian in size with barely enough room for 50 patrons, but nonetheless a nightclub showcase for such big fish as Liza Minnelli.

Admission: Free, with one-drink minimum.

Green Mill, 4802 N. Broadway. ☎ 878-5552.

On the fringes of Uptown, the Green Mill is "Old Chicago" to the rafters. A popular watering hole during the twenties and the thirties, when Al Capone was a regular and the headliners included Sophie Tucker—the Red Hot Mama—and Al Jolson, it still has its speak-easy atmosphere and flavor. On Sunday night the Green Mill hosts the Uptown Poetry Slam, when poets vie for the open mike to roast and ridicule each other's work. Most nights, however, jazz is on the menu, beginning around 9pm and winding down just before closing at 4am.

Admission: $3–$7.

Jazz Bulls, 1916 N. Lincoln Park. ☎ 337-3000.

This is one of the liveliest spots in all Chicago. I was fortunate to catch Insight, the hottest quartet the Bulls books these days. Insight consists of four young musicians—bass, keyboard, drums, and lead guitar/vocalist—individually superb, who collectively play a brand of highly polished new age jazz that is innovative, emotive, intelligent, amusing, and foot-stomping all at the same time. You'll find live musical entertainment here 365 nights a year. The drinks aren't cheap and the cafe-style fare of burgers, fries, and pizza is mediocre. But the music is sustenance enough.

Discount parking is available nearby at 2036 N. Clark, or on the fringes of the park, located only a block to the east.

Admission: Sun–Thurs $5, Fri–Sat $8.

Joe Segal's Jazz Showcase, in the Blackstone Hotel, 636 S. Michigan. ☎ 427-4300.

For jazz in an old hotel nightclub setting, Joe Segal's is a must. Over the years Joe has hosted the best, and still does. The night I attended,

IMPRESSIONS

"I Will" is the unofficial slogan of Chicago: or "I Will," as the columnist Max Royko once suggested, "If I Don't Get Caught."
—James Morris, "Chicago," *Places,* 1972

a local quartet built around an alto-sax soloist played a credible set of bebop to a warm and appreciative audience. Reservations are recommended when a big-name headliner is featured.

Admission: Varies according to performer.

Moosehead Bar & Grill, 240 E. Ontario. ☎ **649-9113.**

Just south of the Loop, a favorite after-work hangout is the Moosehead Bar & Grill. The name derives from the moosehead on the wall, but the rest of the atmosphere is strictly kitsch, the cuisine burgers, and the music light jazz.

Admission: Free.

Oz, 2917 N. Sheffield. ☎ **975-8100.**

Uptown, you'll find live music within the jazz genre at Oz, where the bar is built of glass bricks and the outdoor patio is open during the summer months. With no stage, the musicians crowd into a corner of the room and play their sets Tuesday through Friday after 10pm.

Admission: $5.

The Vu, 2624 N. Lincoln. ☎ **871-0205.**

The eclectic offerings at the Vu encompass everything from jazz jams, country music, and a big band to live turtle races. The Vu begins to fill up by 10:30 or 11pm, and remains open nightly until 4am.

Admission: $1–$3.

Blues

With a few notable exceptions, Chicago's best and most popular blues showcases are located in entertainment districts of the Near North Side.

Blue Chicago, 937 N. State. ☎ **642-6261.**

The Blue Chicago is in the Rush Street area.

Admission: $5–$7.

B.L.U.E.S., 2519 N. Halsted. ☎ **528-1012.**

On the Halsted strip, look for B.L.U.E.S.—the name says it all—which is open from 8pm to 2am Sunday through Friday, until 3am on Saturday, with the show beginning after 9pm.

Admission: $5–$8.

B.L.U.E.S. Etcetera, 1124 W. Belmont (at the corner of Clifton). ☎ **525-8989.**

In New Town, B.L.U.E.S. Etcetera attracts the big names in blues, Chicago style and otherwise, like Junior Wells. It's a bit like a cafeteria or a coffee shop, but you don't go to a blues club for the decor. Opens nightly at 8pm and closes "when it's over"; the show begins around 9pm.

Admission: $4–$8.

Kingston Mines, 2548 N. Halsted. ☎ **477-4646.**

The Kingston Mines is reputed to be one of Chicago's premier blues bars, where musicians come after their own gigs to jam with each other and to socialize. The show begins after 9:30pm, seven nights a week, with two sets and continuous music on the weekends.

Admission: $8–$10.

Lilly's, 2513 N. Lincoln. ☎ 525-2422.

In Lincoln Park, Lilly's still enshrines the old-time blues. There are blues jams every Thursday night, and jazz and blues combos the rest of the week. Shows begin at 9pm and end in the wee hours, when there are no more customers to play for.

Admission: $5.

New Checkerboard Lounge, 423 E. 43rd St. ☎ 624-3240.

On the South Side, despite its location in a marginal neighborhood, the "in spot" is the New Checkerboard Lounge. The music is the real thing here, very close to its Mississippi roots.

Admission: Weekdays $3, weekends $7.

Rosa's, 3420 W. Armitage (at Kimball). ☎ 342-0452.

Friends of mine took me to their favorite nightspot, Rosa's, which has live blues every night of the year. Rosa's is strictly a neighborhood hangout, but it has all the atmosphere that any good blues group requires to fuel its heartfelt lamentations. Most genuine blues groups and music lovers feel right at home here. Rosa's also sponsors a Blues Cruise on Lake Michigan every summer. The doors open at 8pm, and the show starts around 9:30pm and runs until 2am, 3am on Saturday.

Admission: $3–$8.

The Wise Fools Pub, 2270 N. Lincoln. ☎ 929-1510\

The Wise Fools Pub caters to the hottest and the best. The popular blues bar and college hangout has long lines on the weekends. There is a cover charge nightly, and a minimum on Saturday.

Admission: $5–$10.

Rock, Folk & Ethnic ───────────────────

Jazz and blues are musically characteristic of the Chicago club scene, but an even greater number of establishments cater to the tastes of those who like all the other musical forms, from mellow folk to heavy metal, with suave salsa, spicy reggae, melancholy Irish, weepy country, and frenetic gypsy in between.

Rock clubs abound in Chicago; you'll find one or several in most of the North Side neighborhoods, and most of them double up as discos.

Asi Es Columbia, 3910 N. Lincoln. ☎ 348-7444.

You can catch the latest in Latin jazz and samba at Asi Es Columbia. Open Friday to Sunday.

Admission: $9.

Biddy Mulligan's, 7644 N. Sheridan. ☎ 761-6532.

Biddy Mulligan's has a big show daily after 9:30pm that varies from reggae and rock to blues and jazz.

Admission: Fri–Sat $5.

Cabaret Metro/Smart Bar, 3730 N. Clark. ☎ **549-0203.**

The Cabaret Metro has live music Friday, Saturday, and most week-nights. The Smart Bar—at the same location—is a dance club open seven nights a week.
Admission: $3–$6.

Cubby Bear Lounge, 1059 W. Addison. ☎ **327-1662.**

The Cubby Bear, across from Wrigley Field, is a showcase for new bands Friday and Saturday nights. Closed Monday and Tuesday.
Admission: $5–$8.

Heartland Cafe, 7000 N. Glenwood. ☎ **465-8005.**

On the weekends, you'll usually find something happening music-wise at the Heartland Cafe. The musical menu is eclectic—anything from funky rock to Irish.
Admission: $6–$8.

Irish Eyes, 2519 N. Lincoln. ☎ **348-9548.**

This place showcases Irish music on Friday and Saturday nights be-ginning after 9pm, and bluegrass music about once a month. (Check the music section of the weekly *Chicago Reader,* a free entertainment newspaper distributed throughout the city, for current listings.)
Admission: $5.

Irish Village, 6215 W. Diversey. ☎ **237-7555.**

It's St. Paddy's Day every night of the week at the Irish Village.
Admission: Free.

The Lakeview Lounge, 5110 N. Broadway. ☎ **769-0994.**

Uptown is country-music territory, and you'll find it live at the Lakeview Lounge. Open 10pm to 4am.
Admission: Free.

No Exit Cafe, 6970 N. Glenwood. ☎ **743-3355.**

The No Exit Cafe, which has been around for decades, is owned and run today by a woman named Suzanne who first came here as a waitress in 1968. The folk music featured here in the evening is among the tops in the city, and you can linger all day over a cup of coffee, hassle-free. Open Monday through Thursday from 4pm to midnight, on Friday until 1:30am, on Saturday from noon to 2am, and on Sunday from noon to midnight.
Admission: $3–$5.

Phyllis's Musical Inn, 1800 W. Division. ☎ **486-9862.**

This is a small, generally uncrowded club in Wicker Park with live new wave music on Wednesday and Friday through Sunday nights.
Admission: $3–$5.

Vic Theatre, 3145 N. Sheffield. ☎ **248-7277.**

The Vic is a large old theater with candy-cane lettering on the mar-quee that often spells out the names of big-name talent, such as Eric Clapton.
Admission: Varies with the performers.

The Wild Hare, 3530 N. Clark. ☎ **327-4273.**

Number one on Chicago's reggae charts is the Wild Hare, in the shadow of Wrigley Field. When I was first told the name of the club, I thought the name was "wild hair." I was a bit disappointed when I saw what the real name was. But the music is pure Jamaican. Even the atmosphere inside the bar—dark and slightly dingy—might have been transported from a side street in Montego Bay, from the part of town tourists seldom wander through.

Admission: $5–$8.

Dance Clubs/Discos

While the discotheque is not completely a thing of the past in Chicago, most dancing takes place these days in clubs and bars that either specialize in one brand of music or that offer an ever-changing mix of rhythms and beats in an attempt to appeal to different moods and a broader market.

Baby Doll Polka Club, 16102 S. Central. ☎ **582-9706.**

Who didn't secretly love Lawrence Welk? Few could ever feel truly square again after watching Welk start up the band with "a-one and a-two," and then squire a lady from the audience around the floor in a gentlemanly but bouncy polka. Relive those golden memories at the Baby Doll Polka Club and skip-step to the magic accordion of Ed Korosa, weekends only, Friday and Saturday after 9:30 and on Sunday after 5pm.

Admission: $5.

Baja Beach Club, at North Pier, 401 E. Illinois St. ☎ **222-1992.**

This is Chicago's front-rank party club, covering more than 18,000 square feet of fun-and-dance space. Dance show-offs, this is the place. Open seven days a week.

Admission: Free.

Bossa Nova, 1960 N. Clybourn Ave. ☎ **248-4800.**

A thoroughly modern version of the old-fashioned supper club, featuring world beat music and an extraordinary menu of small-platter dishes called "tapas." Live dance music nightly after 10pm.

Admission: Free.

Loading Dock, 3702 N. Halsted. ☎ **929-6108.**

New Town caters to punks, gays, straights, and whoever else descends from the gangplank of the nocturnal ark along and near the Belmont Avenue strip. Local residents who take their dancing seriously, and who save the chitchat for an ambience in the lower decibel range, are said to prefer the Loading Dock, where progressive music is played and the real action only begins in the wee hours—it opens at 11pm.

Admission: $5–$8.

Neo, 2350 N. Clark. ☎ **528-2622.**

For new wave, it's NEO, a bit of a cavern at the end of a lighted alley, a holdover from the short-lived new wave era of the late seventies and early eighties.

Admission: $6–$10.

950 Club, 950 W. Wrightwood. ☎ **929-8955.**

Alternative music à la Patti Smith is the hallmark at the 950 Club, which attracts a mixed crowd aged from 21 to 50.

Admission: $5–$8.

Tania's, 2659 N. Milwaukee. ☎ **235-7120.**

Offering the Latin beat and a primarily Hispanic scene is Tania's, located on the Northwest Side along the so-called Milwaukee Avenue corridor. There's live music Wednesday through Sunday after 10:30pm.

Admission: Free.

Gay/Lesbian Clubs & Bars

Berlin, 954 W. Belmont. ☎ **348-4975.**

Shades of the Weimar period are the intended vibes at Berlin, but the decadence is more style than real, and the crowd a blend of straights and gays. There's a constant background of videos, with male dancers on some weekday nights. Open daily from 4pm to 4am (until 5am on Saturday).

The Closet, 3325 N. Broadway. ☎ **477-8533.**

The Closet is mostly gay, as the name might suggest, but also has a sports crowd.

Manhole, 3458 N. Halsted ☎ **975-9244.**

The Manhole attracts a youthful and late-night clientele with recorded dance music.

Sidetrack, 3349 N. Halsted. ☎ **477-9189.**

Sidetrack is a video bar where the American musical is the sound of choice.

3   The Bar & Cafe Scene

For the atmosphere of a neighborhood tavern, a singles bar, or a so-called sports bar, the visitor must venture beyond downtown into the surrounding neighborhoods. As always, the neighborhood taverns are gathering places; they have their day crowds, their after-work regulars, and a stream of irregulars who stumble upon them while traveling, or who are drawn there by word of mouth (and travel guidebooks). There are three or four entertainment zones on the Near North Side that are saturated with bright, upscale neighborhood taverns, with a few more traditional hangouts scattered around to remind us what bars used to look like before the phrase *theme park* came into the language. The real no-frills "corner taps" are also well represented in the blue-collar neighborhoods of Chicago, and these are for me always a personal pleasure to discover on my own.

IMPRESSIONS

Chicago is never tired.
—James Morris, "Chicago," Places, 1972

AN OVERVIEW   Around **Rush Street** you get the singles bars—a college-aged crowd I'd call it. The bars are always crowded on the weekends and some of the bars successfully maintain the action on weeknights by allowing women free admittance.

Division Street, with its succession of singles bars, is still the street of adolescent dreams where, on any given night, pitchmen stand on the sidewalk before their respective establishments and try to attract customers. Most of the bars have special nights where the price of drinks for women is heavily discounted. The bars line Division Street with names like **Snuggery,** 15 W. Division (☎ **337-4349**); **She-Nannigans,** 16 W. Division (☎ **642-2344**); **Butch McGuire's,** 20 W. Division (☎ **337-9080**); **Lodge,** 21 W. Division (☎ **642-4406**); and **Mother's,** 26 W. Division (☎ **642-7251**).

Old Town has **Wells Street** with Second City and other comedy clubs, and a string of reliable restaurants and bars, many of which traditionally appeal to visiting tourists. In **Lincoln Park,** you have concentrations of in-spots, bars, restaurants, and shops along Armitage Avenue, Halsted Street, and Lincoln Avenue. The same is true for the middle-class demimonde quarter with its slightly New York East Village atmosphere on the blocks surrounding **Belmont Avenue.**

HOTEL NIGHTLIFE   Virtually every hotel in Chicago has a cocktail lounge or piano bar, and in some cases, more than one distinct environment where a guest or patron may take an apéritif before dinner or watch an evening of entertainment (see Chapter 5 for details). In this category, I personally like the lobby bar at the **Nikko Hotel** and the piano bar at the **Pump Room** in the Omni Ambassador East Hotel.

I also liked very much the look of the bars in two of the European-style hotels, the **Raphael** and the **Tremont.** Also extremely pleasant was the Bookmark Lounge at the **Barclay Hotel,** where hot hors d'oeuvres are served at cocktail hour.

BARS & PUBS

Jay's, 930 N. Rush. ☎ **664-4333**.

One of the few "institutions" remaining on Rush Street that reflects the area's bygone honky-tonk character is a real shot-and-chaser bar, Jay's, posing as a singles spot. Anyway, at least by day, Jay's seems to cater to the neighborhood's corner-tavern set, with the TVs on both ends of the bar tuned to some sporting event or movie, and the Italian beef sandwich with hot peppers a treat for $3 while you sip from a bottle of Old Style beer, $1.50. A dartboard and bowling machine complete the picture.

John Barleycorn Memorial Pub, 658 W. Belden. ☎ **348-8899.**

"Se habla Beethoven" announces the legend beneath the sign of the landmark John Barleycorn Memorial Pub, where the western point of this cross street intersects with Lincoln Avenue, a tavern for highbrows who are treated to a background of classical music and

a continuous slide show of art masterpieces. Patrons can order a
meal from the menu, too.

Old Town Ale House, 219 W. North. ☎ 944-7020.

One of Old Town's legendary bars is the Old Town Ale House, a
neighborhood hangout since the late fifties featuring an outstanding
jukebox with a very eclectic selection. It's open daily from noon to
4am (until 5am on Saturday).

Otis, 2150 N. Halsted. ☎ 348-1900.

The Otis is more than a bar, offering live music from southern rock
to reggae and blues 3 nights a week. Wednesday nights feature nothing but acoustic music, and on Tuesday nights, draft beer is only 25¢.
The ambience is attractive, with a beautiful wood floor and unique
wooden fixtures and decorations throughout the bar.

River Shannon, 425 W. Armitage. ☎ 944-5087.

Another "now"-looking bar is River Shannon, a blending of a singles
hangout with a touch of sports-bar ambience. Open Monday through
Friday from 2pm to 2am, on Saturday from 2pm to 3am, and on
Sunday from noon to 2pm.

Sheffield's, 3258 N. Sheffield. ☎ 281-4989.

A neighborhood gathering spot—especially for the theater crowd—
is Sheffield's, one block north of Belmont, on the corner of School
Street. Sheffield's has a working fireplace, a pool table, and a cabaret
stage for live sketches and music. Open Sunday through Friday from
3pm to 2am, on Saturday until 3am. Sheffield's opens at noon on
Sunday when there's a Bears game on the tube.

Sterch's, 2236 N. Lincoln. ☎ 281-2653.

Sterch's is one of the many neighborhood bars that dot Chicago.
Pictures of carrots on the bar's awnings and on the canvas flaps that
flank the doorway apparently refer to a former practice of serving
carrot sticks as munchies instead of chips and pretzels.

Wise Fools Pub, 2270 N. Lincoln. ☎ 929-1510.

The Wise Fools Pub is a popular blues bar and college hangout.

Cafes ────────────────────────────

Java, 909 W. School St. ☎ 545-6200.

A hangout for youngish artists is the Java, a bright and modish cof-
feehouse located just off Clark. Proprietor Cheryl Blumenthal offers
great-looking sandwiches and bakes her turkeys and hams on the
premises. Scones and pastries are also available, and there are many
different brews of coffee, including the popular cappuccino grande,
served in a large bowl with a chunk of milk chocolate on the side
($3.50). The wall art changes every month, and music on the house
piano is provided at the whim of the clientele; open 8am to midnight Monday through Thursday, Friday and Saturday until 1am,
and Sunday from 9am to midnight.

4   More Entertainment

Movies

It's not widely know, but between 1910 and 1918 Chicago was the film capital of the nation. Such classics of the period as Wallace Beery's *Sweedie* and Charlie Chaplin's *His New Job* were shot at the Essanay Studios, then located in a Chicago neighborhood called Uptown. This historical sidebar explains in part why Chicago was blessed with so many of the country's finest film palaces, like the Chicago Theater, mentioned above.

The **Chicago International Film Festival** takes place annually at theaters announced during late October and early November.

For conventional fare, check the local papers for neighborhood theater listings.

Biograph, 2433 N. Lincoln. ☎ **348-4123.**

At the sleek deco-style Biograph, John L. Dillinger saw his last flick before being gunned down in the alleyway next to the theater, fingered by his moll, the Lady in Red. Some of those indentations in the pockmarked telephone pole near the sidewalk end of the alley are said to be bullet holes.

Chicago Filmmakers, 1229 W. Belmont. ☎ **384-5533.**

Chicago Filmmakers is another nonprofit exhibitor, strictly for shorts and documentaries. Here you will see the work of the world's current crop of experimental filmmakers. The group also sponsors workshops in basic filmmaking and performance skills. General admission is $5.

Facets, 1517 W. Fullerton. ☎ **281-4114.**

Nonprofit film exhibitors are also well represented in Chicago. At Facets the program typically features at least one film classic. Facets also supports an experimental theater company and sponsors an annual festival of children's films in October. Facets has daily screenings that mix a broad selection of old favorites with the work of contemporary independents. Admission costs $5; $3 for members.

The Film Center, at the School of the Art Institute, Columbus Dr. and Jackson Blvd. ☎ **443-3737** for a recorded message.

The Film Center screens contemporary feature films that are unlikely to be exhibited by the city's commercial theaters, as well as the great films of the past. Admission is $5, $3 for members.

Fine Arts, 418 S. Michigan. ☎ **939-3700.**

This theater features "arts" and foreign films on a regular basis. No children under 6 are admitted.

Music Box Theatre, 3733 N. Southport. ☎ **871-6604.**

This is a refurbished 1930s movie hall showing double features of golden oldies.

The 3 Penny Cinema, 2424 N. Lincoln. ☎ **935-5744.**

The 3 Penny Cinema, across the street from the Biograph, offers the best in foreign, commercial, and specialized films. Admission costs $4.50, $2.50 on Monday, and $3 for early shows on weekends.

11

Easy Excursions from Chicago

REGRETTABLY, WE MUST NOW LEAVE CHICAGO BEHIND. IN OUR EXPLORATION of the city, we've scratched a fair amount of surface, but left much yet undiscovered for future expeditions, and subsequent editions of this guide. But no city, not even one that is so totally absorbing as Chicago, can be—or ought to be—divorced from its immediate geographic context.

Undeniably, the greatest concentration of diversions for the traveler to Chicago are to be found "in town." Yet numerous drawing cards might tempt a willing party to venture beyond the urban core and the inner circle of neighborhoods to some unique suburban spot. Beyond this near-suburban ring lies the whole, diverse state of Illinois, offering interesting locales that are reasonably close to Chicago, and others—like historic Springfield—that are more in the nature of an overnight side trip.

And there's the added bonus when you visit Chicago of being only an hour and a half from **Milwaukee,** Wisconsin, a favorite destination for Chicagoans seeking a scaled-down, slightly more manageable, version of the urban scene.

1 Day Trips

Certain suburbs right beyond the boundaries of the city line are treated by residents as extensions of Chicago itself. Such is the case with Hyde Park, Evanston, and the environs of O'Hare airport, as well as Oak Park, which makes for a very special excursion. In contrast, one or two of the city's more remote neighborhoods seem to lie beyond the beaten paths, and thus take on characteristics more typical of a less frequented suburb, like the Pullman Historic District, which is described below.

Oak Park—Wright's Shrine

By far one of the most popular side trips from Chicago is to Oak Park, a near suburb on the western border of the city. Oak Park has the highest concentration of houses or buildings anywhere that were designed and built by Frank Lloyd Wright. People come here to marvel at the work of a man who saw his life as a twofold mission: to wage a single-handed battle against the ornamental excesses of architecture, Victorian in particular, and in a more positive vein, to create in its place a new form that would be at the same time functional, appropriate to its natural setting, and stimulating to the imagination.

It is not so much that everyone who comes to Oak Park shares Wright's architectural vision. But there seems to be a widespread recognition, here and abroad, that Wright, more than most artists, was consistently true to his own standards, out of which emerged a unique and genuinely American architectural statement. The reason for Wright's success may stem from the fact that he, himself, was a living metaphor of the quintessential American type. In a deep sense, he embodied the ideal of the self-made and self-sufficient individual who had survived, even thrived, in the rural and frontier society, a quality that he expressed in his utilitarian insistence that each spatial or structural form in his buildings serve some useful purpose. But if he was a puritan, he was also an aesthete in Emersonian fashion, deriving his idea of beauty from natural environments, where apparent starkness or simplicity often hides a finely ordered and subtle complexity underneath the surface of things.

GETTING THERE/ORIENTATION   Oak Park is 10 miles due west of downtown Chicago. If traveling by **car,** take the Eisenhower Expressway (I-290) to exit north of Harlem Avenue (Ill. 43). Follow the brown-and-white signs to the historic district parking lot at Forest Avenue and Lake Street.

By **public transportation,** take the Lake Street/Dan Ryan El to the Harlem/Marion stop, roughly a 25-minute ride from downtown. You will exit onto Harlem Avenue, then backtrack along North Boulevard one block until reaching Forest Avenue, where you turn left (north), walking another block to Lake Street. On this corner you will find the **Visitors Center,** 158 Forest Ave. (☎ **708/ 848-1500**), open daily from 10am to 5pm. Stop here for orientation, maps, guidebooks, and tour tickets.

A THREE-PART OAK PARK ITINERARY   The three principal ingredients of a tour of Wright-designed structures in Oak Park are the Frank Lloyd Wright Home and Studio Tour, the Unity Temple Tour, and a walking tour—guided or self-guided—to view the exteriors of homes throughout the neighborhood that were built by the architect. There are, in all, 30 homes and buildings by Wright in Oak Park, built between the years 1899 and 1913, which constitute the core of the output from his Prairie School period. Tours of another 50 dwellings of architectural interest by Wright's contemporaries, scattered throughout this community and neighboring River Forest, are also worthwhile.

A PACKAGE TOUR   The **Chicago Architecture Foundation** (☎ **312/922-3432** for reservations and tickets) offers a combined tour that includes an informed visit to Unity Temple, a guided walk past homes designed by Wright and his contemporaries, and a visit to the Home and Studio, the latter tour presented by the Frank Lloyd Wright Home and Studio Foundation (☎ **708/848-1976**), where tickets may also be purchased. The tour lasts approximately 2¹/₂ hours, costs $9, and is conducted from March to November at noon or 2pm, and from December to February at 2pm. A bus tour, leaving from downtown Chicago, is offered at a cost of $25. Reservations are required; call **922-3432,** ext. 140.

IMPRESSIONS

Chicago! Immense gridiron of dirty, noisy streets. . . . Heavy traffic crossing both ways at once, managing somehow; torrential noise.
—Frank Lloyd Wright, *An Autobiography*

WALKING TOURS   Apart from the walking tour that joins the visit to Unity Temple to that of the Home and Studio, and only scratches the surface of Wright's domestic architecture in Oak Park, several other options are available. A more extensive tour leaves the **Ginko Tree Book Shop,** installed next to the Home and Studio, at 951 Chicago Ave., weekdays at 11am, 1pm, and 3pm, and continuously on weekends from 11am to 4pm. This tour lasts an hour, whether guided or on cassette, and tickets cost $6 for adults, $4 for youths ages 10 to 18 and seniors, free for children under 10.

A final worthwhile option is to purchase an **"Architecture Guide Map"** from the bookshop of the Visitors Center and fashion a walking tour to fit your own schedule. This map places each subject house schematically on the street plan and includes photos of all 80 sites of interest. Remember that in addition to Wright's work, you will see that of his several disciples, as well as some very charming examples of the Victorian styling that he so disdained.

UNITY TEMPLE

Closest to the Visitors Center, and starting point for the tour described above, is Unity Temple, 875 Lake St. In 1871 a community of Unitarian/Universalists settled near here, and built a Wren-style church, a timber-framed house of worship typical of their native New England, which was destroyed by fire around the turn of the century. Wright, who had joined the congregation, was asked to design an affordable replacement. Using poured concrete with metal reinforcements—a necessity owing to the small budget of $40,000 allocated for the project—Wright created a building that on the outside seems as forbidding as a mausoleum, but that inside contains in its detailing the entire architectural alphabet of the Prairie School that has since made Wright's name immortal. Following the example of H. H. Richardson (Glessner House), Wright placed the building's main entrance on the side, behind an enclosure—a feature much employed in his houses as well—to create a sense of privacy and intimacy.

Front entrances were too anonymous for these two architects. And Wright, furthermore, had complained that other architectural conventions of the church idiom, like the nave in the Gothic cathedral across from the future site of Unity Temple, were overpowering. Of that particular church, he commented that you didn't feel a part of it. Yet his own vision in this regard was itself somewhat confused and contradictory. He wanted Unity Temple to be "democratic." But perhaps Wright was unable to extinguish his personal hubris and hauteur from the creative process, for the ultimate effect of his chapel, and much of the building's interior, is very grand and imperial. Unity Temple is no simple meetinghouse in the tradition of Calvinist iconoclasm. Rather, its principal chapel looks like the chamber of the Roman Senate (perhaps Wright had meant to say "republican" and "patrician," rather than "democratic"?). Even so, the interior is no less beautiful. What often saves Wright from his own tendencies toward an obsession with the "great idea" is the unpredictability of

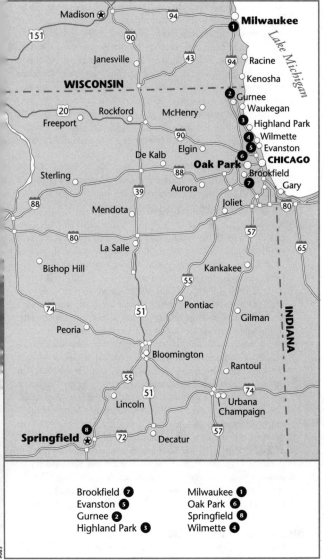

Brookfield **7**   Milwaukee **1**
Evanston **5**   Oak Park **6**
Gurnee **2**   Springfield **8**
Highland Park **3**   Wilmette **4**

his geometric arrangements, and a style of decor that, if it was not directly inspired by Native American art, stems from a kindred inspiration.

Wright used color sparingly within Unity Temple, but the pale, natural effects he achieved are owed in part to his decision to add pigment to the plaster, rather than use paint. Wright's use of wood for trim and other decorative touches is still exciting to behold; his sensitivity to grain and tone and placement was akin to that of an exceptionally gifted woodworker. Wright was a true hands-on, can-do Yankee; he knew, as intimately as the artisans who carried out his plans, the materials that he was using. And his stunning, almost minimalist use of form is what still sets him apart as a relevant and brilliant artist. Other details to which the docent guide will call your attention, as you complete a circuit of the temple, are the great fireplace, the pulpit, the skylights, and the clerestory (gallery) windows. Suffice it to say, Unity Temple—only one of Wright's masterpieces—is counted among the 10 greatest American architectural achievements.

The Unity Temple portion of the tour can be purchased alone for $3 a ticket, $2 for students and seniors on Monday to Friday; $5 a ticket, $3 for students and seniors on weekends.

THE FRANK LLOYD WRIGHT HOME & STUDIO

Known locally as "the" Home and Studio, 951 Chicago Ave. (☎ 708/848-1978), it is first and foremost the magic castle from which Wright was to design and execute more than 130 of an ultimate, and extraordinary, output of 430 completed buildings. The home began as a simple shingled cottage that Wright built for his bride in 1889 at the age of 22, and was remodeled constantly until 1911. During this highly fertile period, the house was Wright's showcase and laboratory, but it also embraces many idiosyncratic features that were molded to his own needs, rather than those of a client. With many add-ons—including a barrel-vaulted children's playroom, and a studio with an octagonal balcony suspended by chains—there is a certain whimsical arrangement to the place that others may have found less livable. Certainly, the vaulted playroom seems an excess of proportion that in and of itself is far from graceful. This, however, was not the architect's masterpiece, but the master's home, and every room in it can be savored for the view it reflects of the workings of a remarkable mind. The schedule for guided tours of this National Historical Landmark is as follows: Monday through Friday at 11am and 1 and 3pm, on Saturday and Sunday every 15 minutes from 11am to 4pm. Additional hours are added in the summertime. General admission is $6, $4 for ages 10 to 18 and over 65, and free for children under 10. Facilities for the handicapped are limited; please call in advance.

ON THE TRAIL OF HEMINGWAY

Frank Lloyd Wright may be Oak Park's favorite son, but the town's most famous native son was Ernest Hemingway. Oak Park has only recently begun to rally around the memory of the Nobel and Pulitzer Prize–winning writer with the opening of a **Hemingway Museum,** 200 N. Oak Park Ave. (☎ 708/848-2222). A portion of the ground floor of this former church, now the Oak Park Arts Center, is given over to a small but interesting display of Hemingway memorabilia. There is also a six-minute video presentation that sheds considerable

Oak Park

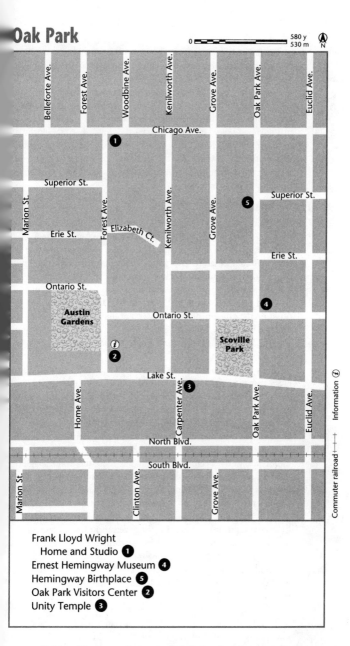

0 — 580 y / 530 m

N

Belleforte Ave.
Forest Ave.
Woodbine Ave.
Kenilworth Ave.
Grove Ave.
Oak Park Ave.
Euclid Ave.

Chicago Ave.

Superior St.

Marion St.

Forest Ave.

Erie St.

Elizabeth Ct.

Kenilworth Ave.

Grove Ave.

Superior St.

Erie St.

Ontario St.

Austin Gardens

Ontario St.

Scoville Park

Lake St.

Home Ave.

Carpenter Ave.

Oak Park Ave.

Euclid Ave.

North Blvd.

South Blvd.

Marion St.

Clinton Ave.

Grove Ave.

Commuter railroad ┼┼┼   Information ⓘ

Frank Lloyd Wright
   Home and Studio ❶
Ernest Hemingway Museum ❹
Hemingway Birthplace ❺
Oak Park Visitors Center ❷
Unity Temple ❸

light on Hemingway's time in Oak Park, where he spent the first eighteen years of his life, and that is particularly good on the writer's high school experiences. The museum's hours are limited; it's open Wednesday and Sunday from 1 to 5pm, and Saturday from 10am to 5pm. There is an admission fee of $2.

To see where Hemingway was born, continue up the block to **339 N. Oak Park Ave.** Here, in the home of his maternal grandparents on July 21, 1899, the author of several great American novels first saw the light. The home was purchased recently by a local foundation to serve as a museum; it has been restored to reflect its appearance during the time of Hemingway's boyhood. Hemingway's actual boyhood home, still privately owned, is located several blocks from here, not far from the Wright Home and Studio, at 600 N. Kenilworth Ave. The hours at the Hemingway Birthplace museum are same as the Hemingway Museum above. A special $5 admission price covers both museums.

The Pullman Historic District

The Pullman Historic District on Chicago's Far Southwest Side is the greatest monument to industrial paternalism in America. George Pullman, inventor of the Pullman railway sleeping car, was not content to compensate for poor wages with symbolic gestures. Rather than follow the more usual Dickensian example of his 19th-century industrialist peers who distributed turkeys at Yuletide, Pullman provided his workers with all the comforts of home—and made a profit on the experiment to boot. Much of the utopian village that Pullman built in the 1880s still stands near the Calumet Expressway between 111th and 115th Streets, and continues today as an active residential community.

Many workers, at least initially, must have counted themselves lucky that their employer had created such a comfortable nest for them. The rents they paid brought them both quality housing and many conveniences. But we are not a people who readily accept a master over our home life, least of all the same man who is our master at work. The residents of Pullman's town quickly rebelled against his rule over their domestic life, and when he began to turn the screw in response to their complaints by holding rents and utilities high during a serious economic depression, they warred against him in his factory as well. The Pullman Strike of 1894, which crippled the nation's rail traffic, was one of the great triumphs and tragedies of the labor movement, and a fascinating episode in American history in its own right. It was broken up by government troops, and was officially a failure that saw the jailing of its leader, Eugene V. Debs, and the weakening of its union, the American Railway Workers. But the public outrage that followed the strike ultimately aided the workers to win many rights and reforms. And in the end, an embittered George Pullman finally bowed to a court order to divest his company of its nonindustrial property.

Time has not been kind to Pullman's reputation in Chicago, where after nearly a century, his name is still mud.

GETTING THERE   By car, take the Calumet/Dan Ryan Expressway to the 111th Street exit, and proceed west. The most direct route to the historic district for travelers without cars is via the **Metra suburban train system,** with stations throughout the Loop, and which stops directly at 111th Street in Pullman. (For Metra information, call **312/322-6777**.) The ride from the Loop takes approximately 30 minutes.

TOURS & SIGHTS   Guided tours of this fascinating community are conducted on the first Sunday of the month from May through October by the Historic Pullman Foundation. Tours begin at 10:30am from the **Historic Pullman Center,** 614 E. 113th St. (☎ **312/785-8181**), where you first view a 22-minute audiovisual slide presentation, and then proceed with your choice of an accompanied walk or bus trip through the neighborhood. The cost is $4 for adults, $3 for seniors, and $2.50 for students.

At all other times, regardless of the season, you may guide yourself through the same itinerary, after first picking up a free walking-tour map at the foundation's headquarters in the **Florence Hotel,** 11111 S. Forestville Ave. (☎ **312/785-8181**). The Florence Hotel, built in 1881 in the Queen Anne style, was the showcase of the Pullman community. Here the owner maintained an elegant suite of rooms, housed his guests and clients, and entertained them amid the grandeur of the hotel's public spaces. Ultramodern in its day, as well as fashionable, the Florence had indoor plumbing, central heat, and a built-in system of bells and alarms to summon servants or to raise the alert in the event of fire. The hotel closed in 1973, after which it was purchased by the foundation, and is now undergoing restoration. The hotel restaurant (☎ **312/785-8900**) continues to function, and lunch is served daily.

What you will see on this tour is a well-planned, hierarchical arrangement of row houses, from fancy to plain, that once housed Pullman's executives and skilled workers, and a few remaining tenements that were reserved for the laborers and single men. Also extant within this parklike environment is the original Greenstone Church that Pullman had built as a nondenominational house of worship, and the Market Hall, a fire-plagued ensemble of buildings setting off a square where community members shopped for foodstuffs and dry goods, now being restored and converted to condos and offices.

THE LAST PULLMAN CAR   The actual Pullman Palace Car Company plant, where railway sleeping cars were manufactured for 114 years, finally closed its doors in 1979. A group of Chicago filmmakers documented the plant's final months of existence, as the local union desperately fought to keep the plant running and to save jobs. Of course, the decision to close the plant was probably one that George Pullman himself would have agreed with. For information on *The Last Pullman Car,* contact **Kartemquin Films,** 1901 W. Wellington, Chicago, IL 60657 (☎ **312/472-4366**).

The Northern Suburbs

Between Chicago and the state border with Wisconsin to the north, there are many attractions. These are the most popular:

EVANSTON

Despite being Chicago's nearest neighbor to the north—and a place much frequented by Chicagoans themselves—Evanston retains an identity all its own. Northwestern University makes its home here, and so once did Frances Willard, founder of the Woman's Christian Temperance Union. **Willard House,** 1730 Chicago Ave. (☎ 708/864-1397), is still the headquarters of the Temperance Union and may be visited. Nine of the 17 rooms in this old Victorian "cottage" have been converted into a museum of period furnishings and temperance memorabilia. Evanston is also known for its examples of fine domestic architecture, which you may view with the aid of a publication entitled *Evanston Architecture: A Sampler of Self-guided Tours,* available in bookstores and newsstands.

Neither cultural nor recreational facilities are lacking in Evanston. The unusual and informative **Mitchell Indian Museum** is located at Kendall College, 2408 Orrington Ave. (☎ 708/866-1395), with a collection ranging from precontact stoneware tools and weapons to the work of contemporary Native American artists. Open Tuesday through Friday from 9 am to 4:30pm; Saturday and Sunday from 1 to 4pm; closed on holidays. A donation of $1 is requested.

For an ecological experience, visit the **Ladd Arboretum,** 2024 McCormick Blvd. (☎ 708/864-5181), a public park, where you will also find the **Evanston Ecology Center,** which houses nature exhibits.

Where to Dine

Café Provençal, 1625 Hinman Ave. ☎ 708/475-2233.
  Cuisine: FRENCH. **Reservations:** Required.
  Prices: Appetizers $4.75–$13.50; main courses $16–$28. AE, DC, MC, V.
  Open: Dinner only, Tues–Sun 7–11pm.

Eating in Evanston requires no privation from the high culinary standards of Chicago's better restaurants. One spot in particular, the Café Provençal, is a superchic and pricey French restaurant that has the reputation of going sauce-for-sauce with any rival in town.

BAHA'I HOUSE OF WORSHIP

Up the road in Wilmette is the most visited of all the sights in the northern suburbs, the Baha'i House of Worship, at Linden Avenue and Sheridan Road (☎ 708/853-2300) a very non–Prairie-style temple, surrounded by well-cultivated formal gardens. The mosquelike structure with its lacelike facade and 135-foot dome, designed by the French Canadian Louis Bourgeois, strongly reveals the Eastern influence of the Baha'i faith's native Iran. Visiting hours May to September are 10am to 10pm daily and October to April from 10am to 5pm daily. Admission is free.

To get there from Chicago, take the Howard Line of the El north to Howard Street. Change trains for Wilmette and go to the end of the line, 4th Street and Linden Avenue. Turn right on Linden and walk two blocks east.

THE CHICAGO BOTANIC GARDEN

Despite its name, the Chicago Botanic Garden is located 25 miles north of the city in the suburb of Glencoe, on Lake-Cook Road just east of Edens Highway (☎ **708/835-5440**). Experience intimately the variations of nature over four seasons in this 300-acre preserve, with its variety of distinct botanical environments, from the Illinois prairie to a garden of English perennials. Also on the grounds are a cafe, a library, a garden shop, and a designated bike path. The grounds are open daily (except Christmas) from 8am to sunset. Parking is $4, which includes admission to the grounds. Train tours, for an additional $3.50, are offered every half hour from 10am to 3:30pm on weekdays, from 10am to 5pm on weekends.

THE RAVINIA FESTIVAL

Ravinia is to Chicago what Tanglewood is to the Berkshires. It's the summer home of the highly regarded Chicago Symphony, which has an eight-week season here. It's also a setting for chamber music, a new music series called New Perspectives, jazz and pop concerts, dance, and music study. Zarin Mehta is music director of the festival, which takes place at Ravinia Park, located in suburban Highland Park (☎ **312/RAVINIA** from May to September). The series runs from mid-June through Labor Day.

Indoor dining, both formal and informal, is available. There's the Rondo, featuring a $13 buffet, and the Cadenza, serving main courses in the $9 to $16 range. These facilities are open from 5:30 to around 8pm, when the concerts begin. Lawn catering is also available for parties of six or more.

Getting to the Ravinia Festival is easy. To reserve a place on a chartered bus, dial **312/RAVINIA,** and then catch the bus at one of seven stops: the Art Institute (Adams and Michigan); the corner of Randolph and Michigan; the Drake hotel (Walton and Michigan); Harbor House (3200 N. Lake Shore Dr.); Sheridan and Hollywood; Sheridan and Devon; or at the Davis Street Station in Evanston. One-way fare is $6; round-trip, $12. Many of the major hotels also charter buses during the season, or you may ride the commuter train from the Chicago and North Western station near the Loop at Madison and Canal, which stops in Highland Park directly at the festival.

SIX FLAGS GREAT AMERICA

This is the Midwest's biggest theme/amusement park. It is located midway between Chicago and Milwaukee on I-94 in Gurnee, Ill. (☎ **708/249-1776**). More than 100 rides are featured, including the brand-new "shock wave," billed as the tallest and fastest steel roller coaster in the country, plus there are shows, restaurants, and theme areas. Admission—$28 for adults, $18 for seniors, $26 for children ages 4 to 10, and free for children 3 and under (not including tax)—entitles you to unlimited use of rides, shows, and attractions. Open seasonally, usually beginning around the first of May and closing by the first week in October.

The Western Suburbs

So many corporations have taken to locating their offices beyond the city limits that today more people work in the suburbs than commute into Chicago. At the hub of this development is O'Hare International, and all around the airport are the kinds of shops, restaurants, and bistros that once only the city could boast of. Those people visiting the Chicago area who are quartered in and around O'Hare also have easy access to a variety of very special museums and nature-oriented facilities.

WHAT TO SEE & DO

Brookfield Zoo, First Ave. and 31st St., in Brookfield.
☎ **708/485-0263.**

This is the Chicago area's largest zoo, with an incredibly varied cast of residents from all branches of the animal kingdom. Have you ever noticed just how big a Kodiak bear is up close, or how squidlike a walrus's face appears when seen from a very short distance? How do those polar bears stay so white with all the grimy urban pollution in the air, and are those great apes really as mean and angry as they look? These and a hundred other questions will be manufactured by your own imagination as you make the rounds from one habitat to another in this make-believe jungle.

Admission: $4 adults, $1.50 seniors and children 3–11. Free on Tues.

Open: Memorial Day–Labor Day, daily 10am–6pm. Labor Day–Memorial Day, daily 10am–5pm. **Directions:** The zoo is located about 14 miles west of the Loop, and is accessible via the Stevenson (I-55) and Eisenhower (I-290) Expressways. **Bus:** RTA no. 304 or 331.

Lizzadro Museum Of Lapidary Art, 220 Cottage Hill, Wilder Park. ☎ **708/833-1616.**

Not far from the zoo, off I-90 in nearby Elmhurst, you will find the Lizzadro Museum. The museum's jade collection is internationally renowned, a fact that is punctuated by the presence of a chunk of jade weighing over half a ton that greets you at the entrance. The word "lapidary," of course, refers to the art of stone cutting, and this repository of that art displays hard-stone carvings, gemstones, mineral specimens, and such oddities as an ivory carving of the Last Supper.

Admission: $2.50 adults, $1.50 seniors and children ages 13–18, free for children under 13. Free admission on Fri.

Open: Tues–Sat 10am–5pm, Sun 1–5pm. **Closed:** Holidays.

Morton Arboretum, in Lisle. ☎ **708/968-0074.**

South and west of the Brookfield Zoo, in Lisle, is this 1,500-acre arboretum off Ill. 53, just north of the East-West Tollway. Not only is this park a nature showcase of flora from around the world, organized into both formal and natural settings, but it is also a wildlife refuge for many forest critters such as foxes and beavers, and of course, birds. There are 40,000 different tree specimens, classified into 4,000 species. Nine miles of roadways allow you to drive through the grounds, but a walk along the more than 25 miles of pathways will give you a more satisfying and intimate view of the plant and woods life.

Admission: $6 per car, $3 per car on Wed.

Open: Daily 7am–7pm.

Lynfred Winery, 15 S. Roselle Rd., in Roselle. ☎ 708/529-9463.

Also off I-90, but closer to the airport, is the Lynfred Winery. This suburban winery purchases grapes from around the country and ferments them here in oak casks. You may sample up to seven of the company's fruit and grape wines for $2.

Admission: Free.

Open: Sat–Sun at 2 and 4pm.

Fermi National Laboratory (Fermilab), in Batavia.
☎ 708/840-3000.

Even the most adamant Nuclear Freeze activist who associates the name of Fermi with the birth of atomic power might want to check out the latest advances in particle physics and get a view, from a safe distance, of the gigantic accelerator at the Fermilab. The main entrance to the laboratory is on Kirk Road, a north-south highway that exits from the East-West Tollway (Ill. 5). Kirk Road intersects with Butterfield Road (Ill. 56) and Roosevelt Road (Ill. 38), which originates in downtown Chicago near the Field Museum. The laboratory entrance is opposite Pine Street in Batavia, between Butterfield and Wilson Roads.

Free guided tours are available, by appointment, for groups of 10 or more people, consisting of an orientation talk and slide presentation, a visit to various laboratory environments, and an opportunity to take in a panoramic view of the accelerator from the 15th floor of the lab's main building. The tour lasts about two hours, after which you are welcome to drive around the 6,800-acre site, to look at the distinctive architecture of the Fermilab buildings, and to see the buffalo and waterfowl that also occupy these lands.

Admission: Free.

Open: Guided tours, Mon–Fri 9:30am–1:30pm. Self-guided tours, daily 8:30am–5pm.

WHERE TO DINE

Carlucci Rosemont, 111 N. River Rd., in the Riverway Complex.
☎ 708/518-0990.

Cuisine: ITALIAN. **Reservations:** Accepted.

Prices: Appetizers $5.95–$7.50; main courses $14.95–$19.95. AE, DC, DISC, MC, V.

Open: Dinner only, Mon–Thurs 5:30–10:30pm; Fri–Sat 5:30–11:30pm; Sun 5–10pm.

Only five minutes by car from the airport is a restaurant that will make you forget that your flight was cancelled and you have to spend the night in an airport hotel. While not exactly offering the same menu as its cousin on Halsted Street in Lincoln Park, Carlucci Rosemont boasts the same superior standards of quality.

Console yourself here with a wonderful meal, beginning with the zuppa—something hearty, say, the lamb-and-bean vegetable soup ($3.95). The appetizers are all superb, like the giant portobello mushrooms with rosemary, roasted in a wood-burning oven ($7.25), or the miniature sweet red peppers stuffed with herb ricotta and sautéed spinach ($6.25). For your entrée, you could not choose better than the roasted quail stuffed with sausage and risotto ($18.95), a true delicacy. The wines are sinfully potable, and I particularly recommend a Tuscan vintage, the 1990 Mastrojanni ($35/bottle). For a strong finish, the tiramisù is a must, creamy mascarpone with marsala and espresso-soaked lady fingers ($4.95).

Le Français, 269 S. Milwaukee, in Wheeling. ☎ **708/541-7470.**

Cuisine: FRENCH. **Reservations:** Required.

Prices: Appetizers $5.95–$17.95; main courses $15.50–$24.95. AE, DC, DISC, MC, V.

Open: Dinner seatings, Tues–Sun at 6:15 and 9:15pm.

A very fine French restaurant, Le Français is located in Wheeling, northwest of O'Hare. The restaurant has two dinner seatings, and the average check is about $85 per person.

EVENING ENTERTAINMENT

Studebaker, 1251 E. Golf Rd., in Schaumburg. ☎ **708/619-3434.**

Former Bears running back and legend Walter Payton owns a raucous nightclub, also near O'Hare, called Studebaker, where patrons have been known to dance on the tabletops to their favorite Motown sounds.

Rosemont Horizon, Mannheim St. between Higgins and Touhy Sts., Des Plaines. ☎ **708/635-6600.**

On the periphery of the airport is the 18,000-seat Rosemont Horizon where big events are scheduled, such as rock concerts, the circus, and important college basketball games. Take the subway/el to O'Hare, then bus no. 220.

Prairie Center for the Performing Arts, 201 Schaumburg Court, in Schaumburg. ☎ **708/894-3600.**

The Prairie Center for the Performing Arts is for big symphony and jazz concerts.

World Music Theater, 19100 S. Ridgeland Ave. ☎ **708/614-1616.**

The new venue for megaconcerts just south of Chicago in suburban Tinley Park, is the World Music Theater.

2 Milwaukee

Milwaukee's fame, the old advertising slogan has it, rests on its beer. An equally one-sided image portrays Milwaukee as a slightly ruined industrial backwater where a Midwestern variant of the "dese, dems, and dose" blue-collar culture holds sway in a slapstick world of lodge halls and neighborhood taverns. Assuming one thinks of Milwaukee at all, it is almost certainly not as a leisure destination. Other than Milwaukeeans themselves, residents of nearby Chicago have probably been the first group of any size to realize that their neighboring city-by-the-lake offers the perfect setting for a bite-sized getaway excursion. Only an hour and a half away by car or train, Milwaukee also represents a bonus for travelers to Chicago who might want to visit two interesting cities for the price of one.

Milwaukee may also be a perfect example of the urban ideal in contemporary America. With more than 600,000 residents, Milwaukee possesses a population density of urban proportions, yet remains in appearance a tidy, uncrowded metropolis blending many cosmopolitan features with the rhythms of a small town. Milwaukee is actually neither too big nor too small, neither too shabby and industrial nor too high-tech and gentrified.

On the upscale side, there are some excellent hotels in the revitalized downtown section, a handful of first-rate gourmet restaurants, and an outstanding cultural menu of theater, symphonic music, and opera that owes its evolution to the many German and Eastern European immigrants who flocked to the city beginning in the 1850s. On the down-home side, Milwaukee retains its brewery image—Miller and Pabst are headquartered here—and its multiethnic, working-class flavor in the many sprawling neighborhoods, where scores of unvarnished shops and family-style restaurants await discovery by the adventurous visitor.

GETTING THERE • By Train   A train called the *Hiawatha* offers a schedule of at least five daily departures from Chicago's Union Station, with additional trains on weekends. The trip takes an hour and a half, and a round-trip excursion ticket costs approximately $25.

• By Car   If you have a car in Chicago, or wish to rent one, simply travel north on Interstate 94, the most direct route. The advantage of car travel, for the visitor not on a tight schedule at least, is the opportunity to explore a bit as you travel through Chicago's legendary North Shore suburban villages.

What to See & Do

The best source of information for what's happening in Milwaukee is the **Greater Milwaukee Convention & Visitors Bureau,** 756 N. Milwaukee St. (☎ 414/273-3950, or toll free 800/231-0903).

Milwaukee calls itself the "city of festivals." Some large-scale, outdoor festival seems to be scheduled for practically every week of the year, with the greatest concentration of events occurring in the summertime. The main event of the year is **Summerfest** in late June or early July at the lakeside Henry Maier Festival Park. Dubbed the Big Gig, the summerfest is preceded by a preliminary barbecue called the Big Pig. Another very popular event, drawing many visitors from out of town, is the **Great Circus Parade,** in effect a street circus and the only event of its kind in the world, also scheduled for early July. Ethnic and seasonal festivals round out the schedule.

SIGHTS

The **Milwaukee Art Museum,** 750 N. Lincoln Memorial Dr. (☎ 224-3200), well-known for its collection of old masters,

German expressionism, and modern and contemporary pieces, also has an unusual and extensive collection of Haitian artworks, and features as well the von Schleinitz collection of 19th-century German paintings. Admission is $4 for adults, $2 for students, free for children 12 and under. Hours are daily from 10am to 5pm, except on Thursdays, when the museum is open from noon to 9 pm. For a view of Milwaukee history, there are interesting exhibits at the **Milwaukee County Historical Society,** 910 Old World Third St. (☎ **273-8288**).

For six-pack culture and professional sports, Milwaukee is also well endowed. Both baseball's **Brewers** (☎ **933-1818**), and basketball's **Bucks** (☎ **272-8080**) make Milwaukee their home. Brewery tours are a popular diversion in this beer capital of the nation. The **Pabst Brewing Company,** 915 W. Juneau Ave. (☎ **223-3709**), and the **Miller Brewing Company,** 4251 State St. (☎ **931-BEER**), both offer continuous guided tours of their plants Monday through Saturday.

A TYPICAL NEIGHBORHOOD

There are many self-contained neighborhoods within walking distance or a short cab or bus ride from downtown Milwaukee, the **Historic Third Ward, Mitchell Street, Riverwest,** and **Neighborhood North,** to name a few. There are a string of interesting shops and cafes on **Downer Avenue,** between Webster Place and Belleview Place, which forms an otherwise nameless urban oasis on the city's upper east side. I am told that many students inhabit this area, and attend the nearby University of Wisconsin, Milwaukee campus.

From the Pfister Hotel, you can head north on Prospect Avenue, hugging the perimeter of Lake Park that runs along the shore. The route will take you past many of Milwaukee's fine old mansions, primarily professional buildings today, with still quite a few beautiful private homes among them. Crossing Brady Street, there are many interesting shops and restaurants along this strip.

In the park itself, at just about this same point, is McKinley Marina, a favorite kite-flying area. Kites may be purchased at the **Gift of Wings** kite shop (a chain with a toll-free number, **800/541-1580**). Kites range from the ordinary to the incredible, costing anywhere from $5 to $400.

Next to the kite shop is the **Highroller** (☎ **273-1343**), a shop renting roller skates, roller blades, and bikes.

A Very Special B&B ─────────────────────────

Marie's Bed and Breakfast, 346 E. Wilson St., Milwaukee, WI 53204. ☎ **414/483-1512.** 4 rms (none with bath).

Rates (including breakfast): $55–$70 single or double. No credit cards.

Across the Milwaukee River from downtown is homey Bay View, "a town within a city," located along the shores of Lake Michigan. Not far off the neighborhood's main drag, Kinnickinnic Avenue, is Marie's

Bed and Breakfast. Hostess Marie Mahan, a multimedia artist who has completely renovated this circa-1896 Victorian home, offers guests four rooms, with two shared bathrooms, and a full gourmet breakfast served in her charming garden, weather permitting. In the spirit of true hospitality, Marie has adapted her home to the comfort of her guests, who keep coming back to visit her year after year. Marie is a talented painter with a collector's eye for just about any object that might both serve some useful purpose and appeal to the eye in a domestic setting. And every object is placed in such a way to make her guests feel just a little bit more at home with each discovery, a table or bed light here, a rocker, a rug, a mirror. Some of her collecting, on the other hand—her primitive baskets and graceful fans—which literally cover the walls in her dining room, is strictly for her own gratification.

Marie's talents in home design do not, moreover, overshadow her skills in the kitchen. I don't think you will be treated in a B&B anywhere to a better, more imaginative full breakfast than the one Marie whips up each morning.

Where to Dine

Eagan's, 1030 N. Water St. ☎ 271-6900.
  Cuisine: AMERICAN SEAFOOD. **Reservations:** Accepted.
  Prices: Appetizers $5.95–$17.95; main courses $7.95–$15.95. AE, DISC, DC, MC, V.
  Open: Sun–Thurs 11am–11pm; Fri–Sat 11am–1am (limited menu after 11pm).

Eagan's is the principal watering hole that now anchors Milwaukee's ever-growing and ever-popular North Water Street theater and nightlife district. The restaurant has an extensive menu that is updated daily, and features many varieties of both fish and shellfish, flown in daily from various points of the compass. Eagan's is spacious and attractive, smoothly efficient yet relaxed and informal at the same time. With its many starters and a well-stocked raw bar, you can enjoy an eclectic meal, alternating between the thin-crust pizza with shrimp and sun-dried tomatoes ($9.95), for example, and the cold seafood combo plate, with oysters, clams, scallops, King crab, steamed mussels, and shrimp ($16.95). Eagan's is also an eco-conscious establishment and takes pride in calling itself, "the leading recycling restaurant in the country"; to prove it, Eagan's operates without a dumpster.

★ **Three Brothers,** 2414 S. St. Clair St. ☎ **481-7530,** or 747-9138.
$ **Cuisine:** SERBIAN. **Reservations:** Recommended on weekends.
  Prices: Appetizers $1.25–$5.95; main courses $10–$15. No credit cards.
  Open: Dinner only, Tues–Thurs 5–10pm. Fri–Sat 4–11pm, Sun 4–10pm.

The Three Brothers is a Serbian-style restaurant, housed in a landmark building—and old corner tavern—on a remote back street within view of both river and lake. Food at the Three Brothers is remarkably like Greek and Turkish food, owing to Serbia's 500-year occupation under the Ottoman Empire, and this restaurant—as well as its genial owner/chef—is highly regarded in Milwaukee.

One of Chef Branko's perennial specialties is roast suckling pig, prepared right on the premises and served with homegrown baked cabbage and rice ($12.95). Roast duck ($12.95) and roast goose ($13.95), both served with stuffing, are also available. Serbian goulash served with dumplings ($10.96) is a house favorite. For lighter fare, there are such Serbian standards as peppers, zucchini, or grape leaves, stuffed with beef and rice ($9.95 each).

Evening Entertainment

For cultural entertainment, the **Pabst Theater,** 144 E. Wells (☎ **271-3773**), provides a stunning setting for music and stage works; the **Milwaukee Symphony Orchestra,** 212 W. Wisconsin Ave. (☎ **291-6000**), is considered "one of America's great virtuoso orchestras." Its director is Zdenek Macal. The **Milwaukee Repertory Theater,** 108 E. Wells (☎ **224-1761**), provides stages for work ranging from experimental to contemporary Broadway hits.

An Excursion to Cedarburg

The restored city of Cedarburg, settled largely by German immigrants in the 1850s, is about a twenty-five minute car ride north from Milwaukee. Heritage tourism has become increasingly popular in the United States, and Cedarburg forms an integral part of a heritage corridor running up the northern shore of Lake Michigan, organized and funded in part by a federal pilot project. Cedarburg has retained much of its nineteenth-century appearance, and currently plays host to a weekend-getaway and seasonal touring crowd throughout the year. The city has several cultural attractions, including a charming small museum with period pieces from the thirties, and two fine inns.

WHERE TO STAY

The Stagecoach Inn, W61 N520 Washington Ave., Cedarburg, WI 53012. ☎ **414/375-0208.** 12 rms. A/C TV TEL

> **Rates** (including continental breakfast): $65 standard rm with bath; $95 deluxe suite with double whirlpool bath. AE, DC, MC, V. **Parking:** Free.

Down the block from the Washington House is the Stagecoach Inn, in a beautifully restored historic building. Somewhat smaller and more intimate than its counterpart, the Stagecoach is the paradigm of the quaint roadside inn you see in all the old movies. Guests gather at night in the pub, which features Milwaukee's favorite root beer, Sprecher's, on tap, in addition to a selection of bottled beers. A continental breakfast is served in the same area in the morning, consisting of homebaked muffins, croissants, juice, and coffee. Beerntsen's Candy, a Wisconsin favorite, also has a small shop on the premises.

Washington House Inn, W62 N573 Washington Ave., Cedarburg, WI 53012. ☎ **414/375-3550** or toll free **800/554-4717.** Fax 414/375-9422. 34 rms. A/C TV TEL

Rates: (including continental breakfast): $59 standard rm with bath; $129 deluxe rm with pencil-post queen bed, fireplace, and oversized whirlpool bath; $139–$159 suite. AE, DISC, DC, MC, V. **Parking:** Free.

The Washington House is more like a fine old provincial hotel than a B&B. The three-story inn offers a wide variety of accommodations, literally something for every pocketbook. The sensuous elegance of certain suites makes the Washington House a good choice as a romantic getaway. Some amenities include free HBO in all rooms, and use of the inn's sauna. A continental breakfast is included in the price of the room, featuring fresh-baked breads and rolls and fresh-squeezed orange juice. There is also an afternoon social hour every day, where complimentary Wisconsin wine and cheeses are served.

3   Springfield & Other Destinations

Were this book a guide to all of Illinois, it would have to continue on for an additional 200 to 300 pages at the very minimum. Illinois is, after all, one of the country's largest, as well as most historic, productive, and populous states. It is also a state well endowed with parks and other areas of great natural beauty. For those who are interested in touring Illinois beyond Chicago, I suggest that you contact the **State of Illinois Office of Tourism,** 620 E. Adams, Springfield, IL 62701 (☎ toll free **800/545-7300**), or 100 W. Randolph, lobby level, Chicago, IL 60601 (☎ **312/814-3306**).

The state capital, Springfield, is by far the most visited destination in Illinois outside of Chicago. Springfield was first settled in 1821, but did not become the state capital until a young politician named Abraham Lincoln skillfully maneuvered the appropriate legislation through the Illinois legislature in 1837. Later that same year, Lincoln himself moved to Springfield. For the next 25 years Springfield was to be the center of Lincoln's law practice, though he spent much of his time riding the circuit and arguing cases in county courthouses all around central Illinois, and politicking—running for one office or another—throughout the state. As a result, one may profitably follow in Lincoln's footsteps over these years and visit dozens of locales in Illinois where his visits and speeches are commemorated in one form or another. The office of tourism will be happy to help you fashion such an itinerary.

In Springfield itself, the principal Lincoln-related sights are the **Lincoln Home National Historic Site,** at 8th and Jackson (☎ **217/492-4150**), open daily (except major holidays) from 8:30am to 5pm, with hours extended to 8pm in the summer, admission free; the **Lincoln-Herndon Law Offices,** at 6th and Adams (☎ **217/785-7289**), open from 9am to 5pm daily, admission free; and the **Lincoln Depot,** on Monroe between 9th and 10th (☎ **217/544-8695**), where on February 11, 1861, Lincoln bade farewell to his Springfield friends and neighbors en route to his inauguration in Washington, D.C., as the United States's 16th president. In the depot you will see a restored waiting room, various exhibits, and a multimedia presentation; it's open free of charge daily from 10am to 4pm from April through August. On the outskirts of the town is the **Lincoln Tomb,** Oak Ridge Cemetery, 1500 N. Monument Ave. (☎ **217/782-2717**), open free of charge from 9am to 5pm daily, the final resting place of Lincoln and his family. June through August there is a flag-lowering ceremony from 7 to 8pm.

Lincoln was by far the state of Illinois's most illustrious citizen, but by no means the only one. In Springfield itself, you may also visit the **home of Vachel Lindsay,** the "Prarie Troubadour," at 603 S. 5th St. (☎ **217/528-9254**). In June, the home is open on Wednesday and Sunday from 10am to 4pm, and in July and August, it is open only on Sundays.

Index

General Information

Resturants by Cuisine

Key to Abbreviations B=Budget; E=Expensive; I=Inexpensive;
M=Moderate